THE ECONOMICS AND POLITICS OF CHOICE NO-FAULT INSURANCE

Huebner International Series on Risk, Insurance, and Economic Security

Other books in the series:

Cummins, J. David and Derrig, Richard A.: *Classical Insurance Solvency Theory*
Borba, Philip S. and Appel, David: *Benefits, Costs, and Cycles in Workers' Compensation*
Cummins, J. David and Derrig, Richard A.: *Financial Models of Insurance Solvency*
Williams, C. Arthur: *An International Comparison of Workers' Compensation*
Cummins, J. David and Derrig, Richard A.: *Managing the Insolvency Risk of Insurance Companies*
Dionne, Georges: *Contributions to Insurance Economics*
Dionne, Georges and Harrington, Scott E.: *Foundations of Insurance Economics*
Klugman, Stuart A.: *Bayesian Statistics in Actuarial Science*
Durbin, David and Borba, Philip: *Workers' Compensation Insurance: Claim Costs, Prices and Regulation*
Cummins, J. David: *Financial Management of Life Insurance Companies*
Gustavson, Sandra G. and Harrington, Scott E.: *Insurance, Risk Management, and Public Policy*
Lemaire, Jean: *Bonus-Malus Systems in Automobile Insurance*
Dionne, Georges and Laberge-Nadeau: *Automobile Insurance: Road Safety, New Drivers, Risks, Insurance Fraud and Regulation*
Taylor, Greg: *Loss Reserving: An Actuarial Perspective*
Dionne, Georges: *Handbook of Insurance*
Sinha, Tapen: *Pension Reform in Latin America and Its Lessons for International Polichmakers*
Lascher, Jr., Edward L. and Powers, Michael R.: *The Economics and Politics of Choice No-Fault Insurance*

THE ECONOMICS AND POLITICS OF CHOICE NO-FAULT INSURANCE

edited by

Edward L. Lascher, Jr.
California State University, Sacramento

Michael R. Powers
Temple University

SPRINGER SCIENCE+BUSINESS MEDIA, LLC

Library of Congress Cataloging-in-Publication Data
The economics and politics of choice no-fault insurance / edited by Edward L. Lascher, Jr., Michael R. Powers.
p. cm. -- (Huebner international series on risk, insurance, and economic security ; 24)
Includes bibliographical references and index.
ISBN 978-1-4613-5605-9 ISBN 978-1-4615-1541-8 (eBook)
DOI 10.1007/978-1-4615-1541-8
1. Insurance, No-fault automobile. I. Lascher, Edward L. II. Powers, Michael R. III. Series.
HG9970 .E36 2001
368.5'728'00973--dc21

2001038233

Originally published by Kluwer Academic Publishers in 2001
Softcover reprint of the hardcover 1st edition 2001

Printed on acid-free paper.

To my mother and step-father, Barbara and Jack Cudmore

ELL

To my parents, Dorothy and John Powers

MRP

CONTENTS

FOREWORD

Michael S. Dukakis
Northeastern University/University of California, Los Angeles

A lot of us have been trying to reform the way we compensate victims of auto accidents for a long time. In fact, I was the first state legislator in the country to sponsor a no-fault auto insurance bill, and it was ultimately approved by the Massachusetts Legislature and the then-governor, Francis W. Sargent, in 1970.

As governor in the 1970s and 1980s, I successfully proposed amendments to the state's no fault law that raised the tort threshold and expanded coverage. I continue to believe that we can do a much better job of protecting people from injuries on our highways at a reasonable cost than the current mishmash of liability laws that govern the way we compensate people for their injuries and losses.

For the current system is still a mess. Despite noble efforts to reform our auto insurance laws in Massachusetts and elsewhere, we are still falling short. Urban motorists in particular are burdened with insurance premiums that are often two and three times what their suburban counterparts pay. In inner city Boston neighborhoods, for example, it cost in excess of two thousand dollars a year for the auto insurance that is required of every Massachusetts motorist, and other major cities are even worse. In fact, when Kitty and I arrived in Los Angeles to take up winter teaching duties at UCLA a few years ago, I found myself paying nearly *three thousand* dollars for insurance for the car we leased in Los Angeles.

A number of states have adopted reform plans, and there was a serious and concerted effort in Congress to legislate national auto insurance reform in the 1970s. Back then, however, those of us who were pushing no fault constantly found ourselves facing the argument from our opponents that by advocating no fault laws, we were depriving people of their right to sue the other guy who might have been at fault. Given the waste and unfairness that is inherent in the liability lottery that passes for an auto insurance system, I never bought that argument. But our adversaries did have a point. There was no question that under certain circumstances we were denying people the right to sue a potential wrongdoer and limiting their ability to collect damages for pain and suffering.

Auto Choice eliminates that objection. It gives motorists the right to exercise their own judgment about how and to what extent they wish to be compensated in a way that denies nobody their right to sue if that is what they want. What it also does-and to me this is the most important feature of the bill-is provide generous relief from sky high insurance rates, especially for the people who live in our older urban neighborhoods. Nothing in our tax system is as regressive as the way we force people in our cities to pay for their auto insurance.

In the meantime, we will hear much from a new administration and a new Congress about the importance of encouraging revitalization and growth in our older cities. Community development block grants and empowerment zones are part of that agenda. We are warned almost daily about the dangers of urban sprawl. But how can we possibly expect to encourage more and more Americans to live, work, and invest in our cities when we make it prohibitively expensive to live there? How can we expect welfare mothers to get off welfare and to work when it costs them over two thousand dollars a year simply to put a car on the road?

Furthermore, the savings from Auto Choice are enormous. In my state alone motorists stand to reap premium reductions of between one billion and two billion dollars a year. Best of all, a large percentage of those billions will be going to the people who need them and deserve them the most-the residents of our urban neighborhoods.

I'm still looking for some explanation from the opponents of Auto Choice as to why it should not be passed overwhelmingly by a bipartisan Congress and accepted enthusiastically by the states. These days their principal argument against it seems to be that people cannot be trusted to make the right choice.

Those of us who strongly support Auto Choice have a lot more faith in the American people. We know that they must make choices about insurance and other products in the marketplace every day, and we know that they are perfectly capable of looking at the options that Auto Choice offers them and making an informed decision. In fact, I will be astonished if the vast majority does not choose the less expensive option auto insurance that will compensate them promptly and generously for their economic losses and save them billions of dollars at the same time.

ACKNOWLEDGMENTS

We wish to thank the contributors for their enthusiastic participation in this project. They greatly eased our work as editors.

We also extend our appreciation to the editorial staff at Kluwer Academic Publishers—especially David Cella and Judith Pforr—for their strong support of this project and their helpful and timely feedback.

Edward Lascher wishes to thank his colleagues in the Graduate Program in Public Policy and Administration at CSUS. Their dedication to excellence in both scholarship and teaching is most appreciated. And he wants to thank his family (Liz, Alex, and Avery) for support in ways too numerous to mention.

Michael Powers wishes to thank the Advanta Corporation for its financial support of this research through the Advanta Center for Financial Services Studies at Temple University's Fox School. He also thanks Deedee Khovidhunkit for her help with Chapter 8, Trudy McGinley for her extensive assistance with the preparation of the manuscript, and his family (Imelda, Thomas, and Andrew) for their help and encouragement.

I. BACKGROUND

1
AN INTRODUCTION TO CHOICE NO-FAULT

Edward L. Lascher, Jr.
California State University, Sacramento

Michael R. Powers
Temple University

1. OVERVIEW OF THE BOOK

"Choice" no-fault automobile insurance refers generally to any automobile accident recovery regime in which individuals purchasing automobile insurance policies are afforded a choice between traditional tort recovery on the one hand, and some variant of no-fault, with a barrier to tort recovery, on the other. Currently, only three jurisdictions in North America—Kentucky, New Jersey, and Pennsylvania—offer insureds some form of choice system. However, choice no-fault has received considerable attention from academics at least since the publication of a seminal 1986 law review article by Jeffrey O'Connell and Robert H. Joost (see O'Connell and Joost, 1986). Furthermore, since 1997, legislation has been pending in both Houses of the U.S. Congress to provide a federal mandate for choice no-fault. Under this plan, each state would be strongly encouraged to offer insureds a no-fault alternative to traditional tort recovery. Additionally, over the past 10 years, legislatures in several states (e.g., Rhode Island) have given serious consideration to bills aimed at establishing choice systems.

Despite the emergence of choice no-fault as a major issue for policy makers and academics, until now no single volume has pulled together the growing research in this area. Our book seeks to fill this void. We have included "classics" in the subject, such as the 1986 article by O'Connell and Joost and the widely cited (and appropriately updated) work by Stephen Carroll and Allan Abrahamse of RAND's Institute for Civil Justice. We have added works addressing the pending federal legislation in more detail. Included as well are pieces written specifically for this volume that examine the track record of existing choice systems in more depth than has been done before. In addition, we have added our own new analyses of the economics and politics of choice no-fault.

With this volume, we hope to reach a broad audience of readers interested in automobile insurance reform. Certainly we hope that the book is useful to the academic community that studies insurance issues. Yet we also hope the book is of interest to many others involved in the public policy debate, or who simply want to understand better "what this 'choice' idea is all about": lawmakers, legislative staff members, regulators, journalists, etc. Consequently this collection is relatively light on highly technical and/or mathematical selections, although some formal modeling is included as appropriate.

As the editors of the volume, we acknowledge our sympathy with the choice approach. We have a "track record" in this regard: Powers was involved in bringing choice no-fault to Pennsylvania, while Lascher editorialized (1995) in favor of a choice system for Rhode Island. We believe that choice no-fault makes sense, addressing many of the concerns raised in opposition to mandatory no-fault. We also believe that many of the arguments against the choice approach are over-stated at best, and erroneous at worst. Finally, we think choice is more politically feasible than other approaches aimed at limiting tort recovery.

Nevertheless, we have sought a degree of ideological balance in this collection. To this end, we have included a piece by Brent Kabler that is expressly critical of the choice approach. In addition, we note that the other chapters are not uniformly and unequivocally in support of choice no-fault. For example, Powers (1992) argues in favor of the "self-determining" system of choice no-fault—in which the tort elector enjoys unrestricted tort rights, but the no-fault elector is subject to restricted tort rights—whereas the federal proposal gives preference to the alternative "no-fault-favoring" approach.

The remaining sections of this chapter broaden the analytical context for the more detailed chapters that follow. In Section 2, we review some of the principal terminology of the no-fault debate. Then, in Section 3, we present some of the key issues relevant to the implementation of a choice system. We complete the introduction with a summary of the chapters that are to follow.

2. THE LEXICON OF CHOICE NO-FAULT

The generalist attempting to make headway in the no-fault insurance literature may be intimidated simply by the amount of jargon that needs to be understood: "BI" and "PIP coverage," "verbal" and "monetary thresholds," "insureds", "tortfeasors", etc. Focusing on the choice approach only adds to the complexity of the language.

We sympathize with those who find some of the language difficult and confusing. At the same time, we recognize that many of the specialized terms offer convenient shortcuts to those "in the know." For example, it is much easier to write "the PIP coverage limit is *X* dollars" than to write "the maximum amount of compensation that a person injured in an automobile accident can obtain from his or her own insurance company for economic losses regardless of fault is *X* dollars." Accordingly, we have left the specialized language in the chapters that follow, and, in this section of the introduction, have attempted to define (sometimes explicitly, and sometimes implicitly through context) the most frequently used terms. Each specialized term is printed in boldface at its first appearance in the text. We encourage the reader to think of this section as a brief primer for what is to follow.

2.1. Automobile Insurance Policies and Coverages

There are two basic types of automobile insurance **policies** sold in the U.S.: (1) **private passenger (personal) automobile** policies, which provide insurance coverage for most sedans, minivans, and other "light" vehicles owned and operated by individuals and families, generally for non-business purposes; and (2) **commercial automobile** policies, which cover virtually all other motor vehicles.

Each automobile insurance policy is written for one or more insured vehicles, and makes reference to one or more insured individuals. The insured individuals whose names are mentioned explicitly on the declarations page of the policy are generally referred to as **named insureds**, whereas other covered individuals, such as dependent family members, employees, and passengers of the named insureds, are referred to simply as **insureds**. (As will be noted later, for statistical and actuarial purposes, it is the individual vehicle, not the policy or the insured, that is considered the fundamental unit of risk.)

When discussing the parties involved in an automobile accident (whether or not they are insured), it is important to distinguish between those who cause injury and those who are injured. To this end, we will use the (somewhat legalistic, but commonly accepted) term **tortfeasor** to refer to the at-fault motorist, and the term **victim** to refer to anyone whose person or property is damaged by a tortfeasor.

Naturally, it is possible for there to be more than one tortfeasor associated with a given accident (i.e., it is possible for one or more motorists to share responsibility for causing the accident), and it also is possible for a tortfeasor to be a victim (of himself or herself and/or of another tortfeasor). The various American states deal with the potential sharing of fault through their **comparative negligence** statutes. "Pure" comparative negligence laws permit a victim to recover damages up to the percentage of fault for which a different tortfeasor is responsible, regardless of how much fault is attributable to the victim (e.g., if Driver A is 25 percent at-fault and Driver B is 75 percent at-fault, then A can recover 75 percent of his or her damages from B, and B can recover 25 percent of his or her damages from A). Many states have **contributory negligence** restrictions that permit a victim to recover damages only if his or her own contribution to fault is no more than that of the other tortfeasor (the "50 percent rule"), or if his or her own contribution to fault is strictly less than that of the other tortfeasor (the "49 percent rule").

The financial protection afforded by an automobile insurance policy is divided into a number of different components, or **coverages**, that respond to different types of personal injury and property damage. Although coverages may be bundled in different ways in different states, the following breakdown is typical of many jurisdictions:

Bodily Injury Liability (BI or BIL) is a **liability** coverage that compensates victims of an insured tortfeasor for any type of **personal injury damage** caused by the insured, including medical services, lost income, pain and suffering, and death. This coverage is often sold with one or more different dollar **limits** (i.e., caps) on the total amount that will be paid by the insurer (on a per-accident and/or per-victim basis). Because BI responds to the claims of those who are not insured by the coverage, it is said to be a **third-party coverage**.

Property Damage Liability (PD or PDL) is a liability coverage that compensates victims of an insured tortfeasor for any type of **property damage** caused by the insured. Like BI, this coverage is often sold with one or more different dollar limits on the total amount that will be paid by the insurer, and it is a third-party coverage.

Personal Injury Protection (PIP) is a no-fault coverage that compensates insured victims for economic personal injury damage, including medical services, lost income, and death, regardless of who caused the damage. Sometimes, this coverage is further subdivided into separate coverages for distinct types of economic loss (**Medical Payments (MedPay), Income Loss**, and **Death**). PIP coverage is often sold with one or more different dollar limits on the total amount that will be paid by the insurer. Because PIP responds to the claims of insureds, it is said to be a **first-party coverage**.

Uninsured Motorist (UM) is a liability coverage that compensates insured victims of an **uninsured** tortfeasor (i.e., a tortfeasor who has not purchased BI insurance) for any type of personal injury damage, including medical services, lost income, pain and suffering, and death. This coverage is often sold with one or more different dollar limits on the total amount that will be paid by the insurer. Although a liability coverage, UM responds to the claims of insureds, and is therefore a first-party coverage.

Underinsured Motorist (UIM) is a liability coverage that compensates insured victims of an **underinsured** tortfeasor (i.e., a tortfeasor whose BI insurance is insufficient to pay for all damages caused) for any type of personal injury damage, including medical services, lost income, pain and suffering, and death. This coverage is often sold with one or more different dollar limits on the total amount that will be paid by the insurer. Like UM, it is a first-party coverage.

Collision (COLL) is a no-fault coverage that compensates insured victims for any type of property damage resulting from a collision, regardless of who caused the damage. This coverage is often sold with one or more different dollar **deductibles**, so that claim amounts below the deductible will not be paid by the insurer. Because COLL responds to the claims of insureds, it is said to be a first-party coverage.

Comprehensive (COMP) is a no-fault coverage that compensates insured victims for any type of non-collision property damage (e.g., automobile theft, vandalism, and glass damage). This coverage is often sold with one or more different dollar deductibles, so that claim amounts below the deductible will not be paid by the insurer. Like COLL, it is a first-party coverage.

The typical coverages described above are summarized in Table 1 below. In most, but not all, of the American states, all motorists are required by state **financial responsibility** laws to purchase one or more of these coverages. Usually, states require that all motorists purchase the third-party liability coverages (BI and PD) up to certain **minimum limits**, as well as some degree of first-party no-fault protection for personal injury (e.g., PIP Medical Payments up to certain limits). These are referred to as the **mandatory** or **compulsory** coverages (as distinguished from the remaining **optional** coverages).

While insurance companies are generally required by state law to make a set of coverages available in the marketplace, they are not necessarily required to sell insurance voluntarily to every motorist who wishes to purchase it. Subject to conditions specified by consumer protection laws and regulations, insurance companies are permitted to **underwrite** their book of business by making **refusals to write**, **refusals to renew**, and **policy cancellations**.

To make sure that all motorists are able to purchase a minimum amount of automobile insurance (and especially any coverages required by law) each state provides for the establishment of a **residual market mechanism** to serve as the "insurer of last resort" for those who cannot obtain insurance in the voluntary market. These residual markets are generally industry-operated entities, and commonly take either of two basic forms: (1) an **assigned risk plan**, through which hard-to-place insureds are allocated randomly among the insurers writing in a given market, or (2) a **joint underwriting association** (JUA) or **insurance facility**, through which hard-to-place insureds are provided insurance by a pooling mechanism in which all insurers in the market share the risks of these insureds.

Table 1
Summary of Typical Automobile Insurance Coverages

	Personal Injury Coverages	**Physical Damage Coverages**
Liability Coverages	Bodily Injury Liability Uninsured Motorist* Underinsured Motorist*	Property Damage Liability
No-Fault Coverages	PIP—Medical Payments PIP—Income Loss PIP—Death	Collision Comprehensive

* *Note that although the UM and UIM are liability coverages, they are actually paid on a first-party basis (i.e., by the insured victim's own insurance company).*

2.2. Recovery Systems and Restrictions

We already have mentioned the impact of comparative negligence statutes, as well as the effects of coverage deductibles and limits, on the recovery of personal injury and property damage losses. We now describe a number of legal and institutional conventions that affect the flows of funds among insurance companies and accident victims, including some of the basic terminology of no-fault automobile insurance.

For any personal injury or property damage claim made by an automobile accident victim, there is (generally) an explicit order in which all relevant policies and policy coverages will apply to pay the claim. This predetermined **priority of recovery** is established through a combination of state law, insurance contract language, and derivative case law. Generally speaking, the no-fault automobile coverages (PIP, COLL, and COMP) enjoy primacy, and so pay first. However, important exceptions to this occur when: (1) the victim is engaged in employment-related activity, in which case workers' compensation coverage is generally primary for personal injuries, or (2) state law or insurance contract language has specifically provided for alternative health insurance coverage to be primary for personal injuries.

Often, there is more than one no-fault automobile coverage that is eligible to respond to a specific type of damage. For example, consider the case of Passenger A, who is riding in Driver B's automobile when it is struck by Driver C. In some jurisdictions, A may be able to collect for personal injury damages from any one of the PIP coverages belonging to A, B, or C, but only as permitted by the priority of recovery. For example, A may be required to seek compensation first from his or her own policy, then from the policy of B, and finally from the policy of C.

Ultimately, after all eligible no-fault coverages have paid their full amounts, the victim may seek further compensation from the liability coverages (BI or PD) of one or more tortfeasors (other than himself or herself) or from the UM/UIM coverages, if a tortfeasor is uninsured/underinsured.

When recovering from more than one automobile insurance coverage and/or policy, the total amount that the victim can receive is governed by **collateral source rules**, which generally prevent the victim from collecting more than once ("double-dipping") for the same damages (whether of a personal injury or property nature). In addition, the total amount of recovery may be augmented or restricted by **stacking rules**, which specify the degree to which the victim can collect from the same type of coverage on more than one policy—for example, whether Passenger A in the above scenario could "stack" the PIP coverages of Drivers B and C on top of his or her own PIP coverage, taking advantage of the full limits of all three coverages. (Often, stacking is particularly relevant—and controversial—in the context of recovery from the UM and UIM coverages when a victim owns more than one automobile, and therefore may have access to UM or UIM coverage from a vehicle that was not even involved in the accident.) Like the priority of recovery, collateral source and stacking rules are established through a combination of state law, insurance contract language, and derivative case law.

In many cases, the insurer that compensates a victim through a no-fault coverage will retain **subrogation rights** to recover part or all of its claim payments from the tortfeasor responsible for the victim's damages. This is especially true in the case of property damage claims, where the victim's insurer first pays the victim through the no-fault COLL coverage, and then seeks recovery from the tortfeasor's PD coverage. Subrogation is less often permitted for personal injury damages.

The explicit purpose of a no-fault recovery system is to achieve improved efficiency and fairness by compensating victims primarily through the no-fault coverages, and by imposing certain barriers to litigation to limit the use of the liability coverages. Within a **mandatory no-fault** recovery system, the barrier to recovery, or **tort threshold**, generally takes either of two forms: (1) a **monetary threshold**, which represents a specified dollar amount that must be reached by the victim's personal injury economic losses before he or she is permitted seek non-economic damages, or (2) a **verbal threshold**, which represents a legal standard of "seriousness" that must be reached by the victim's injuries before he or she is permitted to seek non-economic damages. Rather than imposing a tort threshold on all victims, a **choice** no-fault system offers individual insureds the opportunity to decide whether they would prefer lower automobile insurance premiums in return for some tort restrictions, or higher premiums and no tort restrictions.

2.3. Statistical and Accounting Measures

Insurance companies must keep track of insurance **claim costs** for purposes of setting insurance **rates** (average premium dollar amounts to be charged per unit of risk), and **loss reserves** (total dollar amounts to be set aside to pay future claims). To this end, insurers collect a variety of claim cost experience and accounting data related to each of the various automobile coverages.

As noted above, the basic unit of risk, or **exposure unit**, is the individual vehicle. For a given time period and coverage, an automobile insurance company will keep track of its total **number of exposures**, as well as the associated total **claim count** (i.e., number of claims), total **losses** (i.e., dollars in **claim payments**), total insurance **premiums**, and total **expenses**. Because of the nature of the insurance business, in which an insured's premium dollars are often collected well in advance of the time that any claim payments are made, the various types of experience and accounting data are tracked by the insurer in a number of special ways.

With respect to total losses, one important distinction is between **paid losses**, which already have been paid by the insurer, and **incurred losses**, which include both paid losses and loss reserves. A similar distinction is made between **paid claim counts** and **incurred claim counts**. Premiums are often recorded on a **written** basis, which includes all premiums associated with new and renewed policies underwritten during a given period, as well as an **earned** basis, which includes all premiums associated with the fractions of policies for which coverage is actually provided during the period. Various types of corporate expenses, such as **general company expenses** (overhead), **agent commissions and other acquisition costs**, **state premium taxes**, and **unallocated loss adjustment expenses** (i.e., claim settlement expenses that cannot be attributed to specific claims) are also often kept on both a written and earned basis. **Allocated loss adjustment expenses**, which can be attributed to the settlement of specific claims, are usually included as a portion of losses (paid or incurred).

To compute the underlying rate for a portfolio of automobile exposures, insurers often work with the following useful ratios:

$$\textit{Claim Frequency} = \frac{\textit{Total Claim Count}}{\textit{Total Number of Exposures}},$$

$$\textit{Claim Severity} = \frac{\textit{Total Losses}}{\textit{Total Claim Count}},$$

$$\textit{Pure Premium} = \frac{\textit{Total Losses}}{\textit{Total Number of Exposures}}$$

$$= \textit{Claim Frequency} \times \textit{Claim Severity},$$

$$\textit{Expense Pure Premium} = \frac{\textit{Total Expenses}}{\textit{Total Number of Exposures}},$$

$$\textit{Loss Ratio} = \frac{\textit{Total Losses}}{\textit{Total Premiums}}, \text{ and}$$

$$\textit{Expense Ratio} = \frac{\textit{Total Expenses}}{\textit{Total Premiums}}.$$

Given that the various quantities in the above ratios may be recorded in more than one way (e.g., total losses may be stated on either a paid or incurred basis, and total premiums may be stated on either a written or earned basis), it follows that these ratios themselves may be recorded in a number of different ways.

Ultimately, an individual insured's premium is calculated as the sum of the appropriate **pure premium** and **expense pure premium**. These quantities will include separate adjustments for a variety of **driver class**, **territorial**, and **model-type/model-year relativities** to recognize the disparate levels of risk and expense associated with different demographic, driving record, geographic, and vehicle categories.

3. KEY ISSUES

A thoughtful consideration of any no-fault proposal must address a variety of economic and political issues. From an economic perspective, one can begin with the traditional actuarial issues regarding the impact of choice no-fault on claim frequency and claim severity for the various personal injury coverages involved. These issues, familiar from past debates on mandatory no-fault, involve such questions as:

- What will be the impact of the no-fault barrier to recovery on BI claim frequency?
- How will the reduction in BI claims translate into premium reductions?
- To what extent will BI premium savings simply be offset by increases in PIP premiums?
- What will be the impact of various related laws—e.g., comparative negligence statutes, mandatory basic limits of insurance coverage, and collateral source rules—on forecast premium reductions?
- What will be the long-term impact on insurance-purchasing behavior (i.e., the purchase of optional coverage limits, as well as compliance with mandatory coverage limits)?
- What will be the moral hazard implications for driver behavior?

With the introduction of choice no-fault, these questions become substantially more complicated, in that they must be answered separately for both no-fault electors and traditional tort electors. In addition, there are several new questions related specifically to the operation of the choice mechanism:

- Will cost savings depend on the proportion of insureds that elect the no-fault option? What factors will influence the proportion of insureds electing no-fault?
- Will it be sufficient to set premiums based solely upon the statistical experience of drivers, or will it be necessary to provide no-fault electors with a non-experience-based premium reduction?

- Will the moral hazard implications for driver behavior be the same as in the case of mandatory no-fault?
- What will be the adverse selection implications associated with the election of the no-fault option?

At the political level, one again faces many of the same questions applicable to discussions of mandatory no-fault:

- What level of barrier to tort recovery will be acceptable to consumers/taxpayers?
- How will variations in the type of barrier to recovery affect the political positions taken by insurers? by trial attorneys? and by consumer groups?
- How can policy makers be certain that potential cost savings will be realized? What will influence such certainty?
- To what extent will the issue be framed in terms of whether or not to preserve a consumer's "right" to tort recovery? How will consideration of such a "right" affect the political debate?

In addition, one must confront several new questions related to the nature of the choice proposal, and especially its application under the proposed federal legislation:

- To what extent will there be concern that individuals "really have a choice," rather than being coerced—by either economic hardship or their relationship to a "named insured"—to become no-fault electors?
- Will the choice feature diminish potential opposition from trial attorney groups and/or lawyer-legislators? To the extent that such individuals remain opposed, will the choice feature diminish their ability to win allies among other policy makers?
- How will the uncertainties of cost savings under choice no-fault affect political support from insurers?
- How understandable will the more subtle features of choice no-fault (e.g., provisions for dealing with accidents between insureds electing different options) be to lawmakers? How will any confusion/uncertainty affect support for choice legislation?
- Under the federal proposal, will the flexibility given to states in constructing their own no-fault alternatives, in addition to the possibility of "opting out," be sufficient to maintain the principle of federalism and satisfy constitutional concerns?
- Will there be unforeseen consequences to this model of federalism?

4. CHAPTER SUMMARY

In the pages that follow, we bring together much of the best scholarship relevant to the subject of choice no-fault insurance. Most of this work is specific to the choice option, but some of the broader issues of no-fault insurance are discussed when they offer important implications for the choice debate.

In Chapter 2, **Lascher** and **Powers** complete the "Background" portion of this volume by providing further depth regarding the rationale for choice, the context in which it has emerged, and the tradeoffs it entails. We begin by tracing the recent history of no-fault and summarizing the key variables in choice approaches. We then offer a simple economic model of consumer behavior under choice, focusing especially on the crucial issues of moral hazard and litigiousness, and conclude with an overview of political considerations.

The next five chapters include a number of pieces related to the "Economics and Practice" of choice no-fault. Chapter 3 represents an updated version of the widely cited work of **Stephen Carroll** and **Allan Abrahamse**, in which these researchers describe a methodology for estimating how the implementation of choice no-fault would affect consumer costs, and then offer detailed state-by-state estimates of the impact of such a change.

To provide some philosophical balance, Chapter 4, by **Brent Kabler**, offers "The Case against Auto Choice." Here Kabler makes a strong argument for rejecting the choice approach, using accident and fatality rates from both mandatory no-fault and traditional tort states to emphasize the potential weakening of accident "deterrence" under no-fault, and to question whether the types of savings projected by Carroll and Abrahamse can actually be realized.

The subsequent three chapters, by **David Loughran** (Chapter 5), **Jia-Hsing Yeh** and **Joan Schmit** (Chapter 6), and **Laureen Regan** (Chapter 7), provide extensive empirical analyses of use to policy makers interested in gauging the probable impact of a choice no-fault system. Comparing the experience of mandatory no-fault and traditional tort systems in the U.S., Loughran comes to a sharply different conclusion from Kabler regarding the influence of no-fault on driver behavior. Yeh and Schmit then provide an analysis of actual claim experience data from New Jersey and Pennsylvania, two states that implemented choice systems, and Regan studies the critical issue of what factors cause insureds to select the "limited tort" option in Pennsylvania.

In the final five chapters, we include a number of pieces related to the "History and Politics" of choice no-fault. This portion begins, in Chapter 8, with a reprint of the classic and seminal article by **Jeffrey O'Connell** and **Robert Joost**, laying out the basic principles and potential advantages of a choice no-fault system. We then turn, in Chapter 9, to the article by **Powers**, which explicitly considers the various possible recovery relationships between electors of no-fault and traditional tort, and finds that these different approaches differ substantially in terms of meeting two fundamental equity principles. Powers also explains in detail how issues of insurer fund imbalances and improper underwriting incentives can be handled under the "self-determining system."

In Chapter 10, **Dan Miller** focuses on the distributional effects of automobile injury compensation systems, and argues that the traditional tort-liability approach adversely affects some of the most vulnerable members of society. In Chapter 11, **Peter Kinzler** and **Jeffrey O'Connell** draw from Miller's work, and illustrate how savings from choice no-fault would be realized under a number of different real-world scenarios.

Finally, in Chapter 12, **Lascher** considers the political feasibility of adopting choice no-fault at the national and state levels in the U.S. (contending along the way that the Canadian political environment is more conducive to mandatory no-fault schemes). Lascher argues that at the state level, choice systems indeed offer some specific political advantages over mandatory no-fault, but that choice poses some political dangers as well.

References

Lascher, Edward L., Jr., 1995, "Choice No-Fault" Insurance May Well Work in Rhode Island, *Providence Sunday Journal*, July 9, D7.

O'Connell, Jeffrey, and Robert H. Joost, 1986, Giving Motorists a Choice between Fault and No-Fault Insurance, *Virginia Law Review*, 72, 61-89.

Powers, Michael R., 1992, Equity in Automobile Insurance: Optional No-Fault, *The Journal of Risk and Insurance*, 59, 2, 203-220.

2
CHOICE NO-FAULT INSURANCE: EFFICIENCY AND EQUITY

Edward L. Lascher, Jr.
California State University, Sacramento

Michael R. Powers
Temple University

1. THE GENESIS OF "CHOICE"

Although slightly more that one-half of the fifty American states require automobile insurers to offer no-fault personal injury coverages (i.e., PIP), many of these states fail to provide any accompanying barrier to tort recovery. In fact, fewer than one-third of all states impose any barrier to recovery, and these barriers invariably take the form of a monetary or verbal threshold[1] that must be satisfied before an accident victim can seek recovery for non-economic (pain and suffering) damages. Currently, no state imposes a barrier to third-party recovery for economic damages.

Massachusetts and Florida enacted the first no-fault laws in the early 1970s, and these states were followed by a small flurry of others during the subsequent decade. In the last twenty years, however, few states have enacted or rescinded no-faults statutes, and so the overall picture in the U.S. has changed little. The most notable developments during this time period took place in New Jersey and Pennsylvania, where choice no-fault systems were enacted.

The story in Canada has been quite different. As in the U.S., the Canadian provinces did not impose limitations on tort recovery prior to the 1970s. Yet in the late 1970s, Quebec moved to establish a pure no-fault system (i.e., a system with an insuperable barrier to all tort recovery). Since

[1] A "monetary" threshold requires that a victim's economic damages reach a certain dollar level, whereas a "verbal" threshold requires that a victim's bodily injuries satisfy a legal standard of "serious" injury.

that time, two other provinces, Manitoba and Saskatchewan, have adopted pure no-fault in response to concerns about insurance rate and claim pressures. Furthermore, Ontario, the country's most populous province, adopted a strong verbal threshold no-fault system. Consequently, by the mid-1990s most Canadian drivers were covered by policies that either blocked, or placed severe limitations on, tort recovery. In short, while provincial governments have given some consideration to choice plans, political agendas in Canada have remained more focused on mandatory plans, several of which have been adopted.

While there is little dispute in the academic literature about the reality of BI cost savings under mandatory no-fault systems, it is also generally recognized that these savings can be diminished by the "erosion" of no-fault thresholds.[2] Clearly, the choice no-fault movement—which generally has promoted the use of a strong verbal threshold or an insuperable barrier to recovery of non-economic damages—represents an attempt to take advantage of the cost savings promised by no-fault, while addressing the greatest perceived shortcoming of mandatory no-fault: the requirement that accident victims be restricted *involuntarily* from seeking recovery through the traditional tort system.[3]

Crucial to any analysis of choice no-fault is an understanding of two fundamental characteristics of the choice system: (1) the nature of the no-fault barrier to tort recovery, and (2) the manner in which accidents involving different types of insureds (i.e., both tort and no-fault electors) are resolved.

As noted above, there are three types of barriers to tort recovery currently used in North America: monetary thresholds for non-economic tort recovery, verbal thresholds for non-economic tort recovery, and an insuperable barrier to all economic and non-economic tort recovery. Obviously, there is much room among these three types for novel alternatives, such as monetary and verbal thresholds for economic (as well as non-economic) tort recovery, and insuperable barriers to non-economic (but not economic) tort recovery.

With regard to resolving claims from accidents involving both tort and no-fault electors, there exist three possible systems, as noted by Powers (1992): "tort-favoring", in which both parties enjoy unrestricted tort rights, "no-fault-favoring", in which both parties are subject to restricted tort rights, and "self-determining", in which the tort elector enjoys unrestricted tort rights, but the no-fault elector is subject to restricted tort rights.

---

[2] Over the years, the impact of monetary thresholds tends to be weakened by medical cost inflation; verbal thresholds, which are immune to economic inflation, may still be weakened by "judicial inflation" of what constitutes a "serious" injury.

[3] In Powers (1992), this is described as a violation of the "tort equity principle."

One important aspect of the proposed U.S. federal choice legislation is the flexibility that it allows individual states in determining the appropriate barrier to tort recovery and method for resolving accidents involving both tort and no-fault electors. The proposal gives preference to (i.e., sets as the default) systems with the following characteristics:

(1) an insuperable barrier to all non-economic (but not economic) tort recovery, and

(2) the no-fault-favoring approach.

However, the legislation would permit other combinations of alternatives, including those currently employed in the states with choice no-fault.

2. ECONOMIC BEHAVIORS

To develop a simple framework for describing the basic economic behaviors associated with choice no-fault, we begin with Figure 1, which portrays (Walrasian) equilibrium in the market for PIP coverage under a traditional tort system with "add-on" first-party no-fault benefits. In this figure, the curve D_Q represents hypothetical market demand for PIP coverage, and is formed by solving for the insureds' optimal quantity of insurance associated with each given level of price. Similarly, the curve S_Q represents hypothetical market supply, and is formed by solving for the insurers' optimal quantity of insurance associated with each given level of price. Market equilibrium is found at the point E, the intersection of the two curves.

Now consider Figure 2, which depicts the anticipated impact of a transition from traditional tort/add-on to mandatory pure no-fault (i.e., no-fault with an insuperable barrier to all tort recovery). Clearly, the basic effects of this transition are: (1) to shift the demand curve to the right (to D'_Q) to recognize the transfer in the insureds' resources from the purchase of BI coverage to PIP, and (2) to shift the supply curve to the right (to S'_Q), to recognize the insurers' increased capacity for PIP coverage, as the market for BI evaporates. The net result of imposing mandatory pure no-fault is thus to shift market equilibrium from E to E', increasing the quantity of PIP coverage purchased, with an ambiguous effect on price.

As noted along the right-hand border of this figure, the region of increased PIP quantity is where problems of moral hazard are more likely to occur. In other words, as the equilibrium level of PIP coverage increases, insureds are more likely to take risks in their driving—both because of enhanced first-party no-fault compensation and because of reduced third-party liability risk.

Figure 1
Equilibrium in a Market for PIP Coverage
(under Traditional Tort/Add-on)

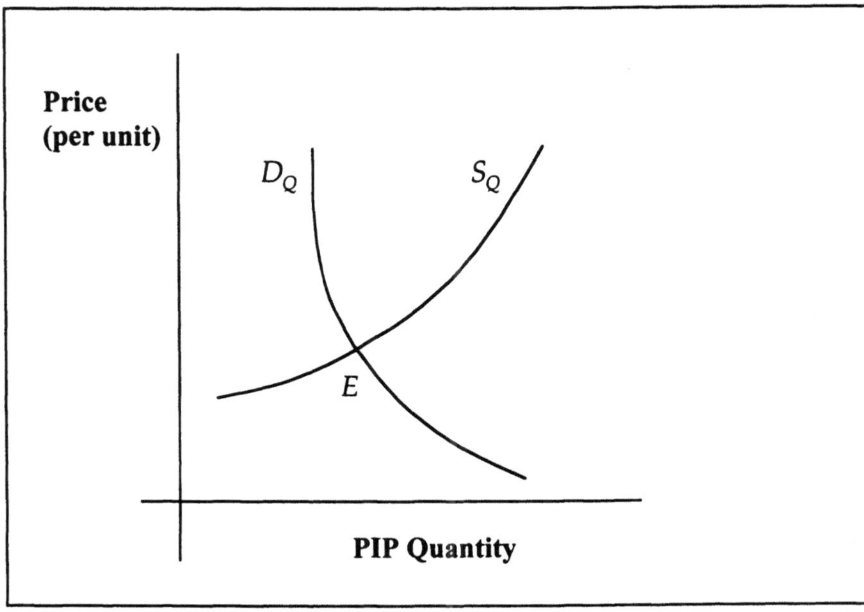

To look more closely at the specific effects of a "choice" mechanism, we now posit an entire continuum of mandatory no-fault systems existing between the extremes of traditional tort/add-on and pure no-fault. (For example, one could start with a monetary threshold of zero, and gradually increase its value through the positive real numbers to infinity, in the limit.) In this model, the insureds/insurers not only would be permitted to select the optimal amount of PIP coverage to purchase/sell, but also would be permitted the "choice" of the optimal tradeoff between reliance on traditional tort (with BI coverage) and pure no-fault (with only PIP).

To depict market demand and market supply under these assumptions would require a three-dimensional coordinate system, as shown in Figure 3. Here, the horizontal (x-) and vertical (z-) axes are identical to those used in

Figure 1, whereas the y-axis represents the degree to which traditional tort is relied on for personal injury recoveries.[4]

Figure 2
Equilibrium in a Market for PIP Coverage
(under Mandatory Pure No-Fault)

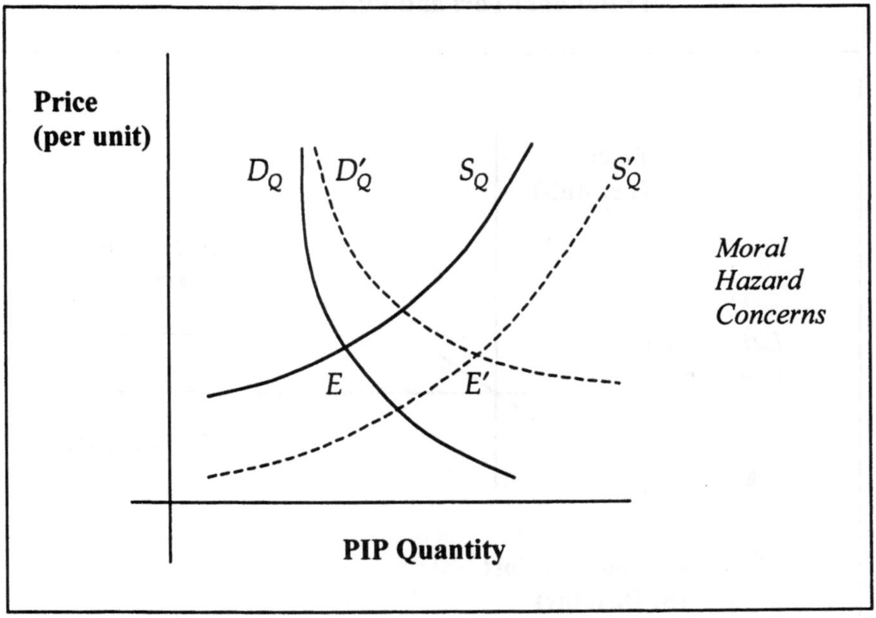

Continuing with this scheme, we see that hypothetical market demand would be given by a two-dimensional surface sloping down (toward the viewer), as in Figure 4, and hypothetical market supply would be given by a two-dimensional surface sloping up (toward the viewer), as in Figure 5. Superimposing these two surfaces would yield an equilibrium "curve", whose endpoints would be found at E' (by slicing along the xz-plane to obtain Figure 2) and E (by slicing along a plane parallel to the xz-plane at the maximum value of y to obtain Figure 1).

Of course, no currently viable legislative proposal provides for individual insureds to select among a continuum of no-fault barriers.[5] However, consideration of the above theoretical market does enable one to

[4] For example, if one were using a monetary threshold, then the value of the threshold would be a decreasing function of y, ranging from infinity to zero.

[5] It is interesting to note that, for a number of years, New Jersey's choice no-fault system actually did permit insureds to select from either of two different monetary thresholds.

evaluate conceptually the effect of a choice system on each of three potentially problematic behaviors of the insurance market: *moral hazard*, *litigiousness*, and *adverse selection*.

Figure 3
Market with Tradeoff "Choice" between Traditional Tort and Pure No-Fault

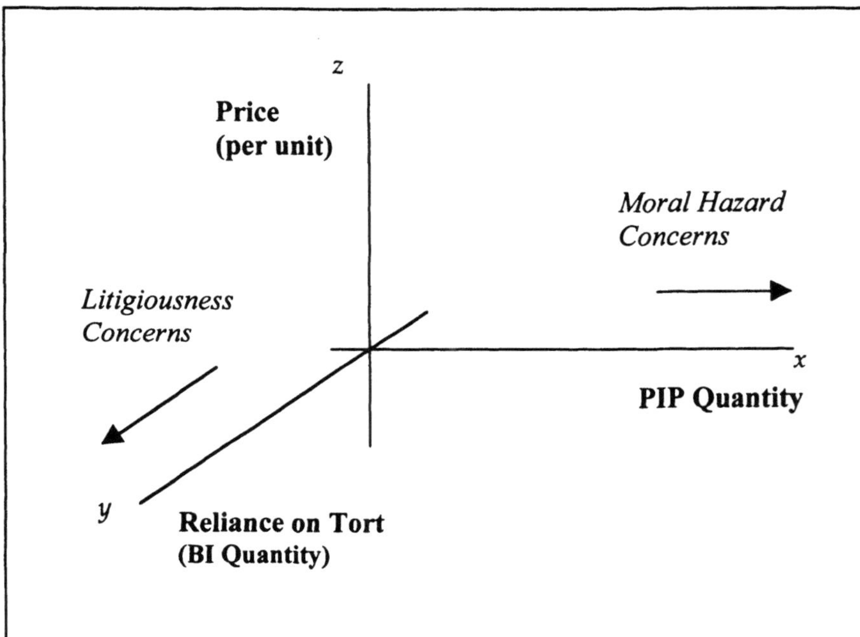

Returning to Figure 3, we see that, at the extreme of mandatory pure no-fault, there may be problems with moral hazard in equilibrium, whereas at the other extreme—traditional tort/add-on—there may be problems with litigiousness (the underlying motivation for no-fault in the first place). Thus, moral hazard and litigiousness may be viewed as conceptually analogous behaviors: the former is the pathology of excessive first-party no-fault insurance, whereas the latter is the pathology of excessive reliance on third-party liability recovery.

This analysis may be carried further. Just as the imposition of the no-fault barrier led to concerns about moral hazard in Figure 2, the imposition of a fixed upper limit on PIP benefits would cause analogous concerns about litigiousness, as accident victims sought additional recovery through the tort system. This is essentially why unlimited PIP medical benefits have always been the ideal of no-fault advocates.

Figure 4
"Choice" Market Demand

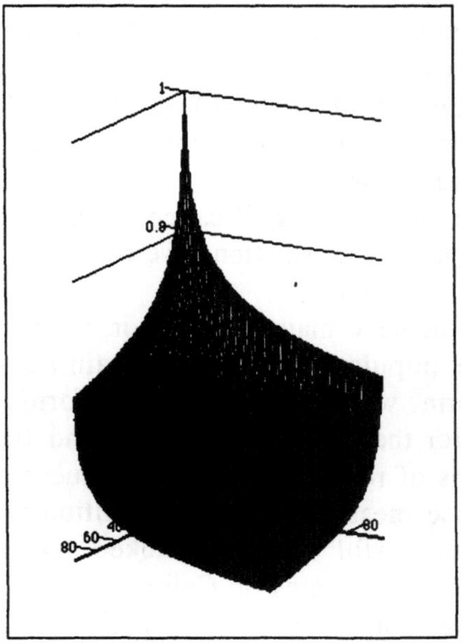

Figure 5
"Choice" Market Supply

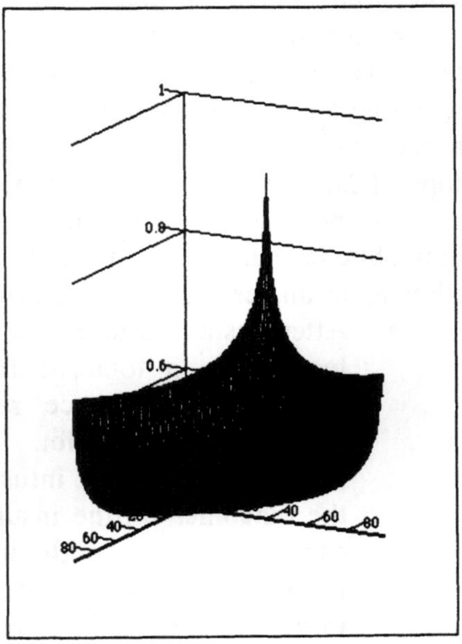

The degree to which adverse selection is a problem would depend on how the insureds distributed themselves along the equilibrium curve formed by the intersection of the surfaces in Figures 4 and 5. Points along this curve closer to the xz-plane would represent insureds preferring no-fault, whereas points farther away would indicate those preferring traditional tort. Thus, if stronger levels of no-fault were disproportionately popular among higher-risk insureds (because no-fault offers some immunity from tort recovery), then the higher-risk insureds would have a tendency to place themselves closer to the xz-plane, forcing up prices and driving out the lower-risk insureds.

Naturally, there does not need to be a continuum of no-fault choices for the problem of adverse selection to occur. Given the discrete choice between traditional tort/add-on (Figure 1) and mandatory pure no-fault (Figure 2), the presence of too many higher-risk insureds electing no-fault may drive lower-risk insureds away from the no-fault option.

3. POLITICAL CONSIDERATIONS

In both the U.S. and Canada, no-fault automobile insurance has been hotly contested at the state/provincial level since the early 1970s. Influential interest groups have staked out sharply different positions on the issue, and fierce, well-funded, political battles have occurred over reform proposals. Choice no-fault is a relative newcomer to this debate, arising in several state legislative initiatives in the mid-1980s as a novel response to dramatically increasing automobile insurance premiums. At the federal level in the U.S., choice no-fault is an even more recent phenomenon, with the current proposal dating back only as far as the mid-1990s.

To provide some flavor of the political significance of no-fault automobile insurance in many North American jurisdictions, we consider the following examples, taken from Lascher (1999, ch. 1):

- After unsuccessful efforts to achieve major changes in the state legislature, a total of five popular initiatives pertaining to automobile insurance reform were placed on California's November 1988 ballot. With the insurance industry and trial lawyers making vast infusions of resources aimed at influencing the outcomes on the insurance measures (e.g., $37 million was expended on a single unsuccessful measure backed by the insurance industry), campaign expenditures on California's ballot initiatives exceeded the total amount of funds spent nationally by the candidates for the 1988 presidential campaign.
- The issue of how to deal with spiraling automobile insurance costs dominated the 1987 provincial election campaign in Ontario. After the Liberal Party's victory, buoyed by Premier David Peterson's promise of a "specific plan to lower rates," the issue was the subject of intensive discussions among top governmental officials. These discussions led in turn to enactment of major no-fault insurance legislation. A subsequent government contemplated a sharply different approach to automobile insurance reform (establishing a public insurance system), but ultimately backed away from this plan.
- After a multi-year battle, Pennsylvania Governor Robert P. Casey in 1990 succeeded in obtaining enactment of comprehensive automobile insurance reform legislation, including choice no-fault. In an interview shortly before his retirement, Casey indicated that this was one of his proudest accomplishments since the legislation addressed the "biggest consumer issue in the state."

- In 1988, Manitoba's governing New Democratic Party (NDP) lost a vote of confidence and subsequently suffered electoral defeat at the hands of the Progressive Conservative Party. Both losses were widely attributed to anger at the NDP for political manipulation of insurance rates under the province's public automobile insurance system. In 1993, the Progressive Conservatives pushed through their own no-fault insurance plan, completely restructuring the existing system.

Although generally supported by insurers and their industry trade associations, no-fault insurance has created one implacable set of enemies: trial attorneys. Throughout North America, trial attorneys have been strongly and almost universally opposed to no-fault in all of its various forms—a position that is well-recognized in both the popular press and the academic literature.

There are two fundamental reasons for the trial attorneys' antagonism to no-fault. First, many trial attorneys stand to lose a substantial amount of income from restrictions on tort actions, because automobile accidents constitute a significant source of tort claims. In fact, a 1992 U.S. Department of Justice study indicated that automobile insurance accidents were by far the most common source of state court cases in the nation's seventy-five largest counties, accounting for fully 60 percent of all tort cases disposed (Smith, et al., 1995). Second, trial attorneys tend to have an ideological attachment to the protection of constitutional and common-law "rights", including the unfettered ability to seek redress through the court system.

The stances of various consumer groups have been less monolithic, and considerably more complicated, than those of the insurers and trial attorneys. In some jurisdictions (e.g., Rhode Island), organized consumer groups were actively involved in insurance reform battles, whereas in others (e.g., Pennsylvania and Manitoba), there was little involvement. Furthermore, where consumer groups have been active, they have been observed to take different positions with respect to no-fault—some have been supportive, while others (especially those closely associated with U.S. consumer advocate Ralph Nader) have allied themselves with the trial attorneys.[6]

[6] The split between consumer groups has been evident in California over the past ten to fifteen years. Voter Revolt, the consumer group that had sponsored *Proposition 103* in 1988, led a successful effort to place a strong no-fault initiative on the spring 1996 primary election ballot. Opposition to the no-fault approach caused one of Voter Revolt's original founders to leave the group and join forces with trial attorneys to urge the measure's defeat. Ultimately, the no-fault initiative was soundly defeated by voters.

Nevertheless, from the perspective of elected officials, the positions of organized consumer groups are not necessarily the most noticeable manifestations of consumer (and therefore broad constituent) opinion. Instead, more forceful input often comes in the form of spontaneous or loosely organized complaints about high automobile insurance premiums, and about the need for elected officials to "do something."

In considering various automobile insurance reform proposals, politicians understand that there are undeniable costs associated with mandatory no-fault, because some accident victims will obtain less compensation than under a traditional tort system. Thus, as noted above, the choice no-fault movement represents an attempt by lawmakers to take advantage of the cost savings promised by no-fault, while alleviating the requirement that accident victims be restricted *involuntarily* from seeking recovery through traditional tort.

There is some evidence to indicate that adoption of choice no-fault is in fact more politically feasible than adoption of mandatory plans, at least in the U.S. It is noteworthy that the only successful 1990s effort to move a state toward a stronger no-fault system (the Pennsylvania legislation referred to previously) included choice provisions. Furthermore, Governor Casey backed the choice option only after previously failing to make headway with a mandatory plan. In Rhode Island, where no-fault legislation progressed further than in most other states during the past decade, a mandatory no-fault plan evolved into a choice proposal after encountering stiff opposition, and the choice plan actually passed one house of the state legislature. Experience in these and other states suggests that the choice option may indeed help to reassure lawmakers worried about involuntary limits on recovery rights, and to weaken some of the arguments made by trial attorneys and other no-fault opponents.

Differences in political capacities may well explain why the choice option has been relatively more prominent in the U.S. than in Canada. While all American states use a separation of powers system modeled after that at the national level, all Canadian provinces operate under a Westminster-style parliamentary system. A growing body of evidence suggests that the multiple veto points and dispersed power of the separation of powers system makes it especially difficult to impose political losses on powerful groups (see Weaver and Rockman, 1993; Pal and Weaver, forthcoming). Significant automobile insurance reforms require imposing such losses. Previous research (see Lascher, 1998; 1999, ch. 7) indicates that U.S.-Canadian political system differences help to explain the different fates of no-fault plans in the two countries. Given the challenges faced in the U.S., it may be that activists for no-fault have largely concluded that only the choice approach is "doable".

At the same time, there are uncertainties as to how much the shift to choice proposals benefits no-fault advocates, and what are the political tradeoffs associated with the different varieties of choice. For example, a "tort-favoring" choice system may best satisfy lawmakers worried about restricting their constituents' recovery rights. However, such an approach may cause insurers to abandon support, or even to oppose such a plan. We will explore the political subtleties of choice no-fault in greater depth in the last chapter of this book.

References

Lascher, Edward L., Jr., 1998, Loss Imposition and Institutional Characteristics: Learning from Automobile Insurance Reform in North America, *Canadian Journal of Political Science*, 31, 143-164.

Lascher, Edward L., Jr., 1999, *The Politics of Automobile Insurance Reform: Ideas, Institutions, and Public Policy in North America*, Washington, DC: Georgetown University Press.

Powers, Michael R., 1992, Equity in Automobile Insurance: Optional No-Fault, *The Journal of Risk and Insurance*, 59, 2, 203-220.

Smith, Steven K., Carol J. DeFrances, Patrick A. Langan, and John Goerdt, 1995, *Tort Cases in Large Counties*, U.S. Department of Justice, Bureau of Justice Statistics, April.

Pal, Leslie, and R. Kent Weaver, forthcoming, *The Politics of Pain: Political Institutions and Loss Imposition in the United States and Canada*, Washington, DC: The Brookings Institution.

Weaver, R. Kent, and Bert A. Rockman, eds., 1993, *Do Institutions Matter? Government Capabilities in the United States and Abroad*, Washington, DC: The Brookings Institution.

II. ECONOMICS AND PRACTICE

3
THE EFFECTS OF CHOICE AUTO INSURANCE ON COSTS AND COMPENSATION

Stephen J. Carroll
RAND Corporation

Allan F. Abrahamse
RAND Corporation

1. INTRODUCTION

In 1999, bills that would establish a choice auto insurance plan in all states were introduced in both the U.S. Senate (S. 837) and the U.S. House of Representatives (H.R. 1475). These bills would establish an auto insurance plan in every state under which consumers are given a choice between a modified version of their state's current insurance system (MCS) and an absolute no-fault (ANF) plan.[1] This analysis uses data for a representative sample of auto accident victims whose claims were closed in 1997 to estimate the effects of a choice automobile insurance plan that embodies the basic principles of the plans being considered in Congress. However, because of data limitations, we do not consider certain provisions of those plans. These are noted below.

In earlier studies,[2] we used data on the compensation provided to representative samples of auto accident victims whose claims were closed in 1987 and in 1992 to estimate the effects of a choice automobile insurance plan on the costs of compensating auto accident victims. This study replicates those earlier analyses, using exactly the same methodology.

---

[1] States would have the right to reject the choice plan and retain their current auto insurance plan.

[2] Abrahamse and Carroll (1995), Abrahamse and Carroll (1997), and Carroll and Abrahamse (1998).

Accordingly, the following description of our data and methodology is largely reproduced from our earlier reports.

2. THE CHOICE PLAN

In the choice plan examined here, all drivers are required to purchase bodily injury (BI) coverage to at least their state's financial responsibility level. Drivers who opt for MCS are also required to purchase a new form of insurance, tort maintenance (TM), to at least that level, and, in the current no-fault states, they are required to purchase the personal injury protection (PIP) coverage now required. Drivers who opt for ANF are required to purchase personal protection insurance (PPI) coverage to at least the state's financial responsibility level.[3] Drivers may purchase the same optional coverages now available under their state's current system: medical payments (MP), uninsured motorist (UM), underinsured motorist (UIM), and, in the add-on states, personal injury protection (PIP).

The rules of a state's current system would govern the compensation available to victims covered by MCS if no other driver were at least partially responsible for the accident or if any other driver at least partially responsible for the accident were uninsured or had also elected MCS. At-fault MCS insured victims covered by first-party, no-fault insurance would be compensated for their medical losses (under MP) or for all their economic losses (under PIP) by their own insurer. MCS insured victims injured by an uninsured driver would be compensated by their own UM insurance, if they had purchased that coverage, for their economic and non-economic losses to the degree the uninsured driver was at fault. MCS insured victims injured by a driver who had also elected MCS would be compensated by that driver's BI insurance for their economic and non-economic losses to the degree that that driver was at fault. In a no-fault state, the tort threshold would apply as in the current system.

MCS insured victims injured by an ANF insured driver in a tort state would seek compensation in fault for both economic and non-economic losses from their own insurer under their TM coverage. In essence, TM insurance would operate as UM coverage does today. In the no-fault states,

---

[3] PPI covers the insured's economic losses (and funeral costs), regardless of fault, to the policy limits. It provides essentially the same coverage as the PIP insurance now required in current no-fault systems and available in many of the current tort states. We use the term personal protection insurance in reference to the coverage purchased by consumers who opt for ANF under choice to distinguish it from the personal injury protection coverage purchased by consumers who opt for the modified current system under choice in a no-fault state.

MCS insured victims injured by an ANF insured driver would be compensated for their economic loss by their own PIP coverage up to the policy limit. If their injuries surmounted the tort threshold, they would seek compensation in fault from their own insurer under their TM coverage for any economic loss not covered by their PIP insurance as well as for non-economic losses.

Accident victims covered by MCS who were injured by an ANF insured driver may seek compensation in tort from that driver for economic losses in excess of their TM coverage. When claims for excess economic loss are pursued, a reasonable attorney's fee is recoverable, in addition to the excess economic loss.

In any state, victims who elected ANF would be compensated by their PPI insurance for any economic losses resulting from the accident, including accidents involving drivers who elected their state's MCS, without regard for fault, to the PPI policy limit. Drivers electing ANF could never seek compensation for non-economic losses. Accident victims covered by ANF may seek compensation in tort from a driver who injured them for economic losses in excess of their PPI coverage. When claims for excess economic loss are pursued, a reasonable attorney's fee is recoverable, in addition to the excess economic loss.

Uninsured drivers injured in auto accidents would proceed as under their state's current system if injured by either a driver who elected MCS or another uninsured driver. Uninsured drivers injured by an ANF insured driver may seek compensation for their economic losses in excess of the mandated PPI limit, to the extent the ANF insured driver was responsible for the accident.

Compensation for injured non-drivers—passengers, pedestrians, bicyclists, and so on—who have purchased auto insurance is governed by the rules relevant to their insurance, even though they were not driving when injured.[4] Compensation for injured non-drivers who have not purchased auto insurance is governed by the rules relevant to the insurance purchased by the driver who injured them.

3. SCOPE AND LIMITATIONS

Both the Senate and House versions of the Choice Plan would include commercial vehicles in the plan. However, because our data describe

[4] Motorists who choose either MCS or ANF bind their resident relatives to that choice.

compensation paid under private passenger auto insurance coverages, we do not consider the effects of including commercial auto insurance in the plan.

We note that both bills would allow a victim to recover under tort when the injury was caused by a tortfeasor's alcohol or drug abuse regardless of either party's choice. And drivers who elected the no-fault option under the choice plan would forfeit their no-fault benefits if they were injured while under the influence of alcohol or illegal drugs. However, data limitations prevent inclusion of these provisions in the plan examined here.

The Senate and House bills would make PPI benefits secondary to other compensation sources such as workers compensation. Because our data do not indicate the availability of benefits from collateral sources, we do not consider the effects of these provisions in the analysis. We assume that auto insurance is primary in this analysis.

Finally, both bills would allow legally uninsured non-drivers to seek compensation under their state's current system from a driver who injured them regardless of that driver's insurance choice. Our data do not identify the insurance status of non-drivers injured in auto accidents. Accordingly, the plan examined here incorporates a provision that appeared in earlier versions of the federal bills. We assume that non-drivers injured in auto accidents are compensated under the option elected by the driver who injured them.

In our study, we assume the distributions of accidents, injuries, and losses observed in the 1997 data for each state would be the same in that state under the choice plan. We estimate the costs of compensating the sample of victims in each state under either its current insurance system or the choice plan described above. The ratio of these estimates indicates the relative cost of compensating the same victims, for the same injuries and losses, under the two plans.[5] Because our results involve relative costs, they do not address whether auto insurance costs will rise or fall if a state adopts the choice plan. Rather, they show the difference between what would happen in that state if the current system were retained and what would occur instead if the choice plan were adopted.

We focus on how the choice plan affects auto insurers' compensation costs, including both the amounts insurers pay in compensation and the transaction costs they incur in providing that compensation.[6] Because the choice plan has no effect on property damage coverages, we do not consider

---

[5] We include all accident victims in these calculations: insured and uninsured drivers, passengers, pedestrians, bicyclists, people injured in single-car accidents, and so on.

[6] Under the choice plan, victims may recover reasonable attorney's fees for a claim for excess economic loss. The attorney's fees paid by insurers as a result of such claims are included in our estimates.

property damage in any of our estimates. To translate our estimates of the effects of the plan on compensation costs into estimates of the effects of the plan on insurance premiums, we assume that the many other factors (e.g., insurers' other expenses, profit margins, and investment income) that play a role in determining insurance premiums all vary in proportion to compensation costs. That is, we estimate savings on compensation costs and then estimate how total premiums for personal injury coverages would have to vary to maintain the existing ratio of total premiums to compensation costs.

We do not attempt to estimate the plan's effects on the costs of any particular coverage. Specifically, we compare the *average* amount insurers pay per insured driver under all coverages in the current system to the *average* amount paid under all coverages on behalf of drivers who choose either MCS or ANF under the choice plan.

For each state, we assume that the distribution of TM policy limits purchased by consumers who opt for MCS under choice would be the same as the distribution of BI policy limits purchased by consumers under the current system. The auto insurance compensation[7] for non-economic loss available to victims injured by a driver insured under the current system in each state is limited to that driver's BI policy limits. The auto insurance compensation for non-economic loss available to victims who elect MCS under choice in each state is limited to the victim's TM policy limits. Consequently, our assumption holds constant the average compensation for non-economic loss available to consumers who elect MCS. If consumers who elect MCS under choice buy higher TM policy limits, on average, than the BI policy limits purchased under the current system, their savings would be lower, and their access to compensation for non-economic loss greater, on average, than our estimates. Conversely, if they buy lower TM policy limits, on average, than the BI policy limits purchased under the current system, their savings would be greater, and their access to compensation for non-economic loss less, on average, than our estimates.

Furthermore, because our focus is on the financial implications of the choice plan, we do not consider the degree to which victims derive satisfaction from being compensated under an insurance policy purchased by the driver who injured them. Nor do we consider the satisfaction that consumers who value access to compensation for non-economic loss derive

---

[7] Because our concern is for the effects of the choice plan on private passenger auto insurance costs, we address only the effects of the plan on the costs incurred by auto insurers in covering private passenger vehicles. People injured in auto accidents may obtain compensation for non-economic loss from other forms of insurance such as personal umbrella or business liability coverages.

from being able to determine for themselves the limits on what they can obtain if injured by another driver in an auto accident rather than facing the uncertainty of the policy limit purchased by that driver.

The current system in most states encourages victims to exaggerate their medical costs as a means of leveraging larger settlements from auto insurers.[8] The ANF option would eliminate this incentive for excess claims. To the extent that the distributions of claimed economic losses reflect excess claiming in response to the current system, drivers who elect ANF under choice would submit fewer, smaller claims than we assume. The choice plan might thus result in greater savings than those reported here.[9]

Hawaii and New Jersey made significant changes to their auto insurance systems after 1997. Since our data do not provide a basis for estimating the effects of a choice plan in those states, we excluded them from this analysis.

Pennsylvania offers consumers a choice plan under which they can elect either tort or a verbal threshold no-fault plan.[10] We performed separate analyses for the effects of each plan. In the subsequent tables, the effects of the plan on Pennsylvania drivers who elected tort, labeled "Penn. Tort," are included in the results for the tort states; the effects of the plan on Pennsylvania drivers who elected no-fault, labeled "Penn. No-F," are included in the results for the no-fault states.

4. DATA

The analysis relies on data from three sources: closed-claim surveys conducted by the Insurance Research Council (IRC);[11] special tabulations compiled at our request by the Insurance Services Office (ISO); and National

---

[8] See, for example, Carroll, et al. (1995) or Insurance Research Council (1996).

[9] Some victims who could not have recovered from any auto insurer under the tort system (e.g., a totally at-fault driver who had not purchased the optional no-fault insurance, MP or PIP, available in the tort state) will be compensated if they elect ANF under the choice plan. These claims are included in this analysis.

[10] Under a verbal threshold auto insurance plan, injured parties may seek compensation for non-economic loss if they have suffered certain injuries specified in the law. Examples of the language found in the various verbal thresholds now in use are "death" (all verbal threshold states), "significant and permanent loss of an important bodily function" (Florida), "permanent serious disfigurement" (Michigan and Pennsylvania), "dismemberment" (New Jersey), and "permanent consequential limitation of use of a body function or system" (New York).

[11] See Insurance Research Council (1999a), which provides a detailed description of the closed-claim surveys.

Association of Insurance Commissioners (NAIC) reports on auto insurance premiums by type of coverage.[12]

The closed-claim surveys obtained detailed information on a national representative sample of auto accident injury claims closed with payment during 1997 under each of the principal auto injury coverages—BI, MP, UM, UIM, and PIP.[13] The data detail each victim's accident and resulting injuries and losses, as well as the compensation each victim obtained from auto insurance. The data were collected by forty insurance companies that, together, accounted for about 67 percent of private passenger automobile insurance by premium volume at the time of the study. In each state and for each coverage, the survey includes a representative sample of all claims closed.[14]

We used the ISO data to estimate insurers' transaction costs,[15] including both allocated loss-adjustment costs—legal fees and related expenses incurred on behalf of and directly attributed to a specific claim—and unallocated, or general, claims-processing costs for each line of private passenger auto insurance.[16] We estimate insurers' allocated loss-adjustment expenses as 1 percent of MP compensation paid, 1 percent of PIP compensation paid, 10 percent of BI compensation paid, and 8 percent of UM or UIM compensation paid. We estimate insurers' unallocated loss-adjustment expenses as 8 percent of paid compensation for each type of coverage. The plan provides that anyone who seeks compensation for economic loss in excess of the mandated PIP limit can recover attorneys' fees; we assume claimants' attorneys' fees average 31 percent of paid compensation.[17]

---

[12] See National Association of Insurance Commissioners (1999).

[13] These are the most recent available data describing the outcomes of a national sample of individual claims.

[14] The sampling fraction differs from state to state. We estimate the effects of the choice plan in each state, using the data for that state. To obtain an estimate of the nationwide effects of the plan, we combine the results across states, weighting the result for each state by the product of the sampling fraction for that state and the number of auto insurance policies sold in the state in 1997. We obtained the data on the number of policies written in each state from the National Association of Insurance Commissioners (1999).

[15] Carroll, et al. (1991) describe the data and methods used to estimate insurers' transaction costs in their Appendix D.

[16] We do not include victims' legal costs, the value of victims' time, or the costs the courts incur in handling litigated claims. Those costs do not affect insurers' costs and hence do not affect auto insurance premiums.

[17] We do not suggest that attorneys will necessarily charge accident victims a 31 percent contingency fee to represent them in seeking compensation for economic loss in excess of policy limits. However, plaintiff's attorneys' fees now average about 31 percent of victims' recovery. If plaintiff's attorneys' compensation in the current system is reasonable and fair, then their fees, whether charged on an hourly basis, as a contingency, or by some

The NAIC (1999) reports private passenger automobile insurance premiums by state and coverage for 1997, the most recent year for which these data are available.

5. RESEARCH APPROACH

For each state, we estimate the relative cost effects of the choice plan in three steps. First, we estimate the average cost of compensating accident victims under the current system. We then estimate the average cost of compensating accident victims on behalf of drivers who elect either MCS or ANF under the choice system. Finally, we calculate relative savings under choice as the percentage difference between the break-even premium—the premium an insurance company must charge to cover exactly what it pays in claims and the associated transaction costs—under choice for drivers who elect either option and the corresponding break-even premium under the current system.

5.1. Estimating Compensation Costs under the Current System

To estimate compensation costs under the current system, we identify the sources of auto insurance compensation that would be available to accident victims, depending on the type of insurance that they, and others, purchase. We then estimate the average amount of compensation and associated transaction costs that would be paid by each source for a representative sample of auto accident victims from each state. Finally, we assume a distribution of insurance-purchase decisions (i.e., the coverages and limits purchased), and compute the expected compensation paid to accident victims, on average, given that distribution. The result is an estimate of the compensation costs, including transaction costs, incurred under each state's current system for the assumed distribution of insurance-purchase decisions.

Table 1 indicates the sources of compensation available to an accident victim under the current system in a tort state, depending on the victim's insurance status, whether another driver was at least partially at fault for the

---

other system, would presumably be approximately as large, relative to the victims' recovery, under the choice plan.

accident[18] and, if so, whether that driver was insured. The corresponding table for an add-on state[19] in which PIP coverage is available, instead of or in addition to MP coverage, would look exactly the same except that insured accident victims (those in the bottom row) would have access to PIP, if they had purchased that coverage. Similarly, the corresponding table for a no-fault state would look exactly the same except that insured accident victims (those in the bottom row) would have access to PIP in every case.

Table 1
Compensation Sources for Accident Victims under the Current System

Insurance Status	**Other Driver at Least Partially at Fault Is:**		**No Other Driver at Fault**
	Uninsured	**Insured**	
Uninsured Victim	0	BI	0
Insured Victim	UM	MP + BI	MP

To estimate compensation costs for each state, we use our data on the compensation (and associated transaction costs) for a representative sample of accident victims, as follows:

We assume that an uninsured victim injured either in an accident caused by a driver who is also uninsured or in an accident in which no other driver is at least partially at fault receives no compensation from auto insurance.

We estimate the costs of compensating an uninsured victim injured in an accident with an insured, at-fault driver as the average compensation paid on BI claims times the probability that an accident victim exceeds the tort

[18] In earlier studies, we assumed that all victims injured in multi-car accidents had access to another driver's third-party coverage with the probability that the other driver was insured. In this study, we assume that victims who were injured in accidents in which no other driver was at least partially at fault would have access only to their own first-party coverage, regardless of the number of cars involved in the accident. Specifically, we assume, using Insurance Research Council data, that 30 percent of victims were injured in accidents in which no other driver was at least partially at fault. We present tests of the sensitivity of the results to alternative assumptions regarding this percentage below.

[19] Add-on states are those in which PIP coverage is available but there is no tort threshold.

threshold.[20] We assume that average transaction costs are 18 percent of BI compensation in all states. We estimate the costs in tort states of compensating a victim injured in an accident caused by an uninsured driver as the average compensation paid on UM claims times the fraction of insured drivers in the state who purchased UM coverage.[21] For the no-fault states, we estimate compensation costs as the average compensation paid on PIP claims, plus the average compensation paid on UM claims times the fraction of insured drivers in the state who purchased UM coverage times the probability that an accident victim exceeds the tort threshold. We assume that average transaction costs are 9 percent of PIP compensation paid and 18 percent of UM compensation paid.

We estimate the costs of compensating an insured victim injured in an accident with another insured driver in tort [no-fault] states as the sum of the average compensation paid on BI claims in that state plus transaction costs plus the average compensation paid on MP [PIP] claims in the state plus transaction costs times the probability that the victim will claim against both his or her own first-party and the other driver's third-party coverages. We use the ratio of MP earned exposures to BI earned exposures in each state as our estimate of the fraction of insured accident victims that have access to MP coverage.[22] We assume that all insured accident victims in the no-fault states have PIP coverage and will seek compensation under that coverage. We assume that transaction costs are 9 percent of MP or PIP compensation paid and 18 percent of BI compensation paid.

We estimate the costs of compensating an insured victim injured in an accident in which no other driver was at fault in tort [no-fault] states as the average compensation paid on MP [PIP] claims times the fraction of insured drivers in the state who purchased MP [PIP] coverage. We assume that transaction costs are 9 percent of MP or PIP compensation paid.

Because state-specific estimates of uninsured motorist rates are not readily available, we take a parametric approach. We assume that the uninsured motorist rate is 15 percent.[23] We then compute the resulting

---

[20] By definition, all accident victims "exceed the tort threshold" in tort states. In a no-fault state, we take the fraction of PIP claims that the claim adjuster judged qualified for a BI tort recovery under the no-fault law, whether or not the victim actually pursued a tort claim.

[21] We use the ratio of UM earned exposures to BI earned exposures in each state as our estimate of the fraction of insured accident victims who have UM coverage. The National Association of Independent Insurers (1998) reports earned exposures by coverage for all states except Massachusetts, North Carolina, South Carolina, and Texas. We use the national average ratio of exposures for these four states.

[22] National Association of Independent Insurers (1998).

[23] Using the ratio of UM claim frequencies to BI claim frequencies to estimate the uninsured motorist rate, the Insurance Research Council (1999b) estimates that, on average,

fraction of accident victims that would be found in each cell of Table 1, multiply that fraction by the corresponding compensation costs, and sum over the cells. The result is an estimate of the average cost of compensating an accident victim in each state under that state's current system. The product of this estimate and the ratio of accident victims to insured drivers in the state is the amount that the state's insured drivers would have to be charged, on average, to recover the costs of compensating all victims. We then vary the assumed uninsured motorist rate and repeat the procedure.

Note that under the assumption that insurance-purchase decisions are statistically independent of subsequent accidents and the resulting injuries and losses, the estimates we obtain for each state are identical to those we would have obtained by estimating expected compensation outcomes for each individual victim and then averaging over the victims in the sample. In other words, the method outlined above essentially takes account of the variations in relevant accident characteristics (e.g., the victim's negligence) and injuries/losses among individual accident victims.

5.2. Estimating Compensation Costs under the Choice System

To estimate what it would cost under the choice system to compensate the same accident victims for the same injuries and losses, we identified the sources of auto insurance compensation that would be available to accident victims under that system. We then estimated the average amount of compensation, and the associated transaction costs, that would be paid by each source, and computed the expected compensation paid to the average accident victim.

Table 2 indicates the sources of compensation available to accident victims in a tort state under the choice plan, depending on their insurance status, whether another driver was at least partially responsible for the accident, and, if so, whether the other driver involved in the accident was insured. The corresponding table for a no-fault state would look exactly the same except that insured accident victims (those in the bottom row) would have access to PIP in every case.

---

about 14 percent of drivers are uninsured nationally. Miller, Rapp, Herbers, & Terry, Inc., an actuarial consulting firm, estimated the frequencies of UM and BI claims in the tort states in the early 1990s. The ratio of their estimates is about 15 percent (private communication).

Under choice, the current system's compensation rules govern in accidents that do not involve a victim or driver covered by ANF. We use the methods described above to estimate compensation in these cases.

An uninsured victim injured in an accident involving another car whose driver switched to ANF is compensated by the other driver's supplemental BI insurance for any economic loss in excess of the mandated PPI policy limit. We estimate the expected value of compensation for excess economic loss, denoted XEL in Table 2, in three steps. First, we compute the difference, if positive, between the victim's economic loss and the mandated PPI limit up to each possible value of the BI policy limit, weighted by the distribution of BI policy limits in the state. We then multiply by one minus the victim's degree of fault for the accident. Finally, we average over all victims in the state. We assume that transaction costs are 49 percent of compensation paid for excess economic loss—18 percent in insurer's costs and 31 percent in plaintiff's attorney fees.[24]

Table 2
Compensation Sources for Accident Victims under the Choice System

Insurance Status	Other Driver at Least Partially at Fault Is: Uninsured	ANF	Current	No Other Driver at Fault
Uninsured Victim	0	XEL[a]	BI	0
ANF Victim	PPI	PPI + XEL	PPI+ XEL	PPI
Current Victim	UM	TM + XEL	MP + BI	MP

[a] *XEL denotes excess economic loss.*

We estimate compensation costs for accident victims covered by ANF under choice as their own PPI coverage plus recovery of XEL. We estimate PPI as the average value of victims' economic losses up to the PPI policy limit. We estimate XEL as described above. We assume that transaction costs are 9 percent of PPI compensation and 49 percent of XEL compensation.

[24] Because the plan provides that victims who seek recovery of excess economic losses may recover their legal costs, we assume that all such victims will seek representation.

Victims covered by MCS who are injured in an accident caused by a driver who switched to ANF are compensated by their own TM coverage. Because the amount an accident victim can recover under TM is governed by the same rules that govern the amount an insured driver can recover under the state's current system, we estimate average TM compensation costs using the methods described above to estimate BI compensation costs under the current system. Drivers who chose MCS are compensated by the other driver's supplemental BI insurance for any economic loss in excess of the TM policy limit. We estimate XEL for victims covered by MCS as the difference, if positive, between the victim's economic loss and his or her TM recovery up to each possible value of the BI policy limit, weighted by the distribution of BI policy limits in the state. We then multiply by one minus the victim's degree of fault for the accident. Finally, we average over all victims in the state. We assume that transaction costs are 18 percent of TM compensation paid and 49 percent of XEL compensation.

A driver who is uninsured under his or her state's current system has declined to purchase the insurance—BI or PIP—mandated under that system. We assume that, under choice, this driver would *not* purchase the coverage that he or she declined before ANF became an option. Thus, under choice, a driver who is uninsured in the current system would either remain uninsured or would opt for ANF under the choice plan. Similarly, a driver who is insured under his state's current system preferred the coverage—BI or no-fault—mandated under that system to going uninsured. Hence, we assume that if a driver *does* have insurance under his or her state's current system, he or she would elect either to retain the modified version of that insurance or to switch to ANF under choice, but would *not* decide to drop automobile insurance coverage altogether.

Given the assumed uninsured motorist rate under the current system and the other parameters that describe claiming patterns under the current system, the distribution of accident victims among the cells in Table 2 depends on the rate at which drivers who would have been insured under the current system opt for ANF coverage and the rate at which drivers who would have gone uninsured under the current system opt for ANF coverage. We have no data that allow us to estimate what either of these rates would be in any particular state. Accordingly, we take a parametric approach. We assume values for each of these rates, estimate the effects of the choice plan conditional on those values, and then revise the assumed values and repeat the analysis.

We assume that drivers' insurance-purchase decisions are statistically independent of whether or not they will cause, or be injured in, an auto accident. We group drivers into three types according to their insurance-purchase decisions and estimate the compensation costs insurers incur on behalf of each type of driver. Specifically, we estimate the costs incurred by insurers under policies purchased by

- *Stayers*: drivers who would be insured under the current system and who select MCS under choice,
- *Insured switchers*: drivers who would be insured under the current system and who select ANF under choice, and
- *Uninsured switchers*: drivers who would be uninsured under the current system and who select ANF under choice.

We use the methods discussed above to compute the probability that an accident victim would fall into each cell in Table 2. We then multiply these probabilities by the corresponding compensation costs and add these quantities together. The result is an estimate of the average costs insurers incur under the choice plan in compensating a representative sample of accident victims in each state on behalf of drivers who make each possible type of insurance-purchase decision. For any state, the estimate for each type of driver, multiplied by the ratio of accident victims paid on behalf of that type of driver to the number of insured drivers of that type, is the average amount insurers would have to charge that type of driver to recover the costs of compensating victims. We lack data on the number of accident victims per insured driver of each type for each state. However, this number will cancel out when we compute the ratio of compensation costs under the current system to compensation costs under the choice plan for each type of driver.

Note again that, under the assumption that insurance-purchase decisions are statistically independent of subsequent accidents and the resulting injuries/losses, the estimates we obtain for each state are identical to those we would have obtained by estimating expected compensation outcomes for each individual victim and then averaging over the victims in the sample. In other words, the method outlined above takes account of the variations in relevant accident characteristics (e.g., the victim's negligence) and injuries/losses among individual accident victims.

5.3. Estimating Relative Savings on Compensation Costs

To calculate the break-even personal injury premium for the current system, assume that there are N drivers, that a driver is involved in k injury-producing accidents per year, on average, and that each injury costs insurers C dollars, on average, including transaction costs (that is, C dollars for *every* injury, including injuries suffered by pedestrians, passengers, bicyclists, and insured and uninsured drivers). On average, insurers will pay kNC dollars a year.

Let X denote the fraction of all drivers that are insured. Let P be the average premium that insurers must charge just to cover what they pay in claims and associated transaction costs. To break even, P must be set such that $XNP = kNC$. Thus, the break-even premium is $P = kC/X$. We know how to calculate C. In estimating relative savings under choice, we will assume the value of X and specify k as an unknown parameter.

To calculate *relative* savings on compensation costs, we extend the above notation to three conceptual insurance companies. The first sells all the insurance policies purchased by drivers in a state under its current system. The second sells all insurance policies purchased by drivers in that state who elect MCS under the choice plan. The third sells all insurance policies purchased by drivers in that state who elect ANF under the choice plan. The effects of the choice plan on the costs insurers incur on behalf of drivers who are insured in the traditional system and who would elect MCS under choice are reflected in the ratio of the second company's break-even premium to the first company's break-even premium. Similarly, the effects of the choice plan on the costs insurers incur on behalf of drivers who are insured in the current system and who would elect ANF under choice are reflected in the ratio of the third company's break-even premium to the first company's premium.

Assume that the fraction of drivers insured in the current system is X_1 and that the company that insures them pays out an average of C_1 dollars for every injury. The corresponding parameters for the company that insures drivers electing MCS under choice are X_C and C_C, respectively. The break-even personal injury premium for the current system company is $P_1 = kC_1/X_1$, and the break-even personal injury premium for the company that insures MCS electors under choice is $P_C = kC_C/X_C$. The ratio of the two companies' break-even personal injury premiums is thus P_C/P_1, and the number of injury-producing accidents per driver per year, k, cancels out of both the numerator and denominator, leaving an expression that depends only on the fraction insured by each company (the Xs) and the average amount of compensation paid for each injury (the Cs).

In our calculations, we have made assumptions about the Xs and have estimated the Cs so that without knowing the accident rate, but assuming that it remains the same, we could compare the relative change in the break-even personal injury premium for drivers who elect either their state's MCS or ANF under choice.

Note that these estimates account for changes in claim frequency that would result from the adoption of a choice plan. Specifically, we divide all accident victims under the current system into six mutually exclusive and collectively exhaustive groups depending on the victim's insurance status (insured or uninsured), whether another driver was at least partially at fault for the accident, and, if so, whether or not that driver was insured. We assume both the uninsured motorist rate and the fraction of victims injured in accidents in which no other driver was at fault. Given these assumptions, we compute the distribution of victims among the groups, including the fractions of victims who fall into those groups in which no compensation is paid. Multiplying the fraction of victims who fall into each group by the expected costs of compensating victims for that group, and summing over the groups, we estimate the expected cost of compensating an accident victim under the current system. Again, because we compute expected compensation costs over all accident victims, the estimate includes those who receive nothing under the current system. We also recognize that the expected compensation paid to the victims in other groups will depend on the fraction of insured drivers who purchase voluntary coverages. For example, we estimate that, in a tort state, the expected cost of compensating an insured accident victim injured in an accident in which no other driver is at fault equals the average compensation paid on MedPay claims in that state times the fraction of insured drivers in the state who purchase MedPay coverage.

We multiply this estimate of expected compensation costs per victim by the average number of injury-producing accidents per driver and divide by the fraction of drivers who are insured. The result is an estimate of the amount each insured driver must pay for insurance so that the sum of all payments is just sufficient to pay the costs of compensating accident victims under the current system (including those who receive no compensation from auto insurance).

We then note that, under choice, all accident victims can be divided into twelve mutually exclusive and collectively exhaustive groups, depending on the victim's insurance status, whether another driver was at least partially at fault for the accident, and, if so, that driver's insurance status. We assume the fractions of insured and uninsured drivers under the current system who switch to the ANF under choice. Given these assumptions, and those we made earlier regarding the uninsured motorist rate and the fraction of victims injured in accidents in which no other driver is at fault, we can compute the distribution of victims among the groups. Multiplying the fraction of victims who fall into each group by the expected costs of compensating victims in that group on behalf of ANF (or MCS) drivers, and summing over the groups, we estimate the total expected costs of compensating accident victims on behalf of ANF (or MCS) drivers. Again, because we compute expected compensation over all accident victims, these estimates include victims who would have received nothing under the current system, would switch to ANF under choice, and, consequently would receive compensation. Multiplying this estimate by the average number of injury-producing accidents per driver and dividing by the fraction of drivers who are insured under ANF (or MCS), we estimate the amount each ANF (or MCS) insured driver must pay for insurance so that the sum of all payments is just sufficient to pay the costs of compensating accident victims on behalf of ANF (or MCS) drivers. We term this number the "break-even" premium for ANF (or MCS).

Finally, we compare the break-even premium under the current system to the break-even premium for drivers who elect ANF (or MCS) to estimate the savings that accrue to insured drivers who switch to ANF (or stay in MCS) under choice. As noted above, the break-even premiums involved in this comparison are based on the expected compensation costs per injury computed over all accident victims whether or not they receive compensation. Hence, our estimates take account of the possibility that some victims who go uncompensated under the current system will receive compensation under the choice plan.

5.4. Estimating Relative Savings on Total Premiums

The calculations described above yield estimates of the average compensation costs insurers will incur on behalf of stayers, insured switchers, and uninsured switchers under choice, relative to the compensation costs they would have incurred on behalf of each type of driver under their state's current system. The NAIC (1997) provides state-specific estimates of both claim costs and other expenses for liability claims.[25] The relationship between claim costs and other expenses for liability claims is highly linear and essentially goes through the origin. The R-squared for a regression of insurers' other expenses on claim costs is 0.97, and the intercept is indistinguishable from zero. Thus, if insurers' other expenses include any fixed costs, these are sufficiently small relative to the variable component of other expenses that other expenses are essentially proportional to claim costs. We assume that insurers' profit margins on MCS

[25] Insurers' other expenses include commissions and other selling expenses, general expenses, state premium taxes, licenses, and fees, and dividends to policyholders.

insureds will be the same as on ANF insureds, and that the return on investment income is independent of the mix of insureds.

To translate the effects on compensation costs under personal injury coverages into effects on total auto insurance premiums, we multiply our estimate of compensation cost savings by the proportion of total auto insurance premiums in each state that were spent for personal injury coverages in 1997, the most recent year for which data are available.

5.5. The Effects of the Choice Plan on Costs and Premiums

We have no data to estimate, for each state, the fraction of drivers currently purchasing insurance who would switch to ANF under choice. We therefore consider a base case in which it is assumed that 50 percent of currently insured drivers switch to ANF. We also consider the case in which all currently insured drivers elect ANF under choice. The savings realized by currently insured drivers who elect ANF under choice do not depend on the percentage of uninsured drivers who elect ANF under choice. Tables 3 and 4 present state-by-state estimates[26] of the average percentage reduction in both personal injury compensation costs and total auto insurance premiums that policyholders who elect either MCS or ANF would realize in each of the states. These estimates assume that:

- 15 percent of drivers in the state are uninsured under the current system;
- either 50 percent or 100 percent of the drivers insured under the current system would opt for ANF if given the choice; and
- one-half of all drivers who were uninsured under the current system would opt for ANF if given the choice.

Averaging over the *no-fault states*, if one-half of the insured drivers were to switch to ANF under the choice plan, the costs of compensating victims on their behalf would be reduced by about 63 percent from what the costs would have been under their state's current system. If insurers' other costs vary in proportion to compensation costs, this would translate into a 29 percent reduction in total auto insurance premiums. Adoption of the choice plan would reduce the costs of compensating victims on behalf of drivers who elect MCS by about 16 percent, resulting in a 7 percent savings on their total premiums.

[26] We report the effects of the choice plan on Pennsylvania drivers covered by tort in 1997 in Table 3. We report the effects of the choice plan on Pennsylvania drivers covered by the verbal threshold no-fault plan in 1997 in Table 4.

We estimate that if half the insured drivers in the *tort states* were to switch to ANF under the choice plan, the costs of compensating victims on their behalf would be reduced by about 54 percent from what they would have been under the traditional tort system. If insurers' other costs vary in proportion to compensation costs, this would translate into a 22 percent reduction in total auto insurance premiums. Adoption of the choice plan would have little effect on the costs of compensating victims on behalf of drivers who choose MCS.

Table 3
Relative Savings under Choice by State: No-Fault States
(All Savings Expressed as Percentages)

	Half-Switch Scenario				**All-Switch Scenario**	
	Switchers		**Stayers**		**Switchers**	
State	Injury Prem.	Total Prem.	Injury Prem.	Total Prem.	Injury Prem.	Total Prem.
Colorado	70	41	11	7	70	40
Florida	61	29	16	8	61	28
Kansas	76	23	14	4	74	23
Kentucky	67	28	15	7	66	28
Mass.	65	33	13	7	65	33
Michigan	42	15	20	7	44	15
Minnesota	63	29	13	6	62	29
New York	70	32	16	7	71	32
N. Dakota	58	18	21	7	58	18
Penn. No-F	82	36	11	5	82	36
Utah	62	25	12	5	61	25
All No-Fault States	63	29	16	7	63	29

Table 4
Relative Savings under Choice by State: Tort States
(All Savings Expressed as Percentages)

	Half-Switch Scenario				All-Switch Scenario	
	Switchers		Stayers		Switchers	
State	Injury Prem.	Total Prem.	Injury Prem.	Total Prem.	Injury Prem.	Total Prem.
Alabama	53	17	6	2	50	16
Alaska	65	26	13	5	66	26
Arizona	51	23	7	3	49	23
Arkansas	57	20	9	3	57	20
California	47	22	6	3	45	21
Connecticut	62	28	7	3	61	28
Delaware	61	31	9	5	55	28
Georgia	52	18	5	2	49	17
Idaho	54	21	0	0	54	21
Illinois	56	20	8	3	52	19
Indiana	58	22	6	2	55	21
Iowa	55	20	6	2	53	19
Louisiana	72	34	13	6	70	33
Maine	65	25	10	4	63	24
Maryland	55	23	7	3	54	23
Mississippi	49	17	5	2	46	15
Missouri	54	19	8	3	52	19
Montana	47	18	3	1	42	16
Nebraska	49	17	1	0	48	16
Nevada	54	28	7	3	51	26
N. Hamp.	52	20	7	3	49	19
N. Mexico	50	23	9	4	51	23
N. Carolina	47	19	6	2	45	18
Ohio	61	24	7	3	58	23
Oklahoma	49	19	7	3	48	19
Oregon	51	22	6	3	50	22
Penn. Tort	54	23	8	3	48	21
R. Island	70	35	18	9	70	35
S. Carolina	56	23	7	3	54	22
S. Dakota	60	24	10	4	60	24

Table 4 (Continued)

State	Half-Switch Scenario				All-Switch Scenario	
	Switchers		Stayers		Switchers	
	Injury Prem.	Total Prem.	Injury Prem.	Total Prem.	Injury Prem.	Total Prem.
Tennessee	49	17	6	2	47	16
Texas	45	22	6	3	45	22
Vermont	63	22	9	3	63	22
Virginia	52	23	8	3	50	22
Washington	55	27	6	3	54	26
W. Virginia	62	28	6	3	61	27
Wisconsin	57	22	7	3	55	21
Wyoming	63	21	5	2	59	19
All Tort States	54	22	7	3	51	21

Averaging over *all states combined,* compensation costs incurred on behalf of insured switchers would be reduced by about 57 percent (see Table 5). This translates into about a 24 percent reduction in total premiums.

Table 5
Relative Savings for Previously Insured Drivers
(All Savings Expressed as Percentages)

			Relative Savings		
Scenario	**Insurance Class**	**Premium**	**Tort States**	**No-Fault States**	**All States**
Half Switch	Switchers	Personal injury	54	63	57
		Total	22	29	24
	Stayers	Personal injury	7	16	10
		Total	3	7	4
All Switch	Switchers	Personal injury	51	63	56
		Total	21	29	23

Assuming that all insured drivers switch to ANF has little effect on the estimates. In the tort states, compensation costs would be reduced about 51 percent, which translates into a 21 percent reduction in total auto insurance premiums. The corresponding estimates for the no-fault states are a 63 percent reduction in compensation costs and a 29 percent reduction in total auto insurance premiums. For all states combined, compensation costs incurred on behalf of insured switchers would be reduced about 56 percent. This translates into about a 23 percent reduction in total premiums.

In both the tort states and the no-fault states, differences among states are relatively small. Whatever differences exist may reflect sampling variation in the data or differences in the extent to which our assumptions apply. In any case, our general results are robust with respect to interstate variations in the distributions of accidents and injuries. This suggests that, even if these distributions vary over time in any state, the variations are not likely to affect the results significantly.

Drivers who opt for ANF under choice are not liable for others' non-economic losses. In the tort states, the compensation costs that insurers incur on behalf of such drivers would be substantially lower than they would have been under the tort system. On the other hand, the amounts paid to these drivers under their PPI coverages generally would exceed what would have been paid to them under MP insurance. In general, the savings obtained by eliminating compensation payments on their behalf for non-economic loss under choice greatly outweigh the additional costs incurred in providing them more generous first-party no-fault compensation—PPI versus MP. Hence, the cost of compensating for personal injuries incurred or caused by tort state drivers who elect ANF would drop substantially—40 percent or more—relative to the costs incurred on their behalf under the traditional tort system. If insurers' other costs declined in proportion, the total premiums charged drivers insured under the tort system who would opt for ANF under choice would be reduced by at least 15 percent in each of the tort states.

The savings that would be realized by insured drivers who switch to ANF under choice are not very sensitive to the fraction of insured drivers who exercise that option. In most states, the savings available to an individual consumer who switches from the current system to ANF are slightly greater if half of those insured under the current system switch to ANF than if all of those insured under the current system switch to ANF. This result stems from the provision that ANF electors are liable to anyone they injure (to the degree they are responsible for the injury) for excess economic loss. Under the plan examined here, we assume that ANF electors purchase the mandated PPI policy limit. Thus, an ANF insured driver who injures someone else covered by ANF is liable for the victim's economic losses in excess of the PPI policy limit. An ANF insured driver who injures someone covered by MCS is liable for the victim's economic losses in excess of his or her TM policy limit. We assume that the distribution of TM policy limits purchased by consumers who elect MCS under choice is the same as the distribution of BI policy limits purchased by consumers under the current system. Because BI limits are at least as large as the mandated PPI limit, and sometimes larger, the expected excess economic losses incurred by victims who are covered by TM are less, on average, than the expected excess economic losses incurred by victims covered by PPI.

A driver who elects MCS and is involved in an accident with a driver who chose ANF is entirely free from liability for non-economic loss; his or her insurer would pay less, on average, under choice than under the current system. But a driver who chooses MCS and is injured in an accident with a driver who chose ANF must turn to his own TM coverage, rather than the other driver, for recovery of non-economic loss. Thus, his or her insurer saves the costs of compensating the other driver for non-economic loss but incurs the additional costs of compensating the insured for his or her own non-economic loss. If there is no adverse selection in the choices made under the choice plan, drivers who choose MCS would have the same average non-economic loss and negligence as would drivers who elect ANF, and these savings would approximately equal the additional costs.

Current no-fault plans already limit accident victims' access to compensation for non-economic loss. Hence, the savings on compensation costs obtained by totally eliminating compensation payments for non-economic loss on behalf of drivers who elect ANF are smaller than in tort states. But current no-fault plans already include PIP compensation, so no new compensation costs are incurred on behalf of drivers who elect ANF under choice in the no-fault states. Thus, compensation costs incurred on behalf of ANF electors in the no-fault states would tend to decline substantially relative to the costs incurred on their behalf under their state's current system. On average, the cost of compensating for personal injuries caused by insured drivers in the no-fault states who elect ANF would drop more than 60 percent in most states—relative to the costs incurred on their behalf under the current no-fault system. If insurers' other costs declined in proportion, the total premiums charged drivers insured under the current system who opt for ANF under choice would be reduced by about 27 percent in the no-fault states.

The savings that would be realized by insured drivers who switch to ANF under choice are not very sensitive to the fraction of insured drivers who exercise that option. The estimated savings to drivers when 50 percent of insured drivers switch to ANF are very similar to the savings estimates when all insured drivers switch to ANF.

As in the tort states, drivers who elect MCS and are involved in an accident with a driver who chose ANF are entirely free from liability for non-economic loss; their insurers would pay less, on average, under choice than under the current system. But drivers who choose MCS and are injured in an accident with a driver who chose ANF must turn to their own TM coverage for recovery of non-economic losses. Their insurers save the costs of compensating the other driver for non-economic loss but incur the additional costs of compensating the insureds for their own non-economic loss. If there is no adverse selection in the choices made under the choice plan, drivers who choose MCS would have the same average non-economic loss and negligence as would drivers who elect ANF, and these savings would approximately equal the additional costs.

5.6. The Effects of the Choice Plan on Compensation

Figure 1 draws on the results for California to illustrate the effects of the choice plan on compensation outcomes. These results are for a scenario in which 50 percent of insured drivers and 50 percent of uninsured drivers elect ANF under choice. The dark bars illustrate how $1,000 in compensation costs are distributed in California under the current system. The dollar figure attached to each bar shows the amounts spent on the associated cost category. The light bars illustrate how these compensation costs would be affected by the choice plan, assuming the base case insurance parameters. The dollar figure attached to each light bar shows the amount that would be spent in that category under the choice system.

For purposes of this comparison, we count all dollars paid to accident victims as compensation for economic loss until the victims have been fully compensated; we include only amounts paid to victims in excess of their economic losses as compensation for non-economic loss. The compensation figures are gross in that they show the amounts paid to accident victims without regard to any legal fees or costs that the victims must pay out of these amounts. We distinguish between drivers insured under the current system and those who are uninsured under the current system. We divide the latter into two subgroups: those who stay uninsured under choice and those who elect to purchase ANF when it is available to them. (Because this illustration assumes that half of the uninsured drivers under the current system would switch to ANF under choice, these subgroups are equal in size.)

Figure 1
Effects of Choice Plan on Compensation Outcomes in California

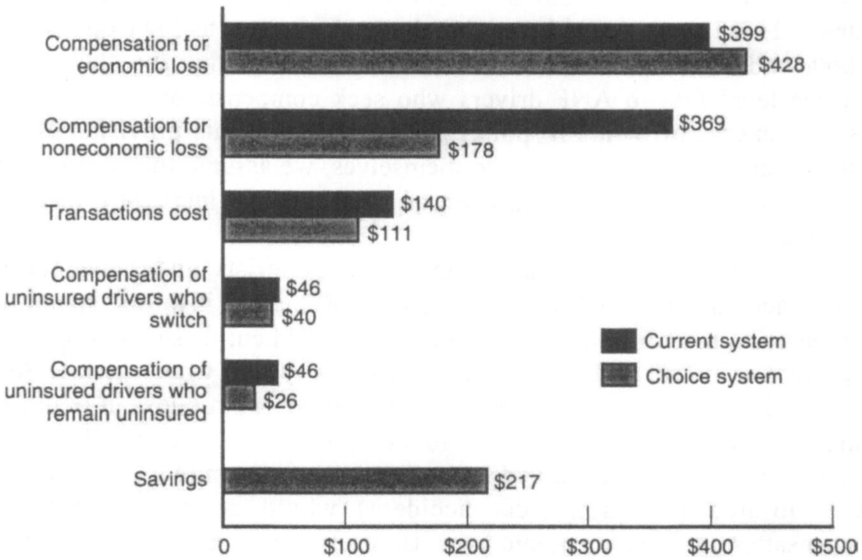

We estimate that if one-half of the insured drivers in California switched to ANF under choice, the amount paid to insured accident victims for economic loss, including both those covered by ANF and those covered by MCS, would be increased by about 7 percent, on average. Out of each $1,000 spent in the current system, about $399 is paid in compensation for economic loss to victims who have purchased insurance. Under choice, the amount of compensation paid to these victims for economic loss would be about $428. There are of course some differences from one victim to another in how the compensation paid for economic loss under the choice plan would compare with the compensation paid under the current system.

About $369 out of each $1,000 spent in the current system is paid to insured victims in compensation for non-economic loss. Under choice, the amount of compensation paid to these victims for non-economic loss would be cut to the extent that drivers switch to ANF. Drivers who elect MCS under choice would receive essentially the same compensation for non-economic loss as under the current system, assuming no change in policy limits. Those who switch to ANF would receive no compensation for non-economic loss. In the example, we assume that half the insured drivers under the current system elect MCS and half switch to ANF. Consequently, the amount paid to insured victims in compensation for non-economic loss under choice would be reduced by about one-half, to $178 out of each $1,000 in compensation costs.

Insurers' transaction costs—defense fees and allocated loss adjustment expenses—account for about $140 out of each $1,000 under the current system. These costs would be cut by about 15 percent, to $111 out of each $1,000, under the choice plan in this example. Note that the choice plan provides legal fees to ANF drivers who seek compensation for economic losses in excess of their PIP policy limits. Because this provision allows victims representation at no cost to themselves, we assume that victims will generally secure representation, even on small claims, increasing insurers' transaction costs for these claims.

The costs of compensating uninsured motorists under the current system account for $92 out of each $1,000 auto insurers spend on compensation in California. The choice plan would cut these costs by about 28 percent. Uninsured drivers under the current system who switch to ANF under choice would waive compensation for non-economic loss in return for being assured compensation of economic loss. Uninsured switchers who would have gone uncompensated under the current system (e.g., an uninsured driver injured in a single-car accident) would do better, receiving compensation for their economic loss. Uninsured switchers who would have obtained compensation from another driver's BI coverage for both their economic and non-economic loss do worse. The net result is a 12 percent reduction in the compensation paid to these victims, on average. The compensation paid to drivers who remain uninsured under choice is cut to 56 percent, on average, of what it would have been under the current system. Uninsured drivers under choice who are injured in an accident with someone who opted for MCS would receive the same compensation they would have received under the current system. But uninsured drivers under choice who are injured in an accident with someone who opted for ANF under choice are compensated only for economic loss in excess of the mandated PPI policy limit.

Overall, the effects of the plan on compensation outcomes generally follow the pattern described above for California.

5.7. Sensitivity Analyses

The estimates presented above are for a base case in which we assume:

- 30 percent of accidents were the injured person's own fault (percent own-fault),

- 50 percent of insured accident victims who were injured by another insured driver and who have purchased MP collect from both the at-fault other driver and from their own MP policy (percent claim-both), and
- 15 percent of drivers are uninsured under the current system (percent uninsured).

To examine the sensitivity of our estimates to these parameters, we replicated the analysis for every combination of the following alternative assumptions:

- the percentage of own-fault accidents is 15, 30, or 60 percent,
- the percentage of claim-both victims is 25, 50, or 100 percent, and
- the percentage of uninsured motorists before choice is 10, 15, or 20 percent.

Further, in each state, we generally find a few large settlements along with a large number of smaller ones. We re-estimated the effects of the plan on insured switchers' compensation costs under each of the above 27 combinations of assumptions, assuming, in every state and for each compensation element, that

- the compensation provided in each of the largest 10 percent of all cases is double the actual value,
- the compensation provided all cases, including the largest 10 percent of all cases, is the actual value, and
- the compensation provided in each of the largest 10 percent of all cases is one-half the actual value.

In all, we developed 81 estimates of the effects of the choice plan on insured switchers' total auto insurance premiums in each state. Figure 2 shows the smallest, base case, and largest of these estimates for each state, assuming that 50 percent of insured drivers elect ANF under choice. The left end of the bar shown for each state is the lowest estimate we obtained for that state. The right end is the highest estimate for that state. The line inside the bar shows the base case estimate. The corresponding figure for the scenario in which *all* insured drivers elect ANF under choice is virtually the same.

For most states, the range of estimates is relatively small. Nothing in these estimates affects our main finding that the personal injury coverage costs of insuring drivers who elect ANF under choice will fall about 55 percent, which translates into savings of about 23 percent on their total premiums.

Figure 2
Relative Savings for Drivers Who Switch if One-Half of Insured Drivers Switch to ANF: Smallest, Base case, and Largest Percentage Savings

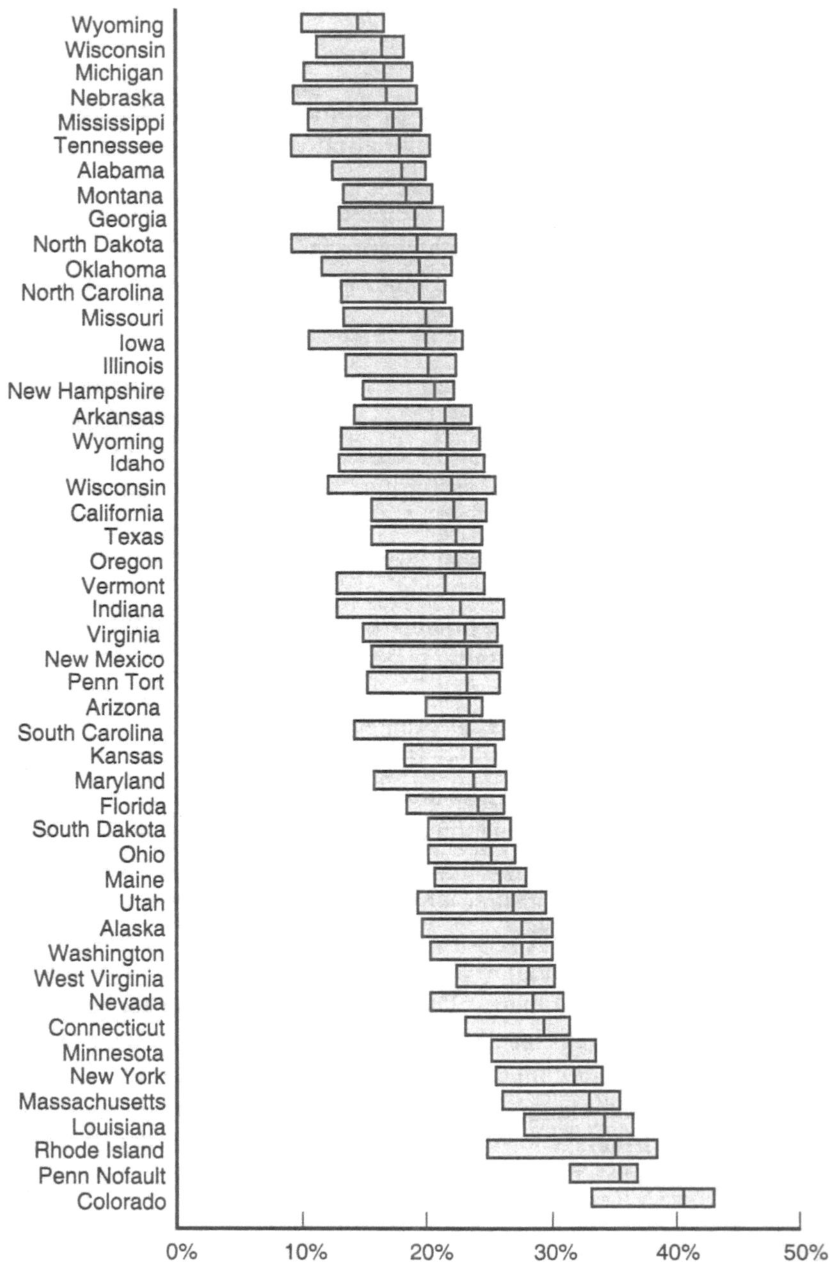

We used the same approach to develop 81 estimates of the effects of the choice plan on total auto insurance premiums for drivers who elect MCS in each state. Figure 3 shows the smallest, base case,[27] and largest of these estimates for each state, assuming that 50 percent of insured drivers elect ANF under choice.

Here, too, the range of estimates is relatively small in most states. Nothing in these estimates affects our main finding that insured drivers who elect their state's MCS under choice will not be noticeably affected by the availability of ANF.

5.8. Adverse Selection and Moral Hazard

We have assumed that insurance-purchase decisions are statistically independent of subsequent accidents and the resulting injuries/losses. That is, we have assumed that bad drivers elect either MCS or ANF with the same probabilities as do good drivers; i.e., that there will be no adverse selection in the choices drivers make under the choice plan.

The available evidence suggests that drivers do not have a clear understanding of their own relative driving performance. A national survey of people who suffered accidental injuries found that auto accident victims attributed their injuries to someone else more than 90 percent of the time and even drivers injured when their vehicle struck another vehicle named themselves as the cause of the accident only 16 percent of the time.[28] If drivers did not perceive themselves as having caused an accident in which they were injured, how likely is it that these same drivers would have labeled themselves before the fact as likely to be involved in an accident? Adverse selection cannot affect the distribution of drivers between plans unless drivers accurately perceive their own driving abilities.

[27] The base case assumes that, in the current system, 15 percent of drivers are uninsured, 30 percent of victims are injured in accidents in which no other driver is even partially at fault, and 50 percent of victims with access to both their own and another driver's auto insurance will pursue claims against both.

[28] Hensler, et al. (1991), p. 143.

Figure 3
Relative Savings for Drivers Who Retain a Modified Version of the Current System if One-Half of Insured Drivers Switch to ANF: Smallest, Base Case, and Largest Percentage Savings

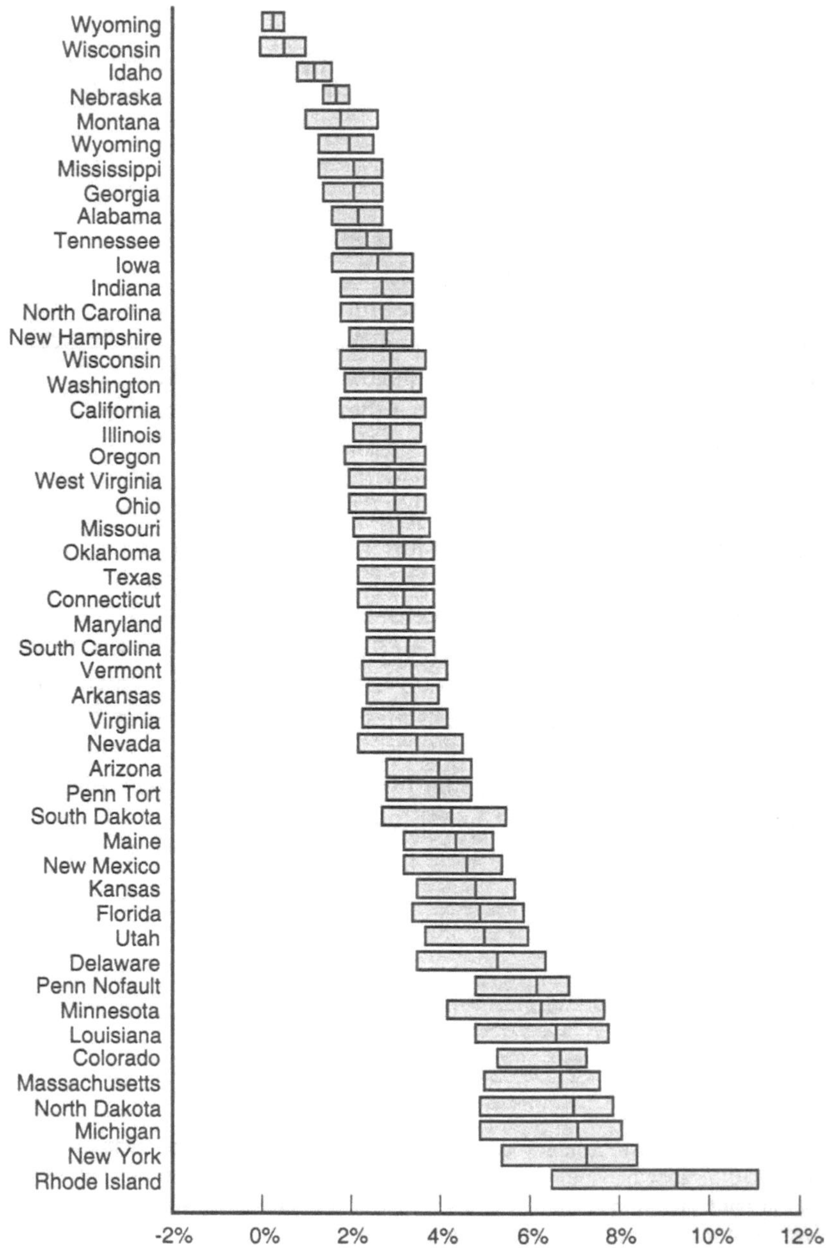

We do not suggest that drivers cannot identify risky behavior. Rather, we argue that drivers seem generally to believe that their own driving behavior does not contribute to the likelihood of an accident. The survey results noted above indicate that drivers who were involved in injury-producing accidents very rarely perceived themselves as having driven in a way that contributed to the accident. A survey conducted by the National Highway Traffic Safety Administration[29] supports this argument. It found that high proportions of the households surveyed routinely encountered others speeding and engaging in other forms of risky driving behavior (p. 94) and thought unsafe driving was a major threat to themselves and their families (p. 183). However, the survey respondents also reported that they themselves routinely engaged in these same behaviors (pp. 120-121). "Less than one in five (18 percent) reported that in the past year they had not done any of the eight or nine unsafe driving acts they were asked about" (p. 131). Similarly, of the respondents who had been involved in a vehicle crash in the last five years and said unsafe driving was a factor in their crash, about four times as many (73 percent) said only the driver of the other vehicle had committed unsafe driving actions as said only the driver of their vehicle (18 percent) had driven unsafely (p. 178).

In sum, drivers may be fully capable of identifying various behaviors as risky. But, at the same time, they routinely engage in those behaviors themselves. If drivers generally believe that their own driving behavior is not related to the likelihood that they will be involved in an accident, there is no reason to believe that they can accurately sort themselves accordingly.

Finally, even if bad drivers or good drivers accurately perceived their own driving abilities, it is not clear which option they would prefer. Drivers covered by ANF who cause accidents impose costs on their insurers for their own economic losses, so insurers have the same incentives to experience-rate drivers who elect ANF under choice as they do to experience-rate drivers who elect MCS. Similarly, drivers who consider themselves "accident-prone" have to consider the tradeoff between (1) the risk that the compensation available to them under MCS will be reduced to the degree that they are responsible for an accident in which they are injured, and (2) the loss of access to compensation for non-economic loss if they elect ANF.

Several studies have examined the effects of no-fault auto insurance on fatality rates, controlling for other factors.[30] However, the results of the empirical analyses of the relationship between auto insurance systems and fatality rates are mixed and, at best, inconclusive. A recent study of the

---

[29] National Highway Traffic Safety Administration (1997).

[30] Loughran (Chapter 5 of this volume) reviews previous studies of the effects of no-fault auto insurance on driving behavior.

relationship between auto insurance and accident rates found no evidence that no-fault insurance plans had any effect on the frequency of accidents and, therefore, on driving behavior.[31]

The concern over moral hazard is based on the assumption that "individuals largely immunized from liability may simply take less care behind the wheel."[32] However, the notion of immunization from liability is essentially irrelevant. Individual drivers very rarely pay compensation to people they have injured out of their own pockets. Surveys conducted by National Family Opinion find that personal payments by at-fault drivers account for less than 5 percent of the compensation auto accident victims obtained from all sources.[33] For all practical purposes, auto insurance immunizes drivers from the direct financial consequences of liability in the tort states just as much as no-fault thresholds do in the no-fault states.

Accident-causing driving can have indirect financial consequences. An auto insurer may boost a driver's premium if he or she has been involved in an at-fault accident. However, as we noted in our discussion, a driver who causes an accident in a no-fault state imposes costs on his own insurer, and insurers in no-fault states experience-rate their insureds' first-party premiums in much the same way as insurers in tort states experience-rate their insureds' liability premiums. In his analysis of the effects of no-fault on deterrence, Schwartz (forthcoming) concludes that

> . . . no-fault insurance premiums—in this regard, surprisingly resembling liability insurance premiums—can be expected to take both the reality and the prospect of bad driving into account. In light of this resemblance, the threat that no-fault poses to the core tort values of fairness and deterrence is much less than has commonly been supposed.[34]

Adverse selection and moral hazard are empirical issues that warrant further study. However, the evidence now available offers no reason to suspect that either adverse selection or moral hazard would be sufficient to affect the results dramatically.

---

[31] Loughran (Chapter 5 of this volume).
[32] Kabler (1999), p. 66.
[33] Insurance Research Council (1999b), p. 37.
[34] Schwartz (forthcoming), p. 3.

5.9. How the 1997 Results Compare to 1992 and 1987

Our updated estimates of savings under the choice plan generally fall between estimates based on the 1987 data and those based on the 1992 data. In most states, our estimates of the savings that would accrue to drivers who opted for ANF based on the 1992 data were lower than the corresponding estimates we had obtained using the 1987 data. These patterns generally reversed themselves, though not in every case, between 1992 and 1997. In most states, our estimate of the savings that would accrue to drivers who opted for ANF based on the 1997 data was greater than the corresponding estimate we had obtained using the 1992 data, though generally not as large as the estimate we had obtained using the 1987 data.

These changes in the savings estimates are largely due to changes in the average economic losses claimed by accident victims. An accident victim covered by ANF would be compensated for economic loss regardless of fault. Because victims injured in accidents in which no other driver is at fault frequently receive less than full compensation for their economic losses under the current system, many of these victims would be more fully compensated, at greater expense to the insurance system, under ANF. Thus, increases in economic losses increase the expected costs incurred on behalf of those who switch to ANF under choice. At the same time, an ANF insured victim injured by another driver does not receive the compensation for non-economic loss that would be provided him or her under the current system. But the amount of compensation for non-economic loss available to a victim is generally limited to the difference between the injuring driver's BI policy limit and the victim's economic loss. Because drivers tend not to increase their policy limits over time, increases in economic loss squeeze compensation for non-economic loss and reduce the extent to which ANF provides savings, relative to the current system.

The victims in the 1992 database claimed economic losses that were much greater, on average, than the losses claimed by the victims in the 1987 database. Hence, the estimated savings attendant on electing ANF were smaller in most states in 1992 than they had been in 1987. Conversely, average claimed economic losses actually declined in about half of the states between 1992 and 1997. In these states, the reduction in claimed economic loss generally led to increased savings for those electing ANF.

6. CONCLUSIONS

Our results suggest that the choice plan can offer dramatically less expensive insurance to drivers willing to give up access to compensation for non-economic loss with little actual effect on those who want to retain access to compensation for both economic and non-economic loss. If insurers pass on cost savings, the adoption of a choice plan would:

- Allow drivers who are willing to waive their tort rights to buy ANF personal injury coverage for roughly 55 percent of what they have to pay for personal injury coverage under their state's current system, which translates into savings on total premiums of about 23 percent, on average.
- Allow drivers who prefer to remain within a somewhat modified version of their state's current system (MCS) to do so, at essentially the same costs as under their state's current system.

References

Abrahamse, Allan, and Stephen J. Carroll, 1995, *The Effects of a Choice Auto Insurance Plan on Insurance Costs*, Santa Monica, CA: RAND Corporation, Institute for Civil Justice.

Abrahamse, Allan, and Stephen J. Carroll, 1997, *The Effects of a Choice Automobile Insurance Plan under Consideration by the Joint Economic Committee of the United States Congress*, Santa Monica, CA: RAND Corporation, Institute for Civil Justice.

All-Industry Research Advisory Council, 1989, *Uninsured Motorists*, Oak Brook, IL: AIRAC.

Carroll, Stephen J., and Allan Abrahamse, 1998, *The Effects of a Choice Automobile Insurance Plan on Insurance Costs and Compensation: An Updated Analysis*, Santa Monica, CA: RAND Corporation, Institute for Civil Justice.

Carroll, Stephen J., and James Kakalik, 1993, No-Fault Approaches to Compensating Auto Accident Victims, *The Journal of Risk and Insurance*, 60, 2, 265-287.

Carroll, Stephen J., et al., 1991, *No-Fault Approaches to Compensating People Injured in Automobile Accidents*, Santa Monica, CA: RAND Corporation, Institute for Civil Justice.

Carroll, Stephen J., et al., 1995, *The Costs of Excess Medical Claims for Automobile Personal Injuries*, Santa Monica, CA: RAND Corporation, Institute for Civil Justice.

Hensler, Deborah R., et al., 1991, *Compensation for Accidental Injuries in the United States*, Santa Monica, CA: RAND Corporation, Institute for Civil Justice.

Insurance Research Council, 1996, *Fraud and Buildup in Auto Insurance Claims*, Wheaton, IL: IRC.

Insurance Research Council, 1999a, *Injuries in Auto Accidents*, Malvern, PA: IRC.

Insurance Research Council, 1999b, *Uninsured Motorists*, Malvern, PA: IRC.

Kabler, Brent, 1999, The Case against Auto Choice, *Journal of Insurance Regulation*, 18, 1, 53-79.

Loughran, David, 2000, *The Effect of No-Fault Auto Insurance on Driver Behavior and Accidents in the United States*, Santa Monica, CA: RAND Corporation, Institute for Civil Justice.

National Association of Independent Insurers, 1998, *Private Passenger Automobile Experience*, Des Plaines, IL: NAII.

National Association of Insurance Commissioners, 1998, *Profitability by Line by State in 1997*, Kansas City, MO: NAIC.

National Association of Insurance Commissioners, 1999, *State Average Expenditures and Premiums for Personal Automobile Insurance in 1997*, Kansas City, MO: NAIC.

National Highway Traffic Safety Administration, 1997, *National Survey of Speeding and Other Unsafe Driving Actions, Vol. II: Driver Attitudes and Behavior*, Washington, DC: U. S. Government Printing Office.

O'Connell, Jeffrey, Stephen J. Carroll, Michael Horowitz, and Allan Abrahamse, 1993, Consumer Choice in the Auto Insurance Market, *Maryland Law Review*, 52, 4, 1016-1062.

O'Connell, Jeffrey, Stephen J. Carroll, Michael Horowitz, Allan Abrahamse, and Paul Jamieson, 1996, The Comparative Costs of Allowing Consumer Choice for Auto Insurance in all Fifty States, *Maryland Law Review*, 55, 1, 160-222.

O'Connell, Jeffrey, Stephen J. Carroll, Michael Horowitz, Allan Abrahamse, and Daniel Kaiser, 1995, The Costs of Consumer Choice for Auto Insurance in States without No-Fault Insurance, *Maryland Law Review*, 54, 2, 281-351.

O'Connell, Jeffrey, and Robert H. Joost, 1986, Giving Motorists a Choice between Fault and No-Fault Insurance, *Virginia Law Review*, 72, 1, 61-89.

Schwartz, Gary T., forthcoming, Auto No-Fault and First-Party Insurance: Advantages and Problems, *Southern California Law Review*.

4
THE CASE AGAINST AUTO CHOICE[†]

Brent Kabler
Missouri Department of Insurance

1. INTRODUCTION

> To consider wrongs as merely incidental to remedies; to inquire for what injuries a particular action may be brought, instead of explaining the injuries themselves, and then asking what action may be brought for their redress; seems to me to reverse the natural order of things . . . .
>
> Francis Hilliard

As a nation, we have collectively adopted a notoriously inefficient, expensive, environmentally unsound, and most importantly for our purposes, unsafe method of simply getting from Point A to Point B. Consider the comparisons in Table 1 below between U.S. automobile fatalities and fatalities associated with historical events of some repute. The death toll on U.S. highways is as relentless as it is astonishing. Considering also non-fatal injuries as well as property damage loss associated with automobile transportation is staggering, and comparable to a continuous war of no small magnitude.

Perhaps due to the public's infatuation with the automobile, a staggering level of loss of life and limb has become acceptable as an unfortunate by-product of life in the modern era. Recently proposed "auto choice" legislation embodies a singularly deterministic attitude towards highway casualties, and represents, at its most profound level, a fundamental rethinking of the nature of "causality". The cause, or "fault", of unfortunate events lies not with the individuals who participate in the events, but results

---

[†] This chapter is a revised version of an article appearing in the Fall 1999 issue of the *Journal of Insurance Regulation* (18, 1, 53-79), and is reprinted with permission.

from reified forces external to those involved in misfortunes. It follows with logical necessity that individuals *ought* not be made liable for damages incurred on the highway.[1] But the proposed auto choice legislation pursues its internal logic a bit further. Not only will no particular individual(s) be responsible for compensating others, *no one will be responsible.* The open secret of the "savings" of auto choice is that a significant portion of the costs associated with automobile transportation will simply be "written off."

Table 1
Automobile Fatality Equivalencies

Time Lapse	Events Responsible for a Comparable Number of Deaths
One Month	U.S. Troops Killed During the Tet Offensive, Vietnam
One Year	Total U.S. Fatalities in the Korean War
Three Years	Deaths from Hiroshima Bomb
7.3 Years	Total U.S. Fatalities in World War II

Source: Author's comparisons.

This chapter seeks to clarify the issues in the proposed dissolution of the current tort system governing automobile liability. After a brief description of the proposed legislation, the sharp philosophical divide that lies at the heart of the debate over auto choice is discussed, namely:

- Are claims of "faultless" accidents reasonable?
- *How* ought we assign "value" to loss?
- *Who* should compensate lost value?

Next, we critically examine some of the purported benefits associated with auto choice. Finally, we discuss the potentially negative consequences of tort reform, and present initial results of an ongoing project to assess the impact of tort reform on driving behavior.

2. AUTO CHOICE

Proposed federal "auto choice" legislation will, if enacted, supplant existing state automobile insurance systems with what is essentially a no-

[1] The use of the term "ought" here is not incidental; many proponents of no-fault or auto choice have explicitly adopted the normative position implied by the term (see below).

fault system with residual elements bearing a verisimilitude to existing tort systems. Consumers in current tort states would be permitted to "opt out" of the tort system and surrender their right to receive non-economic damages. In return, no-fault selectors are immunized from liability for injuries they cause, except in accidents involving drugs or alcohol, or where harm caused through the operation of a motor vehicle was intentional. Injury claims are limited to economic damages, essentially lost wages and medical expenses. Injuries sustained in accidents involving two no-fault selectors would be compensated for both drivers under their own respective policies. Collisions between two tort drivers would be compensated under the traditional tort liability system, with the "at-fault" driver providing compensation for the injuries sustained by the other party. In accidents between tort and no-fault drivers, both drivers would be compensated by their own personal injury protection (PIP) coverage for economic damages. The tort driver retains the right to collect non-economic damages if the other driver is "at fault," but under his or her *own* Tort Maintenance Insurance (TMI).

Proponents of "auto choice" argue that the system will result in a significant reduction in premiums, achieved by limiting awards for non-economic damages, and reducing fraud and litigation. The veracity of these claims will be taken up in a later section. First, we turn to a critical examination of the foundational principles of "no-fault".

3. FAULT

Tort law constitutes the vinculum of civil society, prescribing a generalized civic obligation to take appropriate levels of care not to harm others, and conversely constituting the rights of individuals to be free from such harm. Auto choice represents not merely or even primarily an "insurance reform," so much as a radical abrogation of the binding civil authority that circumscribes the level of risk individuals may impose on others. Of immediate concern, then, is whether automobile transportation is an appropriate arena for tort sanctions, which generally are predicated on some notion of negligence or misfeasance. There is unquestionably an inherent level of risk associated with automobile transportation. However, if a significant portion of accidents is associated with conscious risk-taking, inappropriate levels of care, or a willful disregard for the safety of others, then a compelling case is made for the retention of tort remedies for accident victims. The question may be framed thus: Do traffic crashes result from misfortune or misconduct?

Robert R. Detlefsen, a strong proponent of auto choice, rejects the notion that fault can or ought to be assigned in automobile accidents: "The typical accident is just as likely to be due to mechanical failure, hazardous road conditions, or simply an innocent mistake made by an all-too-human driver" (Detlefsen, 1999, p. 201). The implication is that the tort system incorrectly faults "fallible" human beings for capricious events beyond their control.

Detlefsen's assertion is quite simply and demonstrably untrue in a substantial majority of instances. Insurance rating itself would be impossible if the *typical* accident resulted from a confluence of unpredictable random events as opposed to driver characteristics. An overwhelming abundance of evidence indicates that human judgments and conscious decisions, as opposed to fortuitous happenstance, are prominent causes of accidents. Indeed, the evidence indicates that most crashes serious enough to produce injury result from very egregious misconduct.

Consider Table 2 below, compiled from the 1997 National Highway Transportation Safety Administration (NHTSA) FARS file, which includes data on all fatal accidents in the U.S. The table categorizes accidents by the contributing factor considered, in the author's view, to be the most serious proximate cause. For example, an accident in which drinking was a contributing cause is not included in any of the remaining categories, even if additional contributing factors were also present (speeding, etc). The categories are thus mutually exclusive and jointly exhaustive.

Roughly one-third of all fatal accidents during 1997 involved alcohol or other controlled substances. An *additional* 27.7 percent of fatal crashes were speed-related, or involved a major traffic violation such as improper tailing, improper passing, driving on the wrong side of the road, or "erratic/reckless" driving. Less than a quarter of accidents did not involve a fairly serious driver error. NHTSA (1997) also has concluded that the vast majority of injury-producing accidents are the result of human error, and the Alberta Ministry of Transportation and Utilities (Alberta, 1998) recently concluded that ". . . the bottom line is that the majority of collisions remain preventable, in fact, virtually 89 percent are attributable to driver error."

A fairly voluminous body of research, dating to at least the late 1940s, indicates that a significant proportion of motor vehicle (and well as other) accidents result from imprudent risk-taking, lack of emotional control, anti-sociality, delinquency, aggression, and even criminality (see, for example, Wood, Pfefferbaum, and Arneklev, 1993; Gottfredson and Hirsch, 1990; McGuire, 1976; Evans and Wasielewski, 1983; Mayer and Treat, 1977; and

Tillman and Hobbs, 1949).[2] For example, Michalowski (1977) found that perpetrators of automobile crashes were two and one-half times more likely to have had criminal records than were their victims (38.9 percent to 15.6 percent). Fewer than one-half of perpetrators had neither traffic nor criminal records, compared to 73.7 percent of victims. Such findings are consistent throughout the literature, and indicate that individuals with a consistent history of risk-taking are disproportionately responsible for accidents. Crashes cannot generally be ascribed to discrete "slips" or random "errors", but are more typically the outcome of patterned conduct whose long-term risk of harming others is substantially high.

The notion of "faultless accidents," which ascribes the occurrence of highway injuries and fatalities to a confluence of circumstances beyond anyone's control, is unlikely to resonate with the driving public. A nationally representative survey of 6,000 households conducted by NHTSA (1997) reports that:

- 61 percent of respondents believe that unsafe driving, such as speeding, tailgating, and erratic driving, constitute a "major threat to the personal safety of themselves and their families" (p. xii);
- 70 percent of individuals who regularly drive on urban interstates report that they routinely encounter vehicles traveling at "unsafe speeds" (all or most of the time);
- in addition to speeding, 45 percent of urban interstate drivers say they regularly encounter "weaving in and out," 27 percent report routine tailgating, 17 percent report inattention, and 14 percent reported frequent encounters with "unsafe lane changes" (p. 92); and
- only 13 percent of individuals who frequent urban interstates reported no routine encounters with unsafe driving.

Somewhat surprisingly, respondents were nearly equally critical of themselves. Nearly two-thirds of drivers, 65 percent, admit that they occasionally drive at unsafe speeds, and nearly one in ten claim to do so nearly every day. Other self-reported unsafe driving practices, and time of last occurrence, are presented in Table 3.

---

[2] Lest the reader forget, highway violations, even though widely tolerated, are a form of lawlessness, so that a strong correlation between traffic offenses and other forms of lawlessness is not altogether surprising.

Table 2
Fatal Accidents by Contributory Factors, U.S., 1997

Fatal Accidents Involving:	Number of Accidents	Percentage of All Accidents	Cumulative Percentage
Drinking	11,101	29.8%	29.8%
Drugs	1,164	3.1	32.9
Speeding[a]	6,315	16.9	49.8
Other Major Violation[b]	4,040	10.8	60.7
Drowsiness/ Sleeping	238	0.6	61.3
Rules of the Road[c]	5,317	14.3	75.6
Medication	9	0.0	75.6
Cell Phone/Fax/Etc.	285	0.8	76.4
Other Improper Action[d]	160	0.4	76.8
Inattentive/ Emotional	713	1.9	78.7
Remainder	7,938	21.3	100%
Total Fatal Accidents	37,280	100%	

[a] *Either at least one vehicle exceeded the posted speed limit by at least 10 mph, or "driving too fast" was listed as a contributing factor on the accident report.*
[b] *Includes improper tailing, improper lane change, prohibited passing, passing on wrong side of the road, passing with insufficient distance, "erratic/reckless" driving, driving on shoulder, or driving the wrong way or on the wrong side of the road.*
[c] *Driving in a prohibited trafficway, improper entry/exit, improper start or backup, failure to yield or obey traffic signs/signals, driving around barrier, failure to signal, wrong signal, driving under the minimum speed, improper turning, stopping in road.*
[d] *Left vehicle unattended, improper loading, improper towing, or driving without required equipment.*
Source: Compiled by the author from 1997 FARS data.

A growing body of research supports the contention that individuals are conscious of risks, but nevertheless opt to pursue risky behavior. For example, the Insurance Research Council (1997) recently reported that while 84 percent of cellular phone owners believe that use of the phone while driving increases the risk of an accident, 61 percent choose to talk while driving. Similarly, a 1999 survey of over 5,000 drivers conducted by Old Dominion University found that 55.8 percent of respondents deliberately run red lights, even though over 98 percent recognize that red-light-running carries a significant risk of an accident (Porter, Berry, and Harlow, 1999).

Table 3
Self-Reported Driving Behavior by Most Recent Occurrence

Driving Behavior	Total in Past Yr.	Most Recent Occurrence			
		Today	Past Week	Past Month	Past Year
Entered an intersection just as the light was turning from yellow to red	71%	9%	21%	22%	19%
Drove 10 mph over the speed limit on an interstate highway	60%	7%	16%	17%	20%
Drove 10 mph faster than most other vehicles were going	56%	8%	14%	16%	18%
Went 10 mph over the speed limit on a two-lane rural road	52%	5%	11%	17%	19%
Slowed but didn't completely stop at a stop sign	51%	11%	15%	12%	14%
Went 10 mph over the speed limit in a residential neighborhood	40%	5%	8%	10%	16%
Drove through traffic switching quickly back and forth between lanes	32%	2%	6%	8%	16%
Drove 20 mph over the speed limit on an interstate highway	29%	2%	5%	7%	15%
Drove 20 mph over the speed limit on a rural road	26%	2%	4%	7%	13%

Table 3 (Continued)

Driving Behavior	Total in Past Yr.	Most Recent Occurrence			
		Today	Past Week	Past Month	Past Year
Drove through a light that was already red before you entered an intersection	23%	1%	3%	6%	14%
Tailgated another vehicle on a highway with one lane in each direction	23%	2%	3%	6%	12%
Drove 20 mph faster than most other vehicles were going	21%	1%	3%	6%	10%
Made an angry, insulting, or obscene gesture or comment toward another driver so that they heard or saw it	20%	2%	4%	6%	8%
Cut in front of another car in order to make a turn	18%	1%	2%	4%	11%
Made a U-turn where a sign said not to	16%	1%	2%	5%	8%
Drove through a stop sign without slowing	15%	1%	3%	3%	7%
Crossed railroad tracks when the red light was blinking	13%	<1%	2%	3%	8%
Passed a vehicle in a no-passing zone	10%	<1%	1%	2%	7%
Used the shoulder to pass in heavy traffic	10%	1%	2%	3%	5%
Drove when affected by alcohol	8%	<1%	1%	2%	5%
Raced another driver	6%	1%	1%	1%	3%

Source: NHTSA, 1997, Table 8-1.

Certainly, accidents will occur to the most prudent drivers. Contextual factors, such as poor infrastructure and congestion, unquestionably play a significant role in highway injuries. But the evidence regarding the prominent role of conscious and purposeful behavior in accidents is so overwhelming that auto choice proponents are deprived of the normative claim that "individuals *ought* not be held liable for others' injuries." Indeed, it is simply contrary to another normative claim: individuals *ought* to drive less aggressively and recklessly.

4. VALUE

Auto choice creates a system whereby all insured drivers will be guaranteed compensation for economic damages resulting from personal injury, where economic damages are defined by the act as ". . . any objectively verifiable pecuniary loss . . . ." Economic damage translates primarily into medical expenses and lost wages. Compensation for non-economic damages is relegated to an adjunct coverage for individuals choosing tort maintenance insurance. The projected savings (discussed in more detail below) under auto choice is thus derived primarily by denying compensation for otherwise legitimate claims. As J. Robert Hunter (1997) has pointed out in testimony before the Joint Economic Committee (JEC) of the U.S. Congress, only a small fraction of projected cost reductions are expected from increased "efficiencies" resulting from a reduction in the portion of premiums that are consumed by "transaction costs" (primarily attorneys' fees). Assuming that loss adjustment expenses significantly decline under auto choice to a level equivalent to current costs associated with settling physical damage claims, the resulting savings would amount to only a 1.5 percent decline in insurance prices. The level of savings envisioned by auto choice advocates would only be achieved by a 50 percent reduction in compensation.

Much more optimistic assumptions regarding the level of decline in transaction costs fail to produce significantly different results. The most commonly cited projections among auto choice proponents regarding cost reductions under auto choice can be traced back to a series of studies released by the RAND Institute for Social Justice, co-authored by Stephen Carroll and Allan Abrahamse (see below). However, RAND's own figures indicate that a large majority of projected savings are derived from a reduction of benefit payments. Projections for California provided to the JEC by Stephen Carroll are illustrative of the manner in which savings might be achieved under auto choice, based on the assumption that 50 percent of insureds would opt for no-fault coverage and that transaction costs associated with bodily injury claims would decline by nearly 46 percent. The figures indicate a reduction of injury costs by $327 for every $1000 of costs incurred under California's current reparations regime. However, $276 of the projected cost reduction, nearly 85 percent of savings, would be achieved by a reduction in compensation. Only 15 percent of savings is expected from reduction in transaction costs (author's calculations based on Carroll, 1997, p. 6, Figure 4). A more recent analysis by Carroll and Abrahamse projects no expected efficiency gains associated with a choice system. Under broadly similar assumptions as the earlier study, the authors' figures indicate that while transaction costs equal 17.5 percent of benefits under California's current tort system, such costs are estimated at 17.4 percent of benefits under "choice" (Carroll and Abrahamse, 1999, p. 26; calculated from Figure I).

A significant portion of the true cost of automobile transportation will remain entirely uncompensated under choice. Of course, uncompensated losses do not constitute a "savings" in any meaningful sense of the word. As Richard Abel (1987, p. 446) has noted, ". . . tort claims do not *create* liability costs, they merely *shift* them from victims to tortfeasors. It is the *tortfeasors* who create liability costs by injuring victims" (emphasis in original). Axiomatically, auto choice will shift those costs back to the victim: "The fact is that these costs remain regardless of liability limits which protect the party inflicting . . . injuries from bearing the cost" (Wiggins and Caldwell, 1987, p. 730).

There has been a tendency among auto choice proponents to treat non-economic damages as somehow inherently suspect. Robert Detlefsen (1998, p. 190), for example, has described non-economic damages as ". . . inherently subjective . . ." and ". . . impossible to quantify . . . ." The sentiment is echoed in the proposed legislation itself.

Non-economic damages are indeed more difficult to quantify due to a lack of a transparent market in pain in suffering,[3] but for that reason are no less "real" or "tangible" or "objective" than economic damages. In essence, the distinction rests upon a change in perspective in assessing damages. An assessment of lost wages depends upon the ability of particular human attributes to command a price in the labor market, and therefore involves *others'* valuations of worth. Non-economic damages are designed to compensate individuals based on *their own* experience of loss. The reader may conduct a kind of "thought experiment" to test this proposition by asking himself or herself: (1) How much would the loss of an arm cost in lost wages? (2) How much would be required to undergo voluntarily an

[3] Though such markets can be *inferred*, as recognized at least since Adam Smith.

amputation? While the answer to the second question varies from individual to individual, and is therefore "inherently subjective," it is not arbitrary, and for the majority of individuals the price for the second will almost certainly be considerably higher than that for the first.

In fact, high jury awards for non-economic damages are themselves *prima facie* evidence of the high value our society places upon non-pecuniary losses. In a sense, jury awards over many cases may be interpreted as a form of "deliberative" public opinion. In a meaningful economic sense, the valuations of worth on the part of the public do constitute a measure of value that is as "objective" as any other measure. The primacy of the economic over the non-economic embodied in auto choice is itself an arbitrary imposition of one set of values over another. Through devaluation of activity outside of paid employment, auto choice would reduce accident victims to the legal status of a commodity.

The priorities of compensation under auto choice will inevitably engender perverse results. Relatively minor injuries, such as fractures, may be compensated much more than fatalities, especially the death of a (non-wage-earning) child. The "loss" in the latter case may not be assessed at much more than burial expenses. Instances of severe disfigurement or impairment will not be compensated at all beyond medical expenses and time lost from paid employment.

In any case, the judicial system *has* been effective in producing non-arbitrary valuations of non-economic loss. Evidence indicates that awards for non-economic damages are strongly correlated with injury severity. While data for auto liability awards by injury severity are unavailable, Table 4 presents non-economic awards for personal injury cases. The data consist of cases drawn from Florida and Kansas City between 1973 and 1987. With the exception of death,[4] there is a monotonic relationship between both mean and median awards, as well as awards at both the 25th and 75th percentiles, and injury severity. There is clearly very high variability in awards within injury categories, all of which probably cannot be explained by differing circumstances in individual cases. However, in light of the fact that juries are given only the vaguest of guidance in determining damages,[5] the consistent relationship between damages and injury severity is striking.

---

[4] Awards for cases involving death are generally the result of more restrictive procedural rules. Death has been treated under separate legal doctrines than has injury, under the rationale that deceased individuals no longer experience "pain and suffering".

[5] In many cases courts merely provide instructions for damages of a "reasonable amount" or "fair compensation" (Bovbjerg, Sloan, and Blumstein, 1989, p. 912).

Table 4
Jury Awards, Non-Economic Damages by Injury Severity ($000s)
(Adjusted for Comparative Negligence)

Severity Level	25th Percentile	Median	Mean	75th Percentile
Temporary Injury				
2	0	2	10	7
3	0	9	53	56
4	4	36	63	60
Permanent Injury				
5	3	46	160	152
6	9	292	3,86	598
7	336	1,642	2,309	3,446
8	778	1,832	4,252	8,936
Death				
9	260	545	1,242	1,247

Coding:
2 Temporary Insignificant: Lacerations, contusions, minor scars, rash.
3 Temporary Minor: Infections, mis-set fracture, fall in hospital.
4 Temporary Major: Burns, surgical material left, drug side-effect, brain damage.
5 Permanent Minor: Loss of fingers, loss or damage to organs, other non-disabling injuries.
6 Permanent Significant: Deafness, loss of limb, loss of eye, loss of one kidney or lung.
7 Permanent Major: Paraplegia, blindness, loss of two limbs, brain damage.
8 Permanent Grave: Quadriplegia, severe brain damage, lifelong care or fatal prognosis.
9 Death.
Source: Derived from Table 3, Bovbjerg, Sloan, and Blumstein (1989).

5. THE CONSEQUENCES OF AUTO CHOICE

5.1. Premiums

Auto choice is a departure from existing no-fault reparation systems. All current no-fault systems among the states permit suit for non-economic damages for injuries beyond a threshold of severity. Auto choice would nearly eliminate such suits against what may be a significant proportion of drivers. Consequently, proponents of auto choice have claimed that the consistently unexceptional performance of "actually existing" no-fault systems is not indicative of the likely impact of federal auto choice on premiums.

No-fault systems possess both premium-increasing and premium-decreasing features. Such systems have a tendency to increase premiums significantly by expanding the pool of eligible claimants. On the other hand, proponents argue that under properly designed no-fault systems, reductions in payments for non-economic damages and in transaction costs disproportionately offset claimant expansion.

Inasmuch as the federal version of auto choice has not been instituted, estimates of premium reductions attendant with auto choice have a weak empirical foundation. Essentially, the estimates are derived from projections whose outcome cannot be empirically substantiated. Like all projections, outcomes are determined by initial assumptions. Importantly, virtually all claims regarding lowered costs may be traced back to a series of studies, all produced by the same authors employing the same methodology, authored under the aegis of the RAND Institute for Civil Justice. A 1998 RAND study (based on 1992 data) projects a 20 percent reduction in the private passenger automobile premiums of those who choose no-fault (Carroll and Abrahamse, 1998, p. 20). For tort selectors, the authors predict little change nationally, though they do suggest that individuals residing in some states could see their premiums increase by as much as ten percent.

While there are literally hundreds of discrete assumptions implicit in the analysis, perhaps the most highly questionable is the assumption that there will be no adverse selection. The RAND study assumes that ". . . bad drivers elect either the modified current system or ANF [Absolute No Fault] with the same probabilities as do good drivers . . . ." (p. 28).

Actually, this assumption implicitly entails a more general assumption that accident rates will not vary significantly between tort and no-fault selectors. If this assumption is not valid, the retention of tort rights could become substantially more expensive under auto choice. RAND's projections to the contrary rely upon an outcome in which the total damages paid on behalf of tort drivers, and hence the premiums charged, remain relatively unchanged under auto choice compared to current reparations systems. Tort drivers who are at fault in accidents with no-fault selectors will register a gain with respect to their share of the overall accident compensation burden. Both drivers will be compensated for economic damages by their own insurers without regard to fault. Under the traditional liability system, the same at-fault tort driver would be responsible for compensating his or her victim for both economic and non-economic damages, which the RAND authors generally reckon at twice the value of economic damages alone. However, tort drivers lose relative to the tort system in accidents in which no-fault selectors are at fault. Under auto choice, compensation for these accidents is also charged against the drivers' respective insurers, whereas the liability system would charge the costs entirely against the at-fault driver.

Given the assumptions of no adverse selection/moral hazard, gains and losses ought to have little net impact on premiums paid by tort selectors. However, if there is a large imbalance between safe tort selectors and risky no-fault selectors, the result may well be that the retention of tort rights will become substantially more expensive under auto choice. From a different vantage point, good drivers will incur a considerable responsibility for subsidizing costs imposed by poor drivers.[6]

The authors fail to provide empirical justification for an assumption central to their analysis, other than suggesting that the assumption is ". . . consistent with available evidence in the three states that have adopted choice plans . . . ," though no citations are provided. The only evidence specifically referenced is survey data that reveal that 90 percent of individuals injured in traffic accidents name others (either other individuals or external factors beyond their control, such as the weather or road conditions) as the cause of the accident. The authors conclude that individuals are unable to assess risk accurately, and that "Self selection cannot affect the distribution of drivers between plans unless drivers accurately perceive their own driving ability" (p. 28).

The assignment of fault is complex, emotionally charged, and subject to *post hoc* rationalization. In addition, the survey does not query respondents in a way that is specifically relevant to insurance-purchasing decisions, namely, whether respondents could identify whether they were *legally* at fault. As such, the results of the cited survey are weak evidence against the possibility of adverse selection. Contrary survey evidence, which indicates that individuals *can* and *do* make assessments of risk-taking on the highway, and that they can accurately identify behavior that is well-known to be associated with the risk of an accident, has been presented in a preceding section.

Secondly, the authors fail to discuss additional factors that may contribute to a statistically meaningful association between accident rates and

---

[6] Cost shifting between good and poor drivers will undoubtedly occur, irrespective of the validity of the assumption in question, as is implicit in RAND's own analysis. All tort victims ("good drivers") of at-fault no-fault selectors ("bad drivers") lose. All at-fault tort selectors ("bad drivers") gain. The RAND analysis applies only to tort selectors collectively, not to "good" and "bad" drivers *per se*. See below.

insurance selection. In addition to adverse selection, in which individuals' assessment of the risk of an accident in which they are at fault influences insurance-purchasing decisions, what might loosely be labeled "moral hazard" may influence driving behavior *subsequent* to the purchase of insurance. Individuals largely immunized from liability may simply take less care behind the wheel, as evidence suggested below indicates. In addition, the degree to which premiums reflect risk will provide a strong financial incentive for high-risk individuals to switch to cheaper no-fault coverage. Financial incentives operate independently of individuals' ability to accurately assess risk. For example, one might imagine that young males, a demographic group combining low earnings with high premiums, would be over-represented among "switchers".

The RAND authors do suggest that "adverse selection is an empirical issue that warrants further study" (p. 32). While we would agree that the issue requires further study, considerable evidence already exists which indicates that subtle alterations of expected consequences can produce "adverse selection" and/or "moral hazard" effects. For example, several studies have documented a statistically significant increase in bodily injury claims and driver aggressiveness associated with the presence of automobile airbags (Hoffer, Millner, and Peterson, 1995; Peterson and Hoffer, 1993). Presumably, individuals at greater risk of accident tend to select autos equipped with safety devices (adverse selection), or the presence of safety devices leads drivers to take more risks (moral hazard). Similarly, individuals who drive heavier vehicles tend to drive more recklessly (Adams, 1997). Abundant evidence indicates that the greater the degree of insulation from the consequences of accidents, the greater degree of risk taking. Additional evidence bearing directly on driving incentives associated with no-fault systems is explored in the next section, where preliminary results of our own empirical studies will be presented.

5.2. Deterrence

The principle of deterrence is the philosophic foundation for the tort liability system. The onus of liability, providing the means whereby individuals can be held accountable for deliberate or negligent acts that result in harm to others, is intended to serve a preventive function. In fact, deterrence is probably more central to the theory of torts than is the principle of restitution, since preventing harm altogether is preferable to compensating for harm.

The deterrence issue has not been fully addressed by auto choice proponents. For example, among the more than 24 pages of recent testimony to the JEC supporting auto choice, only two short paragraphs are devoted to the negative impact upon deterrence of the proposed reform, and then only to dismiss the issue summarily.[7] In support of a conclusion that the deterrence effects of auto choice will not compromise public safety, Jeffrey O'Connell states that (1) "RAND's calculations *assume* no such effect" (emphasis added), and (2) auto choice will ". . . create offsetting incentives . . . ." Professor O'Connell acknowledges that ". . . negligent motorists will absorb or 'internalize' less of their loss . . . because they recover even if they cause accidents and they will not be liable for pain and suffering . . . ," but then suggests that ". . . those same motorists [negligent motorists?] will internalize *more costs* because they cannot recover for their own pain and suffering" (emphasis in original). Of course, *negligent* motorists cannot typically recover for their own pain and suffering under current tort liability systems. Similarly, Robert Detlefsen (1998, p. 202) devotes a single paragraph to the question of deterrence in a lengthy article supporting auto choice.

However, there is a body of empirically based literature that suggests that the effect of immunizing drivers from liability is to increase accident rates as well as the incidence of careless or negligent driving behavior. Two studies from 1982 concluded that no-fault systems significantly increase fatality rates, one of which estimated that no-fault systems increase fatalities by as much as 10 percent (Landes, 1982; Medoff and Magaddino, 1982). Sloan, et al. (1994) have estimated that no-fault systems which eliminate at least 25 percent of tort claims are associated with an 18 percent increase in the automobile fatality rate. More recently, Cummins and Weiss (1999) found a statistically significant association between no-fault systems and fatality rates, and Devlin (1999), using micro-level data, found a significant association between no-fault systems and injury severity. Two studies of no-fault systems in New Zealand and the Northern Territory of Australia found increases in auto fatalities of 16 percent and 20 percent, respectively (Swan, 1984; McEwin, 1989). Sloan, et al. (1995) found an increase in driver intoxication associated with no-fault, controlling for such factors as the price of alcohol as well as premium surcharges for DUIs. A summary of the most credible evidence is displayed in Table 5.

---

[7] Auto choice proponents were: Christine Todd Whitman, Governor of New Jersey; Michael Horowitz of the Hudson Institute; Dr. Stephen Carroll, economist for the RAND Corporation (and a co-author of the RAND studies cited above); and Professor Jeffrey O'Connell of the University of Virginia School of Law, and well-known long-time advocate of tort reform. J. Robert Hunter of the Consumer Federation of America was the lone dissenter among those called to testify.

Table 5
No-Fault Automobile Insurance and Moral Hazard Effects

Study	Effect on Fatality/Injuries/Dangerous Behavior
Cummins and Weiss (1999)	Verbal threshold systems associated with 13% increase in fatalities.
Devlin (1992)	Quebec no-fault system associated with approximately 10% increase in fatal accidents.
Devlin (1999)	An increase in the severity of accidents is associated with no-fault systems. Among all claimants, those in no-fault states were more than twice as likely to have injuries in the most serious category.
Gaudry (1992)	Quebec no-fault system increased fatal accidents—3.3% is attributed to adoption of flat-rated premium, 6.8% to increase associated with no-fault. Injury-producing accidents increased by 32%.
Kochanowski and Young (1985)	No significant effects on fatalities.
Landes (1982)	Significant tort thresholds in no-fault states increase fatal accidents by more than 10%.
McEwin (1989)	16% increase in fatalities associated with no-fault systems in New Zealand and parts of Australia. States retaining tort systems did not experience increases in fatalities.
Medoff and Magaddino (1982)	No-fault systems reduce accident deterrence, findings statistically significant.
Sloan (1995)	No-fault associated with statistically significant increase in drunk driving.
Sloan and Reilly (1994)	Thresholds barring more than 25% of tort suits associated with 16% increase in fatality rate. Compulsory PIP, even with surcharges for accidents, also independently contributes to higher fatality rates.
Swan (1984)	No-fault increased fatalities by 20% in New Zealand and parts of Australia.
Zador and Lund (1986)	No significant effects on fatalities.

Certainly, these types of studies have generated controversy, and at least two studies have found no association between no-fault and fatality rates (Kochanowski and Young, 1985; Zador and Lund, 1986). *While further study is needed, we find substantial and credible, if not incontrovertible, evidence to support the contention that no-fault regimes will significantly erode highway safety.* The evidence indicates that systems with the most restrictive tort thresholds entail the most risk.

5.3. Additional Empirical Evidence

It may be useful in this context to present some preliminary findings on a long-term project to document the effects of reparations systems on accident rates. The following model was fit to data aggregated by state and by year, using ordinary least squares regression:

<u>Dependent Variable</u>:

Fatality Rate (ratio of fatalities per million vehicle miles).

<u>Independent Variables</u>:

Age (percentage of registered drivers under 21),

Gender (percentage of registered drivers who are male),

Speed Limit (maximum state speed limit, usually rural interstate),

Traffic Density (ratio of vehicle miles traveled to highway miles),

Rural (ratio of vehicle miles traveled on rural highways to vehicle miles traveled on urban highways),

Belt Use (percentage seat belt use),

Beer Consumption (per capita consumption of beer),

BAC (blood alcohol content limit),

DUI (number of DUI arrests per registered driver),

Verbal Threshold States (dummy variable coded 1 for no-fault states employing a strict verbal threshold and 0 otherwise; verbal threshold states under this criterion are Michigan, Florida, and New York), and

Monetary Threshold No-fault States (dummy variable coded 1 for all other no-fault states—excluding "add-on" states—and 0 otherwise).[8]

The control variables include demographic characteristics known to be associated with the risk of accidents. The variables "rural", "traffic density," "speed limit," and "belt use" are indicative of overall traffic conditions and behaviors that contribute to either the likelihood or severity of accidents. The model also controls for the effects of intoxication. Per capita beer consumption measures what might be termed cultural differences between the states with regard to attitudes towards the use of alcohol. Lower BAC limits have been shown in prior research to reduce the incidence of drunk driving, while DUI arrests are used as an indicator of the degree or effectiveness of law enforcement. Since verbal threshold states are expected to have a far more significant impact on fatality rates, two dummy variables representing the effects of the different reparation systems are included. Tort states serve as the reference category.

DUI arrests are considered exogenous to the type of reparation system in place in a given state, since arrests are considered a function of the effectiveness of law enforcement. Arrests may also be reasonably considered endogenous, in that reparations systems may contribute to the propensity to drive while drunk. The model is thus a conservative measure of the effects of reparations systems on fatalities, since one path by which those effects are manifested is eliminated. Alternative models that did not include DUI arrests had no significant impact on the results displayed below, nor did regression of the non-alcohol-related fatality rates against the above model minus the alcohol-related variables produce different results.

The pooled time series and state cross-sectional data provide 255 observations (including the District of Columbia). Results are displayed below.

[8] Data sources: Information for vehicle miles of travel, roadway miles, and registered drivers were obtained from the Federal Highway Administration; belt use and BAC laws from the National Highway Transportation Safety Administration (NHTSA); speed limit laws from the Insurance Institute for Highway Safety (IIHS); beer consumption per capita from the National Institute on Alcohol Abuse and Alcoholism; and DUI arrests from the FBI. Information on state insurance laws was obtained from the Alliance of American Insurers. Fatalities by state were calculated from NHTSA's FARS data.

Table 6
OLS Regression Results
Dependent Variable: Traffic Fatalities per 1,000,000 Miles of Travel
(Italics Indicates Statistical Significance)

Model	Coefficient	*p*-value
Constant	*-0.781*	*0.401*
Age	6.055	0.002
Gender	*1.193*	*0.498*
Rural	0.517	0.007
Traffic Density	*0.0000001124*	*0.129*
Speed Limit	*0.005738*	*0.282*
Belt Use	*-0.168*	*0.369*
Beer Consumption	0.288	0.001
BAC Law	4.786	0.045
DUI Arrests	10.676	0.096
Verbal	0.20	0.027
Monetary	-0.19	0.001

R^2 = 0.292.
Number of observations = 255.

All of the control variables are in the expected direction, though gender, traffic density, speed limit, belt use, and DUI arrests are not significant at the 0.05 level. Results indicate a positive relationship between verbal threshold states and the fatality rate. Contrary to expectations, monetary threshold states have lower average fatality rates than do tort states. We cannot provide a good explanation for this result at this time. However, the results would seem to indicate that those states which most insulate drivers from suit experience fatality rates higher than can be accounted for by the control variables. The experience of verbal threshold states should most closely resemble what may be expected under auto choice.

The results are robust, and remain virtually unaltered under a variety of different model specifications. A more satisfactory approach would entail a comparison of fatality rates before and after changes in reparations system. Unfortunately, culling data from a variety of different sources over many years entails much time and effort, and is part of a long-term project in progress. Nevertheless, the results can be interpreted in light of a growing body of literature in which similar findings are obtained under different models and assumptions, as cited above.[9]

5.4. Vehicle Safety

Auto choice proponents argue that auto choice will allow insurers to create incentives for individuals to purchase safer cars, a sentiment expressed in the preamble of auto choice legislation itself, faulting tort systems with an ". . . inability to achieve market-based discounts in insurance rates for owners of safer cars . . . ." Jeffery O'Connell also has suggested that ". . . by reducing the relative cost of driving safer cars the plan should, at the margin, necessarily increase the use of such safer cars. Thus, the plan should generate affirmative market incentives that should, in turn, *enhance the overall safety of driving automobiles*" (emphasis added).

New technologies have produced safety enhancements known to reduce injuries significantly. However, feats of engineering have not surmounted simple physics: the weight differential between vehicles is by far the best predictor of whether two-vehicle accidents will result in serious injury or death. The "safer car" referenced above means primarily a heavier car (or truck or SUV). Of course, the same purchasing decisions that protect a vehicle owner has the contrary effect of placing others at greater risk. To the degree that premiums truly reflect the degree to which vehicles protect their passengers, auto choice will produce incentives to purchase vehicles with high "aggressivity", that is, with a much larger potential to harm others.

Consider the following table, calculated from 1997 FARS data for two- and multi-vehicle accidents. The percentage of all traffic fatalities, including vehicle occupants other than drivers, is listed by the weight difference between striking vehicles. The story these numbers tell us is quite unambiguous: a large majority of fatalities occurred to occupants of the lighter vehicle. Almost one-half of all highway deaths occurred to occupants of vehicles that were 500 lbs. or more lighter than the other vehicle, compared to only 12 percent of deaths in vehicles that weighed over 500 lbs. more than the other vehicle. The chances of surviving a collision decline appreciably for occupants of lighter vehicles. The effect of weight can be expected to dwarf the effects of all other safety enhancements.

---

[9] It is the author's opinion that the burden of proof is in the reverse on this question. Even if one were to grant that extant studies are to some degree inconclusive, auto choice proponents confront the onus to demonstrate conclusively that auto choice *will not* lead to substantial increases in injuries and fatalities. Otherwise, if implemented, auto choice would constitute nothing less than an experiment of epic proportion on an unwitting public.

Table 7
Traffic Fatality Percentages by Vehicle Weight Differentials

Vehicle Weight Differential	**Percentage of All Traffic Fatalities**
Over 1000 lbs. Less than Other Vehicle	26%
500 to 999 lbs. Less than Other Vehicle	21
0 to 499 lbs. Less than Other Vehicle	21
0 to 499 lbs. More than Other Vehicle	19
500 to 999 lbs. More than Other Vehicle	8
Over 1000 lbs. More than Other Vehicle	5
Total	100%

Source: Calculated by author from 1997 FARS data.

In general, there is little doubt that no-fault systems impose a premium charge on drivers of lighter vehicles based on costs produced by drivers of heavier vehicles, simply because heavier vehicles protect their own occupants while causing greater injury to occupants of lighter vehicles.[10] If high risk drivers disproportionately select the no-fault option, as seems likely, auto choice may compound the problem by placing bad drivers in vehicles that pose a greater danger to others. In addition, more large vehicles on the highways may increase the frequency as well as the severity of accidents, since drivers of such vehicles tend to be more careless and aggressive than they would be otherwise. Increased traffic safety seems the least likely outcome of auto choice.

5.5. Who Pays?

A fundamental flaw of auto choice is that good drivers will inevitably be forced to pay for bad drivers. Under auto choice, the costs imposed upon society by negligent behavior are "externalized", meaning that such costs are not borne by those who produce them. Externalization occurs in two ways:

---

[10] This feature of auto choice has been noted by the Academy of Actuaries (1998), which has suggested that premium costs will be transferred from commercial to personal lines, since commercial vehicles typically weigh more than private vehicles. There are also indications that liability surcharges based on vehicle weight are finding increasing support within the insurance industry.

- Costs created by poor drivers are borne entirely by injured parties in the form of uncompensated non-economic losses. These costs will not be reflected in premiums for high risks.
- Under "auto choice," the costs of compensating economic damages caused by high-risk no-fault drivers will be passed on to their victims, since fault is not assigned.

George Priest (1998) offers the following example: "You may be the most careful driver in the world, but if your parked car is hit by a drowsy, careless, or inexperienced driver, under auto choice the repair costs would be built into *your* subsequent insurance premiums, not the offending driver's."[11] Essentially, no-fault coverage indemnifies individuals from a risk that is categorically distinct from the risk covered by liability policies, namely, the risk of *being in an accident* versus the risk of *causing an accident.*

Proponents of auto choice have not directly responded to the problem of cost externalization, except to adopt a tactic of denying the very conceptual legitimacy of "fault", as discussed above. Clearly, the issue requires far more empirical investigation.

5.6. Impact on the Poor

Auto choice proponents have equated auto choice with a progressive tax rebate which would primarily benefit poor individuals residing in urban areas (see Joint Economic Committee, 1998).

However, little has been mentioned of the regressivity of the proposed legislation with regard to benefit payments. Under auto choice, poor individuals are literally "worth less." Individuals earning the least, such as those laboring in minimum wage jobs or out-of-work altogether, will be the least compensated for injury. Jeffery O'Connell (1997, p. 5) has testified against tort reparation on the basis that ". . . the poor must pay into the insurance pool the same as the rich even though they will extract much less from the pool," the argument being that the poor ". . . incur less wage loss." Surely this criticism can more appropriately be leveled against auto choice.

Groups who are disproportionately represented among low-income strata, particularly women and minorities, will experience the largest reduction in benefits. Because of exclusion from the labor market and under-

[11] Actually, the analogy isn't entirely correct, since only bodily injury claims are affected under "choice". However, the logic of the analogy still applies if one substitutes "medical costs" for "repair costs."

valuation of domestic work, for example, women have historically received a majority of compensation in non-economic damages (cf. Ruda, 1993).

5.7. Legal Rights

Caps on non-economic damages (or their elimination as in this case) have been increasingly under attack on constitutional grounds.[12] Legislative usurpation of the traditional role of the judiciary in valuing compensation has been said to violate standards of due process of both the federal constitution as well as many state constitutions. Several state courts of last appeal have voided state-mandated caps (cf. Wiggins and Caldwell, 1987). The Supreme Court of Illinois struck down tort reform in 1997, reasoning that the act violated the "separation of powers" due to the inappropriate legislative acquisition of the power of *remittitur*, the traditional prerogative of judges to reduce jury damage awards deemed excessive. Secondly, the court found that the Illinois statute violated the state's constitution by virtue of creating arbitrary classifications. As an example, the court pointed out that damage caps function to harm severely injured individuals, though not those with minor injuries. The state, the court ruled, possessed no compelling rationale for such a distinction (*Best v. Taylor Machine Works*, 1997). How the provisions of auto choice would be effected by such rulings remains an open question.

In addition, family members of those opting for no-fault policies may involuntarily lose their tort rights. The proposed legislation places all "resident relative" household members under the option chosen by a resident driver (and would permit insurers to "encourage" homogeneity of choice within households). Legal rights of residents are governed by the doctrine of "implied consent," so that they are bound by the decisions of others even if they are entirely unaware of them. Testimony before the U.S. House of Representatives presented the following hypothetical:

> A person who has "chosen" no-fault has an elderly, blind relative who is a member of his household. If another driver caused an accident in which the relative is injured as a pedestrian, does the blind person lose the right to bring an action because of his relative's choice of insurance? In other words, would the bill mean that someone who

---

[12] Proponents claim that relinquishing tort rights is voluntary under auto choice. If, as seems likely, auto choice results in a substantial increase in tort premiums, then auto choice infringes on tort rights in a way that cannot be conceptually distinguished from benefit caps.

does not even drive is deprived of the right to be fully compensated by the driver who caused the injury?

Testimony indicated that, indeed, the blind non-driver would have surrendered his tort rights (related in Buchanan, 1998). Similarly, employees are bound by the decisions of their employers, passengers by the choices of vehicle owners, and automobile renters by the choices of the rental business.

6. CONCLUSION: REFORM VERSUS REVOLUTION

Tort liability systems currently in place do suffer from serious defects. Critics are correct to fault the complicated and lengthy procedures that accident victims must negotiate prior to compensation, as well as the fact that these systems tend to compensate severe injuries inadequately. However, a strong case has not been made for a radical dissolution of tort systems based on centuries of common law. Many of the problems associated with tort liability can be confronted with relatively minor adjustments. Under-compensation can be redressed via increases in mandatory coverage limits. Timeliness of compensation is most appropriately achieved via judicial reform or the establishment of alternative arbitration mechanisms.

Ultimately, the surest way to reduce premiums is to reduce accident rates, a task that ought to constitute the Archimedean point and foundational principle of any public policy reform. It appears immoral to this writer to simply "write off" the enormous costs imposed by automobile transportation, and adopt a reparations regime that by doing so essentially accepts those costs as "given". In truth, credible evidence indicates that even a modest public policy effort can very significantly reduce accidents. Of course, this will require a significant change in tactics on the part of safety advocates and policy-makers, so that the current priority upon "things" rather than human behavior is reversed. Essential elements of such an approach must be the safety incentives built into tort systems, and the general social obligation to minimize the potential to inflict harm on others that driving behavior possesses.

References

Abel, Richard., 1987, The Real Tort Crisis—Too Few Claims, *Ohio State Law Journal*, 48, 443-467.

Adams, John., 1995, *Risk*, London: University College London Press.

AIS Risk Consultants, 1998, *Analysis of RAND Report Entitled "The Effects of a Choice Automobile Insurance Plan on Insurance Costs and Compensation, An Updated Analysis"*, Freehold, NJ: AIS Risk Consultants.

Alberta, Province of, 1998, 1997 Traffic Collision Statistics Show Driver Error is Still a Major Factor in Traffic Collisions, Press Release—September 1, Edmonton, Alberta.

Best v. Taylor Machine Works, 1997, Illinois Supreme Court (docket No. 81890-81893), Dec. 17.

Bovbjerb, Randall R., Frank A. Sloan, and James F. Blumstein, 1989, Valuing Life and Limb in Tort: Scheduling "Pain and Suffering", *Northwestern University Law Review*, 83, 908-975.

Buchan, Philip., 1998, "Not-Ready-For-Prime-Time" No-Fault, *Trial*, 34, 11.

Carroll, Stephen J., 1997, Effects of an Auto Choice Insurance Plan on Costs and Premium, Statement before the Joint Economic Committee of the U.S. Congress, March 19.

Carroll, Stephen J., and Allan F. Abrahamse, 1998, *The Effects of a Choice Automobile Insurance Plan on Insurance Costs and Compensation*, Santa Monica, CA: RAND Corporation, Institute for Civil Justice.

Carroll, Stephen J., and Allan F. Abrahamse, 1999, The Effects of a Choice Automobile Insurance Plan on Insurance Costs and Compensation, *Journal of Insurance Regulation*, 18, 8-33.

Cummins, J. David, and Mary A. Weiss, 1999, The Incentive Effects of No-fault Automobile Insurance, in *Automobile Insurance: Road Safety, New Drivers, Risks, Insurance Fraud and Regulation* (Georges Dionne and Claire Laberge-Nadeau, eds.), Boston: Kluwer Academic Publishers.

Devlin, Rose Anne, 1992, Liability versus No-Fault Automobile Insurance Regimes: An Analysis of the Experience in Quebec, in *Contributions to Insurance Economics* (Georges Dionne, ed.), Boston: Kluwer Academic Publishers.

Devlin, Rose Anne, 1999, No-Fault Automobile Insurance and Accident Severity: Lessons Still to be Learned, in *Automobile Insurance: Road Safety, New Drivers, Risks, Insurance Fraud and Regulation* (Georges Dionne and Claire Laberge-Nadeau, eds.), Boston: Kluwer Academic Publishers.

Detlefsen, Robert F., 1998, Escaping the Tort-Based Auto Accident Compensation System: The Federal Auto Choice Reform Act of 1997, *Journal of Insurance Regulation*, 17, 186-212.

Evans, L., and P. Wasielewski, 1983, Risky Driving Related to Driver and Vehicle Characteristics, *Accident Analysis and Prevention*, 15, 121-136.

Gaudry, M., 1992, Measuring the Effects of the No-Fault 1978 Quebec Automobile Insurance Act with the DRAG Model, in *Contributions to Insurance Economics* (Georges Dionne, ed.), Boston: Kluwer Academic Publishers.

Gottfredson, M. R., and T. Hirschi, 1990, *A General Theory of Crime*, Stanford, CA: *Stanford University Press*.

Hoffer, George E., Edward L. Millner, and Steven P. Peterson, 1995, Are Drivers of Airbag-Equipped Cars More Aggressive? A Test of the Peltzman Hypothesis, *Journal of Law and Economics*, 38, 251-64.

Hunter, J. Robert, 1997, Statement before the Joint Economic Committee of the U.S. Congress, March 19.

Joint Economic Committee, U.S. Congress, 1998, *Auto Choice: Impact on Cities and the Poor*, Washington, DC: Government Printing Office.

Kochanowski, Paul S., and Madelyn V. Young, 1985, Deterrent Aspects of No-fault Automobile Insurance: Some Empirical Findings, *The Journal of Risk and Insurance*, 52, 269.

Landes, Elisabeth, 1982, Insurance, Liability, and Accidents: A Theoretical and Empirical Investigation of the Effects of No-fault Accidents, *Journal of Law and Economics*, 25, 49-65.

Mayer, Richard E., and John R. Treat, 1977, Psychological, Social, and Cognitive Characteristics of High-Risk Drivers: A Pilot Study, *Accident Analysis and Prevention*, 9, 1-8.

Medoff, Marshall M., and Joseph P. Magaddino, 1982, An Empirical Analysis of No-fault Insurance, *Evaluation Review*, 6, 373-392.

McEwin, I. R., No-Fault and Road Accidents: Some Australasian Evidence, *International Review of Law and Economics*, 9, 13-24.

McGuire, Frederick L., 1976, Personality Factors in Highway Accidents, *Human Factors*, 18, 433-442.

National Highway Traffic Safety Administration, 1997, National Survey of Speeding and Other Unsafe Driving, Vol II: Driver Attitudes and Behavior, Washington, DC: Government Printing Office.

O'Connell, Jeffrey, 1997, Consumer Choice in the Auto Insurance Market, Statement before the Joint Economic Committee of the U.S. Congress, March 17.

Peterson, Steven P., and George E. Hoffer, 1993, The Impact of Airbag Adoption on Relative Personal Injury and Absolute Collision Insurance Claims, *Journal of Consumer Research*, 20, 657-62.

Porter, Bryan E., Thomas Berry, and Jeff Harlow, 1999, *A Nationwide Survey of Red Light Running: Measuring Driver Behaviors for the "Stop Red Light Running" Program*, Sponsored by DaimlerChrysler Corporation, the American Trauma Society, and the Federal Highway Administration.

Priest, George L., 1998, The Conservative Delusion over Auto Choice, *On the Issues, American Enterprise Institute for Public Policy Research*, August. (A version of the essay is also available in the *Wall Street Journal*, July 21, 1998.)

Ruda, Lisa M., 1993, Caps on Non-Economic Damages and the Female Plaintiff: Heeding the Warning Signs, *Case Western Reserve Law Review*, 44, 197-233.

Sloan, Frank A., et al., 1994, Tort Liability versus Other Approaches for Deterring Careless Driving, *International Review of Law and Economics*, 14, 53-60.

Sloan, Frank A., et al., 1995, Effects of Tort Liability and Insurance on Heavy Drinking and Drinking and Driving, *Journal of Law and Economics*, 38, 49-78.

Swan, Peter L., 1984, The Economics of Law: Economic Imperialism in Negligence Law, No-Fault Insurance, Occupational Licensing and Criminology?, *Australian Economic Review*, 67, 92-108.

Tillman, W. A., and G. E. Hobbs, 1949, The Accident-Prone Automobile Driver: A Study of the Psychiatric and Social Background, *American Journal of Psychiatry*, 106, 321-331.

Wiggins, David J., and Robert S. Caldwell, 1987, Liability-Limiting Legislation: An Impermissible Intrusion into the Jury's Right to Decide, *Drake Law Review*, 36, 723-733.

Wood, P. B., B. Pfefferbaum, and B. J. Arneklev, 1993, Risk-Taking and Self-Control: Social-Psychological Correlates of Delinquency, *Journal of Criminal Justice*, 16, 111-130.

Zador, Paul, and Adrian Lund, 1986, Re-Analyzing the Effects of No-Fault Auto Insurance on Fatal Crashes, *The Journal of Risk and Insurance*, 53, 226-241.

5
THE EFFECT OF NO-FAULT AUTO INSURANCE ON DRIVER BEHAVIOR AND AUTO ACCIDENTS IN THE UNITED STATES

David S. Loughran[1]
RAND Corporation

1. INTRODUCTION

Proponents of no-fault auto insurance claim the system delivers speedier and more equitable compensation at lower cost than traditional tort insurance (e.g., O'Connell, et al., 1996). A similar case is made in favor of choice auto insurance (Carroll and Abrahamse, 1999). However, the essential property of no-fault and choice auto insurance that proponents argue may reduce auto insurance costs—restricted third-party liability—is considered to be among its greatest weaknesses by opponents. Opponents commonly focus their case against no-fault and choice on the basis that individuals should be held accountable for their negligent actions (e.g., Kabler, 1999). This, they argue, provides redress for those injured and, importantly, serves to deter negligent actions overall. No-fault insurance, they reason, significantly weakens this deterrent effect, leading to more negligent driving, higher accidents rates, and ultimately higher auto insurance costs.

This position is echoed in recent debate over choice auto insurance at the federal level. For example, testimony in 1999 by some no-fault opponents in front of the U.S. Senate Committee on Commerce, Science, and Technology on the Auto Choice Reform Act (S. 837), alluded to the potentially deleterious incentive effects of no-fault. The Association of Trial Lawyers of America (ATLA), deeply opposed to the concept of no-fault,

[1] This research was funded by the Institute for Civil Justice (ICJ) at RAND. The conclusions herein do not necessarily reflect the views and opinions of the ICJ, RAND, or its sponsors. The author would like to thank Stephen Carroll, Kanika Kapur, Michelle White, and Beth Giddens for their careful reviews of earlier drafts of this chapter.

referred to this proposed federal Auto Choice legislation as the "Reckless Driver Protection Act" (ATLA, 2000). Other academics, policy makers, and consumer advocates point to recent studies which they claim make it clear that Auto Choice will increase accident rates substantially. After reviewing the empirical literature on the effects of no-fault on accident rates, George Priest, a professor of law and economics at Yale University, writes in the *Wall Street Journal*: "It would be a deep and abiding misjudgment—indeed, quite possibly a deadly one—to eliminate in the name of 'choice' the responsibility that high-risk drivers ought to bear for their own careless driving" (Priest, 1998). The aim of the present research is to investigate whether data on auto fatalities, accidents, and negligence support the claim that a choice auto insurance system would increase driver negligence and accident rates.

Between 1971 and 1976, 16 states passed some form of no-fault automobile insurance reform in the U.S.[2] Differences among states in both the timing of adoption and strictness of these no-fault laws provides variation needed to identify the effect of no-fault insurance on driver negligence and accident rates. Curiously, the question whether no-fault auto insurance encourages careless driving behavior did not play a prominent role in legislative debates over the adoption of no-fault between 1971 and 1976. Instead, the question seems to have arisen first among academics who were interested in evaluating the deterrent effect of the tort system in general. It is not difficult to write down an economic model in which no-fault liability results in higher rates of driver negligence. The intuition behind such a model is simple: No-fault auto insurance lowers the cost of driving negligently by limiting liability for the injuries suffered by third parties in auto accidents. However, whether no-fault auto insurance as enforced in the U.S. in fact lowers the cost of driving negligently (either financially or in utility terms) and to what extent drivers respond to these lower costs are empirical matters.

The empirical literature has focused almost exclusively on the relationship between no-fault and auto fatal accident rates. Landes (1982) first explored this issue, finding that the adoption of no-fault auto insurance increased auto fatal accident rates by as much as 10 percent annually in no-

---

[2] Since then, four of those states have repealed no-fault and returned to a pure tort insurance system, and two states, New Jersey and Pennsylvania, have enacted choice plans that offer drivers the choice between no-fault and tort insurance. Kentucky has always offered a choice plan with virtually all of its drivers choosing no-fault coverage. The Territory of Puerto Rico enacted no-fault in 1970, and the District of Columbia enacted no-fault in 1983 and repealed it in 1986. A number of jurisdictions in Australia, New Zealand, and Canada also have enacted no-fault auto insurance laws.

fault states between 1971 and 1975. This finding prompted a trio of studies in the early 1980s (Zador and Lund, 1986; Kochanowski and Young, 1985; U.S. Department of Transportation, 1985), which all came to the opposite conclusion that no-fault has no effect on fatal accident rates. More recently, several studies have revisited the question with data from Australia, New Zealand, and Canada, as well as more recent data from the U.S. (Devlin, 1992; McEwin 1989; Cummins and Weiss, 1999; Cummins, Weiss, and Phillips, 1999; Kabler 1999).[3] These studies have all found evidence in favor of the hypothesis that no-fault leads to higher fatal accident rates.

If we take the findings of Landes (1982), Devlin (1992), and Cummins, Weiss, and Phillips (1999) at face value, no-fault led to as many as 5,600 additional highway fatalities in no-fault states between 1991 and 1995 alone. If true, it is hard to justify the adoption of no-fault insurance even if it does substantially lower the cost of auto insurance. I think these numbers are implausibly large, however, and believe the results of the present study show convincingly that not only is there no statistically significant relationship between the adoption of no-fault and fatal accident rates but also that there is no statistically significant relationship between no-fault and accident rates overall or other measures of driver care. I argue further that no-fault auto insurance as implemented in the U.S., even in its strictest form, is unlikely to lower significantly the expected cost of an auto accident to the at-fault driver. So, even *a priori*, it seems unlikely that no-fault auto insurance could have a substantive impact on driver behavior. Presumably a switch from tort to Auto Choice, at least in the form proposed by most advocates, could be expected to have similarly negligible effects on accident rates and driver behavior.

In Section 2, I provide a general explanation of the differences between no-fault and tort insurance and how these differences, in principle, could affect driving behavior. I then offer three tests of whether no-fault affects driving behavior and outcomes in Section 3. Section 3.1 reviews the empirical literature on the relationship between no-fault and the fatal accident rate, focusing on econometric weaknesses that cast serious doubt on the conclusions of previous studies. In Section 3.2, I then test the hypothesis that no-fault auto insurance leads to higher fatal accident rates using state-level data that span the period over which no-fault was first implemented in the U.S. Even if no-fault has no discernable impact on the fatal accident rate, no-fault nonetheless could still affect the overall accident rate and the propensity to drive negligently more generally. So in Sections 3.3 and 3.4, I

[3] Cummins, Weiss, and Phillips (1999) is a revised version of Cummins and Weiss (1999). In the remainder of this chapter, I refer only to the revised paper.

test whether such relationships exist using data not previously employed to study the impact of no-fault. I offer some concluding remarks in Section 4.

2. THE RELATIONSHIP BETWEEN NO-FAULT INSURANCE AND DRIVER BEHAVIOR

Under a traditional tort system, at-fault drivers are liable for the economic and non-economic damages they inflict on third parties. In all tort states, drivers must insure themselves against this potential liability. This insurance comes in the form of third-party bodily injury (BI) and property damage (PD) liability insurance that covers the insured against claims for damages made by third parties up to some specified limit. Typically, states require drivers to carry some minimum level of liability coverage specified in both per-person and per-accident terms (e.g., \$10,000 per person/\$20,000 per accident). Thus, the insurance company of the at-fault driver will compensate a third party for the losses sustained in an accident up to the policy limits. The at-fault driver's own insurance covers his or her own injuries (e.g., MedPay) and property damage (e.g., Collision), assuming he or she chooses to carry such insurance.

Under a typical no-fault system, economic damages from injuries sustained in an accident are covered by a driver's own insurance, known as personal injury protection (PIP) coverage, without regard to fault. Thus, compensation for injuries does not depend on the determination of fault; injured parties who were in no way responsible for the accident recover economic damages from their own insurance as does the at-fault driver. Property damages, however, are typically handled under the traditional tort system.[4] (Table 1 summarizes differences in insurance coverages and liability standards by type of damage under typical no-fault and tort insurance systems.)

In addition, no-fault systems restrict compensation for non-economic damages. Injured parties must demonstrate that their economic damages exceed some threshold before they are allowed to sue for non-economic damages. In most no-fault states, economic damages must exceed a dollar threshold before the injured party can pursue compensation for non-economic damages. The mean value of dollar thresholds in 1990 was approximately \$2,600. In three states—Michigan, Florida, and New York—the threshold is expressed in verbal terms. In Michigan, for example, non-economic damages can be pursued only in the case of a fatality, serious

[4] Only the state of Michigan has a no-fault property damage law.

impairment of a body function, or serious permanent disfigurement. Table 2 lists the 17 states (including the District of Columbia) that have enacted no-fault auto insurance laws to date, the year of enactment, the year of repeal (if applicable), whether the tort threshold is verbal or dollar, and, if dollar, the real values (in 1982 dollars) of the dollar threshold both as enacted and in 1990.

Table 1
Insurance Coverages (and Liability Standards) under Tort and No-Fault

Type of Damage	Tort	No-Fault
First-Party		
Property Damage	Optional Collision coverage	Optional Collision coverage
Economic Personal Injury	Optional MedPay or other first-party health/ disability insurance coverage	Compulsory PIP coverage
Non-Economic Personal Injury	No insurance coverage	No insurance coverage
Third-Party		
Property Damage	Compulsory PD insurance (Full liability)	Compulsory PD insurance (Full liability)
Economic Personal Injury	Compulsory BI insurance (Full liability)	Compulsory BI insurance for damages above PIP limits (No liability below statutory PIP limits)
Non-Economic Personal Injury	Compulsory BI insurance (Full liability)	Compulsory BI insurance for damages above statutory threshold (No liability below threshold)

Table 2
State No-Fault Laws

State	Year Enacted	Year Repealed	Threshold (in 1982 $)	
			As Enacted	In 1990
Colorado	1974	*NA*	5,071	1,913
Connecticut	1973	1994	811	306
D. C.	1983	1986	Verbal	*NA*
Florida	1972	*NA*	2,392	Verbal
Georgia	1975	1991	929	383
Hawaii	1974	*NA*	2,788	5,356
Kansas	1974	*NA*	1,014	1,530
Kentucky	1975	*NA*	1,859	765
Massachusetts	1971	*NA*	1,235	1,530
Michigan	1973	*NA*	Verbal	Verbal
Minnesota	1975	*NA*	3,717	3,060
Nevada	1974	1980	1,521	*NA*
New Jersey	1973	1989	450	*NA*
New York	1974	*NA*	1,014	Verbal
North Dakota	1976	*NA*	1,757	1,913
Pennsylvania	1975	1984	1,318	*NA*
Utah	1974	*NA*	1,014	2,295

Note: Three states—Kentucky, New Jersey, and Pennsylvania—currently have choice plans, which offer drivers the choice between no-fault and tort systems.

As White and Liao (1999) note, it is important to distinguish between no-fault as a liability rule and as an insurance system when considering its probable effect on driving incentives. Strictly as a liability rule, the effect of no-fault on driving incentives is relatively unambiguous. If all drivers self-insure, then it is generally agreed that drivers will exercise no more, and possibly less, care under pure no-fault than under tort since drivers are not liable for the economic or non-economic damages they inflict on others.[5] Formal models of the incentive effects of a pure no-fault liability rule can be found in Cummins, Weiss, and Phillips (1999) and White and Liao (1999).

[5] This result may not hold in the presence of uncertainty and risk aversion (Cummins, Weiss, and Phillips, 1999). It is also not clear that no-fault will necessarily reduce incentives to drive carefully when drivers consider the behavior of other drivers. See discussion below for more on uncertainty, risk aversion, and general equilibrium considerations.

It is often pointed out, however, that no-fault is not just a rule of liability; no-fault is an insurance system that has much in common with traditional tort. In fact, I would argue the incentive to drive carefully remains largely unchanged in moving from a tort to no-fault insurance system. Indeed, the principal motivation for exercising care—avoiding injury to oneself and penalties for traffic violations—is unaffected by no-fault insurance. The marginal change in liability under no-fault can at best affect only a minor portion of the overall incentive to drive carefully. Moreover, as many researchers have noted, no-fault, as currently implemented in the U.S. at least, is far from pure. Tort thresholds in most states shield only a small fraction of all accidents from the tort system.

Why might incentives differ for drivers subject to tort and no-fault insurance? And are these differences in incentives likely to matter? I answer these questions by way of example rather than formal modeling. Consider the following thought experiment: A driver gets into his or her car and decides before turning the ignition key how much care he or she will exercise on this trip. Assume for now that this decision is driven solely by the expected financial cost of getting into an automobile accident for which this driver is 100 percent at-fault. The driver may or may not be insured. We can divide the potential costs this driver will incur as a result of the accident into three categories: (1) costs arising from the damages incurred by the at-fault driver, (2) damages incurred by the third party, and (3) changes in the at-fault driver's insurance premiums.

Potential damages to the at-fault driver include property damage, bodily injury, wage loss, and non-economic damages. In both tort and no-fault states, personal collision insurance compensates at-fault drivers for their own property damages and under neither system are the at-fault driver's own non-economic damages eligible for compensation (see Table 1). Consequently, no-fault does not differentially affect incentives through its treatment of the at-fault driver's property and non-economic damages. In terms of bodily injury and wage loss, it is conceivable that no-fault creates an additional moral hazard not present in tort states for those drivers who elect not to carry insurance for economic damages they sustain in accidents in which they are at fault. Under tort, first-party bodily injury insurance is not compulsory. Under no-fault, however, all drivers must carry PIP insurance which compensates them for economic damages regardless of fault. Thus, compulsory first-party bodily injury insurance under no-fault may induce this marginal driver to drive less carefully since his own bodily injury and wage loss will now be compensated whereas under tort they would not be. How important this effect could be is difficult to determine since we have no direct figure on how many drivers in tort states do not insure themselves for their own injuries. Nor do we know how many drivers who did not have coverage for their own injuries in tort states would continue to drive uninsured in no-fault states. Nonetheless, it seems unlikely that this moral hazard alone could affect the incentives of many drivers.

Now let us consider third-party damages. The tort system governs compensation of third-party property damages under both insurance systems (except in Michigan) and so does not alter incentives. For those individuals who carry liability insurance under both regimes, the compensation of third-party economic damages also has no effect on incentives.[6] Under tort, bodily injury liability insurance covers third-party economic damages and, under no-fault, PIP insurance provides coverage. The presence of PIP insurance under no-fault, however, could alter the incentives of those individuals who choose to drive without insurance under no-fault. The reason, of course, is that no-fault drivers are not responsible for third-party economic losses.[7] Under tort, uninsured at-fault drivers can be sued for third-party economic damages. Again, though, it seems unlikely that this difference could affect many drivers. First, states levy significant penalties for driving uninsured in both tort and no-fault states. Second, most uninsured drivers have no assets to protect, and so whether they are financially liable for third-party damages makes little difference in the incentives they face to drive carefully.

The difference in the treatment of non-economic damages is often cited as the major reason why no-fault drivers may exercise less care than tort drivers. The reason is simple: Under pure no-fault the threat of suit for non-economic damages by a third party is substantially less than under tort. It is doubtful, however, that the magnitude of this effect could be very large in the U.S. for three reasons. First, a sizable fraction of no-fault auto claimants can pursue non-economic damages under no-fault law as it currently stands in most states. Second, the average amount of non-economic damages sought by third parties is small, and, third, the probability of being sued for non-economic damages at a level that exceeds the limits of a bodily injury liability policy is low.

The Insurance Research Council (IRC) periodically collects data on a sample of auto insurance claims closed over a two-week period. Using such data from 1977, 1987, 1992, and 1997, the IRC (1999a, 1994) and State Farm (1993) estimated the fraction of PIP claims eligible for non-economic damages in no-fault states. Table 3 reproduces these estimates, which show that about 17 percent of PIP claims in 1977 and 29 percent of PIP claims in 1997 exceeded tort thresholds. In 1977, the percentage of claims eligible for

---

[6] Except in terms of the effect such damages may have on subsequent premiums. See below for discussion of experience rating.

[7] More precisely, they are not responsible for third-party losses below PIP limits.

non-economic damages ranged from 3 percent in Hawaii to 31 percent in Florida. By 1997, this range had increased to between 15 percent (Michigan) and 52 percent (Massachusetts). This increase largely reflects the deterioration in the real value of dollar thresholds over this period (see Table 2). Thus, while no-fault prohibits many claimants from pursuing compensation for non-economic damages, drivers in no-fault states still face a substantial risk of being sued for non-economic damages.

Table 3
Percentage of PIP Claims Eligible for Non-Economic Damages

State	1977	1987	1992	1997
Colorado	16	26	34	30
Connecticut	19	41	63	*NA*
Florida	31	33	37	34
Georgia	24	49	*NA*	*NA*
Hawaii	3	20	36	21
Kansas	13	29	17	22
Kentucky	10	25	33	42
Massachusetts	26	54	63	52
Michigan	6	12	19	15
Minnesota	10	22	34	29
New Jersey	35	63	*NA*	*NA*
New York	27	29	31	22
North Dakota	3	13	*NA*	*NA*
Utah	19	19	23	24

Sources: Connecticut, Georgia, and New Jersey data reproduced from State Farm (1993); all other state data reproduced from IRC (1999a, 1994).

However, even if we were to assume the existence of pure no-fault shielding all claims from non-economic damages, this prohibition would have little effect on the expected cost of an accident. This conclusion comes from examining the distribution of non-economic damages in the 1997 closed claims data (Table 4).[8] Overall, median non-economic damages in tort states totaled $1,609 in 1997. Even in the upper tail of the distribution, non-economic damages are not severe: $8,117 at the 90th percentile and $13,679 at the 95th percentile. In columns two and three, I restrict the sample

[8] These data cover about 60,000 claims from roughly 30 insurance companies representing 60 to 70 percent of the private passenger automobile insurance market.

to those claims in which economic damages fall under $2,500 or involve injuries other than a fatality or permanent disability (typical dollar and verbal thresholds). The median value of non-economic damages in these cases is $1,000 and $1,201, respectively, and even at the 95th percentile, non-economic damages amount to only $4,665 and $8,142. Thus, under a typical no-fault insurance system in the U.S., restrictions on non-economic damages shield at-fault drivers from relatively minor financial liability.

Table 4
Distribution of Non-Economic Damages in Tort States

Non-Economic Damages (in 1997 $)			
Percentile	**All Claims**	**<$2500**	**<Verbal**
50	1,609	1,000	1,201
75	3,900	2,091	3,000
90	8,117	3,500	5,500
95	13,679	4,665	8,142

Notes: Sample restricted to one- or two-car accidents in which the insured was 100 percent at fault and the claimant was either the driver of the other car or a pedestrian. All claims are in tort states and against voluntary policies (n = 12,537). Verbal threshold is defined as a fatality or permanent disability.
Source: 1997 IRC Closed Claims Data.

In any case, most tort drivers carry BI insurance which shields them from all but the most excessive non-economic damage claims. According to the 1997 closed-claim data, only 11 percent of all claims in tort states had combined damages of more than $10,000, and virtually all states require drivers to insure themselves against at least that level of liability. Moreover, in fewer than 5 percent of all cases did total damages paid come within $5,000 of an individual's policy limits. So, while the probability of being sued for non-economic damages is higher in tort states, the expected cost of such a suit to the at-fault driver is actually quite low because of the presence of liability insurance. According to data from the IRC's 1998 survey of auto accident victims, individuals involved in auto accidents receive only a small fraction of total compensation (economic plus non-economic) from at-fault drivers directly, and this fraction does not vary significantly between tort and no-fault states.[9] The expected value of out-of-pocket expenditures for at-fault drivers was $589 in tort states and $622 in no-fault states in 1998, 6.7

[9] See IRC (1999b) for a description of this survey of 5,768 individuals involved in auto accidents some time after January 1, 1995.

and 5.0 percent, respectively, of total reimbursements made to the injured party to date.

A final difference in the expected cost of an accident between tort and no-fault states is in the degree to which premiums reflect negligent driving. Under both systems, we expect total premiums to cover total expenditures. If the assignment of fault in no-fault states is less certain than in tort states, however, it could be that good drivers subsidize bad drivers to a greater extent under no-fault than under tort. This subsidy, in turn, lowers the direct cost of negligent driving to at-fault drivers and so encourages greater negligence under no-fault. It could also be that limited liability for non-economic damages under no-fault implies any given accident will result in a smaller percentage increase in premiums for the at-fault driver. The question, then, is whether insurance companies raise premiums in a comparable fashion in tort and no-fault states in order to account for negligent driving.

It is true that most states prohibit insurance companies from leveling premium surcharges on PIP insurance. Insurance companies in no-fault states, though, can and do level surcharges on property damage insurance, and it is rare that an accident involving an injury does not also involve property damage. In addition, insurance companies in no-fault states level surcharges on bodily injury insurance. Whether these surcharges result in an actuarially fair assignment of total insurance costs to at-fault drivers in no-fault states is an outstanding research question. I am aware of no evidence, however, suggesting that at-fault drivers in no-fault states escape surcharges for their negligence.

The preceding analysis provides an admittedly simplistic comparison of expected accident costs and incentives under no-fault and tort insurance. The effect of no-fault insurance on expected accident costs should also take into account an individual's level of risk aversion and how he or she believes other individuals will behave under a no-fault insurance system. This latter consideration is particularly important. One drives carefully, in part, in order to compensate for the negligent driving habits of others. If individuals choose to drive less carefully under no-fault they may also reasonably believe that others will also choose to drive less carefully. In turn, this behavior may cause individuals to revise their level of care upward to defend against the careless driving of others under no-fault. In short, the benefits of driving carefully are not only avoiding costs associated with an at-fault accident as discussed above, but avoiding accidents caused by others. Note also that the restriction on non-economic damages cuts both ways: no-fault drivers are less liable for non-economic damage suits against them but also forgo the right to sue for non-economic damages themselves. In equilibrium, therefore, it is not a given that even as a pure liability rule no-fault will induce more careless driving.[10]

3. THREE TESTS OF THE NO-FAULT HYPOTHESIS

Let us suppose that no-fault does reduce the expected cost of an accident to a given individual. How might we measure empirically the effect of this savings on driver behavior? The approach employed in the empirical literature to date has been to examine the correlation between no-fault and the fatal accident rate. This approach is popular for two reasons: (1) there is a compelling public interest in reducing fatal accidents, and (2) state agencies compile data on fatal accidents in a consistent and comprehensive manner. While fatalities are certainly well-measured and, moreover, something we care about, many things must be true if we are to observe a causal relationship between no-fault insurance and fatal accident rates. First, drivers must believe the expected cost of getting into an accident is lower under no-fault than under tort. Second, a decrease in the expected cost of getting into an accident must cause drivers to drive less carefully than they would otherwise. Third, the degree of this effect must be large enough to cause a statistically significant change in accident rates generally, and, fourth, this must translate into higher fatal accident rates. Thus, fatalities reside far down the causal chain of events.

Despite this limitation, the fatal accident rate is still an attractive measure of the incentive effects of no-fault. We can be reasonably certain that fatal accidents are well-measured events and the data extend back to the mid-1960s, prior to changes in no-fault laws. Furthermore, as the standard metric of driver care in this literature, fatalities provide a logical starting point for an empirical analysis of the incentive effects of no-fault. I review and critique the empirical literature on the effect of no-fault on fatal accidents in the next section (Section 3.1) and then present my own estimates in Section 3.2.

A rejection of the hypothesis that no-fault leads to higher fatal accident rates does not rule out the possibility that no-fault affects the overall accident rate. Researchers have avoided examining the accident rate, however, because of poor data. Many accidents go unreported to the police and, more significantly, the incentive to report accidents to the police might vary between tort and no-fault states. In Section 3.3, I employ a proxy for the overall accident rate—the ratio of property damage claims to property

---

[10] See White and Liao (1999) for an equilibrium model of no-fault and driver care.

damage exposure—to study the effect of no-fault on accidents in general. I assume the incentive to make property damage claims should be no different under tort and no-fault since property damage is subject to tort liability in all states but Michigan.

The direct effect of no-fault insurance should be to lower the expected cost of driving negligently. Unfortunately, a rigorous empirical test of this claim is not possible since we have little data on how accident costs incurred by drivers vary from state to state. While we cannot observe the cost of negligence, perhaps we can observe negligence itself. That is, if no-fault lowers the cost of driving negligently, we should then observe an increase in negligent driving. Using data from the Department of Transportation's (DOT) Fatal Accident Reporting System (FARS), a census of all fatal accidents in the U.S. between 1975 and 1998, I test in Section 3.4 the hypothesis that fatal accidents in no-fault states are more likely to involve negligent behavior than fatal accidents in tort states. Together, these three analyses of fatal accidents, accidents in general, and negligent driving provide no evidence that no-fault insurance in the U.S. affects driving behavior.

3.1. Literature Review and Methodological Issues

A lengthy empirical literature exists on the relationship between no-fault policy and the fatal accident rate. Landes (1982) was the first to investigate this issue empirically. Using state-level data for the period 1967 to 1975, Landes concluded that the adoption of no-fault policy had increased fatal accidents in states adopting no-fault by as much as 10 percent. This striking result inspired a number of subsequent papers reexamining state-level fatality data (Zador and Lund, 1986; Kochanowski and Young, 1985; U.S. DOT, 1985). These researchers uniformly rejected the hypothesis that no-fault leads to higher fatal accident rates. McEwin (1989) and Devlin (1992) then reported finding large effects of no-fault on fatal accident rates—on the order of 9 to 10 percent—in New Zealand and Quebec. More recent work by Sloan, Reilly, and Schenzler (1994), Cummins, Weiss, and Phillips (1999), and Kabler (1999) using state-level data also reports positive effects of no-fault on fatal accident rates of a substantial magnitude.

The most difficult problem in establishing the effect of no-fault on fatal accident rates or other outcomes is in separating the effect of no-fault itself from the underlying forces that led to the implementation of no-fault in the first place. This basic problem is generally recognized in the research cited above. One approach to solving this problem has involved examining fatal accident rates in tort and no-fault states around the time no-fault laws were first implemented in the early 1970s. Another approach has been to account explicitly for the factors that led some states to enact no-fault and others to retain tort. I begin this section by first outlining what has become a standard approach to identifying policy effects with panel data that cover periods both before and after implementation of a given policy—the method of difference-in-differences. I then note that most of the previous research cited above has failed to employ this technique properly, and so may have produced misleading results. I end by discussing the most recent paper in this literature, Cummins, Weiss, and Phillips (1999), which takes a fundamentally different approach to estimating the effect of no-fault on fatal accident rates from previous papers by explicitly modeling the decision to adopt no-fault policy. I cite a number of weaknesses in their approach and explain why a properly executed difference-in-differences approach will likely produce more reliable estimates of the effect of no-fault on fatal accident rates.

The goal of the panel data approach to identifying the effect of no-fault on fatal accident rates is to establish the counterfactual: What would have happened to fatal accident rates in no-fault states had no-fault not been implemented? The most naive estimate of this counterfactual question would be to examine fatal accident rates both before and after the implementation of no-fault laws in no-fault states. Doing so, we would conclude that the adoption of no-fault laws in no-fault states lowered fatal accident rates by 32 percent; fatal accident rates fell from 4.7 to 3.1 fatalities per 100 million vehicle miles traveled (VMT) between 1970 and 1977 in no-fault states (Figure 1).[11]

Of course, there are many reasons why fatal accident rates fell over that period that have nothing to do with the implementation of no-fault, including greater seat-belt use, declining rates of drinking and driving, and heightened vehicle and road safety. Indeed, in Figure 1, we see that fatal accident rates have fallen steadily in no-fault states since 1967, the earliest point for which we have state-specific data on fatal accident rates. The problem with this simple before and after comparison in no-fault states is that we do not know from these data alone what would have happened to fatal accident rates in no-fault states had they not adopted no-fault. Consequently, we need to form a control group that gives us some basis for comparison. A natural control group in this case is states that retained tort between 1971 and 1976. Again, looking at Figure 1, we see that fatal accident rates declined in

---

[11] Note that the no-fault line is somewhat misleading for the period 1971 to 1976 since only one state, Massachusetts, had no-fault in effect over the entire period.

tort states over this period as well, no doubt for some of the same reasons noted above.

Figure 1
Fatal Accident Rates in Tort and No-Fault States: 1967-95

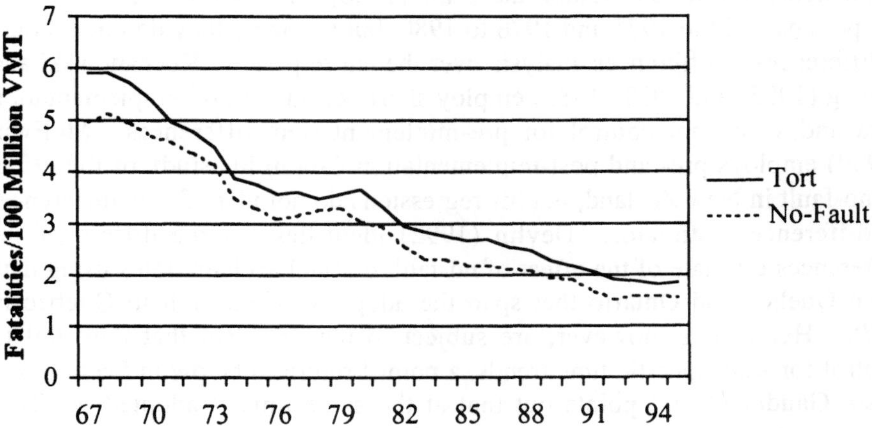

Source: U.S. DOT.

From Figure 1, we see that fatal accident rates are lower in no-fault states than in tort states following the implementation of no-fault laws. No-fault states had lower fatal accident rates than tort states in the pre-implementation period as well, however. This initial difference suggests that the simple difference between no-fault and tort states in fatal accident rates following implementation cannot be attributed solely to the adoption of no-fault since these differences existed before implementation. That is, conditions that cause no-fault states to have relatively low fatal accident rates existed before the adoption of no-fault and so must be controlled for. It is unlikely, however, that the researcher can control for all these conditions, so a common approach to identifying the effect of policy changes with panel data is to compare the difference in the outcome of interest before and after implementation in states that adopted the policy with the same difference in outcomes for states that did not. This "difference-in-differences" estimate represents the effect of no-fault policy on fatal accidents, assuming time-invariant state fixed-effects (see Section 3.2) and the absence of other unobserved factors correlated with the adoption of no-fault and fatal accident rates.

Surprisingly, only one of the studies cited above employs this simple empirical strategy for identifying the effect of no-fault on fatal accident rates. Landes (1982) comes close with data spanning the years 1967 to 1975, but her regressions fail to make the proper pre- and post-implementation comparisons, and the data arguably do not include a sufficiently long post-implementation period. Zador and Lund (1986) run separate regressions for the periods 1967 to 1975 and 1976 to 1980, but strangely they do not conduct a difference-in-differences analysis over the entire period. Kochanowski and Young (1985) and DOT (1985) employ short periods of post-implementation data and so cannot control for pre-implementation differences. McEwin (1989) employs pre- and post-implementation data in his study of the effect of no-fault in New Zealand, but his regressions do not identify the difference-in-differences estimator. Devlin (1992) identifies a large difference-in-differences estimate of the effect of no-fault on fatal accident rates using data from Quebec and Ontario that span the adoption of no-fault in Quebec in 1978. Her results, however, are subject to the criticism that they fail to control for state-specific time trends, a point I return to below in Section 3.2. Also, Gaudry (1992) points out that at the same time it adopted no-fault, Quebec also abolished experience rating, which also might have been expected to lower the incentive to drive carefully. Kabler (1999) reports regression results using post-implementation data for the U.S. indicating states with verbal thresholds have higher fatal accident rates than tort states. His results also show that states with monetary thresholds have lower fatal accident rates than tort states. In neither case, though, do Kabler's estimates identify the difference-in-differences estimator.

The difference-in-differences estimator is not the only way to identify the effect of no-fault on fatal accident rates. Cummins, Weiss, and Phillips (1999) find a large effect of no-fault on fatal accident rates using state-level data between 1982 and 1994, many years after the implementation of no-fault between 1971 and 1976. At first glance, this seems to be a strange finding since from Figure 1, we see that fatal accident rates are on average lower in no-fault states than in tort states over this period. Now, there may be important differences between no-fault and tort states, like the degree of urbanity, that can account for the lower fatal accident rates in no-fault states. Cummins, Weiss, and Phillips (1999) in fact show that after controlling for differences in state characteristics like urbanity there is no statistically significant difference in fatal accident rates between tort and no-fault states.

They go on to argue, however, that there may be other characteristics correlated with fatal accident rates, but omitted from simple analyses, that caused some states to adopt no-fault and others to remain with tort. Failing to control for these characteristics could result in drawing the false conclusion that no-fault has no effect on fatal accident rates. Econometricians often refer to this type of bias as endogeneity bias. An approach to correcting for this type of endogeneity bias is to model the adoption of no-fault policy itself and then use that information in estimating the effect of no-fault on fatal accident rates. Cummins, Weiss, and Phillips (1999) adopt this strategy by employing a two-step estimation method in which they first estimate the probability a given state has a no-fault law in effect as a function of various state characteristics and then include a non-linear transformation of that estimated probability as a control variable in a separate regression predicting the effect of no-fault on fatal accident rates.[12] Using this approach produces an estimate that implies a switch from tort to no-fault increases fatal accident rates by 6.8 percent. They interpret these results as implying that failure to control for unobserved differences between tort and no-fault states correlated with fatal accident rates biases conventional estimates of the effect of no-fault on fatal accidents downward substantially.

There are a number of reasons to be suspicious of the Cummins, Weiss, and Phillips estimates. First, the method they employ requires several strong statistical assumptions that have been widely questioned in the econometrics literature, especially, as is true here, when the estimates come from a small sample.[13] Given the tremendous difficulty in finding credible sources of exogenous variation in the adoption of no-fault laws, the difference-in-differences approach, which admittedly has weaknesses of its own, is nonetheless, I think, a more reliable estimation strategy in this case.

Even if we thought modeling the adoption of no-fault in the manner of Cummins, Weiss, and Phillips were justified econometrically, it is still not clear on *a priori* grounds why conventional estimates of the effect of no-fault on fatal accident rates should be biased downward as they suggest. The adoption of no-fault, they argue, could have been in response to rising auto

[12] See Vella (1998) or Maddala (1983) for detailed descriptions of two-step estimation methods for sample selection bias. This approach is most widely attributed to Heckman (1978).

[13] The selection model relies strongly on the assumption of the joint normality of the error terms in the equation predicting no-fault and the equation predicting fatal accident rates. If this distributional assumption (which is difficult to test) does not hold, the selection model is inherently misspecified. Even with the assumption of joint normality, this identification strategy can still produce seriously biased estimates unless implemented with strong exclusion restrictions (Vella, 1998; Nawata 1993; Greene 1993). The exclusion restrictions employed by Cummins, Weiss, and Phillips (1999)—per day cost of hospital care, percentage of state legislators who are Democrats, presence of a Democratic governor, population density, and percentage of the population living in urban areas—are hard to justify econometrically. It is difficult to find examples in the recent econometrics literature that employ a selection model of this type to address the problem of endogenous policy adoption.

insurance costs, which in turn are more severe in states with high accident rates.[14] This may be true, and if states with high accident rates have high fatal accident rates, the conventional estimate of no-fault on fatal accident rates should be *upwardly* biased. Cummins, Weiss, and Phillips, however, argue that the conventional estimate of the effect of no-fault are *downwardly* biased. To do so, they note that states with high accident rates tend to have *low* fatal accident rates. This also is true but only because accidents are more common in urban areas and urban accidents are less likely to result in fatalities because of the lower speeds involved. Thus, the endogeneity of no-fault is with respect to the accident rate and only incidentally related to the fatal accident rate. This type of spurious correlation is best addressed by controlling for differences between states that cause some to have high accident rates, but low fatal accident rates. Measures of urban concentration, which they include in their basic regression, should be sufficient to control for this spurious correlation. In Section 3.3 below, I go into further detail on the political economy of no-fault and why, if anything, conventional estimates of the effect of no-fault on fatality and accident rates are likely to be upwardly, not downwardly, biased.

A final approach used in the literature to identify the effect of no-fault on fatal accident rates is to exploit variation in dollar thresholds both within and across no-fault states. The idea here is that states with low dollar thresholds can be thought of as having lenient no-fault laws and states with high dollar thresholds as having stricter no-fault laws. The hypothesis, then, is that fatal accident rates should be positively correlated with the level of the dollar threshold. A more stringent form of this test, which I employ in the next section, uses only within-state variation in dollar thresholds to identify the effect of dollar thresholds on fatal accident rates. Sloan, Reilly, and Schenzler (1994) take such an approach in finding that within-state variation in the fraction of claims barred from the tort system between 1982 and 1990 was positively correlated with fatal accident rates in those states.

While there are no studies that examine the effect of no-fault on accident rates, there are two studies that test whether no-fault affects the rate of negligent driving generally. Using self-reported data, Sloan, Reilly, and Schenzler (1995) test whether the frequency of binge drinking and the tendency to drink and drive is higher in no-fault states than in tort states. While they find a small effect of no-fault insurance on the self-reported frequency of binge drinking, they find no effect on the propensity to drink and drive. Drinking and driving, however, is a particularly severe form of

[14] Note that fatalities are relatively inexpensive from an insurance perspective, so it is unlikely that differences in fatal accident rates across states can explain the adoption of no-fault directly.

negligence, so broader tests of this hypothesis may be desirable. Devlin (1999) conducts an indirect test of the negligence hypothesis. She argues that not only should the greater negligence caused by no-fault lead to more accidents, but the severity of those accidents should increase. To test this hypothesis, Devlin uses 1987 IRC closed-claim data on over 28,000 bodily injury claims. The data contain elements describing the severity of the injury-causing accident which Devlin then uses to test whether accidents in no-fault states resulted in more severe injuries. The problem with this approach, though, is that BI claims in no-fault states should on average be more severe than in tort states because BI claims can only be brought in no-fault states if the economic damages caused by the accident exceed some threshold value. In tort states, third-party injuries, no matter how minor, are compensated under BI liability insurance. Not surprisingly, Devlin finds that the injuries reported in the BI claims data are more severe in no-fault states. This result, of course, may simply reflect how injuries are compensated in tort and no-fault states rather than the effect of no-fault on driving behavior *per se*.

3.2. The Effect of No-Fault on Fatal Accident Rates

I begin this analysis by modeling state fatality as a linear function of state characteristics in the post-implementation period of 1977 to 1989:

$$F_{it} = \beta_1^T \mathbf{X}_{it} + \beta_2 NOFAULT_{it} + v_t + \varepsilon_{it}, \qquad (1)$$

where F_{it} is the log of the fatal accident rate in state i in year t. I define the fatal accident rate to be the number of fatalities divided by 100 million vehicle miles traveled. The denominator controls for differences between states in automobile travel. Results are qualitatively similar in models in which the denominator is the state's population ages 18 to 64.[15] The vector $\mathbf{X}_{it}$ includes a variety of state characteristics thought to affect fatal accident rates, including the proportion of vehicle miles traveled on rural highways (*R_VMT*), log population density (*POP_DEN*), proportion of the population ages 18-24 (*POP_1824*), log average annual temperature (*TEMP*), log annual total precipitation (*PRECIP*), log per capita income (*PC_INC*), and

[15] Some researchers (e.g., McEwin, 1989) have questioned whether it is appropriate to express fatalities in terms of VMT or population, fearing these variables themselves could be a function of no-fault policy. We must employ some measure of scale, however, and modeling the choice to drive in terms of no-fault policy seems to me to be of second-order importance.

log bachelor degrees awarded as a fraction of the population ages 18 to 24 (*BA*).[16] I also control for year effects common to all states with the term v_t. I code $NOFAULT_{it} = 1$ for states with no-fault in effect in year t. The data cover the lower 48 states and Hawaii.

No-fault states are different in several important ways from tort states. These differences can be seen in Table 5, which provides the means and standard deviations of the variables listed above. First, over the 20-year period, fatal accident rates were on average 23 percent lower in no-fault states than in tort states. No-fault states are more urban as indicated by the relatively low proportion of vehicle miles traveled on rural highways. Median population density (not shown) and real per capita income is also substantially higher in no-fault states. Although there is no significant difference in mean temperature between no-fault and tort states, the median temperature is substantially lower and mean heating days substantially higher in no-fault states than in tort states. Cummins, Weiss, and Phillips (1999) also show that no-fault states have greater average annual snowfall.

[16] A more complete model might also control for differences in insurance systems (e.g., experience rating) and traffic law enforcement across states. These data are not readily available, however, and it is not clear that systematic differences exist in these variables between no-fault and tort states in any case.

Table 5
Sample Means and Standard Deviations by No-Fault Status: 1970-89

			State Type	
Variable	**Description**	**Source**	**No-Fault**	**Tort**
F	Fatalities/100million VMT	U.S. DOT	2.76 (0.77)	3.58 (1.21)
R_VMT	Rural VMT/total VMT	U.S. DOT	0.42 (0.16)	0.56 (0.15)
DENSITY	Population density (population/sq. mile)	U.S. Census	265.19 (306.53)	381.44 (1,589.32)
POP_1824	Proportion of population age 18-24	U.S. Census	0.13 (0.01)	0.13 (0.01)
TEMP	Area weighted average annual temperature	NOAA	521.05 (92.14)	527.42 (74.52)
PRECIP	Area weighted annual total precipitation	NOAA	3,722.82 (1,571.71)	3,670.16 (1,506.23)
PC_INC	Real per capita income ($1982)	U.S. Census	12,935.80 (2,112.31)	11,369.09 (1,803.68)
BA	Bachelor degrees awarded/population 18-24	U.S. Dept. Education	0.03 (0.01)	0.02 (0.15)

Table 6
OLS Estimates of the Effect of No-Fault on State Fatal and Overall Accident Rates

	Model Specification			
	F_{it}		PD_{it}	
	(1)	(2)	(3)	(4)
NOFAULT	-0.14 (0.02)	-0.05 (0.01)	-0.01 (0.01)	-0.04 (0.01)
R_VMT	*NA*	0.42 (0.08)	*NA*	-0.23 (0.06)
DENSITY	*NA*	-0.03 (0.01)	*NA*	-0.02 (0.01)
POP_1824	*NA*	-1.52 (0.87)	*NA*	2.42 (0.65)
TEMP	*NA*	0.80 (0.05)	*NA*	-0.21 (0.04)
PRECIP	*NA*	-0.13 (0.02)	*NA*	0.10 (0.02)
PC_INC	*NA*	-0.05 (0.07)	*NA*	0.10 (0.05)
BA	*NA*	-0.004 (0.008)	*NA*	-0.01 (0.01)
INTERCEPT	-1.04 (0.03)	-4.40 (0.83)	1.87 (0.02)	1.34 (0.60)
R^2	0.40	0.68	0.62	0.69

Notes: The dependent variable in (1) and (2) is the state fatal accident rate on the log scale. The dependent variable in (3) and (4) is the log of PD claims/100 PD exposures. The period of analysis is 1977 to 1989. Regressions include year effects. Standard errors are given in parentheses.

Since we expect these various state characteristics to affect fatal accident rates, controlling for differences in these characteristics across tort and no-fault states is important in isolating the effect of no-fault itself on fatal accident rates. For example, it may be that much of the difference in fatal accident rates between tort and no-fault states is attributable to the fact that no-fault states are more urban than tort states. This difference is evident in Table 6. In Column (1) of Table 6, the coefficient for *NOFAULT* of -0.14 indicates that fatal accident rates were about 14 percent lower in no-fault states than in tort states after accounting for common year effects. We see in

Column (2), however, that once we control for differences in other characteristics of no-fault and tort states, the difference in fatal accident rates diminishes substantially. The coefficient for *NOFAULT* drops to a statistically significant -0.05. The other covariates of the model generally have the expected signs and explain a substantial portion of the overall variance in fatal accident rates as evidenced by the large increase in R^2 between Columns (1) and (2).[17] In this simple analysis, then, it appears that even after controlling for differences in observable characteristics across tort and no-fault states, no-fault states have lower fatal accident rates than tort states.

3.2.1. A Difference-in-Differences Estimate

The specification in (1), though, does not address the possibility that we have omitted from the model other differences between no-fault and tort states that are correlated with fatal accident rates. These unobserved differences, whatever they may be, could bias the estimated coefficient for *NOFAULT*. The difference-in-differences strategy outlined above addresses this problem by comparing fatal accident rates in tort and no-fault both before and after implementation of no-fault between 1971 and 1976. Perhaps the easiest way to see the logic of the difference-in-differences estimator is to examine Panel A of Table 7, which reports fatal accident rates by year and no-fault status.

Reading along the columns, we see that in the pre-implementation period of 1967 to 1970, fatal accident rates were 0.73 higher in tort states than in no-fault states.[18] In the post-implementation period, this difference fell to 0.38. The difference in these differences, reported in the third column, is 0.35. Similarly, looking at the rows of Table 7, fatal accident rates declined by more in tort states than they did in no-fault states between the pre- and post-implementation periods. The difference in these declines is also 0.35. If we make the assumption that no-fault states would have experienced the same decline in fatal accident rates as tort states over this period were it not for the implementation of no-fault law, then we can interpret the difference-in-differences, 0.35, as the causal effect of no-fault on fatal accident rates. That is, the estimate implies fatal accident rates were

---

[17] The one exception is the negative coefficient for *POP_1824*. We might think fatal accident rates would increase with larger numbers of young drivers. Cummins, Weiss, and Phillips (1999) report a statistically insignificant coefficient for this variable.

[18] Here $NOFAULT_i = 1$ if no-fault were enacted in state *i* between 1971 and 1976.

a little over 10 percent higher (0.35/3.24) in no-fault states in the post-implementation period than they would have been in the absence of no-fault.

This difference-in-differences estimate is expressed in absolute levels. A more appropriate way to model the effect of *NOFAULT* on fatal accidents may be in percentage terms. That is, we might hypothesize that the implementation of no-fault increases fatal accident rates in no-fault states by *x* percent, regardless of the initial level of fatal accident rates in those states. A natural specification for this model is with the fatal accident rate expressed on the log scale. Panel B of Table 7 presents the difference-in-differences estimate for this model.

Here we see that fatal accident rates declined by approximately 46 percent between the pre- and post-implementation periods in tort states and by 43 percent in no-fault states. The difference in these differences is a statistically insignificant 3 percentage points, suggesting that no-fault had no effect on fatal accident rates. The difference-in-differences estimate of Panel B is preferable to that of Panel A because it has the effect of controlling for differences in pre-implementation time trends in fatal accident rates between no-fault and tort states. Close inspection of Figure 1 reveals that fatal accident rates were declining at a faster rate in tort states than in no-fault states in the pre-implementation period. Between 1967 and 1970, fatal accident rates fell by 6 percent in no-fault states and 10 percent in tort states. Thus, fatal accident rates were already converging between tort and no-fault states before no-fault was adopted. We do not want to attribute this pre-implementation convergence to the effect of no-fault.

Table 7
Fatal Accident Rates by Year and No-Fault Status

State type	**1967-70**	**1977-80**	**Difference**
A. Fatality Rates, in Absolute Levels			
Tort	5.72	3.62	2.10
No-fault	4.99	3.24	1.75
Difference	0.73	0.38	0.35
B. Fatality Rates, on Log Scale			
Tort	-0.58	-1.04	0.46
No-fault	-0.72	-1.15	0.43
Difference	0.14	0.11	0.03

Another way to recover the difference-in-differences estimate is in a regression context:

$$F_{it} = \beta_1^{\mathrm{T}}\mathbf{X}_{it} + \beta_2 POST\_76_t + \beta_3 NOFAULT_i + \beta_4 POST\_76_t \cdot NOFAULT_i + \varepsilon_{it}, \tag{2}$$

where $POST\_76_t$ equals one for the years 1977 to 1980 and zero for the years 1967 to 1970. (I drop the implementation years 1971 to 1976 from the analysis.)[19] In this specification, $\hat{\beta}_2$ captures the difference in fatal accident rates across the two periods common to both tort and no-fault states, $\hat{\beta}_3$ represents the difference in fatal accident rates between no-fault and tort states in both the pre- and post-implementation periods, and $\hat{\beta}_4$ tells us whether fatal accident rates changed more or less between periods in no-fault states than in tort states (the difference-in-differences). The advantage of this specification over the simple comparison of means in Table 7 is that it controls for other time-varying state characteristics that influence fatal accident rates.

Controlling for state characteristics in this regression does not appear to affect the simple difference-in-differences estimates of Table 7. Looking first at Column (1) of Table 8, we see that, as in Table 7, fatal accident rates are lower in the post-implementation period for both tort and no-fault states ($\hat{\beta}_{post76}$ = -0.46) and fatal accident rates are, on average, lower in no-fault states than in tort states ($\hat{\beta}_{nofault}$ = -0.11). The statistically insignificant coefficient of 0.03 for the interaction of *POST_76* and *NOFAULT* indicates that fatal accident rates fell equivalently in percentage terms in tort states and no-fault states between the pre- and post-implementation periods. This is the difference-in-differences estimate of Panel B, Table 7. In Column (2), we see that this difference-in-differences estimate is basically unchanged with the inclusion of additional covariates in the model.[20] In Column (3), I show that these results do not change if we perform separate comparisons using states that enacted a strong version of no-fault and those that did not.[21] Finally, in Column (4), I specify the model in first differences (e.g.,

---

[19] The implementation years are dropped in order to form clear treatment and control groups. Experiments with a variety of treatment and control groups over the implementation period, including a full fixed-effects model ($F_{it} = \beta_1^{\mathrm{T}}\mathbf{X}_{it} + \beta_2 NOFAULT_{it} + \lambda_i + v_t + \varepsilon_{it}$) that accounts for the fact that states adopted no-fault in different years, yielded comparable results. The results are not sensitive to the number of years analyzed in the post-implementation period.

[20] Pre-1970 data were unavailable for population density, population ages 18 to 24, and bachelor degrees awarded.

[21] I define strong no-fault states as those with either verbal thresholds or dollar thresholds exceeding $1,000 at the time of enactment.

$\Delta F_{it} = F_{it} - F_{i,t-1}$), which has the effect of controlling for time trends specific to tort and no-fault states that could influence the rate of change in fatal accident rates. Again the basic result does not change; the implementation of no-fault laws did not affect the relative change in fatal accident rates between tort and no-fault states before and after the implementation of no-fault between 1971 and 1976.

Table 8
Difference-in-Differences Estimates

	Model Specification			
	(1)	(2)	(3)	(4)
POST_76	-0.46 (0.03)	-0.38 (0.02)	-0.37 (0.07)	0.06 (0.01)
NOFAULT	-0.11 (0.03)	0.002 (0.024)	*NA*	-0.004 (0.016)
POST_76 * *NOFAULT*	0.03 (0.05)	0.04 (0.03)	*NA*	-0.01 (0.02)
STRONG	*NA*	*NA*	0.10 (0.03)	*NA*
POST_76 * *STRONG*	*NA*	*NA*	0.03 (0.05)	*NA*
R_VMT	*NA*	0.70 (0.07)	0.74 (0.07)	0.39 (0.28)
TEMP	*NA*	0.72 (0.06)	0.72 (0.06)	1.38 (0.26)
PRECIP	*NA*	-0.20 (0.02)	-0.20 (0.02)	-0.07 (0.03)
PC_INC	*NA*	-0.18 (0.07)	-0.22 (0.07)	0.67 (0.21)
INTERCEPT	-1.04 (0.02)	-2.61 (0.97)	-2.32 (0.96)	0.01 (0.01)
R^2	0.52	0.79	0.80	0.12

Notes: The dependent variable in (1) and (2) is the state fatal accident rate on the log scale. The dependent variable and time-varying covariates in (3) and (4) are in first-differenced form. Standard errors are in parentheses.

3.2.2. A Test Using Variation in Dollar Thresholds

There is one more test of this hypothesis I can conduct with the available data. Fifteen of the 16 states that enacted no-fault by 1976 did so with dollar thresholds. These thresholds vary both across and within states over time due to explicit legislative changes and the erosion of the real value of dollar thresholds due to inflation. If we believe a continuum exists between no-fault and tort characterized by the threshold at which individuals can sue for non-economic damages (where tort states essentially have no threshold and verbal no-fault states have a very high threshold), then it is possible that higher dollar thresholds lead to higher fatal accident rates. If that hypothesis is true, then it would lend some credence to the claim that no-fault insurance leads to higher fatal accident rates.

One way to test this hypothesis is to test whether within-state variation in dollar thresholds is correlated with fatal accident rates holding other state characteristics constant. A fixed-effects specification is a common way to do this:

$$F_{it} = \beta_1^{\mathrm{T}}\mathbf{X}_{it} + \beta_2 THRESHOLD_{it} + \lambda_i + \nu_t + \varepsilon_{it}, \tag{3}$$

where $THRESHOLD_{it}$ is the real log value of a no-fault state's dollar threshold and λ_i is a vector of individual state dummy variables. The fixed-effects specification controls for unobserved heterogeneity across states that may simultaneously affect fatal accident rates and the relative sizes of the dollar thresholds.

I estimate (3) with data from 13 no-fault states with dollar thresholds in force sometime between 1970 and 1989.[22] The inclusion of fixed state effects means that the estimation of $\hat{\beta}_2$ comes solely from within-state variation in the dollar threshold. Figure 2 graphs the real value of the dollar threshold between 1970 and 1989 in no-fault states. Much of the within-state variation is due to inflation, which is common across all states. Importantly, however, there is variation across states in the timing of adoption, repeal, and adjustments to thresholds. Hawaii, for example, went from having no threshold in 1974 to a threshold of $2,788 in 1975. This threshold fell with inflation to $2,066 in 1979 and then steadily increased by legislative mandate throughout the 1980s. Discrete jumps in dollar thresholds are evident in other states as well, like Massachusetts, Minnesota, and Kansas.

---

[22] I exclude New York and Florida, which initially adopted no-fault with dollar thresholds, but changed to verbal thresholds shortly thereafter.

The results of estimating (3) indicate that within-state increases in dollar thresholds lead to very small, but precisely estimated, *declines* in fatal accident rates (Table 9).[23] This result is contrary to the hypothesis that fatal accident rates should increase as the no-fault threshold increases, providing further evidence against the claim that the implementation of no-fault laws could have raised fatal accident rates in no-fault states.

Figure 2
Dollar Thresholds in No-Fault States: 1971-89

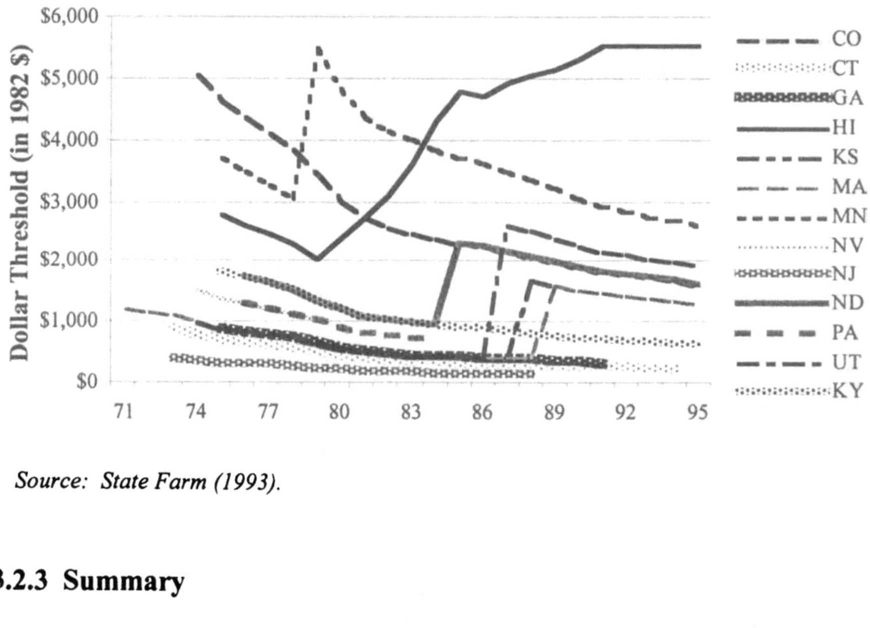

Source: State Farm (1993).

3.2.3 Summary

The difference-in-differences results reported in the final two columns of Table 8 provide no evidence that the implementation of no-fault between 1971 and 1976 had a statistically significant effect on fatal accident rates in no-fault states. The narrowing in the difference in fatal accident rates between tort and no-fault states evident in the first two columns of Table 8

[23] I should also note that this result is contrary to the results of Sloan, Reilly, and Schenzler (1994), who find that within-state increases in the fraction of claims barred from tort liability, which is a positive function of the dollar threshold, increases the fatal accident rate. I prefer these estimates, however, because Sloan, Reilly, and Schenzler could calculate their claims fraction variable for only two years (1977 and 1987). They filled in the intervening years by a linear interpolation of those two data points. While the claims fraction variable is a more direct measure of no-fault stringency, I think the greater within-state variation afforded by using dollar thresholds produces more reliable estimates.

appears to have occurred largely prior to the enactment of no-fault laws. The results in Table 9 using variation in dollar thresholds provide further evidence against claims that no-fault law diminishes the incentive to drive with care, and so increases the fatal accident rate. Although contrary to several recent studies, these results are not surprising given the highly idiosyncratic nature of many fatal accidents. Even if the presence of no-fault insurance diminishes incentives to drive carefully, it is not at all clear that increased negligence would translate directly into higher fatal accident rates. More plausibly, no-fault could affect the overall accident rate, a topic to which I now turn.

Table 9
The Effect of Within-State Variation in Dollar Thresholds on State Fatality and Accident Rates

	Dependent Variable	
	F_{it}	PD_{it}
THRESHOLD	-0.010 (0.004)	0.007 (0.004)
R_VMT	0.71 (0.33)	0.80 (0.31)
DENSITY	-0.05 (0.13)	0.57 (0.14)
POP_1824	3.47 (1.68)	0.88 (1.50)
TEMP	0.15 (0.33)	-0.23 (0.25)
PRECIP	0.03 (0.05)	0.03 (0.04)
PC_INC	0.29 (0.15)	0.07 (0.16)
BA	0.08 (0.05)	0.10 (0.04)
R^2	0.92	0.90

Notes: The regressions control for state and year effects and are restricted to no-fault states with dollar thresholds. The sample period for fatality regression is 1970 to 1989 and for PD regression is 1976 to 1989. Robust standard errors are in parentheses.

3.3. The Effect of No-Fault on Overall Accident Rates

The focus on fatal accident rates in the existing literature is driven largely by data constraints. Unlike fatal accidents, there is no state-by-state census of all automobile accidents available for analysis in the U.S. The DOT does maintain data on a nationwide sample of accidents from local police reports beginning in 1988 in its General Estimates System, but the data cannot be aggregated to the state level. Even if these data could be aggregated to the state level, the resulting sample would not likely be random. A large number of accidents do not get recorded by the police, and it seems likely that these unrecorded accidents are much less serious on average than those that do get recorded.

Here I use data on property damage liability claims collected by the National Association of Independent Insurers (NAII) since 1976. For each state and year, the NAII's auto experience data record the number of property damage claims made as well as the number of property damage policies in effect (referred to as "exposures"). I treat the ratio of these two variables as an unbiased measure of the accident rate to test whether accident rates are higher in no-fault than in tort states. In all states but Michigan, property damage resulting from automobile accidents is handled under the traditional tort system. This uniformity in liability law implies that the incentive to make property damage claims should not vary between tort and no-fault states. Thus, property damage claims normalized by some appropriate factor, say vehicle miles traveled or number of insured vehicles, should provide a consistent estimate of the accident rate over time and across states.[24]

The analysis of accident rates in the post-implementation period parallels the analysis of fatal accident rates:

$$PD_{it} = \beta_1{}^{\mathrm{T}}\mathbf{X}_{it} + \beta_2 NOFAULT_i + \nu_t + \varepsilon_{it}, \qquad (4)$$

where PD_{it} is the log of the accident rate in state i in year t as defined above, and the vector $\mathbf{X}_{it}$ includes the same state characteristics as in (3).[25] I examine the time period 1976 to 1989.

---

[24] The measure probably underestimates the accident rate in both tort and no-fault states because drivers may not report minor accidents if they fear their premiums will rise more than the actual damages sustained.

[25] The auto experience data do not include Massachusetts, North and South Carolina, and Texas, so I drop these states from the analysis. As before, I do not include Alaska or the District of Columbia. Finally, I drop Michigan since it has a no-fault property damage insurance law.

As with fatal accidents, the overall accident rate, as measured by *PD*, fell substantially over the period of analysis (Figure 3). In both tort and no-fault states, *PD* falls by about one third between 1976 and 1981, and remains fairly constant thereafter. In tort states, the ratio of claims to exposure falls from 6.5 to 4.6 claims per 100 policies between 1976 and 1981. In no-fault states this ratio falls from 6.4 to 4.4 over the same period. Between 1976 and 1981, *PD* is lower in no-fault states than in tort states. The difference is generally insignificant between 1982 and 1990, when *PD* in tort states falls below that of no-fault states.

Figure 3
Overall Accident Rates in Tort and No-Fault States

Source: NAII.

The results of fitting (4) indicate that no-fault insurance has little effect on accident rates overall. In Column (3) of Table 6, the coefficient for *NOFAULT* is small and statistically insignificant at conventional levels. In Column (4), we see that the addition of controls for state characteristics to the model causes the coefficient for *NOFAULT* to fall to -0.04. Thus, contrary to the hypothesis, no-fault states appear to have lower accident rates overall than tort states. Where significant, the estimated effects of state characteristics have the expected sign and seem to be of a reasonable magnitude. For example, the coefficients tell us that accident rates are higher in more urban states and in states with lower temperatures, greater precipitation, and a relatively younger population.

We should be cautious in interpreting these estimates, however, since without pre-implementation data, we have no way of controlling for unobservable differences across tort and no-fault states that may simultaneously influence *PD* and *NOFAULT*. The concern is that the adoption of no-fault insurance could be correlated with omitted variables also correlated with either the numerator (claims) or denominator (exposures) of *PD*. I can think of no reason why exposures should be correlated with the adoption of no-fault. It is possible, however, that states with relatively high numbers of PD claims were more likely to adopt no-fault insurance than states with relatively low numbers of PD claims. By most accounts, the adoption of no-fault in the early and mid-1970s was driven largely by concerns over high auto insurance costs (Lascher, 1999).[26] Massachusetts, for example, had the most expensive auto insurance in the nation when it became the first state to adopt no-fault in 1970, and many of the states that followed suit in the heavily urbanized eastern corridor (Connecticut, New York, New Jersey, and Pennsylvania) also had comparatively high auto insurance costs. Harrington (1994) shows a positive correlation between the propensity to adopt no-fault and premium growth between 1966 and 1970, even after controlling for population density. Thus, it is possible that failing to control for factors leading to the adoption of no-fault could bias our estimate of the coefficient for *NOFAULT*. Note, however, that this bias should be upwards, so, if anything, the coefficient for *NOFAULT* should be even more negative than reported in Table 6.

Although I cannot fit a difference-in-differences model, I can examine the effect of within-state variation in dollar thresholds on accident rates. As with fatal accident rates, such an analysis corrects for any unobserved heterogeneity among states correlated with both the size of dollar thresholds and *PD*. The results of this fixed-effects regression, identical to that in (3) with *PD* as the dependent variable, are reported in the rightmost column of Table 9. The coefficient for *THRESHOLD* indicates a small positive effect of within-state changes in dollar thresholds on accident rates, but this effect is not statistically significant at conventional levels.

---

[26] There are a variety of other reasons why no-fault passed in some states and not in others, including the strength of the trial lawyers' bar (Dyer, 1976; Harrington, 1994) and particular political circumstances (Lascher, 1999).

3.4. The Effect of No-Fault on Driver Negligence

Even if no-fault has no measurable effect on the overall or fatal accident rate, it is conceivable we could observe an effect on the level of care exercised by drivers. Lower accident costs, under certain assumptions (see Section 2), should lead drivers to exercise less care under no-fault than under tort. Unfortunately, driver care is difficult to measure in the population at large. It is no surprise, then, that only one study to date has directly tested whether liability laws affect the propensity to drive negligently—Sloan, Reilly, and Schenzler's (1995) test of the effect of no-fault on binge drinking and drinking and driving discussed above.

Here I rely on detailed data from fatal accidents to test whether driver negligence in a variety of forms varies between no-fault and tort states. The most comprehensive state-level data on driver negligence come from the DOT's Fatal Accident Reporting System (FARS), which records information on all fatal accidents in the U.S. beginning in 1975. Among the elements recorded in the FARS data are indicators for whether some traffic violation or other negligent behavior on the part of any of the drivers precipitated the accident. These elements include speeding, improper lane changing, failure to stop or signal, unsafe passing, and other negligent actions. FARS also reports on the blood alcohol content (BAC) of drivers involved in the accident, when available.

The FARS data are derived from reports produced by state transportation agencies, which collect information about fatal accidents from medical examiners, coroners, and emergency medical and police accident reports. While the DOT is confident that the number of fatal accidents is accurately portrayed in these data, substantial variation in the data elements reported across states and over time for each fatal accident may exist. There is some concern, therefore, that the propensity to report negligence in the FARS data might be correlated with state liability laws. Specifically, it is possible that accident officials face more pressure to report negligent behavior in tort states than in no-fault states since the assignment of fault presumably has a greater impact on the distribution of accident costs in tort states. Limiting the analysis to fatal accidents, however, should minimize this type of bias because the seriousness of fatal accidents demands investigation of the possibility of criminal negligence and the incentive to assign criminal negligence should not differ dramatically between no-fault and tort states. Thus, I expect differences in reporting across states to result in potentially noisy measures of negligence in the FARS data, but not biased ones. Analyses of negligence in general accident data could cause us to draw misleading conclusions, as in Devlin (1999).

I use FARS data between 1979 and 1994, and note that the coding of many variables is unreliable in earlier years (DOT, 1996). For each accident, state officials recorded information on the accident itself, each of the vehicles involved in the accident, and then each of the passengers in those vehicles (and pedestrians, if any). I merge data from each of these accident, vehicle, and person files to create a single file with information on all drivers involved in fatal accidents between 1979 and 1994, and I exclude accidents involving special-use vehicles (taxis, emergency vehicles, military vehicles, and school buses). The final data set contains records for 508,773 fatal accidents in 50 states involving 897,985 drivers. I aggregate these data over drivers to the state-year level, weighting the analyses below accordingly. Thus, the dependent variables in the analyses below measure the proportion of drivers involved in a fatal accident in a given state and year who were cited for some type of negligent driving behavior.

State officials identify driver-related contributing factors for each vehicle involved in a fatal accident. These factors range from driving while sleepy, to speeding, to obscured vision due to weather conditions. Out of the total universe of 99 contributing factors, I classified 26 as involving negligent behavior (see the Appendix). By far the most common contributing factors identified in the FARS data are inattentive driver, failure to keep in proper lane, erratic, reckless, or negligent driving, failure to yield right of way, failure to obey traffic signs, and speeding. I classify these six factors as "principal" negligent actions in the tables below. Other examples of negligent driving behavior are improper lane changing, dangerous passing, and following too closely. If no-fault encourages negligent driving, we should observe a higher incidence of negligence as a contributory factor in fatal accidents in no-fault states than in tort states.[27]

There is little variation across states in the proportion of fatal accidents in tort and no-fault states involving negligent behavior. As can be seen from Table 10, approximately 58 percent of drivers involved in fatal accidents in tort states were classified as having engaged in a negligent act compared with 54 percent in no-fault states. This finding is contrary to the hypothesis that negligence should contribute to a higher proportion of fatal accidents in no-fault states than in tort states. In only one category—erratic, reckless, or negligent driving—does the proportion of drivers cited with a negligent action in no-fault states exceed that of tort states significantly (0.14 vs. 0.07).

---

[27] This follows as long as the incidence of negligent driving in a state affects the number of fatal accidents reported as involving negligence more strongly than the number of fatal accidents reported as not involving negligence. A superior test of this hypothesis would employ data on the negligence of all drivers, not just those involved in fatal accidents. Unfortunately, no such data exist.

Table 10 also reports the proportion of fatal accidents in which one or more drivers were thought to be drunk and the proportion of drivers charged with a specific traffic violation in the accident itself or in the previous three years. Once again, little difference exists in the means of these variables across states.

It is conceivable that the propensity to classify a given driver as having engaged in some negligent act depends on the particular circumstances of the accident and the characteristics of the driver. If these circumstances or characteristics vary systematically by whether a state has no-fault insurance, then these simple comparisons of means could be misleading.[28] To address this potential problem, I run weighted least squares regressions with the variables listed in Table 10 as dependent variables and the following accident and driver characteristics as explanatory variables: light and weather conditions, year, month, and day of the accident, number of lanes, urban or rural location, speed limit, number of vehicles and individuals involved, number of fatalities, whether a pedestrian was involved, the vehicle's role in the accident, and the driver's age, sex, and severity of injury.

With few exceptions, negligence rates are no higher in no-fault states than in tort states after controlling for accident and driver characteristics (see Column (1), Table 11). Overall, negligence rates are about 2 percentage points lower in no-fault states. The major exception is in the category of erratic, reckless, or negligent driving. State authorities appear more likely to cite drivers in no-fault states with this particular contributing factor than in tort states. However, this particular contributing factor exhibits more variation both across and within states than any other. In many states, both tort and no-fault, the incidence of this contributing factor varies by 30 or more percentage points from year to year. One explanation for this high level of variation is that state authorities receive varying instructions from year to year regarding citing drivers with erratic, reckless, or negligent driving, which may be related to changes in administrations, insurance, or auto-safety-related legislation. I cannot rule out, though, that erratic, reckless, or negligent driving is more often a real contributing factor in fatal accidents in no-fault than in tort states based on the available data.

---

[28] As noted above, I maintain the assumption that the propensity for state officials to classify an accident as involving negligence does not vary across tort and no-fault states.

Table 10
Proportion of Drivers Involved in Fatal Accidents Cited with Negligent Behavior

	State Type	
Negligent Behavior	**Tort**	**No-Fault**
Negligent Contributing Factors		
All	0.58	0.54
All principal	0.55	0.51
Inattentive driver	0.08	0.04
Failure to keep in proper lane	0.29	0.21
Erratic, reckless, or negligent driving	0.07	0.14
Failure to yield right of way	0.08	0.08
Failure to obey traffic signs	0.05	0.05
Speeding	0.25	0.20
Other Negligence		
Drunk driver	0.29	0.28
Violation charged	0.16	0.18
Previous violation	0.41	0.40

Notes: The sample includes all drivers involved in fatal accidents between 1979 and 1994. Fatal accidents involving special-use vehicles are excluded. Means are weighted by the numbers of observations in each state-year cell.

Again, we might worry that these regressions fail to control for omitted variables correlated with both negligence levels and the adoption of no-fault.[29] To address this concern, I test whether negligence is correlated with changes in the level of dollar thresholds within no-fault states over time. Column 2 of Table 11 shows there is a small positive correlation between changes in dollar thresholds and the incidence of erratic, reckless, or negligent driving and drunk driving. Overall, however, increases in dollar thresholds are associated with decreases in negligence.

In summary, this analysis of negligence data generally rejects the hypothesis that no-fault influences negligence levels in fatal accidents. The small, but statistically significant, positive correlation between no-fault and citations for erratic, reckless, or negligent driving is the one exception. The fact that all other citations for negligent behavior like speeding, improper

[29] The direction of the bias this introduces is unclear since we do not know how the incidence of negligence influences attitudes toward no-fault.

lane changing, and failure to obey traffic signs are the same or lower in no-fault states as well as the high level of within-state variation in this negligence category draws this exception into question, however.

Table 11
The Effect of No-Fault Insurance on Negligent Behavior in Fatal Accidents

	Regressor	
Dependent Variable	*NOFAULT*	*THRESHOLD*
Negligent contributing factors		
All	-0.023 (0.004)	-0.004 (0.002)
All principal	-0.026 (0.004)	-0.003 (0.002)
Inattentive driver	-0.037 (0.006)	-0.004 (0.002)
Failure to keep in proper lane	-0.054 (0.009)	-0.002 (0.003)
Erratic, reckless, or negligent driving	0.020 (0.007)	0.012 (0.004)
Failure to yield right of way	0.001 (0.002)	-0.0003 (0.0009)
Failure to obey traffic signs	-0.003 (0.002)	-0.003 (0.001)
Speeding	-0.019 (0.004)	-0.003 (0.002)
Other negligence		
Drunk driver	0.002 (0.005)	0.006 (0.001)
Violation charged	-0.008 (0.007)	-0.006 (0.002)
Previous violation	-0.014 (0.007)	0.003 (0.003)

Notes: The sample includes all drivers involved in fatal accidents between 1979 and 1994. Fatal accidents involving special-use vehicles are excluded. All regressions control for light and weather conditions, year, month, and day of accident, number of lanes, urban or rural location, speed limit, number of vehicles and individuals involved, number of fatalities, vehicle impact, whether a pedestrian was involved, and the driver's age, sex, and severity of injury. The THRESHOLD *regression includes only no-fault states with dollar thresholds, and also controls for state fixed-effects. The estimates are generated by weighted least squares. Standard errors are in parentheses.*

4. CONCLUSIONS

The evidence presented here casts serious doubt on contentions that no-fault auto insurance as implemented in the U.S. has led to greater driver negligence and higher accident rates. Previous studies finding a positive relationship between no-fault and the fatal accident rate have employed questionable empirical methodologies. Closer inspection of differences in fatal accident rates in tort and no-fault states both before and after the implementation of no-fault (between 1971 and 1976) reveals that no-fault had no effect on fatal accident rates during that time. Moreover, there is little reason to believe that failure to control for factors that influenced the adoption of no-fault, such as rising insurance costs, should bias the effect of no-fault on fatalities toward zero. Additional analyses found little evidence that the overall accident rate or the rate of driver negligence in fatal accidents in no-fault states exceeds that in tort states. If anything, no-fault states appear to have generally lower overall accident rates and lower rates of driver negligence than tort states.

Presumably, the overriding reason to drive carefully is self-preservation, an incentive that does not vary between no-fault and tort states. Indeed, the FARS data show quite clearly that driver negligence is more likely to result in the fatality of a negligent driver than in the fatality of a non-negligent driver. First, 41 percent of all fatal accidents between 1979 and 1994 involved a single vehicle for which the fault for the accident (if any) rests with a single driver. Moreover, in two-car accidents, 52 percent of all negligent drivers died compared with 32 percent of non-negligent drivers. The margin over which no-fault might change the incentive to drive with care seems rather small in comparison. In the U.S., there is little reason to believe that no-fault auto insurance affects incentives for the vast majority of drivers. Thus, there may be reasons to oppose the concept of no-fault auto insurance and, by extension, choice auto insurance, but their effect on driver behavior and accidents should not be among them.

References

Association of Trial Lawyers of America, 2000, *The Reckless Driver Protection Act*, on-line at <http://www.atla.org/homepage/reck0203.ht>, Washington, DC: ATLA.

Carroll, S., and A. Abrahamse, *The Effects of a Choice Automobile Insurance Plan on Insurance Costs and Compensation*, Santa Monica, CA: RAND Corporation, Institute for Civil Justice.

Cummins, J. D., and M. Weiss, 1999, The Incentive Effects of No-Fault Automobile Insurance, in *Automobile Insurance: Road Safety, New Drivers, Risks, Insurance Fraud and Regulation* (G. Dionne and C. Laberge-Nadeau, eds.), Boston: Kluwer Academic Publishers.

Cummins, J. D., M. Weiss, and R. Phillips, 1999, The Incentive Effects of No-Fault Automobile Insurance, working paper, University of Pennsylvania, Wharton School.

Devlin, R., 1992, Liability versus No-Fault Automobile Insurance Regimes: An Analysis of the Experience in Quebec, in *Contributions to Insurance Economics* (G. Dionne, ed.), Boston: Kluwer Academic Publishers.

Devlin, R., 1999, No-Fault Automobile Insurance and Accident Severity: Lessons Still to be Learned, in *Automobile Insurance: Road Safety, New Drivers, Risks, Insurance Fraud and Regulation* (G. Dionne and C. Laberge-Nadeau, eds.), Boston: Kluwer Academic Publishers.

Dyer, J., 1976, Do Lawyers Vote Differently? A Study of Voting on No-Fault Insurance, *The Journal of Politics*, 38, 2, 452-456.

Greene, W., 1993, *Econometric Analysis*, 2nd Edition, New York, NY: Macmillan Publishing Co.

Harrington, S., 1994, State Decisions to Limit Tort Liability: An Empirical Analysis of No-Fault Automobile Insurance Laws, *The Journal of Risk and Insurance*, 61, 2, 276-94.

Heckman, J., 1978, Dummy Endogenous Variables in a Simultaneous Equation System, *Econometrica*, 46, 4, 931-959.

Insurance Research Council, 1994, *Auto Injuries: Claiming Behavior and Its Impact on Insurance Costs*, Malvern, PA: IRC.

Insurance Research Council, 1999a, *Injuries in Auto Accidents: An Analysis of Auto Insurance Claims*, Malvern, PA: IRC.

Insurance Research Council, 1999b, *Paying for Auto Injuries: A Consumer Panel Survey of Auto Accident Victims*, Malvern, PA: IRC.

Kabler, B., 1999, The Case Against Auto Choice, *Journal of Insurance Regulation*, 18, 1, 53-79.

Kochanowski, P. and M. Young, 1985, Deterrent Aspects of No-Fault Automobile Insurance: Some Empirical Findings, *The Journal of Risk and Insurance*, 52, 259-288.

Landes, E., 1982, Insurance, Liability, and Accidents: A Theoretical and Empirical Investigation of the Effect of No-Fault Accidents, *Journal of Law and Economics*, 25, 1, 49-65.

Lascher, E., 1999, *The Politics of Automobile Insurance Reform: Ideas, Institutions, and Public Policy in North America*, Washington, DC: Georgetown University Press.

Maddala, G., 1983, *Limited Dependent and Qualitative Variables in Econometrics*, Cambridge, England: Cambridge University Press.

McEwin, I., 1989, No-Fault and Road Accidents: Some Australasian Evidence, *International Review of Law and Economics*, 9, 13-24.

Nader, R., 1999, Hearing on S. 837—The Auto Choice Reform Act of 1999, Washington, DC: *U.S. Senate Committee on Commerce, Science, and Technology*, June 9.

Nawata, K., 1993, A Note on the Estimation of Models with Sample-Selection Biases, *Economic Letters*, 42, 1, 15-24.

O'Connell, J., S. Carroll, M. Horowitz, A. Abrahamse, and P. Jamieson, The Comparative Costs of Allowing Consumer Choice for Auto Insurance in All Fifty States, *Maryland Law Review*, 55, 160-222.

Priest, G., 1998, *The Wall Street Journal*, July 21, A-15.

Rokes, W., 1971, *No-Fault Insurance*, Santa Monica, CA: Insurors Press, Inc.

Sloan, F., B. Reilly, and C. Schenzler, 1994, Tort Liability versus Other Approaches for Deterring Careless Driving, *International Review of Law and Economics*, 14, 53-71.

Sloan, F., B. Reilly, and C. Schenzler, 1995, Effects of Tort Liability and Insurance on Heavy Drinking and Driving, *Journal of Law and Economics*, 38, 49-77.

State Farm Insurance Companies, 1993, *No-Fault Reference Manual*, Bloomington, IL: State Farm.

U.S. Department of Transportation, 1985, Compensating Auto Accident Victims: A Follow-Up Report on No-Fault Auto Insurance Experiences, Washington, DC: U.S. DOT.

U.S. Department of Transportation, 1996, *Traffic Safety CD-ROM*, BTS-CD-10, Washington, DC: Bureau of Transportation Statistics, U.S. DOT.

Vella, F., 1998, Estimating Models with Sample Selection Bias: A Survey, *Journal of Human Resources*, 33, 1, 127-169.

White, M. and Y. Liao, 1999, *No-Fault for Motor Vehicles: An Economic Analysis*, Paper #99-016, University of Michigan, Department of Economics.

Zador, P., and A. Lund, 1986, Re-Analyses of the Effects of No-Fault Auto Insurance on Fatal Crashes, *The Journal of Risk and Insurance*, 53, 226-241.

Appendix

The following is a list of 99 contributing factors to fatal accidents listed in the FARS database. I classify 26 of these factors as involving negligent behavior (6, 21-24, 26, 36, 38-44, 46-48). These 26 contributing factors are printed in italics. In addition, I classify six contributing factors as being "Principal" because they are by far the most commonly cited (6, 28, 36, 38, 39, 44). These six factors are denoted by an asterisk (*).

Physical/Mental Condition

01 Drowsy, sleepy, asleep, fatigued
02 Ill, passed out/blackout
03 Emotional (e.g., depression, angry, disturbed)
04 Drugs-medication
05 Other drugs (marijuana, cocaine, etc.)
*06 Inattentive (talking, eating, etc.)**
07 Restricted to wheelchair
08 Paraplegic
09 Impaired due to previous injury
10 Deaf
11 Other physical impairment
12 Mother of dead fetus
13 Mentally challenged
14 Failure to take drugs/medication

Miscellaneous Factors

18 Traveling on prohibited trafficways
19 Legally driving on suspended or revoked license
20 Leaving vehicle unattended with engine running, leaving vehicle unattended in roadway
21 Overloading or improper loading of vehicle with passengers or cargo
22 Towing or pushing vehicle improperly
23 Failing to dim lights or to have lights on when required
24 Operating without required equipment
25 Creating unlawful noise or using equipment prohibited by law
26 Following improperly
27 Improper or erratic lane changing
*28 Failure to keep in proper lane or running off road**

29 Illegal driving on road shoulder, in ditch, sidewalk, or on median

30 Making improper entry to or exit from trafficway

31 Starting or backing improperly

32 Opening vehicle closure into moving traffic or vehicle is in motion

33 Passing where prohibited by posted signs, pavement markings, hill or curve, or school bus displaying warning not to pass

34 Passing on wrong side

35 Passing with insufficient distance or inadequate visibility or failing to yield to overtaking vehicle

*36 Operating the vehicle in an erratic, reckless, careless or negligent manner or operating at erratic or suddenly changing speeds**

37 High speed chase with police in pursuit

*38 Failure to yield right of way**

*39 Failure to obey traffic signs, traffic control devices or traffic officers, failure to observe safety zone traffic laws**

40 Passing through or around barrier

41 Failure to observe warnings or instructions on vehicle displaying them

42 Failure to signal intentions

43 Giving wrong signal

*44 Driving too fast for conditions or in excess of posted speed limit**

45 Driving less than posted minimum

46 Operating at erratic or suddenly changing speeds

47 Making right turn from left turn lane. Making left turn from right turn lane

48 Making improper turn

49 Failure to comply with physical restrictions of license

50 Driving wrong way on one-way trafficway

51 Driving on wrong side of road (intentionally or unintentionally)

52 Operator inexperience

53 Unfamiliar with roadway

54 Stopping in roadway (vehicle not abandoned)

55 Underriding a parked truck

56 Improper tire pressure

57 Locked wheel

58 Over correcting

59 Getting off/out of or on/in to moving vehicle

60 Getting off/out of or on/in to non-moving vehicle

Vision Obscured by

61 Rain, snow, fog, smoke, sand, dust
62 Reflected glare, bright sunlight, headlights
63 Curve, hill, or other design features (including traffic signs, embankment)
64 Building, billboard, etc.
65 Trees, crops, vegetation
66 Motor vehicle (including load)
67 Parked vehicle
68 Splash or spray or passing vehicle
69 Inadequate defrost or defog system
70 Inadequate lighting system
71 Obstructing angles on vehicle
72 Mirrors—rear view
73 Mirrors—other
74 Head restraints
75 Broken or improperly cleaned windshield
76 Other obstruction

Avoiding, Swerving, or Sliding Due to

77 Severe crosswind
78 Wind from passing truck
79 Slippery or loose surface
80 Tire blow-out or flat
81 Debris or objects in road
82 Ruts, holes, bumps in road
83 Live animals in road
84 Vehicle in road
85 Phantom vehicle
86 Pedestrian, cyclist, or other non-motorist in road
87 Ice, water, snow, slush, sand, dirt, oil, wet leaves on road

Other Miscellaneous Factors

89 Carrying hazardous cargo improperly
90 Hit-and-run vehicle drive
91 Non-traffic violation charged - manslaughter or other homicide offense
92 Other non-moving traffic violation

Possible Distractions (inside Vehicle)

93 Cellular telephone
94 Fax machine
95 Computer
96 On-board navigation system
97 Two-way radio
98 Head-up display
99 Unknown

6
AUTO INSURANCE CLAIMS IN NEW JERSEY AND PENNSYLVANIA

Jia-Hsing Yeh
Chinese University of Hong Kong

Joan T. Schmit
University of Wisconsin, Madison

Since the introduction of the automobile to modern American society, accidents and their resulting costs have been a source of concern. Naturally, horse-and-buggy, train, boat, and other transportation-related accidents preceded those of the automobile, offering ideas for the proper treatment of auto accident costs. Yet, no prior form of travel had as widespread an effect on the human social structure as did the automobile. The car ultimately touched the lives of all Americans. By the start of the twenty-first century, approximately one in every two Americans owned a car, resulting in over six million automobile accidents and 41,000 deaths annually on U.S. roads and highways.

Two general approaches to management of the risks associated with automobile accident costs are found in the U.S.: (1) the negligence or tort approach of allowing one party to obtain compensation from another party found to be at fault for the accident; and (2) the no-fault approach, which permits compensation for auto accidents only from one's own insurer and regardless of fault. No-fault, furthermore, typically limits compensation to economic harms. The relative benefits of each approach long have been debated and studied, with empirical support for either perspective hampered by particularly severe data limitations.

Automobile liability laws in the U.S. are determined at the state level. While we observe the two general compensation mechanisms mentioned, variations in laws, driving conditions, and general economic and social qualities across states make comparisons of these mechanisms difficult. The body of empirical analyses seems to indicate that no-fault systems with verbal thresholds are more likely to hold down overall insurance costs than are tort systems, although disagreement remains over the extent of cost savings produced by no-fault laws. Furthermore, many commentators have argued that no-fault systems produce moral hazard problems (see also the chapters by Lascher and Powers, Kabler, Carroll and Abrahamse, and Loughran in this book). Accordingly, scholars continue to debate whether no-fault produces net benefits for the driving public.

Resolution of the debate is hampered by the fact that few American states changed their compensation systems over the past twenty years, making longitudinal analysis of policy change difficult. Furthermore, where change has occurred, variations across states make comparisons of "tort" versus "no-fault" challenging. New Jersey and Pennsylvania, however, modified their automobile liability laws within the past fifteen years in such a way that offers both recent data for study as well as an opportunity to compare tort versus no-fault without worry about state variations. That is, both New Jersey and Pennsylvania implemented choice systems, which permit evaluations of tort and no-fault within a single state for the same time period. New Jersey moved from mandatory no-fault to choice in 1989, while Pennsylvania moved from traditional tort to choice in 1990. These two states provide a natural experiment that to date has received little empirical consideration. We believe such an analysis can shed much light on the impact of choice laws.

We have organized this chapter as follows. First, we review the New Jersey and Pennsylvania systems. We continue with a description of the data available for analysis and the results of the analyses conducted. Our analysis focuses on the following areas: relative costs of each system in terms of attorney representation, duration before payment, and extent of payment relative to losses claimed; types of claims made; types and severity of injuries claimed; and form of medical care received. We conclude with implications of the results and suggestions for future work.

1. THE TWO CHOICE SYSTEMS[1]

Beginning in 1989, motorists in New Jersey have been required to choose between two insurance options: "Limitation on Lawsuit Option" or "No Limitation on Lawsuit Option." A motorist who chooses the no limitation on lawsuit option can sue another motorist for payment of non-economic damages regardless of the injury. On the other hand, a motorist

[1] Information presented in this section is summarized in Table 1.

who chooses the limitation on lawsuit option has legal recourse against another motorist for non-economic damages only if one of the statutorily defined serious injuries is sustained. In either case, motorists are allowed to sue for economic damages above their PIP coverage. The current minimum PIP coverage in New Jersey is $15,000.

Pennsylvania enacted a similar law effective in 1990. In Pennsylvania, the options are referred to as: "Full Tort" and "Limited Tort." Motorists who select the full tort option have no restrictions on their right to sue for non-economic damages. On the other hand, motorists who choose the limited tort option are entitled to a statutorily mandated reduction in premium in exchange for limitations on their right to sue for non-economic damages unless one of the following circumstances occurs: (1) the accident causes serious injury, i.e., exceeds the verbal threshold, or (2) the injuries are caused by another driver who was convicted of drunk driving, who was uninsured, or who was insured in another state.

In sum, the two alternative lawsuit options are "Limitation on Lawsuit Option" (no-fault) versus "No Limitation on Lawsuit Option" (tort) in New Jersey, and "Limited Tort Option" (no-fault) versus "Full Tort Option" (tort) in Pennsylvania, with insureds who choose the no-fault option receiving premium savings. In both states, it is important to note that the options generally affect only non-economic losses. In other words, motorists who choose the no-fault option are still able to recover economic damages in excess of their first-party coverage limits from a negligent driver. Meanwhile, the choice of no-fault does not immunize no-fault electors from liability for non-economic damages they cause others, although those liabilities will exist only when injuries exceed the statutory threshold in the case of no-fault victims. No matter which option the insureds choose, bodily injury liability coverage must be purchased.

A noteworthy difference between the choice systems in New Jersey and Pennsylvania is the statutorily dictated (default) option that comes into play when motorists do not actively choose between alternatives. In New Jersey, no-fault is the default option whereas in Pennsylvania tort is the default. Cummins and Tennyson (1992) and Ellis (1989) present evidence of what they term a "status quo bias in decision making," a tendency of the default option to dominate. We are not surprised, therefore, that the data as depicted in Table 2 show more claims subject to the no-fault option in New Jersey and to the tort option in Pennsylvania. This difference is important in a cross-sectional study, which we are not undertaking. Instead we are analyzing outcomes *within* each state before and after choice and *between* claims of tort and no-fault electors after choice has been implemented.

Table 1
Choice Systems in New Jersey and Pennsylvania

	New Jersey	Pennsylvania
Pre-Choice System	No-fault with dollar thresholds	Add-on tort system
Effective Year of Choice Program	1989	1990
Driver Options	Limitation on lawsuit option (No-Fault) No limitation on lawsuit option (Tort)	Limited tort option (No-fault) Full tort option (Tort)
Default Option	Limitation on lawsuit option	Full tort option
Can no-fault electors sue for economic damages above the PIP limit?	Yes	Yes
Can no-fault electors be sued for non-economic damages caused to others?	Yes	Yes

Table 2
Number of BI and PIP Claims in New Jersey and Pennsylvania: Pre- and Post-Choice

		BI	PIP	Total
New Jersey	**Pre-Choice**	1,380	2,854	6,781
	Post-Choice	1,166	1,381	
Pennsylvania	**Pre-Choice**	943	1,094	4,590
	Post-Choice	1,299	1,254	
Total		4,788	6,583	11,371

Source: All-Industry Research Advisory Council (1989), Insurance Research Council (1999).

Table 2 (Continued)
No-Fault / Tort Electors in Post-Choice Claims

		BI	PIP
New Jersey	No-Fault	541	839
	Tort	442	187
	Unknown	183	355
	Total	1,166	1,381
Pennsylvania	No-Fault	212	277
	Tort	756	393
	Unknown	331	584
	Total	1,299	1,254

Source: Insurance Research Council (1999).

2. DATA

The Insurance Research Council (IRC) conducted automobile insurance personal injury closed-claims surveys in 1977, 1987, 1992, and 1997. The surveys focused on closed claims paid under five principal auto injury coverages: Bodily Injury Liability (BI), Uninsured Motorist (UM), Underinsured Motorist (UIM), Medical Payment (MP), and Personal Injury Protection (PIP). Each participating insurance carrier reported a two-week sample of those five types of claims. The questionnaires contained information regarding the claimant, insured, characteristics of the accident, type of injury, medical treatment, losses incurred and payments received, attorney involvement, relevant coverage, and case disposition—creating approximately 250 variables for each claim. Because the participating companies together wrote more than 60 percent of U.S. private passenger automobile insurance at the time the data were collected, these data sets provide a representative source for the analysis of auto compensation systems in the U.S.

To consider the effect of choice, we utilize the 1987 and 1997 claim data for New Jersey and Pennsylvania, representing similar data pre- and post-choice. Furthermore, we focus on the BI and PIP coverages because these are most relevant in comparing tort and no-fault systems, and because the other claim categories have insufficient data for effective analysis. Table 2 reports the number of observations in each state and across the following claim categories for BI and PIP: pre-choice, post-choice no-fault, post-choice tort, and post-choice unknown. An interesting observation from the work reported here is the large number (over one-third of all observations) of claims for which the claims adjuster did not record (did not know?) the legal option to which the claim was subject.

3. ATTORNEY REPRESENTATION, AMOUNT, AND TIMING OF PAYMENT

Early U.S. no-fault laws were implemented with the intention of addressing various concerns with the tort system, including: (1) large administrative costs; (2) extensive delays in compensation; (3) and significant uncompensated losses. Consideration of how choice responds to these three concerns, therefore, gives some indication of its effectiveness. Table 3 presents pre- and post-choice data on the relative use of attorneys, the reimbursement ratio (the amount of compensation relative to the claimed economic damages), and the duration between the date of accident and closure of the claim both pre- and post-choice for BI and PIP claims.

We are interested in attorney involvement for several reasons. One is its indication of administrative expense. When attorneys are employed, administrative expenses are likely to be higher than when they are not. Additionally, the relative incidence of attorney involvement provides some indication of how adversarial the process is.

Table 3
Attorney Usage, Reimbursement Ratio, and Settlement Time

Pennsylvania

	BI Claims				PIP Claims			
	N^a	A^b	R^c	T^d	N^a	A^b	R^c	T^d
Pre-Choice (Add-On)	848	69%	2.14	369.5	1,028	40%	1.00	151.5
Post-Choice All	1,041	64%	1.62	360	1,138	25%	0.67	122
***p*-value of *t*-test**	*NA*	.0098	.8367	.0021	*NA*	$<10^{-4}$	.0078	$<10^{-4}$
Post-Choice NF	172	55%	1.00	285.5	245	22%	0.68	109
Post-Choice Tort (Default)	603	64%	1.74	357	342	30%	0.65	131
Post-Choice Unknown	266	69%	1.76	387.5	551	23%	0.67	122

New Jersey

	BI Claims				PIP Claims			
	N^a	A^b	R^c	T^d	N^a	A^b	R^c	T^d
Pre-Choice ($ NF)	1,273	94%	2.79	480	2,680	43%	1.00	174
Post-Choice All	997	85%	1.51	683	1,182	51%	0.65	253.5
***p*-value of *t*-test**	*NA*	$<10^{-4}$	.0706	$<10^{-4}$	*NA*	$<10^{-4}$	.8837	$<10^{-4}$
Post-Choice NF (Default)	468	82%	1.48	725	705	47%	0.61	241
Post-Choice Tort	371	91%	1.54	615	169	72%	0.71	290
Post-Choice Unknown	158	83%	1.57	688	308	47%	0.67	253

[a] *Number of valid responses.*
[b] *Ratio of attorney involvement.*
[c] *Median reimbursement ratio.*
[d] *Median number of days from accident report date to settlement date.*

The data indicate a lower incidence of attorney involvement in Pennsylvania following implementation of choice, but a slight increase in attorney involvement in New Jersey. Both of these differences are significant at the 0.01 level. Because New Jersey switched from no-fault to choice, however, this result is not especially surprising. One would expect greater use of attorneys once tort became an option. Furthermore, much of the post-choice increase is found in claims by drivers who selected the tort option, and especially among the tort electors who experienced PIP claims.

We might expect tort electors to be more oriented toward use of attorneys, given their active selection of the tort scheme, and we do find the differences in use of attorneys between tort and no-fault electors to be statistically significant at the 0.001 level for both BI and PIP claims.

More difficult to explain is the consistent decrease in the median reimbursement ratio across claim type and state pre- and post-choice, although the decrease is statistically significant only for Pennsylvania PIP claims. In Pennsylvania, the drop might be due in part to the required PIP coverage even for tort electors, this value being paid prior to collection of any tort compensation. In New Jersey, however, the answer to why the reimbursement ratio declined is unclear, given that it was a no-fault state prior to choice. Recall that claims reported to IRC are only those closed *with payment*, which could offer a partial explanation.

Similarly unclear is why the median settlement time in New Jersey rose following choice. The duration rose substantially in both the BI and PIP claim categories for both tort and no-fault electors. Pennsylvania, in contrast, reveals a change in median claim duration that we can explain. The duration between the accident date and settlement date was substantially lower for the BI claims of no-fault electors than for the pre-choice BI claims, while the post-choice and unknown choice BI claims were of approximately the same duration as pre-choice BI. All categories of post-choice PIP claims in Pennsylvania showed shorter duration than the pre-choice PIP claims.

In general, relatively fewer BI and PIP claimants use attorneys if they are no-fault electors than if they are tort electors. Additionally, the median reimbursement ratio is lower and claim duration shorter for no-fault electors than for tort electors, except in the case of BI claims in New Jersey, in which the median duration for no-fault electors was longer than for tort electors.

4. TYPES AND SEVERITY OF INJURIES

An interesting question regarding no-fault versus tort is whether or not no-fault encourages moral hazard. Because the data available are only claim data, rather than insured data, we cannot test this question directly. We are, however, able to provide information about general categories of injuries, numbers of injuries claimed, and extent of disability claimed, all of which provide indirect information toward answering the question.

Strains/Sprains: Others (e.g., Derrig, et al., 1994) have documented the incidence of fraud and build-up in auto claims, finding a disproportionate share of fraud and build-up in soft-tissue claims. The relative frequency of soft-tissue injuries, therefore, is taken as a potential measure of improper claiming behavior. In Tables 4 and 5, we present various groupings of injuries to highlight the relative incidence of soft-tissue (strains/sprains) claims pre- and post-choice and between tort and no-fault electors. The general trend is for relatively fewer claims of only strain/sprain injuries for post-choice claims and among no-fault electors. These results are consistent with a reduction in fraud and build-up of claims, although we have insufficient data to test this hypothesis directly. Additionally, the differences before and after implementation of choice are statistically significant only for the PIP claims.

An earlier IRC (1996) study discussed the vulnerability of auto insurance systems to unnecessary and inflated payments and revealed that fraud and/or buildup appeared in more than one-third of all auto BI claims. The report showed a correlation between the presence of sprains or strains and the appearance of buildup. That is especially the case for BI coverage under which individuals have an opportunity to collect payments for non-economic damages, which provide financial incentives that may influence the behavior of claimants. As shown in Table 5, the percentages of claimants reporting only non-sprain or non-strain injuries are smaller for tort elector claimants (18 percent in Pennsylvania and 10 percent in New Jersey) than for no-fault elector claimants (20 percent in Pennsylvania and 20 percent in New Jersey), a result consistent with the hypothesis.

Table 4
Sprains or Strains as Share of All Injuries

Pennsylvania

	BI Claims			PIP Claims		
	N	Sprains/ Strains	Non-Sprains/ Strains	*N*	Sprains/ Strains	Non-Sprains/ Strains
Pre-Choice (Add-On)	937	65%	35%	1,085	59%	41%
Post-Choice (All)	1,285	65%	35%	1,224	55%	45%
p-value of *t*-test	*NA*	.8437	*NA*	*NA*	.0228	*NA*
Post-Choice NF	210	63%	37%	269	54%	46%
Post-Choice Tort (Default)	745	66%	34%	385	57%	43%
Post-Choice Unknown	330	63%	37%	570	53%	47%

Table 4 (Continued)

New Jersey

	BI Claims			PIP Claims		
	N	Sprains/ Strains	Non-Sprains/ Strains	*N*	Sprains/ Strains	Non-Sprains/ Strains
Pre-Choice ($ NF)	1,370	70%	30%	2,839	68%	32%
Post-Choice (All)	1,155	65%	35%	1,356	65%	35%
p-value of *t*-test	*NA*	.0571	*NA*	*NA*	.0057	*NA*
Post-Choice NF (Default)	537	59%	41%	821	62%	38%
Post-Choice Tort	437	70%	30%	185	69%	31%
Post-Choice Unknown	181	69%	31%	350	67%	33%

Note: Excludes "no injury" and "unknown injuries" claimants and fatalities.

Table 5
Sprains or Strains as Share of All Claimants

Pennsylvania

	BI Claims			PIP Claims		
	Sprains/ Strains	Sprains/ Strains+ Non-S/S	Non-Sprains/ Strains	Sprains/ Strains	Sprains/ Strains+ Non-S/S	Non-Sprains/ Strains
Pre-Choice (Add-On)	49%	26%	25%	40%	23%	37%
Post-Choice (All)	48%	34%	18%	37%	28%	34%
Post-Choice NF	50%	30%	20%	36%	29%	35%
Post-Choice Tort (Default)	50%	33%	17%	39%	28%	32%
Post-Choice Unknown	43%	37%	19%	36%	28%	35%

Table 5 (Continued)

New Jersey

	BI Claims			PIP Claims		
	Sprains/ Strains	Sprains/ Strains+ Non-S/S	Non-Sprains/ Strains	Sprains/ Strains	Sprains/ Strains+ Non-S/S	Non-Sprains/ Strains
Pre-Choice ($ NF)	54%	33%	13%	51%	23%	26%
Post-Choice (All)	43%	43%	15%	45%	37%	18%
Post-Choice NF (Default)	34%	48%	18%	43%	38%	20%
Post-Choice Tort	51%	38%	11%	49%	41%	10%
Post-Choice Unknown	50%	38%	13%	49%	32%	19%

Notes: Excludes "no injury" and "unknown injuries" claimants and fatalities. Numbers of valid responses are the same as those in Table 3. Percentages in some rows do not sum to 100 percent because of rounding.

Measures of Severity: Injury severity can be measured in a number of ways. Two methods available to us are the type of disability (if any) claimed and the type of hospital stay (if any) experienced. Table 6 shows the extent of disability for claimants associated with BI and PIP claims in Pennsylvania and New Jersey. Because of the need to exceed first-party benefits, more BI claimants would be expected to—and actually did—experience some extent of disability than did PIP claimants. The data also indicate a pattern across the different categories of insureds, with fewer recorded disabilities following choice than before choice. Fifty-one percent of post-choice Pennsylvania BI claimants experienced no disability, compared with 36 percent of such claimants before choice. Sixty-eight percent of post-choice Pennsylvania PIP claimants experienced no disability, compared with 56 percent of such claimants before choice. In New Jersey, the percentages were up from 34 percent to 53 percent for BI claimants and up from 55 percent to 66 percent for PIP claimants. The reduction in claims of disability following implementation of choice is statistically significant in both states and for BI as well as PIP claims.

Table 6
Extent of Claimant Disability

Pennsylvania

BI Claims	None	Temp. Disab.	Perm. Partial	Perm. Total	Death	Valid Responses
Pre-Choice (Add-On)	38%	56%	5%	1%	1%	937
Post-Choice All	56%	38%	5%	1%	1%	1,277
Post-Choice NF	49%	41%	8%	1%	<0.5%	208
Post-Choice Tort (Default)	57%	37%	4%	1%	1%	748
Post-Choice Unknown	56%	39%	4%	1%	<0.5%	321
PIP Claims	**None**	**Temp. Disab.**	**Perm. Partial**	**Perm. Total**	**Death**	**Valid Responses**
Pre-Choice (Add-On)	57%	39%	2%	<0.5%	1%	1,089
Post-Choice All	73%	25%	1%	<0.5%	1%	1,231
Post-Choice NF	77%	21%	<0.5%	<0.5%	1%	271
Post-Choice Tort (Default)	72%	26%	1%	<0.5%	2%	388
Post-Choice Unknown	71%	27%	1%	<0.5%	1%	572

Table 6 (Continued)

New Jersey

BI Claims	None	Temp. Disab.	Perm. Partial	Perm. Total	Death	Valid Responses
Pre-Choice ($ NF)	34%	55%	10%	1%	1%	1,370
Post-Choice All	56%	34%	10%	1%	<0.5%	1,125
Post-Choice NF (Default)	52%	36%	11%	1%	1%	524
Post-Choice Tort	68%	25%	6%	<0.5%	<0.5%	424
Post-Choice Unknown	37%	48%	14%	1%	1%	177
PIP Claims	**None**	**Temp. Disab.**	**Perm. Partial**	**Perm. Total**	**Death**	**Valid Responses**
Pre-Choice ($ NF)	56%	41%	3%	<0.5%	1%	2,841
Post-Choice All	67%	30%	2%	<0.5%	1%	1,349
Post-Choice NF (Default)	68%	29%	2%	<0.5%	1%	819
Post-Choice Tort	68%	31%	1%	<0.5%	<0.5%	186
Post-Choice Unknown	64%	33%	2%	<0.5%	1%	344

Note: Percentages in some rows do not sum to 100 percent because of rounding.

The treatment of injuries can serve as a further indicator of injury severity. Table 7 records the hospital treatment provided claimants for BI and PIP claims in Pennsylvania and New Jersey. Similar to the results just reported, those presented in Table 7 demonstrate that fewer claimants sought hospital treatment post-choice than pre-choice. Together, these results indicate a greater proportion of less-severe claims made post-choice than pre-choice; however, the reduction in the severe injuries is a national phenomenon over this time period and therefore might not be linked to choice itself. As pointed out in the IRC report (1999), "the continuing decline in the percent of claimants admitted to a hospital reflects changes in the attitudes and practices of health-care providers as well as a decrease in the injuries sustained by claimants." The national hospital admission rate per 1,000 population declined from 168.3 in 1977 to 141.8 in 1987, 131.1 in 1992 and 125.5 in 1997, according to American Hospital Association Health Forum, *Hospital Statistics*. Additionally, the IRC (1999) indicates that there are a number of developments in motor vehicle safety that may have contributed to the decline in hospital admissions and disabilities resulting from auto accidents. Among these developments are improvements in vehicle design, such as airbags and side-impact test standards.

Table 7
Hospital Treatment

Pennsylvania

BI Claims	No Hospital	E. R. Only	Over-night	2-7 Days	Over 7 Days	Valid Responses
Pre-Choice (Add-On)	22%	61%	2%	10%	5%	928
Post-Choice All	31%	59%	2%	6%	2%	1,270
Post-Choice NF	26%	63%	1%	8%	2%	207
Post-Choice Tort (Default)	33%	57%	2%	5%	3%	744
Post-Choice Unknown	31%	60%	2%	6%	1%	319
PIP Claims	**No Hospital**	**E. R. Only**	**Over-night**	**2-7 Days**	**Over 7 Days**	**Valid Responses**
Pre-Choice (Add-On)	20%	66%	1%	9%	5%	1,085
Post-Choice All	26%	66%	3%	3%	2%	1,211
Post-Choice NF	29%	66%	3%	2%	<0.5%	265
Post-Choice Tort (Default)	27%	65%	3%	3%	2%	381
Post-Choice Unknown	25%	67%	2%	4%	2%	565

Table 7 (Continued)

New Jersey

BI Claims	No Hospital	E. R. Only	Over-night	2-7 Days	Over 7 Days	Valid Responses
Pre-Choice ($ NF)	30%	55%	1%	8%	6%	1,350
Post-Choice All	36%	57%	1%	3%	3%	1,133
Post-Choice NF (Default)	31%	61%	1%	3%	4%	527
Post-Choice Tort	38%	56%	1%	2%	3%	430
Post-Choice Unknown	45%	49%	1%	5%	1%	176

PIP Claims	No Hospital	E. R. Only	Over-night	2-7 Days	Over 7 Days	Valid Responses
Pre-Choice ($ NF)	26%	64%	1%	6%	3%	2,837
Post-Choice All	38%	56%	2%	3%	2%	1,333
Post-Choice NF (Default)	35%	59%	1%	3%	2%	807
Post-Choice Tort	53%	40%	2%	4%	1%	182
Post-Choice Unknown	38%	58%	1%	2%	1%	344

Note: Percentages in some rows do not sum to 100 percent because of rounding.

Table 8
Percentage of Claimants Using Various Medical Providers

Pennsylvania

	BI Claims			**PIP Claims**		
	E.R.	**Chiro-practor**	**Phys. Therap.**	**E.R.**	**Chiro-practor**	**Phys. Therap.**
Pre-Choice (Add-On)	64%	10%	24%	71%	9%	21%
Post-Choice (All)	47%	20%	33%	63%	18%	21%
***p*-value of *t*-test**	<.0001	<.0001	<.0001	.0002	<.0001	.8459
Post-Choice NF	51%	18%	27%	60%	13%	19%
Post-Choice Tort (Default)	44%	21%	35%	64%	22%	24%
Post-Choice Unknown	50%	18%	31%	65%	17%	20%

Table 8 (Continued)

	New Jersey					
	BI Claims			PIP Claims		
	E.R.	Chiro-practor	Phys. Therap.	E.R.	Chiro-practor	Phys. Therap.
Pre-Choice ($ NF)	48%	28%	20%	61%	21%	16%
Post-Choice (All)	40%	44%	27%	48%	38%	23%
***p*-value of *t*-test**	.0001	<.0001	<.0001	<.0001	<.0001	<.0001
Post-Choice NF (Default)	47%	42%	29%	52%	35%	21%
Post-Choice Tort	34%	50%	24%	31%	54%	24%
Post-Choice Unknown	34%	33%	28%	48%	38%	28%

Notes: Excludes "no injury" and "unknown injuries" claimants and fatalities. Numbers of valid responses are the same as those in Table 3. Percentages in some rows do not sum to 100 percent because categories are not mutually exclusive and collectively exhaustive.

5. MEDICAL PROFESSIONALS

Table 8 shows three types of medical treatment used by auto injury claimants: emergency room (E.R.) visits, chiropractor care, and physical therapist care. Among the comparisons of pre-choice versus post-choice, there exist a consistent reduction in the use of E.R. treatment and a consistent increase in the use of chiropractor and physical therapist care across coverages and states. The reduction in the use of the E.R. ranged from 3 percentage points for New Jersey BI coverage to 9 percentage points for New Jersey PIP coverage. The reverse situation occurred for chiropractors and physical therapists. For New Jersey PIP claims, 36 percent of post-choice claimants were treated by a chiropractor, growing from 21 percent of their pre-choice counterparts. Forty-one percent of post-choice New Jersey BI claimants were treated by a chiropractor, up from 29 percent of their pre-choice counterparts. The use of chiropractors was generally less in

Pennsylvania than in New Jersey. However, it was also up for both coverages: from 13 to 20 percent for BI coverage and from 10 to 15 percent for PIP coverage. The same increase in usage was true for physical therapists, although not as pronounced.

6. CONCLUDING COMMENTS

Americans spent about $120 billion in private passenger automobile insurance in the year 2000, an astounding amount, and one which calls for an effective and efficient compensation system. Despite nearly half a century of debate, controversy remains about whether a third- or first-party system works best. The intent of this chapter has been to contribute something new to the debate by reviewing recently available claim data from New Jersey and Pennsylvania before and after implementation of their hybrid systems, and across tort and no-fault insureds.

These data offer new insight into automobile compensation mechanisms. In general, no-fault claimants appear less likely to employ attorneys, more likely to complete settlement of cases quickly, and less likely to pad claims than tort claimants. That is, overall, their claims appear to be managed more efficiently.

As is often hypothesized, no-fault claimants also appear to receive a lower payment per dollar of economic harm. Recall, however, that the data available are claims closed *with payment*, leaving unaccounted the claimants with zero payment. Tort claimants are more likely than no-fault claimants to receive no payment, thus biasing the result towards larger reimbursements of overall costs than actually occurs.

A question not answerable from the available data is whether or not choice encourages hazardous driving behavior. This question is left open for future studies based on more detailed data. We strongly encourage such future studies, believing the results reported here offer support for potential efficiencies of choice systems—efficiencies that if not offset by hazardous driving ought to be considered by state legislators looking for ways to lower the significant expense of automobile insurance. While the results reported here focused on univariate analyses, we urge researchers to undertake future studies that incorporate multivariate analyses for purposes of controlling for differences between no-fault and tort claimants, and between choice and non-choice systems.

References

All-Industry Research Advisory Council, 1989, *Compensation for Automobile Injuries in the United States*, Oak Brook, IL: AIRAC.

Cummins, J. David, and Sharon Tennyson, 1992, Controlling Automobile Insurance Costs, *Journal of Economic Perspectives*, 6, 2, 95-115.

Derrig, Richard A., Herbert I. Weisberg, and Xiu Chen, 1994, Behavioral Factors and Lotteries under No-Fault with a Monetary Threshold: A Study of Massachusetts Automobile Claims, *The Journal of Risk and Insurance*, 61, 2, 245-275.

Ellis, Randall P., 1989, Employee Choice of Health Insurance, *Review of Economics and Statistics*, 71, 2, 215-223.

Herbers, Joseph A., 1994, Choice No-Fault: Actuarial Costing Methods, *Casualty Actuarial Society Forum, Ratemaking Call Papers*, Winter, 564-607.

Insurance Research Council, 1996, *Fraud and Buildup in Auto Injury Claims: Pushing the Limits of the Auto Insurance System*, Malvern, PA: IRC.

Insurance Research Council, 1999, *Injuries in Auto Accidents: An Analysis of Auto Insurance Claims*, Malvern, PA: IRC.

Lascher, Edward L., Jr., 1999, *The Politics of Automobile Insurance Reform: Ideas, Institutions and Public Policy in North America*, Washington, DC: Georgetown University Press.

Powers, Michael R., 1992, Equity in Automobile Insurance: Optional No-Fault, *The Journal of Risk and Insurance*, 59, 2, 203-220.

7
DETERMINANTS OF THE SELECTION OF FULL OR LIMITED TORT AUTO INSURANCE IN PENNSYLVANIA: AN EMPIRICAL ANALYSIS

Laureen Regan[1]
Temple University

1. INTRODUCTION

In response to rapidly rising insurance prices, Pennsylvania was one of several states to adopt no-fault auto insurance in the 1970s. The Pennsylvania no-fault law, passed in 1975, included a $750 monetary tort threshold and unlimited no-fault medical benefits. However, because of the easily reached tort threshold, the new law failed to stabilize costs; and so, in 1984 the legislature acted again, this time repealing the tort threshold, while leaving in place an "add-on" system of no-fault "CAT Fund" benefits capped at $1,000,000 (see Powers, 1989).

The repeal of no-fault seemed only to make matters worse, with insurance prices rising almost 10 percent annually between 1982 and 1988 (see Powers, 1992). Therefore, by 1990, Pennsylvania introduced a "choice" no-fault auto insurance reform, designed to control some of the incentives for cost increases under the traditional tort system, while offering insureds the opportunity to restrict voluntarily their rights to seek full recovery under tort in exchange for a premium reduction. This election is referred to as the limited tort option (as opposed to the full tort option, which is the traditional model).

The Pennsylvania plan requires an insured to elect affirmatively the limited tort option. If a person fails to make an election, he or she is assumed

[1] Support for this research was provided in part by a grant from the Fox School of Business and Management. The author would like to thank Jen McDonald for her assistance in gathering and formatting the data used in this analysis.

to have opted for full tort coverage.[2] There is significant variation in the rate of limited tort election across Pennsylvania counties, ranging from 25 percent of insureds in Montour County to 50 percent in Philadelphia County, in 1991.[3] This is similar to the distribution of auto losses across Pennsylvania counties, with Philadelphia County having the highest average loss costs of any county in the state. However, the rate of limited tort election has increased steadily in all counties, with a statewide average of 31 percent choosing limited tort in 1991, and 44 percent choosing limited tort in 1996, the last year for which data are available.

An interesting question is what determines full versus limited tort election. Insurance prices and loss costs vary widely across Pennsylvania. Differences in tort election across counties have implications for overall loss costs in Pennsylvania. One might expect that a higher rate of limited tort election in high-cost counties might have a greater impact on loss costs than a similar rate of election in a lower cost area. Indeed, Lascher (1999) argues that a higher rate of limited tort election overall would result in reduced loss costs in Pennsylvania. Moreover, the determinants of tort election in Pennsylvania may have implications for other choice no-fault proposals. If limited tort election is based on cost alone, then other measures that reduce costs might be expected to reduce the proportion of insureds electing limited tort coverage. However, if other factors influence the rate of limited tort election, this has implications for both expected loss costs and the design of regulation. This might be particularly relevant to the choice auto insurance reform bill that was introduced at the federal level in 1999. Annual savings of $45 billion are expected to result from passage of the bill, based on estimates of the number of insureds likely to opt to restrict their rights to sue (Fisher, 1997; Detlefsen, 1998).

The political economy model of regulation is used here to analyze the determinants of full versus limited tort choice under the Pennsylvania reform. Under this model, interested parties invest resources to influence the outcome of regulation in their favor. This model has been applied to the analysis of regulatory stringency in insurance (Meier, 1998), state decisions to adopt no-fault auto legislation (Harrington, 1994), and the existence of private rights of action under unfair claims practices laws (Carroll and Regan, 1998). In this chapter, the political economy model is used to analyze the election of individual auto insureds in response to the regulation, rather than in the

---

[2] New Jersey also has a choice no-fault system, but the default is limited tort if the insured fails to make an election. Some authors argue that Pennsylvania's default has caused too few insureds to choose limited tort; see, for example, Detlefsen (1998).

[3] These data were provided by the Pennsylvania Insurance Department.

analysis of the decision by lawmakers to implement the choice no-fault law in Pennsylvania.

Section 2 below briefly reviews the arguments supporting the effectiveness of no-fault auto insurance in general. The key elements of Pennsylvania's choice no-fault are also discussed. In Section 3, we use the arguments of political economy theory to explain the relationships among elements of the law and the incentives of affected groups to influence the choice of limited or full tort. Of course, consumer election of limited tort will also be influenced by insurance prices, and these are also examined in detail in Section 3. Section 4 discusses the empirical analysis, and Section 5 concludes.

2. NO-FAULT AND THE PENNSYLVANIA CHOICE ACT

2.1. Effectiveness of No-Fault

The debate surrounding auto insurance reform in the U.S. has been a long and complex one. Under the traditional tort system, those injured in auto accidents for which another driver is found to be at fault can recover economic costs, such as medical expenses and lost wages, and can also recover non-economic damages to compensate for intangible injuries such as pain and suffering. To recover, the injured party must bring a civil lawsuit against the allegedly at-fault motorist, whose insurance company has the duty to defend against such suits. The injured party is awarded damages if negligence is proved in a court of law, or if the at-fault driver's insurance company settles the claim out of court. The attorney representing the injured party is typically paid a fee that is a proportion of the amount awarded, but receives compensation only if the injured party recovers damages. Proponents of the traditional tort system argue that it is fair in that the burden for accident costs is borne by the responsible party. This in turn should cause drivers to exercise more care to protect themselves against potential liability. It is argued that this will reduce accident frequency and severity, thereby benefiting society in general.

Opponents of the tort system argue that the system is costly and inefficient. Specifically, the system is argued to be inequitable because some injured parties receive no compensation, others with relatively minor injuries may be overcompensated, and those with the most severe injuries tend to be undercompensated.[4] It has also been argued that the tort system encourages fraud and claims inflation. This is because injured parties can receive benefits greater than their losses, since it is costly for insurers to investigate relatively small claims. Also, an incentive to inflate claims is created because intangible costs (and plaintiff attorney fees) are generally related to the level of economic damages suffered (see, e.g., Weisberg and Derrig, 1992; Carroll, Abrahamse, and Vaiana, 1995; Schwartz, 2000).[5] The system has also been found to generate high transaction costs, as well as to delay payments to injured parties.

Various forms of no-fault insurance have been proposed to replace the traditional tort system. Under any no-fault proposal, those injured in auto accidents give up the right to sue responsible drivers in exchange for the certainty of recovery under first-party auto insurance benefits. In a pure no-fault system, tort suits for non-economic costs are barred. In a modified no-fault model, injured parties give up the right to sue for non-economic losses unless injuries exceed a certain threshold. Injuries must be either *serious* as defined in the state law, or exceed a certain dollar level of medical expenses. Suits are barred for injuries below the threshold level. States may also adopt a *choice* no-fault plan, which allows drivers to restrict voluntarily their own rights to sue, but does not restrict the rights of those who choose to remain in the full tort system.

Adoption of no-fault is argued to reduce insurance premiums through savings in transactions costs, lower court costs, reduction in incentives for fraud and inflated claims, and elimination of compensation for intangible costs such as pain and suffering. Studies on the ability of no-fault to reduce costs have shown mixed results (see, e.g., Cummins and Weiss, 1991; Johnson, Flanigan, and Winkler, 1992). However, a study of actual claims by Carroll and Kakalik (1993) shows that no-fault reduces compensation paid to claimants relative to a tort system, both through transaction cost savings and in reduced payments of non-economic losses. Transaction cost savings estimates range from 80 percent under a complete tort ban, to 20 to 40 percent under a no-fault model where only seriously injured parties are permitted to bring suits. This study also shows that compensation is received much faster under the no-fault system than under tort, with an average improvement in speed of payment of approximately two months for no-fault benefits.

---

[4] This argument was first made by Keeton and O'Connell (1965) in their influential work on auto insurance reform.

[5] See Cummins and Tennyson (1996) for a discussion of the lottery aspect of tort recovery for auto injury costs.

Pennsylvania was one of 16 states to enact no-fault auto reform in the 1970s in response to increasing premiums. Because of dissatisfaction with the results of the law, however, it was repealed in 1984, just eight years after it was enacted, and replaced with a tort system. Although restrictions on the right to sue were removed in the 1984 reform, insurers were required to offer minimum levels of first-party benefits. Insurance rates continued to increase, especially in Philadelphia and surrounding counties, and proposals for reform were again launched. In 1990, the tort system was replaced with a choice no-fault model with a verbal threshold that is still in place today. Those insureds that elect the limited tort option give up their right to sue for non-economic losses unless injuries are serious, while full tort electors retain unlimited rights to sue. The law also includes medical care cost containment provisions, and required an initial rate rollback.

2.2. Key Elements of the Pennsylvania Law

Pennsylvania's choice no-fault law, commonly referred to as *Act 6* of 1990, made significant changes to existing regulation. The law requires insurers to notify insureds, using standardized language, of the right to choose between limited and full tort, and the consequences of the choice (75 Pa.C.S.A., Sec. 1705). Notice was initially required upon first renewal of existing policies after July, 1990. However, the initial choice remains effective for all renewals thereafter, unless the insurer receives a "properly executed form" electing the other option. At every renewal, insurers are required to notify insureds that they have the right to change their tort election. If no choice is made, full tort coverage is the default option. Those electing to give up their rights to sue for intangible losses arising from minor injuries can recover economic losses, including medical care costs, rehabilitation, and lost income, from their first-party insurance. Alternatively, injured insureds may seek recovery from the at-fault driver through the tort system to the extent that costs are not recovered under first-party benefits, but damages are limited to economic losses only.

The right to recover non-economic losses is not restricted for serious injuries, however. A serious injury is defined in the statute as "a personal injury resulting in death, serious impairment of body function or permanent and serious disfigurement" (75 Pa.C.S.A., Sec. 1702). Since the vast majority of claims for bodily injury in the U.S. are very small, restricting the right to sue for minor injuries is likely to reduce greatly the use of the tort system to resolve auto accident claims for those choosing the limited tort option. For example, in 1996, the average severity of bodily injury claims in the U.S., including payment of intangible losses, was just under $9,200 (Insurance Research Council (IRC), 2000).

The 1990 law also mandated a rate rollback of at least 10 percent for those choosing full tort, and at least 22 percent for those choosing limited tort (Sec. 1799.7). This discount applied to total premiums for any selection of coverages based on the rate that prevailed on December 31, 1989. In addition, to prevent insurers from preemptively raising rates before the law's effective date, an immediate rate freeze was imposed until July 1, 1990, based on rates as of December 31, 1989, and previously approved rate increases were disallowed. Rate increases thereafter were limited to increases in the CPI and other approved indices of cost increases.

In addition to reducing the costs associated with resolving claims through the tort system, the reform also targeted medical costs as a significant driver of premium increases. *Act 6* includes a health-care cost containment provision which limits reimbursement levels for medical care incurred as a result of an auto accident to 110 percent of the prevailing Medicare rate. Prior to the inception of *Act 6*, medical care costs that were deemed reasonable were reimbursed at the usual, customary, and reasonable (UCR) rate that would prevail for an uninsured treatment. Furthermore, there was no procedure in place to allow an insurer to dispute medical charges under the 1984 law. *Act 6* created a mechanism to allow insurers to challenge medical care treatments through a peer review process (75 Pa.C.S.A., Sec. 1797 (b)). Under the peer review mechanism, private organizations, usually sponsored by physician groups, contract with insurers to evaluate the necessity of medical treatment. If the peer review organization determines that the treatment rendered was not medically necessary, the insurer may refuse payment. The law does contain provisions whereby a provider or insured may challenge an insurer's refusal to pay, however (Duggan, 1993).

3. DETERMINANTS OF FULL VERSUS LIMITED TORT ELECTION

3.1. The Political Economy Model

Early research on the process and outcome of regulation examined the ability of interest groups to control regulators (Stigler, 1971). More recent theories have argued that no single interest group can capture a regulatory body, but rather that regulation is a result of a complex political process (see, e.g., Peltzman, 1976). That is, the motive for regulation might arise from some real or perceived market failure, but the specification of the regulation is likely to be a function of complex negotiation and lobbying among competing interest groups. Then, regulatory processes and outcomes are thought to depend on the magnitude and incidence of the costs and benefits of the regulation, as well as underlying economic conditions. This theory was first applied to insurance regulation by Meier (1988), who argued that insurance industry groups, lawmakers, and other groups affected by provisions of proposed laws, including consumers, all have a stake in attempting to influence the final form of law or regulation.

The theory to date has focused on the legislative process leading up to the adoption of a law or regulation. Tests of the theory have generally examined the form of regulation *ex post* to determine if the regulation benefits a relatively stronger interest group (see, e.g., Meier, 1991; Harrington, 1994). In most cases, a law or regulation once passed becomes binding on all parties, and the costs and benefits are allocated accordingly. Thus, lobbying efforts *ex post* will not change the burdens under the law unless the law itself is changed.

In the case of Pennsylvania auto insurance reform, however, the law allows insureds to choose to maintain their position as it existed prior to implementation of the law, or to accept newly imposed restrictions. In either case, the consumer is entitled to a premium reduction, but the size of the reduction depends on the election of the consumer. Of course, the provisions of the law with respect to rate rollbacks and medical care cost containment are binding on all parties, but the ultimate impact of the provisions is determined by the distribution of consumer choices. Therefore, interested parties may continue lobbying efforts once the legislation is passed, but the target of the effort will necessarily change from lawmakers to consumers. Indeed, members of affected groups may continue to exert casual or organized effort to influence limited or full tort election. For purposes of the analysis that follows, the form of the law is taken as given, and focus is on the incentives of groups to influence consumer choice to elect the limited or full tort option under the law.

3.1.1. The Insurance Industry

Since insureds are required to take a positive action to choose limited tort in Pennsylvania, it is likely that the initial election is very important. In addition, since it is well known that most insureds do not read or understand their insurance policies, an effort would have to be made by insurers, agents, or government to effect widespread change. Because insurers were faced with an initial mandatory rate rollback, they might have been reluctant to support the law. This is especially the case if insurers were not sure of reducing loss costs by a like amount after the law took effect. Since rollbacks were significantly higher under the limited tort option, insurers might have preferred to retain more full, rather than limited tort consumers. Also, since those choosing limited tort are still at risk of being sued for damages by full tort electors in the event of an at-fault accident, yet premiums for limited tort electors must be reduced to reflect the tort restrictions, full tort electors are argued to be less costly to insure on an individual basis (Detlefsen, 1998). Lascher (1999) reports that insurance interest groups actively opposed the bill before it became law, so it seems plausible that insurers made little effort beyond that required by the law to encourage consumers to elect the limited tort option.

Insurance agents, likewise, might have little incentive to recommend to clients that they choose the limited tort option. One reason for this might be concern about potential liability claims against agents by disgruntled clients arguing that the agent did not fully explain the rights they were giving up. However, a more important reason might be due to agent compensation schemes. The bulk of agent compensation is through a commission based on premium volume. If premiums are reduced, all else being equal, agent compensation is reduced.[6] It might be the case, however, that those electing limited tort purchase higher amounts of first-party coverage than they would otherwise. In this case, reductions in unit premium prices may be offset by volume increases, thus leaving agents no worse off whether insureds choose limited or full tort.

3.1.2. Medical Care Providers

Health-care professionals are another group that might have an interest in consumer response to the law. Overall compensation of health-care providers is likely to be lower under *Act 6* because of the replacement of reimbursement at UCR rates with reimbursement tied to Medicare rates. In addition, the ability of insurers to refuse to pay for medical treatment that is found to be unnecessary by a peer review organization would tend to exert downward pressure on prices, which was the intent of the law. Lascher

[6] The majority of auto insurance in the U.S. is distributed through non-employee agents, who may be classified as either independent or exclusive. Both types of agents are compensated on a commission basis, although exclusive agents receive relatively lower commission rates. However, it seems reasonable to expect independent and exclusive agents to be similarly affected by the law.

(1999) reports that medical professional societies did lobby against passage of the law. Also, unsuccessful challenges to the constitutionality of the peer review and reimbursement provisions were brought by medical professional organizations soon after the law was implemented.[7]

Since these provisions are effective *ex post* regardless of whether an auto accident victim is covered under limited or full tort, there does not seem to be a reason to expect medical care providers to have an incentive to exert effort to influence consumer choice on this basis. Duggan (1998), however, argues that insurers tend to challenge medical treatments covered under first-party benefits more often than those covered under third-party benefits. To the extent that peer review results in denial of compensation, this might tend to increase medical professionals' preference for providing coverage under third-party benefits.

Alternatively, medical care professionals might prefer to provide care under first-party rather than third-party reimbursement schemes. This is because there is less uncertainty surrounding payment for care rendered under first-party benefits. Benefits are payable up to policy limits, subject to approval by a peer review organization. However, as noted above, some injured parties who receive medical care will be uncompensated under the tort system. Therefore, to the extent that the reform increases the proportion of people with first-party coverage for injuries sustained in auto accidents, it would tend to reduce the amount of uncompensated care provided by physicians and hospitals, and thus would reduce uncollectible hospital debts (Harrington, 1994). Thus, if the reduction in reimbursements were offset by an increase in collectible debt, medical care providers might support the limited tort election, rather than the full tort option.

3.1.3. Legal Professionals

Any restrictions on the right to sue for damages tend to reduce attorney income, and thus are likely to be strongly opposed by attorney groups. While both plaintiff and defendant attorneys are affected by any measure that reduces the volume of potential cases, plaintiff attorneys tend to be more organized and more vocal in opposition to laws that restrict tort rights. For example, the plaintiff attorneys' lobby was the main source of funds used to defeat auto no-fault proposals *Proposition 104* and *Proposition 200* in California, as well as a comprehensive no-fault proposal in Hawaii in 1995 (Sugarman, 1998). Lascher (1999) notes that the Pennsylvania Trial

[7] See, e.g., *Hospital Ass'n of Pennsylvania, Inc. v. Foster*, 624 A.2d. 1055, (Cmwlth.1993); *Lynn v. Prudential Property and Cas. Ins. Co.*, 619 A.2d 779, (Super.1993).

Lawyers Association, which represents plaintiffs in personal injury cases, was in active opposition to the reform proposal. Empirical research has supported the relationship between greater attorney involvement in claims and higher loss costs (Meier, 1988; Browne and Puelz, 1996). The framers of *Act 6* specifically recognized that attorney involvement in claims led to higher prices, and designed the law to reduce attorney involvement, and courts have upheld this objective.[8]

However, despite failing to stop passage of the law, attorneys might still minimize its impact by encouraging consumers not to give up their rights to sue. Indeed, casual observation indicates that attorneys continue to advertise the importance of maintaining tort rights in auto accident cases. Attorney-backed groups also continue to be vocal opponents of no-fault in any form, and regularly publish articles and editorials to this effect. For example, Public Citizen, an advocacy group formed by Ralph Nader, publishes many articles and editorials arguing against the adoption of no-fault.[9] This type of effort, to the extent that it reaches Pennsylvania residents, and that residents are convinced of its merits, may reduce the adoption of the limited tort option in Pennsylvania.

3.2. Insurance Prices

The choice of limited or full tort auto insurance is also linked to insurance prices. The Pennsylvania reform was introduced at a time of high and rising costs for insurance, and those consumers who valued the benefit of lower costs might choose limited tort for purely economic reasons. Auto insurance premiums are based on insurers' expected loss costs. Loss costs may be generated by bodily injury claims, property damage liability claims, and first-party benefit (PIP) claims.[10] The largest portion of insurance premiums is attributable to liability claims costs, rather than first-party benefits, and that will be the focus of the analysis here. For example, first-party benefits accounted for approximately 27 percent of total loss costs, whereas bodily injury and property damage liability accounted for 73 percent on average across the U.S. in 1996 (IRC, 2000). Average loss costs are defined as total insured losses allocated over all insured autos in the pool.

---

[8] *Motorists Ins. Companies v. Emig*, 664 A.2d 1338, (Super.1994), appeal denied.

[9] The group's website has an area devoted specifically to arguments against no-fault auto insurance (see <http://www.citizen.org/congress/civjus/home.html>).

[10] Data on losses associated with first-party property claims for damage to vehicles were not available. However, these types of losses are not significant drivers of overall loss costs in any case, since the maximum loss is limited to the value of the insured vehicle.

Figure 1
Liability Loss Costs

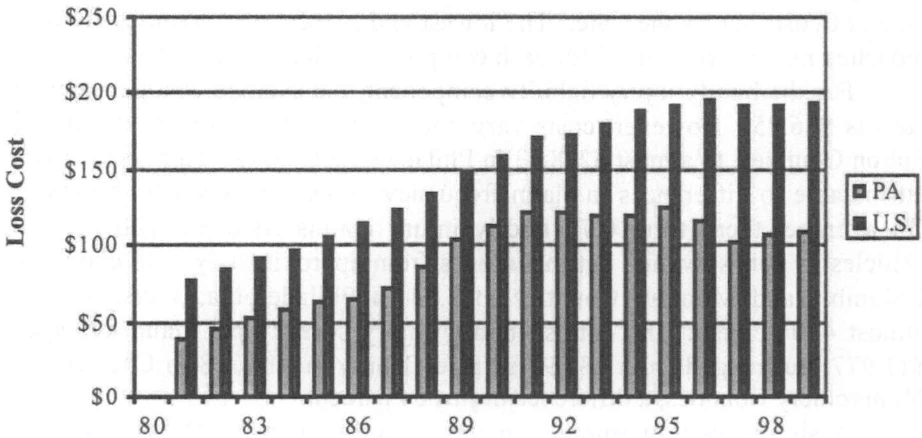

Source: Data are from Trends in Auto Injury Database, *Part A, IRC (2000).*

Figure 1 compares the average level of liability claims costs in Pennsylvania with U.S. averages over the period from 1980 to 1998. Although Pennsylvania average liability loss costs are lower than those of the U.S., Pennsylvania costs increased by 177 percent between 1980 and 1998, whereas U.S. costs increased just over 151 percent. Most of the increase in Pennsylvania occurred before 1990, when loss costs rose from $39.38 in 1980 to $120.77 in 1990. Between 1990 and 1998, Pennsylvania liability loss costs actually declined to $109.27, while U.S. costs continued to rise. The decline in Pennsylvania loss costs after 1990 might be attributable to election of the limited tort option in response to high prices.

It is well known that Philadelphia is ranked among the highest cost areas in the country for auto insurance, but there is a wide variation in insurance costs across Pennsylvania (Smith and Wright, 1992). If election of limited or full tort reflects underlying costs, then we would expect to see insureds choose limited tort more often in higher cost areas. Table 1 shows liability loss costs and loss cost ranges across Pennsylvania counties, based on 1995 to 1997 averages.[11] Loss costs are shown for bodily injury and

[11] This was derived from data compiled by the IRC, which shows loss costs by rating territory averaged over the 1995 to 1997 period. The majority of rating territories are defined at the county level. Those territories that cross borders were aligned with counties using information provided by the Pennsylvania Insurance Department. The county, rather than the

property damage liability costs here, and further decomposed into frequency and severity elements. Columns 2 and 3 of the table show the statewide averages and associated standard deviations, while columns 4 and 5 show the range of costs across the state. The lowest and highest cost counties are also indicated in columns 4 and 5 for each component of liability loss costs.

For the bodily injury liability component, the average cost per insured auto is $86.95. However, costs vary widely, from $62.06 in Bedford and Fulton Counties, to almost $278.73 in Philadelphia County. This seems to be attributable to differences in claim frequency rather than severity, however. On average, there were 0.72 bodily injury claims filed per 100 insured vehicles in Pennsylvania, but this ranges from approximately 0.48 claims in Columbia and Montour Counties to 2.74 in Philadelphia, a disparity of almost 420 percent. In contrast, bodily injury severity per claim averaged $11,977, but ranged from $8,698 in Erie County to $14,728 in Chester and Montgomery Counties, a difference of just 64 percent.

A similar pattern emerges in the property damage liability loss cost data. The average loss cost per 100 insured autos in Pennsylvania is $72.47. Bedford and Fulton Counties have the lowest level of property damage liability loss costs at $56.37, while costs are highest in the Philadelphia suburban area, with average costs of $113.00 in Chester and Delaware Counties. However, while Bedford and Fulton Counties have the lowest frequency of property damage liability claims, the area responsible for the highest frequency is Erie County, with 7.45 property damage claims per 100 insured autos. Philadelphia and surrounding counties experience approximately 5 claims per 100 insured autos, but claim severity tends to be higher, with Delaware and Chester Counties experiencing the highest average severity for property damage liability claims at $2,315, while Erie is lowest, at just $1,357.[12] Overall, these data support the idea that loss costs vary across the state, and further, that there seem to be systematic differences between urban and rural counties, with Philadelphia and the surrounding counties experiencing the highest costs for both bodily injury and property damage liability.

---

territory, is used as the unit of analysis because the demographic data used later in the chapter are available only at the county level.

[12] This might be because Erie receives more snow than any other county in the state, generating relatively more low-speed accidents.

Table 1
Liability Loss Costs across Pennsylvania

Variable	Mean	Stand. Dev.	Minimum (County)	Maximum (County)
Bodily Injury Liability Loss Costs ($)	86.95	34.80	62.06 Bedford, Fulton	278.74 Philadelphia
Bodily Injury Frequency	0.719	0.28	0.479 Columbia, Montour	2.49 Philadelphia
Bodily Injury Severity ($)	11,977	962	8,698 Erie, Allegheny	14,728 Bucks, Montgomery
Property Damage Liability Loss Costs ($)	72.47	12.92	56.37 Bedford, Fulton	113.00 Delaware, Chester
Property Damage Frequency	4.32	0.56	3.44 Bedford, Fulton	7.45 Erie
Property Damage Severity ($)	1,678	202.9	1,357 Erie	2,315 Delaware, Chester

The loss cost data do not allow us to measure differences in amounts paid for insurance across the state, however. Although unit premiums are based primarily on loss costs, elective coverages, physical damage costs, choices of limits and deductibles, and differences in insurer loading and marketing costs, all affect the ultimate price paid by consumers. Consumers are not likely to make insurance purchasing decisions based on underlying costs, but rather on out-of-pocket costs. If there are significant differences in premiums across counties that are attributable to factors other than loss costs, these might also influence insureds to opt for limited rather than full tort to offset the higher cost. Comparing premium levels across counties allows us to capture these differences.

Table 2 indicates that premiums vary significantly across the state. These are based on premiums charged for a model insurance package by the top insurers in each county as of 1999.[13] Premiums are shown for both

[13] The number of insurers shown for each county varies slightly, but most counties show data for 18 companies. The data are available from the Pennsylvania Insurance

limited and full tort options. The premium for the full tort package is $1,032.00 on average across the state, with a minimum average price of $817.81 in Franklin County, and a maximum average price of $2,885.75 in Philadelphia. Similar price differentials are observed for the limited tort package, with an average premium of $870.87 across the state. Franklin County again has the lowest offering prices on average at $691.33, and Philadelphia the highest at $2,413.64.

Table 2
Average Statewide Premium Levels
(Model Policy*)

	Mean	Minimum	Maximum
Full Tort	1032.2	817.8 Franklin	2,885.75 Philadelphia
Limited Tort	870.87	691.33 Franklin	2,413.64 Philadelphia

**See footnote 13 for a description of the model policy.*

There are also significant differences in premiums charged within counties for the same package of coverage. Figures 2 and 3 show the average, minimum, and maximum offering prices for both the limited tort and full tort model polices for a sample of counties. These counties represent a mix of urban and rural areas, and include the highest and lowest cost counties for each package.

The full tort package is offered at prices ranging from $481 to $1,755 in Montour County, whereas Philadelphia County prices range from $1,935 to $5,086. For the limited tort policy, the lowest offering price is also in Montour County at $408, and the highest is in Philadelphia, at $4,178.50. Note, however, that the relative difference in prices between the full and limited tort packages is consistent across both high- and low-cost counties, ranging from 18 to 19.5 percent higher offering prices for the full tort model

Department's website at <http://www.insurance.state.pa.us/html/cauto.html>. The information shown is based on a married male, age 35, with no chargeable accidents or violations, driving a Ford Taurus SE with dual airbags and anti-lock brakes, with a 10-mile round-trip commute to work, and 12,000 miles driven annually. The model policy has bodily injury liability limits of $50,000 per person, $100,000 per accident, a property damage liability limit of $25,000, uninsured and underinsured motorists coverage limits the same as those for BI, and physical damage comprehensive and collision coverage with $100 and $500 deductibles, respectively.

policy. Therefore, there is little reason to expect that differences in tort election are based on differences in relative savings across counties.

Figure 2
Limited Tort—Model Policy Price Range

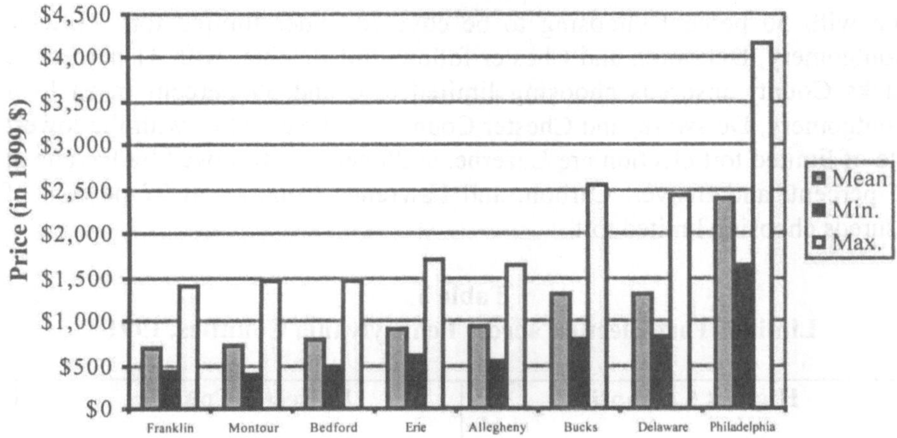

Figure 3
Full Tort—Model Policy Price Range

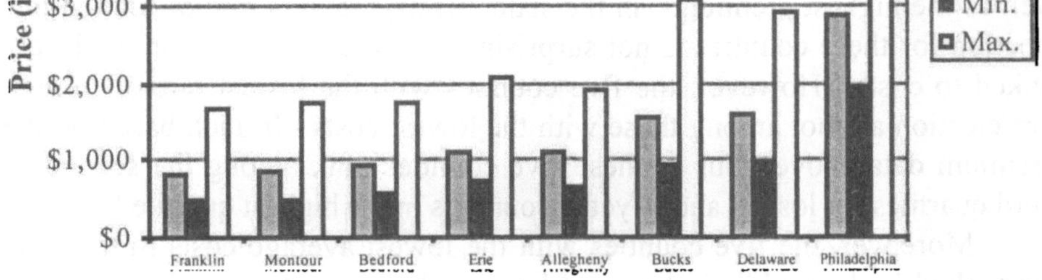

Information on the rate of limited tort election across Pennsylvania counties for the period 1991 through 1996 was obtained from the Pennsylvania Insurance Department, and this can be related to the information on loss costs and premium levels to determine if limited tort election is related to price. Table 3 shows the five counties with the highest and lowest rates of limited tort election in 1991. *Act 6* became effective in February, 1990, so all existing policies would have been renewed by the end of 1991. The first column in Table 3 shows the counties with the highest rates of tort election in 1991. Approximately 32 percent of Pennsylvania insureds chose the limited tort option in 1991, while Philadelphia is ranked first with 50 percent choosing to be covered under limited tort. Bucks, Montgomery, Delaware, and Chester follow Philadelphia, with 41 percent of Bucks County insureds choosing limited tort, and 39 percent in each of Montgomery, Delaware, and Chester Counties. The counties with the lowest rate of limited tort election are Luzerne, at 25 percent, followed by Fayette at 26 percent, and Beaver, Carbon, and Lawrence Counties at 27 percent of insureds choosing limited tort.

Table 3
Limited Tort Election across Pennsylvania Counties, 1991

Highest 5 Counties		Lowest 5 Counties	
Philadelphia	50%	Luzerne	25%
Bucks	41%	Fayette	26%
Montgomery	39%	Beaver	27%
Delaware	39%	Carbon	27%
Chester	39%	Lawrence	27%

Although data on loss costs and premium rates are not available for 1991, it seems likely that the pattern of loss costs across Pennsylvania counties is relatively stable over the short term. The analysis above indicates that Philadelphia and surrounding counties experience the highest losses, as well as the highest premiums, in the state. Thus, the high rate of limited tort election for these counties is not surprising if limited tort election is closely linked to costs. However, the five counties with the lowest rate of limited tort election are not among those with the lowest costs. In fact, based on the premium data above, four of these five counties rank among the second or third quartiles for losses, and Fayette County is in the highest quartile.[14]

Moreover, the five counties with the lowest average costs in the state are ranked in the middle in terms of limited choice election, with 35 percent of insureds in these counties choosing limited tort. This is illustrated in Table 4. Column 1 lists the five counties with the lowest rates of limited tort

[14] This also holds when liability loss costs, rather than premium levels, are used to determine county rankings.

election for 1991. Average premiums for the model limited tort policy are also shown for these counties in column 2, along with the rank of the county in terms of premiums. The five counties with the lowest rate of limited tort election generally fall into the higher end of the distribution for premium levels. Column 3 lists the five counties with the lowest average premium rates in the state for 1991. Limited tort election in these five counties falls into the midrange for the state, and not into the lowest range, as might be expected if limited tort election were based solely on insurance prices. These statistics suggest that factors other than costs may drive the election of limited versus full tort in Pennsylvania.

Table 4
Limited Tort Election Compared to Premium Rates

Lowest Limited Tort Counties	Average Premium (quartile)	Lowest Cost Counties	Limited Tort Election (quartile)
Luzerne	$937.94 (3rd)	Franklin	35% (3rd)
Fayette	$1,124.39 (4th)	Adams	35% (3rd)
Beaver	$1,037.03 (3rd)	Union	35% (3rd)
Carbon	$951.67 (3rd)	Snyder	35% (3rd)
Lawrence	$1,045.10 (3rd)	Lancaster	35% (3rd)

The proportion of insureds choosing limited tort increased across all counties from 1991 to 1996, with just over 44 percent of all Pennsylvania insureds choosing limited tort by 1996.[15] Limited tort election ranges from 34 percent in Luzerne to 62 percent in Philadelphia, similar to the pattern that prevailed in 1991. Limited tort election increased by 27 percent across the state, by 36 percent for Luzerne County, and 24 percent for Philadelphia. The counties with the five highest and lowest proportions of limited tort electors for 1996 are shown in Table 5.

Note that there is no change in the counties with the five lowest proportions of limited tort electors, although there is some sorting among them as compared to 1991. However, there are striking differences in the

[15] No county saw a net decline in limited tort election over this period.

group making up the top five in 1996. While Philadelphia still has the highest proportion of insureds choosing limited tort, Venango, Wyoming, and Sullivan Counties are ranked two, four, and five, respectively. Limited tort election in Venango County increased from 31 percent in 1991 to 54 percent in 1996, an increase of over 74 percent, while Wyoming's and Sullivan's limited tort election increased from 38 percent to 51 percent over the period. These are not high-cost counties on any measure. For example, both Sullivan and Wyoming County are ranked in the 2nd quartile for insurance prices, while Venango falls into the 3rd quartile.

Thus, although premium levels and loss costs do seem to play a role in differences in tort election, price factors alone do not seem capable of explaining the pattern of limited tort election in Pennsylvania. It is likely that other economic factors, such as relative income level across counties, might also influence limited tort election. Further, the political economy model discussed above suggests that interest groups may have an incentive to influence the choice of full or limited tort, but the ability to exert influence might also vary across counties. However, these factors cannot be accounted for simply by comparing limited tort election proportions and relative insurance prices and loss costs.

Table 5
Limited Tort Election across Pennsylvania Counties, 1996

Highest 5 Counties		Lowest 5 Counties	
Philadelphia	62%	Luzerne	34%
Venango	54%	Carbon	36%
Bucks	51%	Fayette	36%
Wyoming	51%	Beaver	37%
Sullivan	51%	Lawrence	37%

4. ECONOMETRIC MODEL

Ordinary least squares regression analysis is undertaken to examine more carefully the relationship among limited tort choice, economic factors, and the predictions of political economic theory. The dependent variable of interest is the proportion of insureds in each county choosing limited tort. The log-odds ratio of limited tort election is used because the proportion of insureds electing limited tort is constrained to fall between zero and one by definition. Although the analysis of changes in tort election across time in Pennsylvania above includes a number of years, data on insurance prices and loss costs are not available for the entire time period. Therefore, our analysis is confined to a single cross-sectional set of observations for 1996, the final year for which the limited tort election data are available.[16]

4.1. Explanatory Variables

The analysis of loss costs and premiums above indicates that limited tort election is likely to be influenced by insurance prices. Because insurance consumption choices are more likely to be related to actual expenditures rather than underlying loss costs, average premium levels for the model insurance policy shown above are used as the measure of insurance prices [*PRICE*].[17]

Several other variables are included to control for other factors which might influence limited tort election. Income is likely to be an important determinant of limited tort choice, even after controlling for insurance prices. Insurance is relatively more expensive for lower-income insureds on average. For example, Miller (1998) reports that auto insurance accounts for seven times the percentage of income for those families in the lowest income quintile as for those in the top quintile. Thus, the premium savings resulting from limited tort choice might be relatively more valuable for lower-income families. However, the marginal benefits of tort recovery are likely to be higher, especially for less severe injuries. The income measure used here is median household income, rather than per capita income [*INCOME*]. This is because insurance is usually a household purchase, rather than an individual purchase.

There are also significant differences in population density across Pennsylvania counties, ranging from approximately 12 people per square mile in Forest County to just under 11,100 people per square mile in Philadelphia County. Population density tends to be positively related to accident frequency, but severity tends to be lower for densely populated areas because accidents occur at slower speeds. There are more single-car

---

[16] This year was chosen since it shows the highest rates of limited tort election across Pennsylvania counties. This also controls for the effect of those who might initially have been reluctant to switch from limited to full tort. However, the analysis was also conducted using the first year of observations, as well as the average rate of limited tort election across the time period, as the dependent. Results are robust to these specifications of the dependent variable.

[17] Analysis shows that average liability loss costs and premiums are highly related, with a correlation coefficient of 91.68 percent. Note that the regression analysis was also performed using average liability costs rather than premium levels, with no significant differences in the results. Therefore, only the results of the analysis using premiums as the measure of insurance prices are discussed here.

accidents in rural areas, and these generally involve more serious injuries (see, e.g., Insurance Institute for Highway Safety, 2000).

The impact of population density on insurance prices will be reflected in premium difference across counties. However, there might be other differences in urban versus rural counties that influence the limited tort choice. For example, residents of small towns in rural areas might be less likely to sue in the event of an auto accident because of stronger community ties. Research has shown that the likelihood of filing a lawsuit to recover damages in an auto accident claim is significantly higher in urban areas, even after controlling for differences in accident severity (see, e.g., Miller, 1998). To control for these differences, a measure of traffic density is included in the analysis of limited tort choice. Traffic density, rather than population density, is used to reflect the fact that limited tort election is made only by those who own cars, rather than by the population as a whole. The ratio of car-years earned to county area is included to control for differences in traffic density across counties [*TRAFFIC DENSITY*].

The rate of unemployment in a county might also influence limited tort election. If unemployment creates an incentive to reduce costs, then it might be that limited tort choice is higher in counties with relatively higher rates of unemployment, all else being equal. Alternatively, it might be that the right to sue for non-economic costs under the tort system is more valuable when unemployment increases. There was considerable variation in the unemployment rate across Pennsylvania for the period of this analysis, ranging from 4.6 percent in Chester and Cumberland Counties to 12.4 percent in Huntingdon County. The unemployment rates published by the Pennsylvania Bureau of Labor Statistics are used to control for the variation in unemployment across counties [*UNEMPLOYMENT*].

Younger drivers tend to have more accidents than more experienced drivers,[18] and there is a wide range in the proportion of youthful population across the state. Younger drivers might experience lower severity per accident, because income losses might be lower, injuries less severe, autos driven less expensive, or time to recovery shorter. Therefore, the right to seek recovery for non-economic damages might be less valuable for younger drivers. Also, because premiums tend to be higher for younger drivers, the savings from limited tort election might outweigh the benefits of retaining suit rights. The proportion of the population between ages 18 and 24 is included in the analysis to control for this effect [*YOUNG*].

Similarly, accident frequency tends to be higher for male drivers. Accident statistics for Pennsylvania indicate that more male drivers were

[18] This is well documented. See, e.g., Insurance Institute for Highway Safety (2000).

involved in accidents than females in 1999, and this holds across all age categories, even after controlling for differences in miles driven (Pennsylvania State Data Center).[19] Male drivers are also involved in more fatal accidents than are females, and this is consistent across time (Fatality Facts, 2000). Therefore, the savings arising from limited tort election might be more valuable for male drivers. Moreover, recent research has shown that males are less risk-averse than females, both in making financial decisions (see, e.g., Bajtelsmit, 1999) and in making lifestyle choices (Hersch, 1999), and this might also influence limited tort election as compared to females. However, because males tend to have higher incomes as well as higher accident costs, the right to sue for non-economic damages might be relatively more valuable for male insureds. The proportion of the county population that is males is included to control for these effects [*MALE*].

Finally, the proportion of the population that drives to work is included as a control for driving intensity [*DRIVE*]. Those insureds who drive more might be more likely to choose to retain the right to sue if they believe the risk of loss increases with driving. Alternatively, insurance prices usually increase with miles driven, so relative price savings offered by limited tort coverage might be preferred.

Several additional variables are included in the analysis to capture the effect of interest groups on limited tort election. Meier (1988) notes that political institutions play a role in influencing legislative outcomes, and thus might have a role in influencing limited tort choice. Meier (1991) argues that Democratic politicians are more likely to pursue goals of fairness and social responsibility than are Republicans. Sugarman (1998) similarly argues that Democratic politicians are likely to support measures that protect individuals rather than corporations, and further argues that Democrats tend to be closely aligned with plaintiff attorney groups. Democratic voters might also be more likely than Republicans to align themselves with populist causes, and less trusting of insurance companies (Sugarman, 1998). Thus, we might expect Democrats to be less likely than Republicans to limit voluntarily their rights to sue, even after controlling for other factors.

However, the auto insurance reform bill in Pennsylvania was sponsored by a coalition of Republican and Democratic legislators, and had backing in both the House and the Senate. Lascher (1999) reports that the bill was strongly backed by then Governor Casey, a Democrat. To the extent that voters trusted the message sent by the bipartisan support of the law, this might have influenced Democrats to elect limited, rather than full tort. The influence of political affiliation is captured by including a variable equal to

---

[19] This can be found at <http://www.pasdc.hbg.psu.edu/pasdc/briefs/brief576.html>.

the ratio of Democrat to Republican votes in the county. Although voter registration by county was not available, the number of Democratic and Republican voters in the 1992 presidential election is used as a proxy for political affiliation [*DEMOCRAT*].

The insurance industry also might have an incentive to influence the choice of limited tort. Previous research has measured the strength of the insurance industry based on industry premium volume or market share (Harrington, 1994; Regan and Carroll, 1998). However, this type of data is not publicly available at the county level. To capture any influence the insurance industry might exert on limited tort election, the proportion of insurance sales agents in the county is included [*AGENT*]. Since sales agents are the primary contact with insureds, they might be better able to influence the selection of insurance policy options. A negative sign on the coefficient for this variable indicates that counties with relatively more insurance agents per capita have lower levels of limited tort election, all else being equal.

To measure the influence of attorneys on limited tort election, a variable equal to the proportion of lawyers employed in the county is included [*LAWYER*]. If attorneys successfully reduce limited tort election, the coefficient for this variable should be negative. A similar variable is included to control for any influence the medical community may exert on the choice of limited or full tort. This variable measures the proportion of people employed in health-care services in the county, rather than the number of doctors, to capture any effect of nurses, physicians' assistants, or health-care administrators, on the limited or full tort choice [*MEDICAL*].

Table 6 below shows the variable names and definitions, as well as the sources of the data used in this analysis.

Table 6
Variable Definitions

Variable	Definition (and Source)
CHOICE	Proportion of insureds electing limited tort auto insurance (Pennsylvania Insurance Department)
PRICE	Average premium for a model policy (Pennsylvania Insurance Department)
INCOME	Median Household Income (County and City Databooks, U.S .Census)
TRAFFIC DENSITY	Car years earned / area (IRC, *Trends in Auto Injury Claims*, 2000)
UNEMPLOYMENT	Proportion of unemployed working population (Pennsylvania Bureau of Labor Statistics)
YOUNG	Proportion of the population age 18-24 (County and City Databooks, U.S. Census)
MALE	Proportion of the population that is male (Pennsylvania Bureau of Labor Statistics)
DRIVE	Proportion of the population that drives to work (County and City Databooks, U.S. Census)
DEMOCRAT	Ratio of Democratic to Republican voters in the 1992 presidential election (<http://fisher.lib.virginia.edu/ccdb/>)
AGENT	Licensed insurance agents/population (Pennsylvania Bureau of Labor Statistics)
LAWYER	Attorneys/population (Pennsylvania Bureau of Labor Statistics)
MEDICAL	Proportion of the population employed in health-care services (County and City Databooks, U.S. Census)

4.2. Results

Two models of limited choice election across Pennsylvania counties are fit. If limited tort election is driven by cost considerations alone, then the inclusion of the measures used to capture the influence of interest groups should not improve the estimation results. To test this, Model 1 is estimated including only the economic and demographic variables, and Model 2 includes the full panel of explanatory variables. The summary statistics for the variables used in the sample are shown in Table 7.

Regression results are shown in Table 8. The results are generally consistent across models. The regression results strongly support the hypothesis that limited tort election is related to insurance prices. The coefficient for the price variable is positive and significant at the 1 percent level for both models, even after controlling for other factors. Thus, if insurance prices continue to increase, limited tort election should also increase, all else being equal.

Table 7
Summary Statistics

Variable	Mean	Standard Deviation	Minimum	Maximum
CHOICE	44.31	5.222	34	62
PRICE	951.54	253.48	754.56	2649.69
INCOME	31637	6718	23004	54770
TRAFFIC DENSITY	676.48	1294.5	20.869	7943.75
UNEMPLOYMENT	8.125	1.833	4.6	12.4
YOUNG	10.262	3.1	6.5	28.2
MALE	47.8	1.23	42.5	51.3
DRIVE	73.64	5.51	44.7	80.6
DEMOCRAT	1.032	0.522	0.425	3.26
AGENT	0.218	0.108	0	0.854
LAWYER	0.133	0.122	0	0.642
MEDICAL	1.247	0.634	0.393	5.634

The results also indicate that limited tort election is positively related to the proportion of males in the population, and to the rate of unemployment in the county. The coefficient for unemployment is positive and significant at the 10 percent level in Model 1. However, when the full panel of explanatory variables in included in Model 2, unemployment rate, while still positively related to limited tort election, is no longer a reliable determinant of limited tort election. Household income is also positively related to limited tort election. This is contrary to the notion that lower-income households value the savings from limited tort relatively more than higher-income households. Perhaps the potential benefits from a tort suit for even minor injuries outweighs the increased price of insurance for lower-income households. However, it might be that higher-income households would not find it worthwhile to sue for costs associated with minor injuries even in a tort system, perhaps because they have other sources of recovery, or because they are better able to bear the costs on their own. This supports the idea that those who would not sue in any case for minor injuries may elect to receive the benefits that accrue to the system as a result of their choices (Powers, 1992).

Traffic density is a significant determinant, but is negatively related to the limited tort choice, and this finding is consistent across models. As traffic density increases, the proportion of insureds choosing limited tort declines, even after controlling for insurance prices. This suggests that there is a greater preference for retaining the right to sue in urban areas as compared to rural areas. The proportion of people that drive to work is also a significant predictor of limited tort choice, but is inversely related. As the proportion of people driving to work increases, limited tort election declines. This seems counterintuitive, since insurance prices are adjusted upward as driving increases. Perhaps this indicates that people who drive relatively more perceive themselves to be at a higher risk for a minor accident. However, this area is beyond the scope of the present research.

The variables used to measure the influence of interest groups on limited tort choice do add to the explanatory power of the model. Model 1 explains approximately 51 percent of the variation in limited tort election across Pennsylvania counties, while including the political economy variables in Model 2 increases the explanatory power to 57.6 percent. This provides support for the theory that limited tort choice might be influenced by external factors. As expected, the coefficient for the variable that measures the potential influence of attorneys in the county is negative and statistically significant at the 7 percent level. This means that as the number of lawyers per capita increases, the rate of limited tort election declines, even after controlling for other factors that might influence choice, suggesting that lawyers can influence insureds to elect the full tort option.

Interestingly, the coefficient for the variable that measures political affiliation is also negative and significantly related to limited tort election. This indicates that Democrats are less likely than are Republicans to elect voluntarily to limit their rights to sue for non-economic costs associated with minor injuries in auto accidents. However, the variables that represent the influence of insurance agents and medical professionals are not significantly related to limited tort choice. Moreover, the signs on these variables are positive, rather than negative as expected. This finding does not support the theory. However, it might be that the data studied are not detailed enough to capture the expected effects. Alternatively, it might be the case that insurance agents and medical professionals have not suffered an income loss associated with the limited tort election, or instead, that they simply represent the best interests of their clients/patients.

Table 8
OLS Regression Estimates
Dependent Variable = Log-Odds Ratio of Limited Tort Election, 1996

	Model 1	**Model 2**
Explanatory Variable	**Coefficient (*t*-Statistic)**	**Coefficient (*t*-Statistic)**
PRICE	0.000354*** (2.744)	0.000592*** (4.172)
INCOME	2.057*** (4.695)	1.735*** (3.079)
TRAFFIC DENSITY	-0.0000828*** (-3.253)	-0.0000745** (-2.534)
UNEMPLOYMENT	0.256* (1.77)	0.1467 (0.975)
YOUNG	-0.00577 (-0.88)	-0.00366 (-0.566)
MALE	2.973* (1.695)	2.872* (1.715)
DRIVE	-0.0259*** (-5.215)	-0.02389*** (-3.979)
DEMOCRAT	*NA*	-0.1392** (-2.448)
AGENT	*NA*	0.3163 (1.132)
LAWYER	*NA*	-0.4954* (-1.841)
MEDICAL	*NA*	0.0018 (0.306)
Adjusted R^2	50.87%	57.57%

*Note: *** indicates statistical significance at the 1 percent level, ** at the 5 percent level, and * at the 10 percent level.*

5. CONCLUSION

On average, auto insurance premiums in Pennsylvania have fallen since *Act 6* was adopted. To the extent that limited tort election has contributed to this decline, the determinants of limited tort election are important for public policy. This chapter documents wide variations in auto insurance loss costs and prices across counties in Pennsylvania. Although the rate of limited tort election has increased across Pennsylvania since 1991, there are wide variations in the rate of limited tort election across the state as well. Moreover, the rate of limited tort election does not correspond precisely to price ranges across the state.

The regression estimation results indicate that limited tort election is positively related to insurance prices. That is, insureds in higher-cost counties are more likely to elect limited choice auto insurance. This suggests that price savings are important determinants of auto insurance purchases. However, other factors also play a role in the election of limited tort. For example, males are more likely than females to choose limited tort, and the limited tort election increases with household income. Insureds in areas with greater traffic density are less likely to choose limited tort, supporting the findings of prior research that liability suits arising out of auto accidents are much more frequent in urban that rural areas.

When variables are included to represent the ability of interest groups to influence limited tort election, the results indicate a positive and significant relationship between attorneys per capita and full tort auto insurance purchases. This is consistent with the notion that attorneys discourage the adoption of auto reforms that might reduce the volume of litigation, and further, that influence efforts of attorney groups may be effective even after the implementation of a law that is viewed as unfavorable to attorney interests.

The ratio of Democratic to Republican voters also is positively related to the purchase of full tort auto insurance, even after controlling for other factors such as price. This result is interesting, and suggests that Democrats might be less trusting of institutions such as insurance companies, and might value the option to have an attorney represent them, even for minor claims. However, further research is necessary before drawing a conclusion from the relationship found here.

No significant effect was found for insurance industry interest groups or medical groups. It might be that the data used are not sufficient to detect an effect if one exists. It might also be that insurance industry and medical professional groups are unsuccessful at influencing the insured's election of limited or full tort, or simply that such groups do not exert effort to influence the insured's decision.

References

Bajtelsmit, Vickie, 1999, Evidence of Risk Aversion in the Health and Retirement Study, paper presented at the Risk Theory Seminar, University of Minnesota.

Carroll, Anne, and Laureen Regan, 1998, Insurer Exposure to Extracontractual Liability under State Unfair Claims Settlement Practices Acts: An Empirical Analysis, *Journal of Insurance Regulation*, 1, 1-15.

Carroll, Stephen, Allan Abrahamse, and Mary Vaiana, 1995, *The Costs of Excess Medical Claims for Automobile Passenger Injuries*, Santa Monica, CA: RAND Corporation, Institute for Civil Justice.

Carroll, Stephen, and James Kakalik, 1993, No-Fault Approaches to Compensating Auto Accident Victims, *The Journal of Risk and Insurance*, 60, 265-287.

Cummins, J. David, and Sharon Tennyson, 1996, Moral Hazard in Insurance Claiming: Evidence from Automobile Insurance, *Journal of Risk and Uncertainty*, 12, 29-50.

Cummins, J. David, and Mary Weiss, 1991, The Effects of No-Fault on Automobile Insurance Loss Costs, *The Geneva Papers on Risk and Insurance*, 16, 20-38.

Detlefsen, Robert R., 1998, Escaping the Tort-Based Auto Accident System, *Journal of Insurance Regulation*, 17, 186-212.

Duggan, John F., 1993, Comment: The Use and Abuse of Peer Review Organizations in Pennsylvania: An Analysis of the Private Enterprise Peer Review System under the Motor Vehicle Financial Responsibility Law of 1990, *Dickinson Law Review*, 463.

Fisher, Mary Jane, 1997, Senators Propose "Auto-Choice" Reform Bill, *National Underwriter*, 101, 2.

Harrington, Scott E., 1994, State Decisions to Limit Tort Liability: An Empirical Analysis of No-Fault Automobile Insurance Laws, *The Journal of Risk and Insurance*, 61, 276-294.

Hersh, J., 1996, Smoking, Seat Belts and Other Risky Consumer Decisions: Differences by Gender and Race, *Managerial and Decision Economics*, 17, 471-481.

Insurance Institute for Highway Safety, 2000, *Fatality Facts*.

Johnson, Joseph E., George B. Flanigan, and Daniel T. Winkler, 1992, Cost Implications of No-Fault Automobile Insurance, *The Journal of Risk and Insurance*, 59, 116-123.

Keeton, Robert E., and Jeffrey O'Connell, 1965, *Basic Protection for the Traffic Victim: A Blueprint for Reforming Automobile Insurance*, Boston: Little, Brown, and Co.

Lascher, Edward L., Jr., 1999, *The Politics of Automobile Reform: Ideas, Institutions, and Public Policy in North America*, Washington, DC: Georgetown University Press.

Meier, Kenneth J., 1988, *The Political Economy of Regulation: The Case of Insurance*, Albany, NY: State University of New York Press.

Meier, Kenneth J., 1991, The Politics of Insurance Regulation, *The Journal of Risk and Insurance*, 58, 700-713.

Miller, Dan, 1998, *Auto Choice: Impact on Cities and the Poor*, Joint Economic Committee of the U.S. Congress.

Peltzman, Sam, 1976, Toward a More General Theory of Regulation, *Journal of Law and Economics*, 19, 276-294.

Powers, Michael R., 1989, *Automobile Insurance in Pennsylvania: Problems and Solutions*, internal report, Pennsylvania Insurance Department.

Powers, Michael R., 1992, Equity in Automobile Insurance: Optional No-Fault, *The Journal of Risk and Insurance*, 59, 203-220.

Schwartz, Gary T., 2000, Auto No-Fault and First-Party Insurance: Advantages and Problems, *Southern California Law Review*, 73, 611.

Smith, Eric, and Randall Wright, 1992, Why Is Automobile Insurance in Philadelphia so Damn Expensive?, *American Economic Review*, 82, 756-772.

Stigler, George J., 1971, The Theory of Economic Regulation, *Bell Journal of Economics*, 2, 3-21.

Sugarman, Stephen D., 1998, Quebec's Comprehensive Auto No-Fault Scheme and the Failure of Any of the United States to Follow, *Universite Laval, Les Cahiers de Droit*, 39, 303.

Weisberg, Herbert I., and Richard A. Derrig, 1992, Massachusetts Automobile Bodily Injury Tort Reform, *Journal of Insurance Regulation*, 10, 3, 384-440.

III. HISTORY AND POLITICS

8
GIVING MOTORISTS A CHOICE BETWEEN FAULT AND NO-FAULT INSURANCE[†]

Jeffrey O'Connell
University of Virginia

Robert H. Joost
U.S. Commodity Futures Trading Commission

Since insurance ranks right up there with photosynthesis on the ho-hum scale, the only way to muddle through this controversy is to inject a little drama into it. Don't think of auto insurance as auto insurance. Think of it as a prize fight. A real knock-down, drag-out marathon slugfest. In one corner is "Killer" Tort, the slow-footed, hard-punching veteran who represents the "you-smashed-into-my-car-and-now-I'm-going-to-sue-your-pants-off" old school of claims settlement. His opponent is "Kid" No-fault, a quick-moving young challenger who has never quite lived up to his potential. The "Kid" takes the gentlemanly approach to all accidents: Why get uptight about who's at fault? Let's just get the bills paid and the cars on the road.

Like any good fight this one has a lot riding on the outcome, namely the $2.5 billion annually spent on car insurance in the state. Given the stakes it's no wonder the pugs are being managed by a couple of hard-bitten pros. "Killer" Tort has New Jersey's legal establishment behind him, while "Kid" No-Fault is in the good hands of the insurance industry.

What makes this boxing match unique is that it's the spectators, not the fighters, who take the pounding. The Killer and The Kid trade jabs, but the consumer is the one getting bruised and bloodied . . . .

. . . [T]he good news from ringside is everybody agrees that, although auto rates are destined to be high, they don't have to be that high. The problem is that nobody agrees on how to ease the financial burden on

---

† This chapter originally appeared as a 1986 article published in the *Virginia Law Review* (72, 61-89), and is reprinted with permission.

motorists. Last February Joseph Tomeo, a 44-year-old millwright from Pennsville, organized a consumer group called New Jersey AIR (Automobile Insurance Reform) partly to find out why, as a married man with a perfect driving record, he is paying $1400 a year to insure two automobiles. "When you talk to a lawyer, he blames it on the insurance agent," says Tomeo, who uses his vacation days to lobby in Trenton. "When you talk to an insurance agent, he blames it on the lawyers. You talk to a legislator, he's either a lawyer or an insurance agent."[1]

The original proponents of no-fault auto insurance[2] promised that it would provide greater compensation to accident victims at the same or lower cost than traditional tort-based liability insurance. Almost half the states accepted that promise and have used some form of no-fault auto insurance for over ten years. The performance of no-fault insurance in those states has been mixed, partially vindicating the claims of its original supporters, yet also displaying some unforeseen problems. No-fault insurance compensates more accident victims[3] more expediently[4] and with lower transaction costs[5] than traditional liability insurance. The cost of no-fault insurance in some states, however, has been unexpectedly high. Traditional tort-based liability insurance also continues to have the problems that led to no-fault reforms, including high administrative costs and inadequate compensation to seriously injured accident victims.

Presently, motorists in any given state cannot choose between no-fault and traditional liability insurance. The structure of current traditional and no-fault insurance schemes prevents both systems from existing in pure form within one state. Currently, states use either an exclusive system of traditional liability insurance or a system of no-fault insurance plus liability coverage.

No-fault auto insurance is a very controversial political issue that generates considerable public debate and lobbying by special interest groups. The result of this pressure in many states has been the enactment of hybrid

---

[1] Dunkel, Battle for the Bucks, New Jersey Monthly, Nov. 1984, at 76.

[2] All discussion of no-fault insurance in this article, including the suggested reforms, concerns only bodily injury claims and not property damage claims. Only one state, Michigan, applies no-fault insurance to property damage. U.S. Dep't of Transp., Compensating Auto Accident Victims: A Follow-Up Report on No-Fault Auto Insurance Experiences 18 (1985) [hereinafter cited as DOT Report]. Therefore, property damage claims, even after adoption of the reforms urged in this article, would still be governed under traditional tort liability and current property damage coverages.

[3] Id. at 3.

[4] Id. at 4.

[5] Id.

insurance schemes that essentially graft no-fault benefits on top of an existing traditional liability system, without sufficiently reducing the scope of the traditional system. Although these statutes may be politically expedient, they have not always served the public well.

As an alternative to the concept of an exclusive state auto insurance system, this article proposes a new scheme that allows motorists a choice between purchasing no-fault and traditional insurance. This simple innovation would be easy to implement and would provide significant advantages over existing no-fault and traditional insurance schemes. Part 1 of this article compares the performance of traditional and no-fault insurance schemes in recent years. Part 2 describes the proposed system in which motorists would have the option to select either traditional liability or no-fault insurance.

1. COMPARING THE PERFORMANCE OF NO-FAULT AND TRADITIONAL AUTO INSURANCE

1.1. In-Balance and Out-of-Balance No-Fault States

No-fault auto insurance compensates policyholders for personal injuries suffered in an auto accident irrespective of who caused the accident. In contrast, tort or traditional auto insurance compensates only accident victims who prove that a policyholder was at fault. In the usage of this article, a no-fault state is one that requires that all motorists be offered or purchase a prescribed amount of no-fault auto insurance. A traditional state is one that does not require the sale or purchase of no-fault insurance and instead relies exclusively on a tort-based liability insurance system.

As seen in a recent U.S. Department of Transportation (DOT) study, no-fault states are usefully divided into two groups: "no-lawsuit" no-fault states and "add-on" no-fault states.[6] No-lawsuit no-fault states have legal restrictions that often bar accident victims from bringing a lawsuit in tort against the person who allegedly caused the accident.[7] The rationale for barring such suits is that they are unnecessary if victims are guaranteed no-

[6] Id. at 21. The DOT report presents a comprehensive comparison of traditional and no-fault insurance and an exhaustive survey of the different jurisdictions' no-fault schemes. It generally concludes that no-fault insurance is more effective than traditional insurance, although existing no-fault systems do have some problems. See id. at 3-6. The DOT report's release attracted scant media attention, but the authors recommend it highly for anyone interested in this area.

[7] Id. at 23-24.

fault benefits. (The term "no-lawsuit" is somewhat misleading because these states do allow lawsuits in limited circumstances.[8]) In contrast, add-on no-fault states provide accident victims with both the traditional right to sue the wrongdoer and some no-fault insurance benefits. The right to receive no-fault benefits in an add-on state supplements, rather than replaces, the traditional right to claim in tort.[9]

A good no-fault law should strike a balance between the amount of no-fault benefits paid to victims and the degree of restriction on tort lawsuits and tort damage payments. To provide generous no-fault benefits at a reasonable cost, states must restrict victims' rights to recover in tort. If no-fault is simply grafted on top of an existing tort liability system, the result will be higher insurance premiums because the savings from reduced tort litigation will not be sufficient to finance the new no-fault benefits without a premium increase. Following the terminology of the DOT report, an "out-of-balance" no-fault law results in higher insurance premiums because the total no-fault benefit payments exceed the reduction in tort liability payments.[10] In contrast, an "in-balance" no-fault law[11] causes no increase in insurance

---

[8] Id. at 1.

[9] Id. at 1-2. The average amount of no-fault benefits available per victim in an add-on state is significantly less than the amount of no-fault benefits available in a no-lawsuit state, as the following chart indicates.

Add-On States		No-Lawsuit States	
Arkansas	$15,920	Colorado	$129,925
Delaware	$10,000	Connecticut	$5,000
Maryland	$2,500	D.C.	$124,000
Oregon	$20,570	Florida	$10,000
Pennsylvania	$15,000	Georgia	$5,000
South Carolina	$1,000	Hawaii	$15,000
Texas	$2,500	Kansas	$16,180
Washington	$24,380	Kentucky	$10,000
		Massachusetts	$2,000
		Michigan	Unlimited
		Minnesota	$30,000
		New Jersey	Unlimited
		New York	$50,000
		North Dakota	$15,000
		Puerto Rico	Unlimited
		Utah	$14,180
Average	$11,484	Average	$120,393

This chart was prepared from state-by-state data in id. at 25-49. To calculate the average, unlimited no-fault benefits were arbitrarily valued at $500,000.

[10] Id. at 86.

[11] Id.

premiums (adjusted for inflation) because the no-fault benefit payments approximately equal the concomitant reduction in tort liability payments.[12]

Michigan, for example, has an "in-balance" no-fault law. The Michigan statute provides for the payment of substantial no-fault benefits: unlimited medical and rehabilitation expenses plus compensation for lost wages of up to $29,000 annually for three years.[13] Michigan victims or their

---

[12] The following chart, which is reprinted from the DOT report, is based on a chart in a research paper prepared by the Alliance of American Insurers. The Alliance computed the average personal injury pure premium in 1982 in 18 states that have had no-fault insurance laws for many years. It then projected what the pure premium rates would have been in those 18 states if no-fault laws had never been enacted. The Alliance compared the difference between actual (with no-fault rates) and the likely (without no-fault) rates for the 18 states and found enormous differences. A "+" mark in the chart means that premiums were *higher* by the amount shown than they would have been if no-fault had never become law. A "-" mark means that premiums in 1982 were lower by the amount shown than they would have been without no-fault. No-lawsuit states with "+" marks in the right-hand column have "out-of-balance" no-fault laws, and states with "-" marks in the right-hand column have "in-balance" no-fault laws.

Change in Personal Injury Insurance Costs Resulting from No-Fault	
Verbal Threshold Only	
Florida	-21%
Michigan	-17%
New York	-6%
Dollar Threshold of $1,000 or More	
Hawaii	+37%
Minnesota	-2%
Kentucky	-29%
North Dakota	-19%
Dollar Threshold of Less than $1,000	
Pennsylvania (repealed as of 10/01/84)	+53%
Colorado (threshold raised to $2,500 in 1/85)	+15%
Georgia	+15%
Kansas	-9%
Massachusetts	-33%
Utah	-13%
Connecticut	+14%
New Jersey	+65%
No-Threshold	
Oregon	-8%
Delaware	+17%
Maryland	+26%

Id. at 87, 96.

[13] See Mich. Comp. Laws Ann. § 500.3107 (West 1983 & Supp. 1985). The statute ties the limit on no-fault benefits to the rate of inflation. Id. See generally Mich. Comp. Laws

estates can recover tort damages, however, only for death, permanent disfigurement, or serious impairment of bodily function.[14] This limitation has reduced tort recoveries by an amount approximately equal to the total payments of no-fault benefits. Accordingly, insurance premiums have remained steady. Michigan's average auto insurance premium rose from $93.60 in 1976 to $153.72 in 1983, a rate of growth roughly equivalent to the increase from $110.16 to $166.43 in the average traditional fault-based insurance state.[15]

Pennsylvania (before a 1984 repeal of its no-fault law) and New Jersey are examples of "out-of-balance" states. Pennsylvania's former no-fault law granted victims unlimited medical and rehabilitation benefits plus wage-loss benefits up to $5,000. At the same time, victims could pursue tort claims if medical losses exceeded a mere $750.[16] Because the $750 restriction was easily met, too many accident victims brought suits for damages in tort while simultaneously receiving benefits under the no-fault coverage. This "double-dipping" resulted in insurance premiums in Pennsylvania rising about twenty percent per year after 1975, the year no-fault was enacted.[17] After years of unsuccessfully struggling to bring Pennsylvania's law into balance—with effective opposition by tenacious and well-financed trial lawyers—the Pennsylvania legislature, in 1984, eliminated restrictions on lawsuits, lowered no-fault benefits, and made Pennsylvania an add-on state.[18]

New Jersey's problems—as the excerpt at the beginning of this article illustrates—have been even worse. Despite unlimited no-fault medical and rehabilitation benefits plus no-fault wage-loss benefits of $5,200, a traffic victim could claim in tort if medical expenses exceeded only $200.[19] The New Jersey trial bar also long resisted efforts to bring the law into balance, but finally, in 1983, the law was amended. The statute now establishes no-lawsuit coverage with deductibles of $500, $1,000, or $2,500 for medical

---

Ann. §§ 3101-3179 (West 1983 & Supp. 1985) (Michigan Motor Vehicle Personal and Property Protection Act). For a summary of Michigan's no-fault law, see DOT Report, supra note 2, at 34.

[14] Mich. Comp. Laws Ann. § 500.3135 (West 1983).

[15] DOT Report, supra note 2, at 68-69.

[16] Pennsylvania No-Fault Motor Vehicle Insurance Act, Pa Stat. Ann. tit. 40, § 1009.101.701 (Purdon Supp. 1985) (repealed 1984). For a summary of the repealed statute, see DOT Report, supra note 2, at 46. The legislature never revised the $750 threshold despite the high inflation of 1976-1984. Id. at 72.

[17] What Ever Happened to No-Fault? 49 Consumer Rep. 511, 512 (1984).

[18] See Pa. Stat. Ann. tit. 40, §§ 1701-1798 (Purdon Supp. 1985). For a summary of Pennsylvania's new law, see DOT Report, supra note 2, at 46.

[19] See N.J. Stat. Ann. 5 39:6A-8 (West 1973) (amended 1983). For the current version of the New Jersey Automobile Reform Act, see N.J. Stat. Ann. §§ 39:6A-1 to 39:6A-35 (West Supp. 1985).

expenses and gives policyholders a choice of medical expense tort thresholds of $200 or $1,500.[20]

The new threshold choice device was intended to save New Jersey motorists money on their auto insurance. A higher threshold means that fewer accident victims can bring lawsuits in tort. Reducing the number of lawsuits decreases the total amount of tort damage payments, which results in cost savings and possibly lower premiums. Under New Jersey's new system, however, the cost savings do not accrue to the motorist who purchases the higher threshold insurance. Instead, they accrue to the person who was at fault in causing the accident. The higher threshold simply reduces the chances of recovering in tort against the person at fault, which saves money for his insurer but not for the insurer of the motorist who purchased the higher threshold policy. To avoid this problem, the New Jersey law sets up a cumbersome "risk exchange" to reallocate the money saved by the motorist at fault back to the motorist who selects the higher threshold,[21] but the device is expensive and inefficient. Consequently, the New Jersey no-lawsuit law will continue to be seriously out of balance until further amendment is made.

1.2. Evaluating the Performance of No-Fault Insurance

The DOT study contains some useful statistics that compare, in no-fault and traditional states, the cost of insurance and the amount of payments to victims. These statistics generally show that payments to accident victims in recent years have increased at a greater rate in no-fault states than in traditional states. The cost of auto insurance also has increased at a greater rate in no-fault states, especially in out-of-balance states. As explained below, both recoveries and the cost of no-fault insurance are high because in many no-fault states accident victims frequently can recover tort damages in addition to no-fault benefits.

In particular, the DOT study shows that during 1976 and 1983, accident victims in the average no-lawsuit state received more compensation through no-fault benefits and bodily injury (BI) liability payments than victims in the average traditional state received in liability payments.[22] More

[20] See N.J. Stat. Ann. §§ 39:6A-4.3, 39:6A-8 (West Supp. 1985). For a summary of New Jersey's no-fault law, see DOT Report, supra note 2, at 36.

[21] Pub. Relations Dep't, State Farm Ins. Cos., No-Fault Press Reference Manual: A Continuously Updated Informational Service on Car Insurance Reform, at N.J. 100-21, 200 (Jan. 1984).

[22] DOT Report, supra note 2, at 91.

importantly, however, the differential between the two systems increased significantly between 1976 and 1983. In 1976, the total payout per 100 insured cars was 54 percent greater in the average no-lawsuit state than in the average traditional state; in 1983, that differential rose to 79 percent.[23]

The DOT study also found that, over the same time period, the payments grew more rapidly in out-of-balance states than in in-balance states. From 1976 to 1983, the total payout of no-fault benefits plus liability payments per 100 cars increased 77 percent in in-balance states, as compared to 149 percent in out-of-balance states.[24] Total liability payments in the average traditional state increased 67 percent during the same time period.[25] Significantly, the BI liability payments to auto accident victims, per 100 insured cars, rose at a somewhat higher rate between 1976 and 1983 in in-balance no-fault states than in traditional states—77 percent versus 67 percent—but it grew more than twice as much in out-of-balance states than in traditional states—150 percent versus 67 percent.[26]

These findings are by no means all bad. A key purpose of auto insurance is to compensate accident victims, and increased payouts mean greater compensation. No-fault's prime virtue, originally claimed and now substantiated, is the increased compensation for traffic victims. Because no-fault makes many persons eligible for benefits who are ineligible under traditional insurance, for example one-car accident victims, the total payout under no-fault insurance is greater than under traditional systems.

Nevertheless, significant increases in payouts to victims, especially in the out-of-balance states, indicate that the cost of auto insurance also may have dramatically increased. The trade-off, implicitly promised more than a decade ago by advocates of no-fault insurance, was that consumers would pay no more for no-fault auto insurance than for traditional insurance because reductions in tort liability recoveries, including recoveries for pain

[23] In 1976, the total payout per 100 insured cars in the average traditional state was $2,897, while the total payout in the average no-lawsuit no-fault state was $4,455. In 1983, the comparable figures were $4,843 for the average traditional state and $8,679 for the average no-lawsuit no-fault state. Id.

[24] Id. at 90.

[25] Id.

[26] Id. at 90-91. BI liability payments might be expected to increase faster in add-on states than in traditional, in-balance, or out-of-balance states. In fact, BI liability payments per 100 insured cars in add-on states increased from $2,769 in 1976 to $5,055 in 1983, a change of 83 percent. Id. at 91. This rate of increase was greater than the rate of increase of traditional and in-balance states, but interestingly, it was less than the rate of increase for out-of-balance states. This result might be explained by three factors: (1) add-on states generally are not as populous as out-of-balance states; (2) add-on states are not as aggressively litigious as out-of-balance states; and (3) add-on states generally pay lower no-fault benefits, thus fewer benefits subsidize tort claims. See infra text accompanying note 31.

and suffering, would finance the payment of no-fault benefits. This trade-off was never made, unfortunately, in out-of-balance states. The significant increase in costs in the out-of-balance states is disturbing, as the following charts[27] indicate:

Comparison of 1976 and 1983 Average Premium			
Type of State	**1976**	**1983**	**% Increase**
Out-of-Balance No-Fault	$123.70	$279.85	126%
In-Balance No-Fault	$117.64	$181.35	54%
Traditional	$110.16	$165.43	50%

Comparison of Average Premium Charged by a Leading Auto Insurer	
Type of State	**% Change from 1977 to 1983**
Out-of-Balance No-Fault	+ 73.3%
In-Balance No-Fault	+ 38.7%
Traditional	+ 35.3%

These comparative premium figures raise the following questions. Why have premiums increased so dramatically in out-of-balance states? Why has the rate of growth of all personal injury payments increased faster in no-fault states than in traditional states? Why has the rate of growth of total payments been higher in out-of-balance states than in in-balance states? Why has the rate of growth in BI liability payments been higher in no-fault states than in traditional states, and especially higher in out-of-balance no-fault states?

The answer to these questions, as suggested earlier, is related to the overlap between no-fault benefits and traditional tort recoveries. All no-fault states, including no-lawsuit states in certain circumstances, allow traffic victims to sue in tort in addition to collecting no-fault benefits. Permitting both types of recoveries has several effects.

First, in the out-of-balance states, double recovery raises the average victim's total compensation, thereby also increasing insurance costs. Second, no-fault thresholds arguably encourage victims to inflate their claims to exceed the threshold for bringing a lawsuit.[28] Moreover, the more medical

---

[27] The charts in the text are excerpted from charts in DOT Report, supra note 2, at 68, 70.

[28] See U.S. Dep't of Transp., State No-Fault Automobile Insurance Experience: 1971-1977, at 77 (1977); O'Connell, Operation of No-Fault Auto Laws: A Survey of the Surveys, 56 Neb. L. Rev. 23, 33 (1977). But see I. Rolph, J. Hammitt, R. Houchens & S. Polin,

expenses and wage losses victims accumulate, within limits, the more they can recover in tort for both economic and non-economic losses (compensation for pain and suffering is often a multiple of economic loss). Permitting victims to profit from additional trips to the doctor or from staying away from work increases both no-fault and tort liability insurance rates. Such inflated claims violate insurance's basic principle of indemnity, which decrees that the "value of insurance benefits [should] not exceed the loss to the insurance beneficiary."[29]

Third, no-fault payments would seem to subsidize BI liability claims analogous to the way that workers' compensation benefits subsidize victims of industrial accidents who are permitted to bring product liability lawsuits against third parties. A workers' compensation recipient pursuing a third-party tort claim is a much more aggressive claimant than a claimant whose basic losses have not already been compensated. Because workers' compensation recipients are assured of compensation for their basic losses, they are better able to hold out against unsatisfactory settlement offers than impecunious injury victims who have mounting bills to pay and accumulating wage losses.[30]

Automobile Accident Compensation: Who Pays How Much How Soon? 19, 30 (1985) (a RAND Corporation report) [hereinafter cited as Automobile Accident Compensation]; Hammitt & Rolph, Limiting Liability for Automobile Accidents: Are No-Fault Tort Thresholds Effective?, 7 Law & Pol'y 493, 503-04 (1985); Rolph, Hammitt & Houchens, Automobile Accident Compensation: Who Pays How Much How Soon?, 52 J. Risk & Ins. 667 (1985).

The explanation for the conclusion that insureds do not "pad" claims is the absence of a disproportionate distribution of medical losses above the tort thresholds. See Hammitt & Rolph, supra, at 503-04. The RAND study does not consider using collateral sources to increase the size of the BI liability claim once the threshold is exceeded. For a discussion of this phenomenon, termed "post accident inflation" of claims, see O'Connell, A Proposal to Abolish Defendants' Payment for Pain and Suffering in Return for Payment of Claimants' Attorneys' Fees, 1981 U. Ill. L. F. 333, 334-39 [hereinafter cited as O'Connell, A Proposal].

The RAND study is based on states with modest medical expense thresholds. In such states, claimants may refrain from padding because it is unnecessary and because they already may be able to recover two or three times for the same medical expenses (once from no-fault auto insurance and once from medical payment insurance). As thresholds become higher and larger amounts of no-fault benefits become available, padding is encouraged. The RAND study is careful to state that "[although] our estimates suggest tort thresholds have a large effect on limiting the number of accident victims who are able to collect from BI [liability] insurance . . . the more serious claims are not excluded by tort thresholds; hence the effect on total payments is much less." Automobile Accident Compensation, supra, at 20.

[29] O'Connell, A Proposal, supra note 28, at 344; see id. at 344-48 for a discussion of this principle.

[30] Plaintiffs' attorneys have defended their aggressive pursuit of third-party tort liability by arguing, with some merit, that workers' compensation benefits are inadequate. See J. O'Connell, The Lawsuit Lottery: Only the Lawyers Win 216 (1979). But query if tort

Similarly, a traffic victim who receives no-fault compensation for much or most of his economic losses, yet is also permitted to pursue a tort liability claim, does not have the same incentive to settle the claim or to compromise demands for non-economic damages as do victims in a traditional state. The auto accident victim in a no-fault state has greater bargaining power than the victim in a traditional state because his basic needs (medical bills and compensation for lost wages) have already been met. That greater bargaining power probably enables the average victim in a no-fault state to win a larger liability settlement than a victim with the same claim in a traditional state. The no-fault payee's stronger bargaining position also helps explain why the average total amount of BI liability damages per victim is larger in a no-fault state than in a traditional state.[31] Ironically, no-fault laws apparently have turned out to benefit their fiercest opponents, the trial lawyers, because the laws enable plaintiffs to recover larger tort claims.[32]

In summary, allowing accident victims to sue in tort and receive no-fault benefits often increases insurance costs, encourages inflation of claims, and subsidizes tort liability claims. Consequently, personal injury payments, including tort liability payments, have grown at a greater rate in no-fault states than in traditional states. Unfortunately for the consumer, however, tacking no-fault benefits onto traditional systems also has caused insurance premiums to increase dramatically in many states.

1.3. Controlling No-Fault Insurance Costs

As demonstrated above, allowing claimants simultaneously to sue in tort and to receive no-fault benefits has caused a precipitous rise in insurance rates in many no-fault states. The challenge today is to reduce these costs with the least possible impact on the availability of benefits for accident victims. Data suggest that the cost of personal injury auto insurance in in-balance, and even in out-of-balance, no-lawsuit no-fault states disproportionately reflects the costs of liability coverage, not the costs of no-

claims are an optimal way for society to supplement inadequate workers' compensation benefits.

[31] See DOT Report, supra note 2, at 88-89. Another explanatory factor is that tort thresholds in no-fault states eliminate smaller bodily injury liability claims, making the average amount of damages larger.

[32] Health insurance generally, and later Medicare and Medicaid, turned out to be a financial boon to health-care providers, who initially bitterly opposed them. Significantly, reactive steps are now being taken to control resulting increases in health-care costs, just as steps should also be taken to control resulting increases in no-fault/tort costs.

fault coverage.[33] Therefore, cutting the cost of liability insurance has greater potential for reducing total insurance costs. Furthermore, no-fault insurance provides greater insurance coverage to motorists at less cost than traditional insurance. Consequently, the key to controlling the cost of insurance in no-fault states is to reduce the cost of the BI liability component.

Data from New Jersey, an out-of-balance state, and New York, an in-balance state, illustrate that no-fault insurance provides greater insurance protection at less cost than traditional insurance. New Jersey's no-fault insurance pays unlimited medical and rehabilitation expenses plus up to $5,200 in lost wages and up to $4,380 for the cost of providing essential services formerly performed by the injured victim.[34] In 1983, the average premium for these generous benefits was $82.[35] As for the BI liability component of New Jersey's insurance, the required liability insurance limits are $15,000 per person and $30,000 per accident, which are clearly lower than the no-fault benefits.[36] The cost of the average liability insurance in 1983, however, was $175, or more than twice as much as the more generous no-fault benefits.[37]

New York's experience illustrates that even in in-balance states, liability insurance is disproportionately expensive compared to no-fault insurance. New York's no-fault insurance pays medical expenses and wage losses up to a combined total of $50,000.[38] In contrast, the limits on the required tort liability insurance are $10,000 per person and $20,000 per accident.[39] In 1983, the average no-fault premium was $46, while the average BI liability premium was $118.[40] In other words, no-fault insurance costs less than half as much as BI liability insurance, but the no-fault coverage automatically pays benefits up to $50,000 per injured person while the liability coverage pays much less and only upon proof of fault.

A similar situation exists in all other no-lawsuit no-fault states. The premium for required no-fault insurance guarantees higher benefits for

---

33 DOT Report, supra note 2, at 4.

34 Id. at 36. The figures cited here and below concern the average premium paid for BI liability coverage in the state. This average includes persons who buy more than the minimum coverage required by law. In more populous states, about 10 percent of the motorists purchase only the minimum liability coverage, whereas the figure for more rural states is about 30 percent. The nationwide average is approximately 15 percent. Telephone interview with Mavis Walters, Vice President of the Insurance Services Office (Jan. 9, 1986).

35 DOT Report, supra note 2, at 4.

36 Id.

37 Id.

38 See N.Y. Ins. Law § 5102(a) (McKinney 1985).

39 DOT Report, supra note 2, at 37.

40 Id. See generally N.Y. Ins. Law §§ 5101-5108 (McKinney 1985) (Comprehensive Motor Vehicle Insurance Reparations Act).

accident victims than the required "residual" liability insurance. The relative cost of the no-fault component would seem much less, however, than the cost of the liability component.[41]

1.4. Controlling Total Auto Insurance Costs

Following the example of workers' compensation insurance laws is the most ambitious way to end the escalation of auto insurance costs. This approach would provide unlimited,[42] or at least very high, no-fault benefits and eliminate tort claims entirely. The experience of New Jersey and New York illustrate the financial feasibility of such a step. In 1983, the average premium in New Jersey for BI liability coverage, sometimes with relatively

---

[41] See DOT Report, supra note 2, at 25-40.

[42] Workers' compensation medical benefits normally are unlimited in amount, 2 A. Larson, The Law of Workmen's Compensation § 61.11 (1983), and wage loss benefits, while having an internal cap of $300 per week, for example, are often unlimited in duration. 4 A. Larson, supra, App. B, Table 8. Insurers, however, stoutly resist unlimited exposure in other areas such as no-fault auto insurance. Nevertheless, a 1978 Michigan Insurance Bureau Report found that the cost of providing unlimited no-fault benefits was nominal:

> A $100,000 ceiling [on Michigan's no-fault medical benefits, as opposed to the unlimited benefits provided under the law] since the inception of no-fault would have saved only about $6 per car per year, based on claim reserves of the state's six largest insurers. One large insurer estimates the cost of paying claims in excess of $100,000 as no more than the cost of insuring against the theft of CB radios. Providing protection against the catastrophic loss represents the essence of insurance. To attempt to place the burden of catastrophic losses on the individuals suffering the loss, when its average cost is only a few dollars, is inconsistent with the provision of insurance.

Ins. Bureau, Mich. Dep't of Commerce, No-Fault Insurance in Michigan: Consumer Attitudes and Performance 76 (1978).

On the other hand, a 1977 study of no-fault insurance by the U.S. Department of Transportation addresses actuarial confusions and hesitations over the determination of the cost of no-fault systems:

> [T]he "cost" of the product that the insurance company sells is, from its perspective, not finally determinable until every claim arising in a given period is paid. Many claims, . . . especially those involving serious injuries, may not be finally settled for years or even decades . . . . Insurance companies attempt to deal with this uncertainty by establishing loss reserves, i.e., estimated set asides of funds in amounts they believe may be needed to meet the future loss costs of a claimant as the losses develop over time. While insurance actuaries have a number of sophisticated analytical tools to help them establish these loss reserves, judgment does play a large role. In the case of a relatively unfamiliar situation such as no-fault, judgment becomes particularly important in determining this perception of "cost", especially from the viewpoint of the insurance industry.

U.S. Dep't of Transp., supra note 28, at 64; see DOT Report, supra note 2, at 125-28. See also infra note 55 and accompanying text.

low limits and always contingent on proof of tort liability, was $175, compared to $82 for no-fault coverage providing very high benefits.[43] Prohibiting all lawsuits in tort, without increasing the amount of the no-fault benefits, would save each New Jersey motorist much of his annual BI liability insurance premium. Shifting to pure no-lawsuit no-fault in New Jersey could thus save each motorist well over $100 per year per car! In 1983, the average premium in New York for relatively limited BI liability coverage was $118.[44] Prohibiting lawsuits altogether would permit New York to finance an increase in its no-fault benefits out of only a portion of the $118 that motorists now spend on BI liability insurance.

Similar cost savings and compensation increases are possible in all other no-lawsuit states.[45] Limits on no-fault benefits could be removed or raised, with the elimination of tort liability insurance paying for this increased no-fault coverage. Motorists' total personal injury premiums would not increase, yet accident victims would obtain greater coverage. This analysis illustrates that Pennsylvania, in changing its auto insurance law, got it exactly wrong. Instead of eliminating the requirement of no-fault coverage and retaining the requirement of liability coverage, it should have done the opposite. Nevertheless, switching to a purely no-fault system, with a concomitant abandonment of common-law liability, would raise serious political controversies.

The one group that stands to lose from enactment of a workable no-lawsuit no-fault law—the trial lawyers—is overrepresented in state legislatures.[46] Trial lawyers often excoriate no-fault insurance by arguing that it abrogates the "right to sue," a right that they claim the average citizen cherishes.[47] The casualty insurance companies might well oppose no-fault because the complete elimination of liability could expose them to "invasion" of their market by life and health insurance companies, who stay out of the casualty market today because they lack experience in handling liability claims. In addition, some motorists may prefer a traditional system because it gives victims a chance of winning a very large recovery.

---

[43] DOT Report, supra note 2, at 36.

[44] Id. at 37.

[45] See supra note 41 and accompanying text.

[46] On the political clout of the trial bar, see J. O'Connell, The Lawsuit Lottery 158-59 (1979).

[47] For a summary of empirical evidence that most motorists are risk averse and thus are likely to prefer prompt, certain payment to the uncertainties of the tort system, see O'Connell & Beck, Overcoming Legal Barriers to the Transfer of Third-Party Tort Claims as a Means of Financing First-Party No-Fault Insurance, 1980 Wash. U.L.Q. 55, 59-60.

2. A PROPOSAL FOR REFORM

2.1. Allowing Motorists to Choose between No-Fault and Traditional Insurance

Opponents of no-fault auto insurance insist that traditional liability is consistent with, and supported by, the public's perception of simple justice. Supporters of no-fault, on the other hand, point out that compensating accident victims by traditional liability insurance grossly disserves the public. Political pressures have prevented any state legislature, even in no-lawsuit states, from completely abandoning common-law liability in favor of no-fault.[48] Instead, many legislatures have simply created additional problems by enacting poorly designed compromise statutes that increase costs as well as benefits.

With such a deep division of opinion, it makes sense to eschew the zero-sum game of a legislative mandate of either no-fault or traditional insurance for all citizens. Why not allow individual motorists to select the kind of insurance they want? Why not let the consumer decide?

Removing this decision from the politicians and giving it to individual motorists is sensible. Individual motorists should have the same right to choose, in a free-enterprise economy, whether they want traditional or no-fault protection, as they now have to choose whether they want an automatic or a manual transmission in their automobile. Allowing individual choice between insurance systems would satisfy motorists who prefer the traditional liability system as well as those who believe that no-fault offers a superior method of claims resolution. The most practical and politically acceptable method of eliminating no-fault's problems while respecting the preferences of advocates of traditional insurance is to operate both systems, giving consumers the choice.

In addition to increasing the consumers' alternatives, a system providing individual choice would allow the no-fault and traditional systems to compete in the marketplace. If all producers in a particular field are required, by law, custom, or technological limitation, to make or offer the same product or service, the resulting monopolistic situation leads to higher prices, lower quality, and less innovation. Consumers have no way to reward efficient producers who offer better products or services for lower prices, or to punish by rejection products or services that they find less desirable or more expensive. This absence of marketplace control in a monopoly-product

48 See DOT Report, supra note 2, at 1 (stating that each no-lawsuit state sometimes allows lawsuits).

situation eventually makes all the producers—and the resultant product—less efficient. Open competition between no-fault and traditional insurance may reveal that no-fault is superior, or that traditional insurance is superior, or that one is better for some, but not all, motorists. In any event, the competitive pressures of giving motorists a choice should improve the performance of both systems, and consumers would benefit.

2.2. Designing an Insurance System to Allow Consumer Choice

Motorists today do not have a choice between fault and no-fault auto insurance. The motorist in a traditional state cannot purchase no-fault auto insurance.[49] The motorist in a no-lawsuit no-fault state (other than Kentucky[50]) cannot reject no-fault benefits or lawsuit restrictions in favor of traditional insurance, nor can he increase the limits of his lawsuit immunity. And the motorist in an add-on no-fault state cannot opt for restrictions on lawsuits.

Choice is unavailable today because a workable system has not yet been developed to accommodate the simultaneous use of both kinds of auto insurance in a single state. To illustrate the problem with permitting choice, consider the impact of the possible combinations of insurance coverage in a two-car collision if a state offered fault and no-lawsuit no-fault insurance:

(1) both vehicles could be covered by no-lawsuit no-fault insurance;

(2) both vehicles could be covered by traditional liability insurance; or

---

[49] According to the Department of Transportation:

> All motorists in all States have some power of choice regarding auto insurance. Each motorist, for example, has the power to choose whether to buy a bodily injury liability insurance policy that has as its limits the State's financial responsibility or compulsory minimum or some higher amount; whether to buy . . . medical payments insurance and, if so, in what amount . . . .
>
> Although important, these choices are all supplemental rather than basic. Under the law today motorists do not have the right to make basic choices regarding auto insurance, such as:
>
> (1) What kind of auto insurance do you wish to buy (no-lawsuit, add-on, or traditional)?
>
> (2) Do you wish to reject a particular kind of auto insurance that State law or industry practice favors?

Id. at 121.

[50] See Ky. Rev. Stat. § 304.39-060 (Supp. 1984). See generally Ky. Rev. Stat. §§ 304.39010 to 304.39-340 (1981 & Supp. 1984) (Motor Vehicle Reparations Act). For a summary of Kentucky no-fault law, see DOT Report, supra note 2, at 32.

(3) one vehicle could be covered by no-lawsuit insurance and the other by traditional insurance.

Resolving claims and transferring accident losses is easy for the first two coverage combinations. If two no-lawsuit insureds collide, they would recover under their respective no-fault policies without bringing a lawsuit. If two traditional insureds collide, they would recover as they do in traditional states today. Resolving claims and transferring losses is problematic for the third combination, a collision between a no-lawsuit insured and a traditional insured. The no-lawsuit motorist would recover under his no-fault policy, but the traditional insured who was not at fault in causing the accident would not recover unless he was permitted to sue the no-lawsuit motorist.

Prohibiting such lawsuits would wrongly prevent the traditionally insured motorist from receiving compensation for losses caused by the fault of another. Allowing the traditional insured to sue the no-fault insured, however, is equally unsatisfactory because the cost of the no-fault insured's insurance would increase inordinately. Such a scheme would require a no-lawsuit insured to carry tort liability insurance (or expose his personal assets to the risk of tort recoveries) as well as no-fault insurance. This system would create a strong disincentive against purchasing no-lawsuit no-fault insurance because the traditional insured would have to pay only for cut-rate tort liability insurance: he would never be liable to any no-lawsuit insured because the no-lawsuit insured has surrendered his right to sue.

The solution to this problem is to establish a mandatory auto insurance "connector" to bridge the gap between traditional insurance and no-fault insurance, thereby enabling the two to coexist without unfairness. With a workable connector, a controversial political issue could be decided in the marketplace. Specifically, a modified form of uninsured motorist (UM) insurance should be the connector.[51]

A conventional UM policy insures against injury caused by an uninsured motorist or a hit-and-run vehicle. His own insurer compensates the insured to the same extent that he could have recovered if the other motorist were insured. Nineteen states require all motorists to purchase UM

---

[51] For a similar proposal, see Holtum [sic, Holtom], Proposal: "Choose-Your-Own" Auto Insurance, National Underwriter (property & casualty ed.), Nov. 22, 1985, at 43, cols. 1-4. But see National Underwriter (property & casualty ed.), Mar. 14, 1986, at 16, colt 34, for an apology by Robert Holtom for failing to reveal in publishing his Nov. 22 article, that prior to writing that article he had available to him a draft manuscript of this article by O'Connell and Joost.

insurance, and virtually all insured motorists voluntarily purchase it in the other thirty-one states.[52]

To form the connector, UM insurance should be extended beyond its current scope to compensate traditional insureds who are injured by a no-fault insured. This coverage extension would solve the problem that arises when a traditional insured collides with a no-fault insured, and it would eliminate the prejudice and unfair benefit that would otherwise exist in a choice system. Giving consumers a choice in auto insurance would then be a practicable alternative for state legislatures.

With the UM connector in place, a traditional insured who is injured in a collision with a no-lawsuit insured would recover tort liability damages on the same basis as in a current tort-based system. The traditional insured, however, would recover under his own extended UM insurance policy rather than from a liability insurance policy or the personal assets of the no-fault insured. The UM connector would not disadvantage traditional insureds even though they would pay more for UM coverage than at present because of its extended coverage. This additional cost would be offset by lower liability insurance premiums because traditional insureds are immune from suits by no-fault insureds.[53] Actually, the average victim's recovery under UM insurance is likely to be larger than the average recovery under traditional liability insurance, which would seem to have countervailing advantages in benefits and disadvantages in cost.

Because the traditional insured receives compensation through his UM policy, the issue of whether to subject a no-fault insured to suit no longer arises. Thus, the no-lawsuit insured receives the full benefit of no-fault

---

[52] See All-Industry Research Advisory Council, Uninsured Motorists: Facts & Figures 34 (1984) [hereinafter cited as AIRAC]. The percentage of private passenger automobile insureds who choose to buy UM coverage in twelve states where insureds can reject UM coverage without doing so in writing is as follows: Alabama-98 percent; Alaska-92 percent; Arkansas-95 percent; Colorado-94 percent; Montana-100 percent; Nebraska-91 percent; North Carolina-99 percent; Ohio-100 percent; Rhode Island-98 percent; Utah-96 percent; Washington-100 percent; Wyoming-99 percent. Id. One would expect even higher figures where insureds must reject this coverage in writing.

[53] The All-Industry Research Advisory Council (AIRAC) examined the records of personal injury claims that were closed in 1977. It compared 2,600 claims paid under UM insurance with 22,000 claims paid under bodily injury liability insurance. Average total payment per claim under UM coverage was $3,316, while the average total under another person's BI liability coverage was $2,955. Assuming these figures are valid today, they mean that an accident victim who recovers benefits from his own insurer under UM insurance is likely to recover 12.2 percent more for the same injury than an accident victim who recovers under the BI liability insurance of the driver who was at fault. See AIRAC, supra note 52, at 35. The higher payment probably occurs because insurers tend to be more generous to their own insureds than to strangers.

insurance without needing to purchase additional liability insurance to protect his personal assets.

To establish the connector and to create a choice-based auto insurance system, state legislatures should pass a statute[54] with the following provisions:

(1) The statute should declare that no-fault insureds are uninsured motorists for the purposes of all UM policies sold in the state. Furthermore, the statute should provide that any purchaser of a UM policy and any occupant of a motor vehicle owned or operated by such a person is conclusively deemed to have waived his right to sue a no-fault insured, and instead to have elected to recover from the UM policy any tort liability damages resulting from an accident with a no-fault insured.

(2) The statute should authorize insurers licensed in the state to sell no-fault insurance if their policy provides a high ceiling on no-fault benefits (for example, at least $500,000)[55] to each insured named in the policy and to each relative of a named insured living in the same household.[56]

(3) The statute should bar a no-fault insured from suing another motorist in tort to recover for injuries suffered in an auto accident.

(4) The statute should provide that a motorist satisfies the financial responsibility or compulsory insurance requirement of the state if he maintains a policy of either: (A) no-fault motor vehicle

---

[54] The connector does not eliminate, or even reduce, the traditional right to sue in tort, but it does change the party against whom the right can be asserted. Such a significant change in common-law rights probably should be made by statute rather than by regulation.

[55] See supra note 42 and accompanying text. A $500,000 cap is very high but, unlike workers' compensation, it is not unlimited. Many insurers fear that unlimited benefits for no-fault insurance might be prohibitively expensive, despite the superficial similarity between auto and industrial accident. Auto accident victims, in the insurers' view, tend to be much more seriously injured and are younger than seriously injured industrial accident victims. Additionally, employers arguably can use their influence to encourage rehabilitation and the return to work, a "centralized" factor not available for auto accident victims. These factors, in some insurers' eyes, make the cost of unlimited auto no-fault more threatening than the cost of workers' compensation.

[56] Arguably, permitting the insured's coverage choice to bind guests, passengers, pedestrians, or bicyclists injured in his car is not a good idea. If the victim were a member of a car-owning family, the law could permit him to claim against his own company for either no-fault or extended UM benefits, depending on the coverage applicable to his family car. But if the injured party were not a member of a car-owning family, the statute could provide that he be paid under the no-fault insured's coverage under either no-fault or tort coverage, whichever the victim chooses. (The no-fault insured's policy would have to include special liability coverage.) This solution raises problems of adverse selection—those with valid tort claims will press such claims and others will agree to no-fault compensation.

insurance with a high established limit on benefits; or (B) motor vehicle insurance that pays tort damages, up to a specified limit, to persons who are injured by the fault of the insured, and that pays to the insured tort damages attributable to the fault of a hit-and-run, an uninsured, or a no-fault insured motorist.[57] Furthermore, the statute could provide that an owner of a motor vehicle who does not maintain either kind of insurance is not entitled to either tort or no-fault coverage.

Variations on this basic insurance scheme are possible. For example, a state could give motorists three different options. The first option would be the current compulsory package now offered by a no-fault state plus extended UM coverage that applies if the tort threshold is exceeded. This option combines extended UM coverage with an existing no-fault package. The second option would be a no-lawsuit no-fault policy that provides a very high limit on benefits and prevents the no-fault beneficiary from suing or being sued in tort. The third option would be liability insurance with current limits, plus extended UM coverage.

A state could actually create an unlimited number of options by selecting different combinations of no-fault benefit levels, internal benefit limits (for example, total and monthly limits on wage-loss compensation), and thresholds.[58] The states should, however, keep the number of options small enough to permit motorists to comparison shop for their insurance.

---

[57] The proposed statute also could authorize the motorists who choose no-fault insurance to coordinate the medical portion of their no-fault insurance with their comprehensive health insurance plan. For example, Michigan's no-fault law requires insurers to "offer, at appropriately reduced premium rates, deductibles and exclusions reasonably related to other health and accident coverage on the insured." Mich. Comp. Laws Ann. § 500.3109a (West 1983). If a motorist permits his auto no-fault benefits to duplicate other collateral sources, he will, on the average, spend 77 percent more in no-fault premiums. Letter to authors from James M. Edwards, Vice President & General Counsel, League Insurance Group (Jan. 16, 1986). Under the proposed statute, other states could make similar rules applicable, on a voluntary basis, for coordination between no-fault and health coverage.

[58] For more on possible options, see infra note 65 and accompanying text. States may also prefer to have special statutory provisions for accidents between large commercial vehicles and passenger cars. The weight of a vehicle affects the severity of injury to passengers in the other vehicle in the collision. For example, a collision with a large truck is likely to do more damage to a passenger car than a collision with another car. Additionally, commercial vehicle owners may be in the best position to reduce or transfer these accident costs through their influence on the driver's conduct, vehicle design, and ability to pass the accident costs through to the price of the commercial products. States may prefer to modify their insurance scheme which allows choice to reflect the damage differential and risk-bearing ability associated with commercial vehicles. A statute could require the commercial vehicle (a truck or taxi, whether covered under fault or no-fault insurance) to pay no-fault benefits to the

2.3. Comparative Appeal of the Proposed Reform

The liability option might be a "better deal" than the no-fault option for individuals who have very high limits of both health insurance and income continuation insurance. It might also be preferred by individuals who view auto accidents as opportunities to "win" a large sum of money, rather than as misfortunes that can result in permanent injury, and who believe that there is no real danger of losing, because Medicare, Medicaid, and welfare will provide for them if they do not win a liability award. The liability option would seem to be more attractive to people who like to sue, who dream of making a "big killing," or who distrust insurance companies. The liability option would pay relatively more money than the no-fault option if the accident victim involved is one who has suffered only moderate injuries, such as back strain, whiplash, or fracture. Moderate injuries cause only limited medical expense and work loss, but they can cause a great deal of pain and suffering, compensable under liability insurance but not under no-fault insurance.

The no-fault option would be better for individuals who want to be sure that catastrophic losses will not outstrip their own coverages no matter how high. It would certainly be better for individuals who do not have very high limits of both health insurance and income continuation insurance. It would also be the preferred choice of motorists who do not want to be paid for their pain and suffering but who do want swift, sure, and complete payment of their accident-caused personal economic losses. This option would be more attractive to people who dislike gambling, who eschew litigation, or who distrust lawyers. In general, the no-fault option would assure relatively more money than the liability option to an accident victim who suffers very severe injuries such as a severing of the spinal cord or a serious brain concussion. The economic loss of such victims can easily outstrip the limits of the average liability insurance policy.

Choice is an approach under which the two involved special interest groups, the trial lawyers and the insurance industry, could compromise and make peace after twenty years of conflict about no-fault. Trial lawyers prefer the contingent fee income that the liability system generates, while many casualty insurance companies prefer to pay benefits to their own

---

occupants of a no-fault insured car. The law also could provide that when a fault-insured car collides with a commercial vehicle, the commercial vehicle remains liable in tort. For a further discussion of the reallocation of such losses between differing types of vehicles and a presentation of a more complicated reallocation scheme contained in the Uniform Motor Vehicle Accident Reparation Act drafted by the Commission on Uniform State Laws, see J. O'Connell & R. Henderson, Tort Law, No-Fault & Beyond 402-15 (1975).

policyholders so that they can generate good will. Choice could conceivably meet the needs of both groups because accident victims who are litigious are the ones who generate fees for trial lawyers; these are also the motorists who are likely to select the liability option. On the other hand, claimants who are likely to be satisfied by their own insurance company's handling of their own claims are the ones who will generate good will and new business for insurance companies; they are the motorists who are likely to select the no-fault option.

2.4. Evaluating the Proposed Reform

The proposed reform is not solely a remedy for a state like New Jersey that has a wildly out-of-balance no-fault law. Motorist choice would also benefit in-balance or slightly out-of-balance no-fault states and traditional states. First, this proposal would remove a highly controversial issue from the political arena and let consumers decide it for themselves. Second, the new scheme would increase the range of consumer choice, allowing those who prefer either traditional or no-fault insurance to select the policies they prefer. Third, compelling no-fault and liability insurance to compete with each other in the marketplace would mean that the most efficient and less costly form of insurance ultimately would prevail. Fourth, no-fault coverage would no longer subsidize the aggressive, but patient, pursuit of BI liability claims.[59]

The proposal will also increase the amount of benefits available to accident victims, thus eliminating a serious problem under the no-fault and traditional systems in force today. According to the DOT report, "[t]ypical auto insurance benefits in both no-fault and traditional States fall short of the needs of catastrophically injured victims."[60] The National Highway Traffic Safety Administration in 1982 studied different classes of auto accident injuries and estimated that the average economic costs of "critical" injuries were $235,828, and that the economic costs of "severe" injuries were $51,487.[61] Only six of the twenty-four no-fault jurisdictions provide medical benefits (including rehabilitation) of at least $50,000;[62] thus, the majority do

[59] See supra notes 30-31 and accompanying text. Under the choice system, those buying add-on coverage will be in a position to make and pay for a subsidized BI liability claim against their own insurer.

[60] DOT Report, supra note 2, at 5.

[61] Id. at 20.

[62] The six jurisdictions and their limits on no-fault are as follows: Michigan-unlimited; New Jersey-unlimited; Puerto Rico-unlimited for 2 years, unlimited thereafter if board approves; D.C.-$100,000; Colorado-$100,000; New York-$50,000. Id. at 25-39.

not automatically protect motorists and pedestrians against the risk of catastrophic injury. Many of the other no-fault jurisdictions do not even provide enough no-fault benefits to meet the costs of victims with "serious" injuries, which average $10,257 per victim. Some states are even unable to meet the costs of "moderate" injuries, which average $4,080 per victim.[63]

Massachusetts' insurance scheme illustrates the problem of undercompensation. Massachusetts provides only $2,000 in no-fault benefits, which cannot begin to meet the staggering medical rehabilitation expense of quadriplegia, paraplegia, or brain injuries in catastrophic auto accidents. (Given the low no-fault limits, even the low Massachusetts threshold of $500 in medical expenses[64] does not make the law out-of-balance.) Adopting the proposed reform would permit Massachusetts motorists to elect a no-fault policy providing very high coverage. Similarly, a law allowing choice would permit motorists who dislike the current mixed law to elect solely a BI liability policy with extended UM coverage. To add additional flexibility to the scheme, motorists who choose that option also could select, for example, $5,000 in no-fault benefits on an add-on basis. Of course, Massachusetts could also allow motorists who prefer their current insurance package to retain it.[65]

---

[63] The no-lawsuit no-fault jurisdictions provide the following required no-fault benefit for medical and rehabilitation treatment: Connecticut-$5,000; Florida-$10,000; Georgia-$5,000; Hawaii-$15,000; Kansas-$4,000; Kentucky-$10,000; Massachusetts-$2,000; Minnesota-$20,000; North Dakota-$15,000; Utah-$2,000. Id. at 25-40. The add-on no-fault states provide the following no-fault benefit for medical and rehabilitation treatment: Arkansas-$5,000; Delaware-$10,000 for 2 years; Maryland-$2,500; Oregon-$5,000; Pennsylvania-$10,000; South Carolina-$1,000; Texas-$2,500, Washington-$10,000 for 1 year. Id. at 41-49.

[64] See Mass. Gen. Laws Ann. ch. 90, §§ 34A, 34M (West Supp. 1985); see also id. ch. 231, § 6D (restrictions on tort recovery for pain and suffering). See generally id. ch. 90, §§ 34A-34O (Compulsory Motor Vehicle Liability Insurance Act). For a summary of Massachusetts no-fault law, see DOT Report, supra note 2, at 33.

[65] A state can build in even greater flexibility by allowing lower no-fault limits than the suggested maximum of $500,000. This could be accomplished by providing by statute that a no-lawsuit insured cannot claim or be claimed against in tort for either special or general damages in an amount less than the limits of no-fault benefits provided in the no-fault policy. Separation of special from general damages would entail the use of special verdicts.

For a discussion of the reasons justifying a separate tort exemption for general damages in addition to that for special damages, see R. Keeton & J. O'Connell, Basic Protection for the Traffic Victim 68, 442 (1965). If no tort exemption for pain and suffering were provided, the victim normally could still pursue his tort claim profitably. Although his claim for special damages would be reduced by the amount of the special damages exemption, general damages are often measured as a multiple of special damages. Consequently, the victim could still hire a lawyer on a contingent fee basis to pursue his tort claim for general damages, thus eviscerating the purpose of the tort exemption in eliminating tort suits.

Some casualty insurance companies may oppose the suggested reform because of the difficulty of pricing two entirely different kinds of auto insurance used simultaneously in a single market. If insurers sell both types of auto insurance, they will never know in advance how many people will select no-fault coverage and how many will select tort liability coverage. Pricing may be difficult without this information because the number of people who select no-fault coverage affects the risk of loss for those who elect liability insurance. It alters the probable payout on traditional insureds' UM coverage and on their BI liability coverage. As the number of no-fault purchasers increases, the average UM premium should go up and the average BI liability premium should go down, but the exact amount of the increase and decrease will not be known in advance. Accordingly, casualty insurance companies may conclude that actuarial science cannot price liability coverage in a choice system.

This pricing problem arises from regulations that require insurers to price BI liability coverage and UM coverage separately.[66] Establishing individual prices is difficult because of the interaction between BI liability and UM coverage under the proposed choice scheme. The solution, however, is to allow insurance companies to establish a single price for a package of BI liability plus extended UM coverage. The package price should be easier to determine because it should not be affected by the number of motorists who opt for no-fault coverage. As motorists switch back and forth between no-fault and liability coverage, the cost of BI liability and UM coverage should change by approximately offsetting amounts. Package pricing is also appropriate because insurers will usually sell these two forms of coverage together rather than individually. The insurance industry most likely would support the proposed reform if the prices of BI liability and UM coverage were merged.

Insurance companies may also object to the choice proposal on the ground that it will make auto insurance more costly to administer and will

---

Where the tort claim is large enough to pierce the UM deductible, the tort claim under the UM coverage and under the other motorist's liability coverage could be consolidated. At that point, the claim would resemble a case where different insurers provide multiple layers of insurance coverage. It would be desirable, though, to amend the UM statute to allow a traditional insured to bypass any arbitration requirement if his UM claim is based on an alleged tort by a no-fault insured. See R. Keeton, Basic Text on Insurance Law § 7.3(c), at 454-55 (1971).

[66] Ranked in order of inflexibility, insurance rate regulations may require (1) "prior approval" by the insurance regulators, (2) "file and use," subject to insurance regulatory disapproval of excessive rates and resultant rate rebates, and (3) "open competition" (or "no filing" laws). See R. Keeton, supra note 65, § 8.4(a), at 564. Arguably, only states requiring prior approval would require change to implement the proposed reform.

confuse agents and consumers as they attempt to evaluate the different options. These might have been meaningful objections several years ago when information processing was less sophisticated and almost all auto insurance policies were difficult reading for non-lawyers.[67] Today, however, neither cost nor confusion are obstacles to the proposed reform. Insurance companies are making their policies easier to read and understand.[68] Also, the desk-top computers that are generally available to insurance agents can generate printouts that compare the alternative policies. As a result, agents and consumers can understand options and make informed choices today that would have been more difficult in the past.[69]

Furthermore, a system using the UM connector probably is not vulnerable to constitutional challenge. Courts have almost universally upheld the constitutionality of personal injury no-fault schemes, especially when such laws replace the tort remedy with an "adequate substitute."[70] UM insurance provides an adequate substitute remedy for fault-based recovery because the prerequisites for recovery are the same and the amount of compensation is not reduced.[71]

---

[67] A noted linguist, Dr. Rudolph Flesch, developed a "readability" scale under which a score of zero means a document is unreadable, and a score of 100 means it is totally readable. Insurance policies scored a 10 on this scale, compared with 82 for magazine ads, 65 for the Reader's Digest, and 52 for Time Magazine. R. Flesch, How to Write Plain English 26 (1981). See infra note 68.

[68] Sentry Insurance Company's "Plain Talk Car Policy" scored 47.98 on the Flesch scale compared with a score of 13.9 for its predecessor. See R. Flesch, supra note 67, at 26; Reutershan & Kunze, Who Wants a New Insurance Policy?, 24 Drake L Rev. 753, 756 (1975) (applying the Flesch test to the new Sentry policy).

[69] Insurers may face two additional problems under a choice system. First, insurers must decide what to do with insureds who, despite clear requests from their insurers, simply fail to make a choice. To solve this problem, the statute could provide that an insured will be deemed to have selected a specified coverage; the statute should designate this as either traditional or no-fault coverage. Arguably, because no-fault is the newer and more novel coverage, the statute should provide that a motorist will receive traditional coverage if he does not choose. On the other hand, if, as the authors believe, no-fault coverage is the more socially beneficial coverage, see supra notes 39-41 and accompanying text, no-fault should be the applicable coverage, absent a designated choice.

Second, insurers must be able to forestall claims by insureds who assert after the fact that they were inadequately informed about the possible choices. To avoid this problem, the statute could provide that if an insurer provides the insured with a written description of the choice, conforming to terms specifically prescribed in the statute, the insurer will be immune from liability for inadequately informing an insured as to the available choices.

[70] For a survey of relevant constitutional decisions, see DOT Report, supra note 2, at 146-53 App. A. For an extensive discussion of the constitutionality of a proposal analogous to that being advanced in this article, see J. O'Connell & J. Souk, Is it Constitutional? in Ending Insult to Injury 204-45 (1975).

[71] See supra note 53.

Some commentators perceive traditional tort law as a deterrent to accident-producing conduct.[72] Even if this were so, substituting no-lawsuit no-fault insurance for traditional liability insurance arguably will not diminish the deterrent effect. Professor Richard Epstein points out that shifts in liability rules create offsetting incentives;[73] this is also true for no-lawsuit insurance. For example, under no-lawsuit coverage, accident victims internalize less of their loss than at common law because they recover even if they cause accidents. Conversely, insurance premium payers internalize more costs because they lose the defense that they were not at fault. Similarly, premium payers internalize less loss because they no longer bear liability for damages for pain and suffering, yet accident victims internalize more loss because they cannot receive damages for pain and suffering.[74]

---

[72] For an analysis of the comparative effect on deterrence of no-fault and traditional tort law, see DOT Report, supra note 2, at 141-43, 159-66; Kochanowski & Young, Deterrent Aspects of No-Fault Automobile Insurance: Some Empirical Findings, 52 J. Risk & Ins. 269 (1985). The study concludes that "fears of a dramatic escalation of fatal accidents because of no-fault insurance are unfounded. Even on a theoretical basis such fears have weak underpinnings. On an empirical basis, they appear to have no foundation whatsoever." Id. at 287. For a study questioning use of fatality statistics to appraise no-fault insurance laws (all of which preserve traditional tort actions for fatalities), see O'Connell & Levmore, A Reply to Landes: A Faulty Study of No-Fault's Effect on Fault?, 48 Mo. L. Rev. 649, 650-51 (1983).

[73] Epstein, Automobile No-Fault Plans: A Second Look at First Principles, 13 Creighton L. Rev. 769, 785 (1980).

[74] If significantly more unsafe drivers opt for no-lawsuit insurance than for liability insurance, insurance premiums for traditional insureds might rise disproportionately over current costs. Traditional insureds' UM insurance would pay for losses that unsafe drivers would otherwise absorb except for their no-lawsuit insurance immunity. No *a priori* reason, however, indicates that disproportionate numbers of safe or unsafe drivers will prefer one form of insurance over the other. Economic analysis might suggest that unsafe drivers, knowing their lesser likelihood of recovering in tort, will opt for no-lawsuit insurance, and conversely, safer drivers, knowing their greater likelihood of recovering in tort, will opt for traditional insurance. But one can just as persuasively argue that safer drivers are more likely to be risk averse and therefore will opt for the more certain, no-fault insurance payments, even if they are lesser in amount. Conversely, unsafe drivers, being risk-preferred, will arguably opt for higher (if less sure) traditional tort insurance payments.

The proposal of giving motorists a choice between fault and no-fault insurance has the additional advantage of encouraging motorists to purchase automobile safety devices such as passive restraint equipment. Traditional auto insurance does not offer this advantage. For example, air bags installed in an automobile reduce the risk of death or injury in a collision. Widespread use of air bags would cut insurance costs by reducing the amount of claims brought by accident victims. If these savings could be passed on in the form of lower premiums to individual motorists who install air bags, motorists would have a financial incentive to purchase such safety equipment. In essence, the lower insurance cost could be used to finance the safety equipment.

Unfortunately, no such incentive exists with traditional insurance. Under traditional insurance, accident victims are compensated by the insurer of the driver who caused the accident. Therefore, any savings in insurance cost from the use of air bags accrues to the

3. CONCLUSION

Allowing individual motorists to choose the kind of auto insurance they want has many advantages. It will permit consumers to decide the issue for themselves rather than surrendering the decision to politicians in the state legislature. Those who prefer traditional insurance and who value the right to sue can purchase traditional liability insurance, and those who desire coverage providing timely compensation without resort to a lawsuit can purchase no-fault insurance. The proposal will enhance efficiency by expanding the range of consumer choice and by creating competition between two systems in the marketplace. Most important, the proposal probably offers the best way to solve the problems that have arisen in states currently using no-fault insurance.

All of the twenty-four jurisdictions that now require the purchase or offering of no-fault insurance have "monopoly" auto insurance statutes, which give the motorist little or no choice in the matter. Many of the monopoly statutes appear to reflect a political compromise in the state legislature between advocates of no-fault and opponents of no-fault, who favor maximizing the availability of lawsuits in tort. These compromised monopoly statutes are costly, however, and do not provide sufficient benefits to compensate the catastrophically injured. The proposed reform will allow insurance companies to sell auto insurance that does not reflect a political compromise. Uncompromised insurance should be less costly, yet more effective.

---

insurer of the motorist at fault rather than to the insurer of the owner of the air bag-equipped car. The insurer of the air bag-equipped car is unable to pass on any cost savings to the motorist who installed the air bags. Consequently, traditional insurance does not encourage the installation of auto safety equipment.

Allowing individual motorists to choose no-lawsuit no-fault insurance and establishing extended UM insurance as a connector would solve this problem. Motorists who choose no-lawsuit insurance would have a strong financial incentive to buy safer cars. Insurance companies would presumably offer lower premiums to no-fault insureds who install air bags because the savings created by their use would accrue to the no-fault motorist's insurer rather than to another insurance company. For the new car buyer, the savings under the new insurance system might pay for the safety system over time.

The proposed reform would automatically give persons selecting no-fault insurance an incentive to purchase passive safety devices. To increase the incentive, however, the connector device could be tied explicitly to the use of passive restraints. Specifically, the statute enacting the connector device could provide that only persons who purchase no-fault insurance and who install passive safety devices will receive the connector's protection from traditionally insured motorists' tort claims. Linking the connector to safety devices is not a necessary part of the proposed reform, but it is one option available to a legislature, and it illustrates the flexibility of the proposed insurance system. Either state or federal law could institute a scheme for financing safety equipment through insurance.

9
EQUITY IN AUTOMOBILE INSURANCE: OPTIONAL NO-FAULT[†]

Michael R. Powers
Temple University

1. INTRODUCTION

Throughout the past decade, automobile insurance premiums have escalated in many jurisdictions. Excessive litigation and the over-utilization of medical services have been primary forces pushing the price of automobile insurance beyond the reach of many consumers. Nationally, automobile insurance premiums increased an average of 9.6 percent annually, about three times the average rate of increase in the Consumer Price Index, from 1982 through 1988 (see A. M. Best Company, 1990). In Pennsylvania, where major automobile insurance reform has been enacted recently, the rate of increase was almost identical to the national average during this period of time.

In Philadelphia County, where the price of automobile insurance has grown most dramatically, the frequencies of both bodily injury liability and first party benefit claims were more than three times those in the rest of the state between 1983 and 1987 (see Insurance Services Office and National Association of Independent Insurers, 1988, p. 38). This region, where automobile insurance has been the least affordable, is also the area with the greatest proportion of uninsured motorists.

To make automobile insurance more affordable in Pennsylvania, Governor Robert P. Casey introduced a package of reforms in June 1989 aimed at bringing both excessive litigation and automobile-related medical costs under control. The Governor's program, based upon research conducted by the Pennsylvania Insurance Department, included both an optional no-fault system and provisions to cap medical reimbursements and

[†] This chapter originally appeared as an article in the June 1992 issue of *The Journal of Risk and Insurance* (59, 2, 203-220), and is reprinted with permission.

implement medical provider peer review. This package was passed by the Pennsylvania General Assembly and signed into law as *Act 6* in February 1990.

Pennsylvania's optional no-fault system is conceptually very similar to the optional no-fault system implemented in New Jersey in 1989. Under both systems, all private passenger named insureds are given the opportunity to elect either a tort or no-fault option that is binding on both themselves and other members of their households who are not named insureds, so that all private passenger automobile insureds[1] may be classified as either tort electors or no-fault electors. Tort electors continue to enjoy their traditional tort rights in all situations, whereas no-fault electors relinquish their right to seek recovery for non-economic (pain and suffering) damages except when their injuries satisfy a verbal tort threshold (i.e., are sufficiently serious, as defined in the law). In return for restricting their tort rights (including the tort rights of other household members), no-fault insureds receive a substantial reduction in their bodily injury liability and uninsured/underinsured motorist premiums.

In the face of strong opposition to no-fault from Pennsylvania's trial bar, it was necessary to develop a system that was clearly equitable to all parties. Thus, only a system that gave consumers the freedom to choose between retaining their traditional tort rights, and restricting their tort rights in return for reductions in premiums, was acceptable. Also, it was imperative that the election of one insured not affect the tort rights of other automobile accident victims (except those from the same household). For these reasons, optional no-fault, rather than mandatory no-fault, was pursued by the administration and legislature.

2. EQUITY IN AUTOMOBILE LIABILITY INSURANCE

From the time the no-fault concept was first proposed for automobile insurance by Keeton and O'Connell (1965), its proponents have supported it with both efficiency and equity arguments. Specifically, it is argued that by compensating victims on a no-fault basis for their economic (medical and income) losses, and restricting traditional tort rights: (1) the recovery system is more efficient, because victims are compensated more quickly, and less

---

[1] Hereafter, the term "insured" is taken to mean "named insured." Individuals who are insured as household members of a named insured are specifically identified, when appropriate.

money is spent on attorneys' fees and court costs, and (2) the recovery system is more equitable, because there is less over-compensation of victims with minor injuries, and more adequate compensation of victims with serious injuries.

Numerous studies conclude that no-fault automobile insurance has, on the whole, achieved both the efficiency and equity goals for which it was proposed.[2] Victims in mandatory no-fault jurisdictions are compensated more quickly than those in traditional tort jurisdictions, and, when there is a strong barrier to tort recovery (such as a verbal or substantial dollar tort threshold), a far greater portion of insurance loss dollars is used to compensate economic losses under mandatory no-fault than under traditional tort.

This author proposes two fundamental equity principles to justify optional no-fault systems, without even bringing to bear the traditional arguments in support of no-fault. These concepts are: (1) The tort equity principle: automobile accident victims should not be restricted involuntarily from seeking recovery through the tort system; and (2) The rate equity principle: less litigious insureds should receive premium reductions to recognize, as precisely as possible, their contribution toward reduced losses.

The tort equity principle is a general affirmation of an individual's traditional tort rights. However, this principle allows individuals to agree, voluntarily, to restrict their tort rights *a priori*. For less litigious individuals, this type of restriction simply formalizes the restraint that they normally demonstrate on an informal basis. While the tort equity principle is satisfied in all jurisdictions preserving traditional tort rights, it is obviously violated by all mandatory no-fault laws, such as those existing in Massachusetts, Florida, Connecticut, and Michigan. In these jurisdictions, all automobile accident victims are barred from seeking recovery for non-economic damages unless a verbal or dollar tort threshold is reached.

The rate equity principle states that less litigious individuals should be rewarded financially for the savings that they create by their voluntary restraint in seeking recovery through the tort system. Because it is impossible to identify different degrees of litigiousness among uninjured automobile insureds, this principle suggests that, whenever possible, insureds be afforded rate reductions in return for voluntary formal restrictions on their tort rights.

In later sections, it will be shown that the rate equity principle can, in theory, be satisfied in all jurisdictions with a mandatory no-fault law, but

---

[2] Most recently, for example, see All-Industry Research Advisory Council (1989), Smith (1989), U.S. Department of Transportation (1985), Rolph (1985), and Hammitt (1985).

that, in practice, this principle is not achieved in these jurisdictions. Also, this equity principle is not satisfied in any jurisdiction maintaining traditional tort rights, because automobile insureds retain an unrestricted right to seek recovery, whether they want it or not.

The rate equity principle requires premium reductions for less litigious insureds that are conceptually similar to loss control discounts in workers' compensation insurance, or wellness and non-smoker discounts in health insurance, in that they reward insureds for behavior that reduces losses for insurers. However, unlike loss control, wellness, and non-smoker programs, the loss savings produced by a less litigious insured are spread across all insurers, rather than accruing directly to the insured's own insurer. Thus, to justify reducing the premium of a less litigious insured, there must be some mechanism to make sure that the insured's own insurer, which must provide the premium reduction, is compensated properly.

The fact that no traditional tort or mandatory no-fault jurisdiction is able to satisfy both equity principles simultaneously illustrates the shortcomings of the *status quo* in most jurisdictions. It is to provide relief from these inequities that optional no-fault systems have been proposed and enacted in several jurisdictions.

3. OPTIONAL NO-FAULT SYSTEMS

An optional no-fault system gives insureds a choice between two types of bodily injury recovery: traditional tort recovery, or some variant of no-fault (such as a tort threshold that must be reached before a claim is made). If two parties in an automobile accident are both tort electors or both no-fault electors, then all recoveries can proceed under the mode of recovery that both have elected. However, if one party is a tort elector and the other a no-fault elector, then the system must provide a rule to decide which recovery mode prevails.

3.1. Varieties of Optional No-Fault

There are three decision rules that can be used to determine the appropriate manner of recovery in an accident between a tort elector and a no-fault elector: (1) tort-favoring, in which both parties have unrestricted tort rights; (2) no-fault-favoring, in which both parties have restricted tort rights; and (3) self-determining, in which the tort elector has unrestricted tort rights and the no-fault elector has restricted tort rights. Interestingly, the only optional no-fault systems that currently exist, i.e., Kentucky's optional $1,000 tort threshold and the New Jersey/Pennsylvania optional verbal tort threshold, correspond to the first and third of these decision rules, respectively, whereas the optional no-fault approach proposed by O'Connell and Joost (1986) corresponds to the second rule.

3.2. Evaluating Automobile Insurance Recovery Systems

In analyzing the relative merits of the three types of optional no-fault systems, it is helpful to consider how well they are able to satisfy the tort equity and rate equity principles described above. Table 1 indicates whether or not each of the two equity principles can be satisfied, in theory, under traditional tort, mandatory no-fault, and the three optional no-fault systems.

Table 1
Equity Principles under Various Recovery Systems

	Tort Equity	**Rate Equity**
Traditional Tort	Yes	No
Tort-Favoring (KY)	Yes	Variant
Self-Determining (NJ/PA)	Yes	Yes
No-Fault-Favoring (O'Connell, Joost)	Variant	Yes
Mandatory No-Fault	No	Yes

This table reveals that the three optional no-fault systems provide a spectrum of alternatives between the extremes of traditional tort and mandatory no-fault. In so doing, the optional no-fault systems are able, in theory, to satisfy both equity principles in varying degrees. The term "variant", used to describe the tort-favoring program's ability to satisfy the rate equity principle and the no-fault-favoring program's ability to satisfy the tort equity principle, simply indicates that the relevant equity principle can be achieved in some circumstances, but not in others.

In the tort-favoring case, the rate equity principle can be satisfied only if all insureds elect the no-fault option. This is because a no-fault elector is forced to retain full tort rights when he or she encounters a tort elector, and so there are not enough savings to make the premiums of the no-fault insureds as low as they would be if everyone elected the no-fault option. In practice, this has not been a problem in Kentucky because the proportion of no-fault insureds is close to 100 percent, and the premium savings increase as the proportion of no-fault insureds increases. However, there is no guarantee that such a high proportion of consumers would elect the no-fault option in other jurisdictions.

In the no-fault-favoring case, the tort equity principle is satisfied only if all insureds elect the tort option. This is because a tort elector is involuntarily deprived of his or her unrestricted recovery rights when he or she encounters a no-fault elector. Because this type of optional no-fault system has never been introduced in any jurisdiction, it is not possible to say what proportion of insureds are likely to elect the tort option. However, there is no guarantee that all or nearly all consumers would elect the tort option in practice.

O'Connell and Joost (1986) have argued that the recovery rights of tort electors need not be restricted under the no-fault-favoring system because the system creates sufficient savings for a tort insured to purchase an additional "connector" coverage that would permit the unrestricted ability to seek recovery from his or her own insurer. This coverage would operate on a first-party basis, in a manner analogous to uninsured motorist coverage. However, having the ability to recover from one's own insurer through the connector coverage is not the same as being able to recover from the actual no-fault tortfeasor in an accident, because the tort elector is prevented from seeking damages greater than the limits of his or her connector coverage, and because he or she is not able to recover from the personal assets of the no-fault tortfeasor.

Table 1 and the preceding discussion make it clear that the only automobile insurance recovery system that can always satisfy both equity principles simultaneously is the self-determining system adopted by both New Jersey and Pennsylvania. This optimal property of the self-determining system was the principal reason that it was proposed by the Casey administration in Pennsylvania.

4. CALCULATION OF RATES

As noted previously, no-fault insureds are entitled to substantial premium reductions on both their bodily injury liability and uninsured/underinsured motorist coverages in return for restricting their tort rights. Whereas appropriate reductions in uninsured/underinsured motorist premiums will ultimately be dictated by the loss experience of no-fault insureds (because this coverage operates on a first-party basis), the calculation of appropriate reductions in bodily injury liability premiums is more complex and interesting. In this regard, it is important to recall that, under the rate equity principle, the rate that applies to an insured must be based not only upon his or her projected loss experience, but also upon the contribution to reduced losses that he or she makes through any applicable tort restrictions. Rates based only upon an insured's projected loss experience will be called experience-based; rates that take into account the projected reduction in losses attributable to an insured's election will be called contribution-based.

For purposes of evaluating and comparing various automobile insurance recovery systems, it will simplify matters to consider only the pure premium portion of the insurance premium—that is, only the portion of the premium that covers expected losses (including allocated loss adjustment expenses (ALAE)). The underwriting expense and profit provisions that comprise the remainder of the premium will be assumed to be adjusted appropriately to comport with changes in the pure premium, with fixed expenses remaining constant and variable expenses changing proportionately with the total premium.

4.1. Experience- and Contribution-Based Pure Premiums

For a given rating territory, R, consider an individual insured by insurer h who occupies driver class i, and who purchases limit j of the bodily injury liability coverage. Let L_{hij} denote the expected loss to insurer h from this insured's policy during a specified policy period. Assume that if an insured with bodily injury liability limit j is the tortfeasor in an accident with a victim with restricted tort rights, then the tortfeasor's insurer's expected losses from the accident will be reduced by the loss elimination ratio r_j, where $0 < r_j < 1$ (e.g., if an expected loss of \$100 is reduced to \$55, then $r_j = .45$).

Note that the loss elimination ratio, r_j, depends on the tortfeasor's bodily injury liability limit, j, but not on the tortfeasor's driver class, i. This is because the restriction of the victim's tort rights reduces L_{hij} by removing a certain proportion of claims from the size-of-loss distribution, and, for a fixed rating territory, there are generally insufficient data to quantify how the shape of the size-of-loss distribution varies with the driver class of the tortfeasor. If sufficient data are available, then r_j may simply be replaced by r_{ij} in all subsequent analysis. Of course, r_j may vary across rating territories as the size-of-loss distribution varies.

Note further that r_j is actually a weighted average of two elimination ratios, one that captures the reduction in expected losses exclusive of ALAE and one that captures the reduction in expected ALAE. Because the restrictions of the victim's tort rights will primarily remove claims from the lower end of the size-of-loss distribution, and because the distribution of ALAE, which includes the legal defense costs associated with any claim, is usually less positively skewed than the distribution of losses exclusive of ALAE, it follows that the elimination ratio for expected ALAE will tend to be larger than the elimination ratio for expected losses exclusive of ALAE.

Let each victim and tortfeasor in an automobile accident that generates a bodily injury liability claim be classified as one of two types, k, where $k = T$ for private passenger automobile insureds (and their household members) bound by the tort option, and N for private passenger automobile insureds (and their household members) bound by the no-fault option. For the moment, it is assumed that victims and tortfeasors cannot be commercial automobile insureds, uninsured motorists, individuals that are neither motor vehicle operators nor insured under any automobile policy (non-operator non-insureds), or out-of-state residents. Later, these additional types will be addressed in the case of the self-determining optional no-fault system.

The experience-based pure premium for an insured of type k, L_{hijk}, is simply the weighted average of what the expected loss would be if all victims were tort electors, and what it would be if all victims were no-fault electors. Thus, for rating territory R:

$$L_{hijk} = L_{hij} \sum_{k'=T,N} \left\{ I(k',k) + \left(1 - r_j\right)\left[1 - I(k',k)\right] \right\} p_V(k'), \tag{1}$$

where $I(.,.)$ is the indicator function such that $I(k_1, k_2) = 1$ if a victim of type k_1 has an unrestricted right to recover from a tortfeasor of type k_2 under the relevant recovery system, and 0 otherwise, and $p_V(k')$ is the proportion of victims of type k' among all victims in the given rating territory.

The contribution-based pure premium for an insured of type k, L^*_{hijk}, is determined by subtracting from L_{hij} the total expected reduction in losses contributed by the insured. Thus:

$$L^*_{hijk} = L_{hij} - \sum_{h',i',j',k'} L_{h'i'j'} r_{j'} p_V(A)[1 - I(k,k')] p_A(h',i',j',k'), \quad (2)$$

where the summation is taken over all insurers h', driver classes i', bodily injury liability limits j', and types k', $p_A(h',i',j',k')$ is the proportion of insureds with characteristics h', i', j', and k' among all private passenger automobile insureds in rating territory R, and $p_V(A)$ is the proportion of victims insured under a private passenger policy among all victims in the given rating territory. Note that although Equation (2) excludes loss reductions contributed by insureds who have accidents with victims from rating territories other than territory R, this omission is offset by the inclusion of loss reductions that are actually contributed by insureds from other rating territories who have accidents with victims from territory R. Note also that because of the simplifying assumption that there are no commercial automobile insureds, no uninsured motorists, no non-operator non-insureds, and no out-of-state residents, $p_V(A)$ must equal 1.

Tables 2 and 3 present, respectively, the experience-based and contribution-based pure premiums determined by applying Equations (1) and (2) to the five automobile insurance recovery systems spanning the range from traditional tort to mandatory no-fault. For ease of exposition, the notation Lr is used to denote the weighted average of the $L_{h'i'j'}r_{j'}$ over all h', i', j', and k', and $L^N r^N$ to denote the weighted average of the $L_{h'i'j'}r_{j'}$ over all h', i', and j', for $k' = N$.

Table 2
Experience-Based Pure Premiums

	Tort Insureds	No-Fault Insureds
Traditional Tort	L_{hij}	Not Applicable
Tort-Favoring	L_{hij}	$L_{hij}[1 - r_j p_V(N)]$
Self-Determining	$L_{hij}[1 - r_j p_V(N)]$	$L_{hij}[1 - r_j p_V(N)]$
No-Fault-Favoring	$L_{hij}[1 - r_j p_V(N)]$	$L_{hij}(1 - r_j)$
Mandatory No-Fault	Not Applicable	$L_{hij}(1 - r_j)$

The expressions in Tables 2 and 3 were derived from Equations (1) and (2) by assuming that $p_V(A)=1$, and recognizing that $I(T,T)=1$ and $I(N,N)=0$ under all optional no-fault systems, $I(T,N)=1$ under the tort-favoring and self-determining systems, $I(T,N)=0$ under the no-fault-favoring system, $I(N,T)=1$ under the tort-favoring system, and $I(N,T)=0$ under the self-determining and no-fault-favoring systems.

Table 3
Contribution-Based Pure Premiums

	Tort Insureds	No-Fault Insureds
Traditional Tort	L_{hij}	Not Applicable
Tort-Favoring	L_{hij}	$L_{hij}-L^N r^N p_A(N)$
Self-Determining	L_{hij}	$L_{hij}-Lr$
No-Fault-Favoring	$L_{hij}-L^N r^N p_A(N)$	$L_{hij}-Lr$
Mandatory No-Fault	Not Applicable	$L_{hij}-Lr$

Note that only two of the entries in Table 3 are dependent on the proportion of insureds electing the no-fault option: those for no-fault insureds under the tort-favoring system, and tort insureds under the no-fault-favoring system. These dependencies illustrate mathematically the failures of the tort-favoring and no-fault-favoring systems to satisfy the rate and tort equity principles, respectively, as noted in connection with Table 1.

With respect to the tort-favoring case, Table 3 shows exactly how this system fails to satisfy the rate equity principle in all cases except when $p_A(N)=1$. For the no-fault-favoring case, Table 3 shows how, because of the expected loss reductions created by tort electors restricted from seeking recovery from no-fault electors, the no-fault-favoring system provides tort insureds with pure premium savings in all cases but the one in which $p_A(N)=0$.

4.2. Assuring Rate Equity

To be truly rate equitable, an automobile insurance recovery system must base an insured's pure premiums not only upon his or her expected losses, but also upon his or her expected contributions to loss reductions for insurers. Thus, the fact that the pure premiums in Tables 2 and 3 are not identical, entry by entry, suggests that the use of experience-based rates under optional or mandatory no-fault systems may often lead to rate inequities, even in cases where the system could, in theory, satisfy the rate equity principle, according to Table 1.

Table 4 presents the differences between the contribution-based pure premiums of Table 3 and the experience-based pure premiums of Table 2, and thus reveals the extent to which the contribution-based pure premiums are higher or lower than the corresponding experience-based pure premiums.

Table 4
Differences in Pure Premiums
(Contribution-Based Less Experience-Based)

	Tort Insureds	**No-Fault Insureds**
Traditional Tort	0	Not Applicable
Tort-Favoring	0	$L_{hij}r_j p_V(N) - L^N r^N p_A(N)$
Self-Determining	$L_{hij}r_j p_V(N)$	$L_{hij}r_j p_V(N) - Lr$
No-Fault-Favoring	$L_{hij}r_j p_V(N) - L^N r^N p_A(N)$	$L_{hij}r_j - Lr$
Mandatory No-Fault	Not Applicable	$L_{hij}r_j - Lr$

From Table 4, it can be seen that the contribution-based and experience-based pure premiums are identical in only two cases: for all insureds under the traditional tort system, and for tort insureds under the tort-favoring optional no-fault system. It can also be seen that the difference between the contribution-based pure premium and the experience-based pure premium is always positive for tort insureds under the self-determining system. The other entries in Table 4 may be positive in some cases and negative in others, depending on the insured's driver class, i, and bodily injury liability limit, j. Because Lr is the weighted average of the $L_{hij}r_j$ over all h, i, j, and k, and $p_V(N) = p_A(N)$ under the assumption that all victims are insured under a private passenger automobile policy, it follows that, if $L^N r^N$ is approximately equal to Lr, then all but one of the remaining entries will be close to 0 on the average. In the case of no-fault insureds under the self-determining system, the difference will tend to be negative as long as $p_V(N) < 1$.

The fact that the experience-based pure premiums are sometimes greater than the contribution-based pure premiums for all but the traditional tort system demonstrates that no mandatory or optional no-fault system that uses pure premiums based solely upon an insured's expected losses can ever truly satisfy the rate equity principle. This is because some insureds will have their tort rights restricted in return for less of a premium reduction than that to which they are entitled.

In practice, the rate inequities created by the effect of some consumers purchasing higher (or lower) bodily injury liability limits than others may not be very significant, because the increase (decrease) in L_{hij} brought about by a higher (lower) limit purchased may be canceled out by the concomitant decrease (increase) in r_j. Thus, with respect to the index j, the product $L_{hij}r_j$ may be relatively constant. However, the effect of the driver class, i, on the rate inequities may be dramatic, because the application of driver class factors can, in some cases, make the base pure premium, L, three or more times as great as L_{hij}. Therefore, for insureds in the lower-rated driver classes, the experience-based pure premiums used under the optional no-fault system in Kentucky and the mandatory no-fault systems in Massachusetts, Florida, Connecticut, Michigan, and other jurisdictions, are clearly excessive. This is true even though Kentucky's tort-favoring system could, in theory, be rate equitable with its large proportion of no-fault insureds, and even though these other systems could theoretically be rate equitable with their mandatory thresholds.

5. THE SELF-DETERMINING SYSTEM

In an earlier section, it was noted that only one automobile insurance recovery system, the self-determining form of optional no-fault used in New Jersey and Pennsylvania, is able to satisfy both the tort and rate equity principles in all cases. Later, it was noted that in optional and mandatory no-fault systems that could, in theory, satisfy the rate equity principle, the use of experience-based rates, in practice, violates that principle. This section examines various details of how both tort equity and rate equity can practically be achieved through the use of the self-determining optional no-fault system with contribution-based pure premiums.

5.1. Insurer Imbalances

Up to this point, the discussion of pure premiums has largely been from the insured's point of view; now, the necessary balance between projected losses and contribution-based pure premiums will be considered from the insurer's perspective. Previously, it was observed that no-fault electors, as less litigious individuals, provide reductions in expected losses that are spread across all insurers. Thus, to justify reducing the premium of a specific no-fault insured, there must be some mechanism to make sure that the insured's own insurer is compensated properly. The question that will now be addressed is whether this mechanism can be implemented separately within each insurer's own accounts, or whether it must operate on a systemwide basis.

To be as precise as possible with respect to the balance between the losses expected to be sustained by insurers and the contribution-based pure premiums charged, the universe of potential victims and tortfeasors will now be expanded beyond those employed in the previous section. Specifically, four categories of victims or tortfeasors will be added to the two types used before, so that a victim or tortfeasor can have one of six types, k, where $k = T$ for private passenger automobile insureds (and their household members) bound by the tort option, N for private passenger automobile insureds (and their household members) bound by the no-fault option, C for commercial automobile insureds, U for uninsured motorists, W for non-operator non-insureds, and F for out-of-state residents.

To simplify Equations (1) and (2), the indicator functions $I(.,.)$ implied by Pennsylvania's *Act 6* will be used. Under *Act 6*, only private passenger insureds are offered the tort and no-fault options, no-fault electors have an unrestricted right to recover only from uninsured motorists (but not from the uninsured motorist coverage) and out-of-state motorists, and uninsured motorists have the same tort restrictions as no-fault electors. Thus,

$$\begin{aligned}&I(N,T) = I(N,N) = I(N,C) = I(N,W)\\&= I(U,T) = I(U,N) = I(U,C) = I(U,W) = 0,\end{aligned}$$

and $I(k,k')=1$ for all other choices of k and k'. Table 5 presents both the experience- and contribution-based pure premiums for both tort and no-fault insureds, obtained by substituting this indicator function into Equations (1) and (2).

Table 5
Self-Determining Optional No-Fault Pure Premiums

	Experience-Based	**Contribution-Based**
Tort Insureds	$L_{hij}\{1-r_j[p_V(N)+p_V(U)]\}$	L_{hij}
No-Fault Insureds	$L_{hij}\{1-r_j[p_V(N)+p_V(U)]\}$	$L_{hij}-Lrp_V(A)$

Consider insurer h's expected losses for rating territory R for the specified policy period:

$$\begin{aligned} L_h &= \sum_{i,j,k} L_{hijk} n_{hijk} \\ &= \sum_{i,j} L_{hij}\{1-r_j[p_V(N)+p_V(U)]\} n_{hij}, \end{aligned} \tag{3}$$

where n_{hijk} is the number of private passenger automobile insureds with characteristics h, i, j, and k in the given rating territory, and $n_{hij}=\sum_k n_{hijk}$. At the same time that it expects to incur these losses, the insurer will, if it charges the contribution-based pure premiums of Table 5, collect pure premiums for rating territory R equal to

$$\begin{aligned} L^*_h &= \sum_{i,j,k} L^*_{hijk}\, n_{hijk} \\ &= \sum_{i,j} \left[L_{hij} n_{hij} - Lrp_V(A) n_{hijN}\right]. \end{aligned} \tag{4}$$

As long as L^*_h is approximately equal to L_h, insurer h's inflows and outflows of funds will be in balance for the given rating territory. However, if L^*_h falls short of L_h, then insurer h will not collect sufficient pure premiums to cover its losses, and if L^*_h exceeds L_h, then the insurer will collect excessive pure premiums. To see how these situations may occur, consider the difference between the two quantities, L^*_h and L_h:

$$L^*_h - L_h = \{L^h r^h [p_V(N) + p_V(U)] - Lrp_V(A)p_h(N)\} n_h, \tag{5}$$

where $L^h r^h$ denotes the weighted average of the $L_{hij} r_j$ over all i, j, and k, $p_h(N)$ is the proportion of no-fault insureds among insurer h's private passenger insureds in rating territory R, and $n_h = \sum_{i,j} n_{hij}$. (The algebraic derivations of Equation (5) and all subsequent equations are provided in the Appendix.) Summing the differences $L^*_h - L_h$ over all insurers, h, it can be shown that

$$\sum_h (L^*_h - L_h) = Lrp_V(U)n, \tag{6}$$

where $n = \sum_h n_h$. Because the expression in Equation (6) is positive, it follows that, if insureds pay the contribution-based pure premiums identified in Table 5, then, for rating territory R, insurers will collectively receive a net gain from the optional no-fault system.

To eliminate this windfall to the insurance industry, one could simply require that the contribution-based pure premium for no-fault insureds in Table 5 be reduced by $Lrp_V(U)/p_A(N)$, one no-fault insured's share of the savings created by restricting the tort rights of uninsured motorists. This yields a pure premium of

$$L^{*\prime}_{hijN} = L_{hij} - Lr[p_V(N) + p_V(U)]/p_A(N). \tag{7}$$

Using this pure premium for no-fault insureds, it can be shown that

$$L^{*\prime}_h - L_h = \{L^h r^h - Lr[p_h(N)/p_A(N)]\}[p_V(N) + p_V(U)] n_h, \tag{8}$$

and

$$\sum_h (L^{*\prime}_h - L_h) = 0. \tag{9}$$

Thus, for rating territory R, the inflows and outflows of funds are exactly in balance.

From Equation (8), it is clear that even though the system may be in balance in the aggregate, it is possible for an individual insurer's inflows and outflows to be seriously out of balance. For example, Equation (8) reveals that $L^{*\prime}_h - L_h$ is positive when $p_h(N) < p_A(N)$ and $L^h r^h > Lr$, and negative when $p_h(N) > p_A(N)$ and $L^h r^h < Lr$. Thus, if insurer h writes a disproportionately large share of insureds that make the no-fault election (so that $p_h(N)$ is significantly greater than $p_A(N)$), and if the insurer writes a disproportionately large share of insureds in lower-rated driver classes (so that $L^h r^h$ is significantly less than Lr), then the difference $L^{*\prime}_h - L_h$ may be substantially negative.

Even when an insurer's funds are not out of balance, there is still a potential problem in that the insurer will find it financially advantageous, at the margin, to write insurance for tort insureds, and disadvantageous to write insurance for no-fault insureds. This is because, as can be seen from Table 5, the contribution-based pure premium of a tort insured is always greater than the experience-based pure premium, whereas the contribution-based pure premium of a no-fault insured tends to be less than the experience-based pure premium. Thus, the increase in expected losses associated with an additional tort insured is more than compensated by the tort insured's contribution-based pure premium, whereas the opposite is true for a no-fault insured. This phenomenon explains why $L^{*\prime}_h - L_h$ is greater when $p_h(N) < p_A(N)$, and less when $p_h(N) > p_A(N)$.

5.2. Balancing Methods

There are two principal approaches to addressing the issues of insurer fund imbalances and disincentives for insurers to write no-fault insureds: the escrow method and the risk exchange method.

In Pennsylvania, *Act 6* employs the escrow method to resolve both of these problems by requiring that insurers set aside, up front, the total amount of expected loss reductions for rating territory R from the optional no-fault system, and then return these savings to their no-fault insureds in the same rating territory. Although this redistribution mechanism will not actually be implemented until the second year under the new law, it could potentially operate in much the same way as a policyowner dividend program; that is, the amount of the premium savings to be given to each no-fault insured would depend on the insurer's actual proportion of no-fault insureds in rating territory R, and would be awarded at the end of the policy period.

In effect, employing the escrow method means that the contribution-based pure premium for no-fault insureds presented in Table 5 is replaced by the following expression:

$$L^{*\prime\prime}_{hijN} = L_{hij} - L^{h}r^{h}\left[p_V(N)+p_V(U)\right]/p_h(N). \tag{10}$$

It then follows that

$$L^{*\prime\prime}_{h} - L_h = 0. \tag{11}$$

The escrow method thus protects an insurer from the potential fund imbalances discussed above by making the total pure premium savings provided to the insurer's no-fault insureds in rating territory R no greater than the total expected loss reductions experienced by the insurer for this rating territory. This method also eliminates an insurer's incentive to write tort insureds instead of no-fault insureds by forcing the insurer to identify, prior to the policy period, the total number of dollars it will return to no-fault insureds through reduced premiums, so that the writing of one additional no-fault insured will only lower the average amount of premium savings provided to no-fault insureds, and will have no adverse impact on the insurer. While this mechanism may result in some no-fault insureds paying more than their contribution-based pure premiums (as expressed in Table 5), such differences should be very slight, because the pure premium in Equation (10) is reduced to account for the expected loss reductions created by restricting the tort rights of uninsured motorists, whereas the pure premium in Table 5 is not.

Another approach to the potential problems of fund imbalances and improper underwriting incentives is the creation of a risk exchange, such as New Jersey's Automobile Insurance Risk Exchange (AIRE), to redistribute premiums and expected losses so that insurers return all of the savings realized from the optional no-fault system to the no-fault insureds who create the savings. Although there are doubtlessly many different ways that this type of mechanism could be structured, its essential purpose is to collect $L^{*\prime}_{h}$ in pure premiums from insurer h for rating territory R, and return L_h. The overall fund balance of the risk exchange for this rating territory is thus equal to the sum of the $L^{*\prime}_{h} - L_h$ over all insurers h. From Equation (9), it is known that this sum is exactly 0, and so the risk exchange will always achieve an exact balance of inflows and outflows. It can also be seen that the existence of a risk exchange removes an insurer's incentive to prefer tort insureds to no-fault insureds by compensating the insurer exactly for the risk of writing either type.

6. CONCLUSIONS

In this article, two fundamental equity principles—the tort equity principle and the rate equity principle—have been used to evaluate and justify optional no-fault systems. It has been shown that only one type of optional no-fault system—the self-determining system implemented in New Jersey and Pennsylvania—can always satisfy both of these equity principles simultaneously, and that to be truly rate equitable, an automobile insurance recovery system must require that contribution-based pure premiums, rather than experience-based pure premiums, be employed.

A detailed examination of the self-determining optional no-fault system reveals that insurer fund imbalances and disincentives for writing no-fault insureds may occur without some sort of mechanism to eliminate these potential problems. Two such mechanisms are the escrow method, to be used in Pennsylvania, and the risk exchange method, currently used in New Jersey. Both of these approaches are able to eliminate satisfactorily the problems of insurer fund imbalances and improper underwriting incentives, to achieve a thoroughly equitable system.

Appendix

Derivations of Equations (5) through (11) from the text are provided below:

Equation (5)

$$L^*_h - L_h = \sum_{i,j}\{L_{hij}r_j[p_V(N)+p_V(U)]n_{hij} - Lrp_V(A)n_{hijN}\}$$
$$= L^h r^h[p_V(N)+p_V(U)]n_h - Lrp_V(A)p_h(N)n_h$$
$$= \{L^h r^h[p_V(N)+p_V(U)] - Lrp_V(A)p_h(N)\}n_h.$$

Equation (6)

$$\sum_h (L^*_h - L_h) = \sum_h \{L^h r^h[p_V(N)+p_V(U)] - Lrp_V(A)p_h(N)\}n_h$$
$$= Lr[p_V(N)+p_V(U)]n - Lrp_V(A)p_A(N)n$$
$$= Lr[p_V(N)+p_V(U)]n - Lrp_V(N)n$$
$$= Lrp_V(U)n.$$

Equation (7)

$$L^{*\prime}_{hijN} = L_{hij} - Lrp_V(A) - Lrp_V(U)/p_A(N)$$
$$= L_{hij} - Lrp_V(N)/p_A(N) - Lrp_V(U)/p_A(N)$$
$$= L_{hij} - Lr[p_V(N)+p_V(U)]/p_A(N).$$

Equation (8)

$$L^{*\prime}_h - L_h$$
$$= \sum_{i,j}\{L_{hij}r_j[p_V(N)+p_V(U)]n_{hij} - [Lr[p_V(N)+p_V(U)]/p_A(N)]n_{hijN}\}$$
$$= L^h r^h[p_V(N)+p_V(U)]n_h - Lr[p_V(N)+p_V(U)][p_h(N)/p_A(N)]n_h$$
$$= \{L^h r^h - Lr[p_h(N)/p_A(N)]\}[p_V(N)+p_V(U)]n_h.$$

Equation (9)

$$\sum_h (L*'_h - L_h) = \sum_h \{L^h r^h - Lr[p_h(N)/p_A(N)]\}[p_V(N)+p_V(U)]n_h$$
$$= Lr[p_V(N)+p_V(U)]n - Lr[p_V(N)+p_V(U)]n$$
$$= 0.$$

Equation (10)

$$L*''_{hijN} = L_{hij} - \{1/[p_h(N)n_h]\}\sum_{i',j'} L_{hi'j'}r_{j'}[p_V(N)+p_V(U)]n_{hi'j'}$$
$$= L_{hij} - L^h r^h[p_V(N)+p_V(U)]n_h/[p_h(N)n_h]$$
$$= L_{hij} - L^h r^h[p_V(N)+p_V(U)]/p_h(N).$$

Equation (11)

$$L*''_h - L_h$$
$$= \sum_{i,j}\{L_{hij}r_j[p_V(N)+p_V(U)]n_{hij} - [L^h r^h[p_V(N)+p_V(U)]/p_h(N)]n_{hijN}\}$$
$$= L^h r^h[p_V(N)+p_V(U)]n_h - L^h r^h[p_V(N)+p_V(U)]n_h$$
$$= 0.$$

References

All-Industry Research Advisory Council, 1989, *Compensation for Automobile Injuries in the United States*, Oak Brook, Illinois: AIRAC.

A. M. Best Company, 1990, Average Auto Premiums by State—1988, *Best's Insurance Management Reports (Property/Casualty)*, Release No. 4.

Hammitt, James K., 1985, *Automobile Accident Compensation, Volume II: Payments by Auto Insurers*, Santa Monica, CA: RAND Corporation, Institute for Civil Justice.

Insurance Services Office and National Association of Independent Insurers, 1988, *Factors Affecting Urban Insurance Costs*, New York, NY: ISO and NAII.

Keeton, Robert E., and Jeffrey O'Connell, 1965, *Basic Protection for the Traffic Victim*, Boston: Little, Brown.

O'Connell, Jeffrey, and Robert H. Joost, 1986, Giving Motorists a Choice between Fault and No-Fault Insurance, *Virginia Law Review*, 72, 61-89.

Rolph, John E., 1985, *Automobile Accident Compensation, Volume I: Who Pays How Much How Soon?*, Santa Monica, CA: RAND Corporation, Institute for Civil Justice.

Smith, Brian W., 1989, Reexamining the Cost Benefits of No-Fault, *CPCU Journal*, March.

United States Department of Transportation, 1985, *Compensating Auto Accident Victims: A Follow-Up Report on No-Fault Auto Insurance Experiences*, Washington, DC: Government Printing Office.

10
AUTO CHOICE: IMPACT ON CITIES AND THE POOR[†]

Dan Miller
Joint Economic Committee, U.S. Congress

1. INTRODUCTION

The current auto insurance system suffers from numerous shortcomings, and these problems are painfully felt by virtually everyone who buys auto insurance. Excessive and unnecessary fraud, litigation and injury claims have pushed the average insurance premium to more than $774 in 1996. The cost to insure an automobile is rising one-and-one-half times faster than the rate of inflation, outpacing the growth in costs for food, energy, housing, and even medical care.[1] Despite more money being paid into the system, however, accident victims with serious injuries are not being fully compensated for their losses. The current system of compensating people through a third-party tort liability system, therefore, results in the worst possible combination: high costs and low benefits.

The problems of cost and compensation are felt by everyone who purchases auto insurance, but some of the biggest losers are low-income families and inner-city residents. For these consumers, the way the current system operates often appears extremely inequitable. The intensity of feelings on auto insurance is reflected in an editorial from the African-American newspaper *The Philadelphia Tribune*:

[†] This chapter originally appeared as a March 1998 publication of the Joint Economic Committee of the U.S. Congress.

[1] National Association of Insurance Commissioners, *State Average Expenditures & Premiums for Personal Automobile Insurance in 1996* (Kansas City, MO: NAIC, 1998), Table 3; and U.S. Department of Labor, Bureau of Labor Statistics, "Consumer Price Indexes" (1998), on-line at <http://stats.bls.gov/cpihome.htm>.

> There is one issue that impacts more Philadelphians than all of the crimes committed in any given month and that is the (criminal) auto insurance rates Philadelphians are FORCED to pay simply because they live within the city.
>
> Because state law mandates that all motor vehicle owners must have insurance to drive those vehicles and because many Philadelphians are required to pay auto insurance rates far in excess of the value of the vehicles they drive, many Philadelphians are committing a crime because they are driving without the legally required auto insurance.
>
> Curiously, none of these tough on crime candidates is addressing the issue of usurious auto insurance rates which has turned thousands of otherwise law-abiding Philadelphians into criminals. Many city residents see a better option in becoming petty criminals than impoverishing themselves by paying the highest auto insurance rates in the nation.[2]

The fact that insurance costs, and as a result premiums, are higher in inner cities adds to a perception that the system is corrupt and unfair. Since inner cities are disproportionately poor and non-white, some critics have described the problem as a "black tax" or a "poor tax."[3] The problem, however, results not so much from who the policyholders are as from the flawed tort liability system that pushes up costs. Unfair or not, premiums are set to reflect the expected costs of paying claims under a liability system that encourages fraud, abuse, and litigation. As this chapter documents, all of these problems are worse in urban areas. Inner-city residents are therefore beset by what is best termed a "tort tax."

The problem of high rates paid by inner-city residents often is exacerbated by large disparities in premiums between cities and suburbs. In Philadelphia, for example, a relatively limited insurance policy for a married adult with no accidents or traffic violations costs approximately $1,800 each year. Moving to one of the nearby suburbs, however, could cut that amount by more than half—a savings of over $900 just by moving out of Philadelphia County.[4]

---

[2] Editorial, *The Philadelphia Tribune*, October 21, 1994. (Capitalization for emphasis in original.)

[3] See, for example, Mary A. Mitchell op-ed, *The Chicago Sun-Times*, July 21, 1996.

[4] Pennsylvania Department of Insurance (Harrisburg: 1995), cited in Insurance News Network, "Pennsylvania Auto Insurance Premiums" (1997), on-line at <http://www.insure.com/states/pa/auto/premiums/>.

The plight of cities is illustrated by the experience of Washington, D.C. Between 1985 and 1994, the number of auto accidents in the District of Columbia fell by 22 percent (Figure 1). Over roughly the same time period (1985 to 1995), however, the number of accident-related lawsuits increased by 137 percent.[5] Clearly, there is a problem with the insurance system when the number (as well as the severity) of accidents is declining, while the number of lawsuits is climbing rapidly.

Figure 1
Accidents and Related Lawsuits in Washington, DC (1985-95)

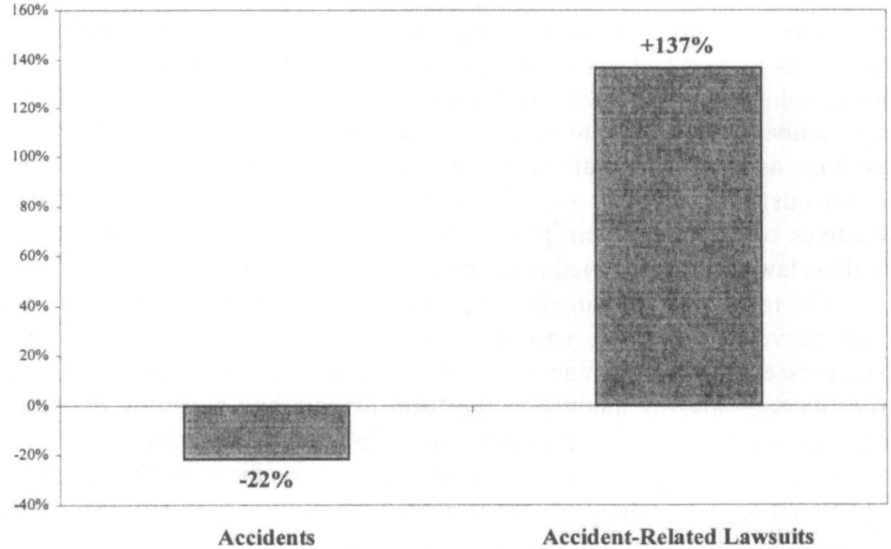

Source: The Washington Post, *June 23, 1996.*

The pinch of higher premiums is perhaps felt most keenly by low-income families. Data from the Bureau of Labor Statistics indicate that when families in the bottom income quintile (bottom 20 percent) buy auto insurance, they spend seven times the percentage of their household income on auto insurance as do families in the top quintile.[6] The problem is even worse for the very poor. A study of families earning less than half of the poverty line found that when such families buy auto insurance, they spend an average of about one-third (31.6 percent) of their family income.[7] Moreover,

---

[5] *The Washington Post*, June 23, 1996.

[6] See infra note 112 and accompanying text.

[7] Robert Lee Maril, "The Impact of Mandatory Auto Insurance upon Low-Income Residents of Maricopa County, Arizona" (unpublished manuscript, 1993), 17.

the study revealed that one-half of all families making less than twice the poverty line had to put off paying for other major expenses such as food, rent or a mortgage payment in order to pay their auto premium. Not surprisingly, when faced with having to make such sacrifices, some drivers choose instead to enter outlaw status as an uninsured driver.

The problems are not just isolated to low-income and urban drivers. Suburban and middle-class families also suffer from the same problems in terms of cost and compensation. The financial burden of auto insurance is magnified for these families by the fact that the average middle-income household owns two vehicles.[8] Excessively high premiums take money from the family budget that could be better spent on items such as education, health care, or a home mortgage. For example, middle-income families on average spent two-and-one-half times more on vehicle insurance in 1995 than on education.[9] In addition, high premiums in urban areas result in a large number of uninsured motorists. Suburban residents not only pay higher premiums as a result, but also are threatened with financial hardship if they are seriously injured by an uninsured motorist. Finally, the perverse incentives of the tort system put all drivers at risk of being the target of a frivolous lawsuit or being victimized by a criminal fraud ring.

The root cause of many of the problems associated with auto insurance is the perverse incentives embedded in the tort liability system. These incentives encourage claimants to inflate actual losses in order to recover larger damage awards, mainly in the form of pain and suffering damages. Legal scholar Charles Wolfram notes that "[p]ain and suffering and similar non-monetary damages probably average three times the monetary damages in personal injury claims."[10] Since pain and suffering awards are often calculated as three times medical and wage loss, there is a powerful incentive to inflate one's claimed economic damages and pursue legal action.

The incentive of pain and suffering awards is clearly seen in the experience of state reforms. In an effort to reduce unnecessary litigation, some states have enacted tort "thresholds" that set a minimum amount of economic loss that must be sustained before litigation can occur. In many cases, the outcome of such reforms is that the threshold becomes a target for claimants who simply inflate their medical claims through additional and often unnecessary visits to the doctor in order to reach the threshold. After Massachusetts raised its threshold from $500 to $2,000 in 1988, the median

---

[8] U.S. Department of Labor, Bureau of Labor Statistics, "1995 Consumer Expenditure Survey" (1997), on-line at <http://stats.bls.gov/blshome.html>.

[9] Ibid. Does not include educational expenses funded through tax payments.

[10] Charles W. Wolfram, *Modern Legal Ethics* (St. Paul, MN: West Publishing Co., 1986), 528 at note 21.

number of doctor visits rose from 13 to 30 per auto injury claim.[11] In Hawaii, where the threshold was $7,000 in 1990, the median number of visits for claimants who went to chiropractors was 58 per claimed injury.[12] Overall, the RAND Institute for Civil Justice estimates that between 35 and 42 percent of all medical claims occur in response to the incentives of the tort liability system, resulting in $13 to $18 billion in higher premiums in 1993.[13]

The tort liability system is also extremely inefficient at compensating accident victims. According to the RAND Institute for Civil Justice, accident victims with relatively minor injuries (under $5,000 in economic loss) generally receive compensation worth two to three times the size of their damages. In contrast, victims with economic losses between $25,000 and $100,000 are compensated for roughly one-half (56 percent) of their losses on average, and those with damages over $100,000 can expect to recoup just 9 percent of their losses (see Figure 2).[14] As consumer advocate Andrew Tobias described it, "It's like homeowner's insurance that pays triple if your stereo's stolen (or you say it was) but only 9 percent if the house burns down."[15]

---

[11] Sarah S. Marter and Herbert I. Weisberg, "Medical Expenses and the Massachusetts Automobile Tort Reform Law: A First Review of 1989 Bodily Injury Liability Claims," *Journal of Insurance Regulation*, 10, 4 (Summer 1992), 512.

[12] Insurance Research Council, *Automobile Injury Claims in Hawaii* (Oak Brook, IL: Insurance Research Council, 1991), 26.

[13] Stephen Carroll, Allan Abrahamse, and Mary Vaiana, *The Costs of Excess Medical Claims for Automobile Personal Injuries* (Santa Monica, CA: RAND, 1995), 23.

[14] Stephen J. Carroll, James S. Kakalik, Nicholas M. Pace, and John L. Adams, *No-Fault Approaches to Compensating People Injured in Automobile Accidents* (Santa Monica, CA: RAND, 1991), 187.

[15] Andrew Tobias, "Ralph Nader is a Big Fat Idiot," *Worth* (October 1996), 102.

Figure 2
Compensation of Economic Loss under the Tort System

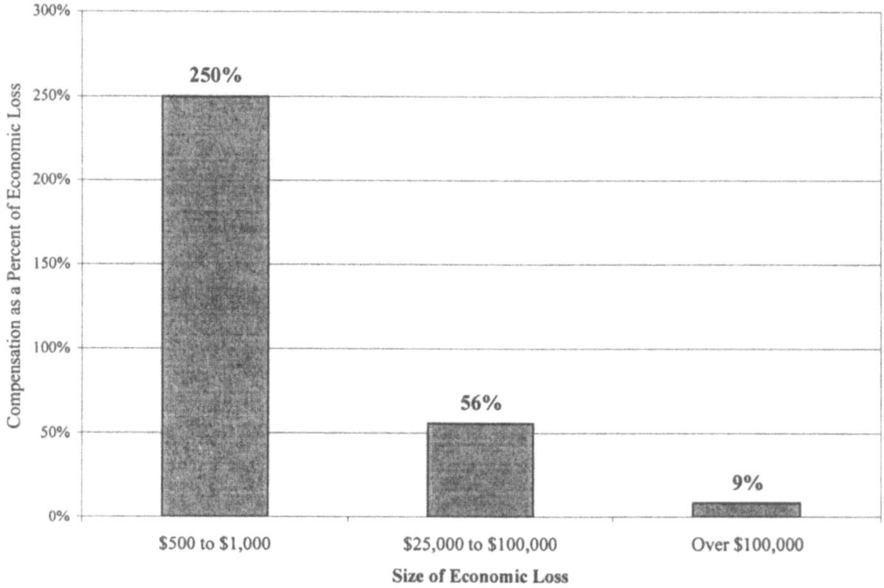

Source: Carroll, et al., (1991).

One reason for this failure is that only a small portion of each premium dollar paid for bodily injury liability actually ends up as compensation for real injuries. Based on data from the Insurance Information Institute, less than 15 percent of each premium dollar paid for bodily injury (BI) liability actually goes to cover legitimate medical costs and wage loss (see Figure 3).[16] The pain and suffering awards associated with these claims net claimants an additional 16.9 percent of the premium dollar. Payments made for fraudulent and excessive claims account for at least 12.6 percent of the premium. More than 28 percent of the BI premium dollar goes towards lawyers' fees (both plaintiffs and defendants). The remaining premium is consumed by state taxes and license fees (2.3 percent), commissions and costs associated with selling policies (15.2 percent), and other overhead expenses (10.1 percent). Overall, the tort liability system spends close to $6 on other expenses for each $1 it covers in actual medical and wage loss resulting from auto accidents.

[16] The basic breakout of the BI premium is from the Insurance Information Institute (New York, NY: III, April 30, 1997). This analysis uses RAND's lower bound estimate of excessive claiming behavior to identify the component of the BI premium attributable to fraudulent and excessive claiming.

Figure 3
Distribution of Bodily Injury Premiums

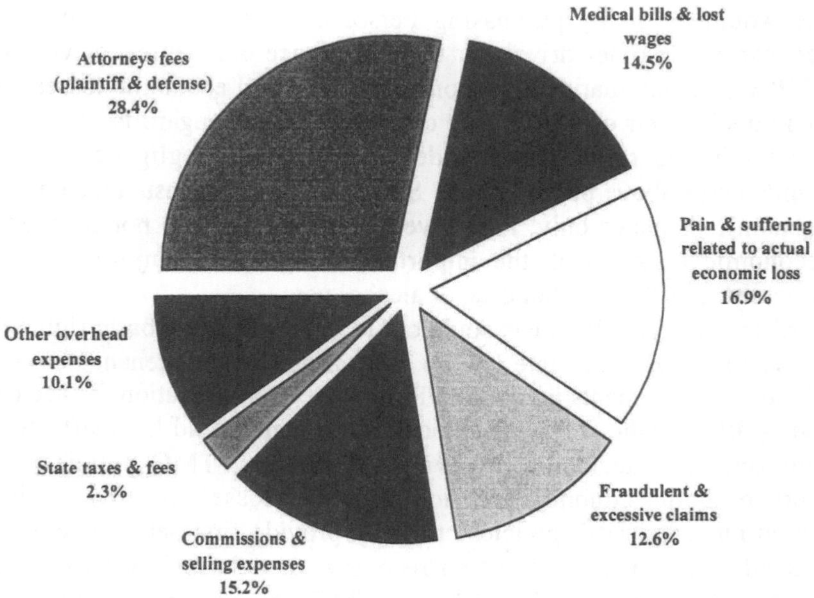

Source: Joint Economic Committee calculations and Insurance Information Institute data.

1.1. Auto Choice Reform

One reform that would help address these problems is Auto Choice, a proposal developed by Jeffrey O'Connell of the University of Virginia School of Law, and Michael Horowitz of the Hudson Institute.[17] Auto Choice gives consumers the option of exiting the current third-party liability system in favor of a primarily first-party insurance system that costs less and provides quicker and more complete compensation for all economic losses.[18] In effect, Auto Choice would make insurance coverage for pain and suffering

---

[17] The proposal is more fully described in Jeffrey O'Connell, Stephen Carroll, Michael Horowitz, Allan Abrahamse, and Paul Jamieson, "The Comparative Costs of Allowing Consumer Choice for Auto Insurance in All Fifty States," *Maryland Law Review*, 55, 1 (1996), 160-222. See also O'Connell, et al. (1995) and O'Connell, et al. (1993).

[18] Economic damages refer to direct measurable losses such as medical expenses, lost wages and income, and funeral costs. The term "pain and suffering" is loosely used to refer to all non-economic damages, including physical and emotional pain, stress, and other psychological damages.

optional. Drivers who wish to remain with their state's current insurance system could do so at essentially no extra cost.[19]

Individuals who want to exit the liability system's pain and suffering regime would do so by purchasing Personal Protection Insurance (PPI). Rather than suing other drivers or their insurance companies, drivers who elect PPI would automatically be compensated for all economic losses up to policy limits by their own insurance company, without regard to fault.[20] PPI drivers retain the right to sue under existing state negligence laws for economic losses above policy limits. Since PPI provides insurance coverage for economic damages only, PPI drivers could neither sue nor be sued for non-economic losses, with the important exceptions of injuries inflicted intentionally or as the result of drug or alcohol use.

Alternatively, individuals could opt to retain the same basic rights they now have under existing state law by purchasing tort maintenance coverage (TMC) to cover accidents involving PPI drivers. Compensation for accidents involving drivers who stay with the current system would be unaffected by this reform. For accidents involving PPI drivers, TMC policies allow recovery of both economic and non-economic losses, much as existing uninsured motorist (UM) policies currently provide first-party coverage for such accidents. Thus, the limit on recovery for pain and suffering losses caused by a PPI driver is chosen by the TMC driver.[21] If economic losses exceed TMC policy limits, TMC drivers can sue negligent PPI drivers for all of the remaining economic loss.[22]

Auto Choice seeks to preserve the traditional state role in regulating auto insurance. First, state laws defining negligence and other legal concepts are left largely intact. Second, state insurance commissioners can block the reform if they determine that their state would not experience a specified minimum amount of savings in premiums for bodily injury liability. Finally, and most importantly, the Auto Choice proposal allows states to repeal the federal reform altogether or to modify it to suit their state's needs. New Jersey Governor Christine Todd Whitman has called the federal Auto Choice

---

[19] See sources indicated in infra note 122.

[20] Fault would no longer matter with respect to injury compensation only. State-based rate regulations could continue to penalize negligent drivers with higher premiums.

[21] Under the current tort system, the limit on pain and suffering recovery is often set by the negligent driver's insurance policy, or set at zero in the case of uninsured drivers.

[22] The version of Auto Choice examined here requires PPI drivers also to purchase supplementary liability insurance to provide additional coverage for certain situations, such as injuries to pedestrians and excess economic losses.

legislation "a model of federalism in that federal law would represent the first word, rather than the last word, on the subject."[23]

2. INSURANCE COST FACTORS IN URBAN AREAS

The most glaring problem with auto insurance in cities is that premiums are too high. However, the fundamental reason that premiums are higher in cities is that the costs to provide insurance are also higher. A review of the empirical research on the subject of urban auto insurance reveals five factors that are primarily responsible for higher liability insurance costs in inner cities:[24]

- frequency of injury claims,
- average injury cost per insured vehicle,
- fraud and claim buildup,
- transaction costs and litigation, and
- uninsured motorists.

This section of the chapter reviews some of the existing empirical research on these factors. Not all urban areas are alike. Some cities have greater problems than others do, even within the same state. Philadelphia, for example, has more serious problems with auto insurance than does Pittsburgh. Similarly, Los Angeles is worse off than San Diego. There are also important territorial distinctions to keep in mind. For instance, one report may compare a city with the rest of the state, whereas another study may compare a city to the surrounding suburbs. Additionally, results may differ from study to study depending on the cities included, the time period examined, or the data used in the analysis.

2.1. Claiming Frequency, Injury Severity, and Loss Costs

The underlying cause of higher insurance costs in urban areas is the higher frequency of injury claims per accident. Even though car crashes in urban areas are generally less severe (because they occur at a lower rate of speed), accidents in urban areas are more likely to result in an injury claim

[23] Christine Todd Whitman, Governor of New Jersey, Testimony to the Joint Economic Committee, U.S. Congress, March 19, 1997.

[24] Property damage and auto thefts are also much higher in cities but are not considered here because they would not be affected by the Auto Choice reform.

being filed with an insurance company. As a result, the average loss per insured vehicle (or average loss cost) is also higher.

To illustrate the magnitude of such differences in claiming behavior, Table 1 presents data for 10 cities and states on the number of bodily injury claims per 100 accidents (measured here as the number of property damage claims). In the state of California (excluding Los Angeles), there are close to 45 claims of bodily injury for every 100 accidents. In Los Angeles, the claimed injury rate is more than double the rest of the state: for every 100 property damage claims, there are approximately 99 bodily injury claims. In Philadelphia, the claimed injury rate is three and one-half times the average for the rest of the state – more than 78 injury claims per 100 accidents.

Table 1
Number of Bodily Injury Claims per 100 Property Damage Claims

	Bodily Injury Claims per 100 Property Damage Claims		
City and State	**City**	**Rest of State**	**Ratio**
Los Angeles, CA	98.8	44.5	2.22
Newark, NJ	79.6	32.8	2.42
Philadelphia, PA	78.5	22.4	3.50
Baltimore, MD	62.1	36.6	1.69
Charlotte, NC	58.1	41.8	1.39
Milwaukee, WI	43.9	29.4	1.49
Cleveland, OH	40.8	28.5	1.43
Memphis, TN	35.7	25.3	1.41
Miami, FL	29.4	18.2	1.62
New York, NY	27.6	10.3	2.67

Source: Joint Economic Committee calculations and Insurance Research Council (1995).

Because each city listed in Table 1 and Table 2 is unique in terms of its state's legal and insurance system, population and vehicle density, overall crime rates, and geographic size, it is sometimes difficult to estimate precise relationships that hold for all cities. Nonetheless, a review of the empirical research reveals a consistent pattern: claiming frequency and insurance costs are higher in cities than they are in other parts of the same state, even though injury severity tends to be the same or lower.[25]

2.1.1. Survey of 49 Cities

To supplement and build on the existing research, we examined insurance data for 49 cities in the U.S. The results of this analysis, presented in Table 2, confirm the findings of earlier research. Figures for each city represent the percentage difference between the city territory and the rest of the state for that indicator. The two primary types of coverage considered here are bodily injury (BI) liability and personal injury protection (PIP) policies.[26] Figures were calculated based on territorial definitions and 1989 to 1991 claim data published by the Insurance Research Council (IRC).[27]

This analysis examines three types of insurance systems: traditional tort, no-fault with a dollar or weak verbal threshold, and no-fault with a strict verbal threshold. Under traditional tort systems, there are no restrictions on the right to sue, and accident victims recover damages primarily from the negligent driver's liability policy.[28] No-fault systems with a dollar or weak verbal threshold allow lawsuits only when a certain amount of medical bills have accumulated (dollar threshold) or when the injuries meet broad descriptive criteria (weak verbal threshold). Drivers in no-fault states with a strict verbal threshold can bring a lawsuit only in cases where the injuries meet specific descriptive criteria (strict verbal threshold).[29] Averages for the

---

[25] See sources listed at infra notes 35, 59, 104, and Highway Loss Data Institute, *Atlas of Automobile Injury and Collision Losses in Large Metropolitan Areas* (Arlington, VA: Highway Loss Data Institute, 1995).

[26] According to data from the National Association of Independent Insurers, these two coverages accounted for 80 percent of all personal injury auto insurance payments in 1994.

[27] Insurance Research Council, *Trends in Auto Injury Claims*, 2nd ed. (Wheaton, IL: IRC, 1995), Appendix B, and unpublished data from the IRC. Criteria for city selection include 1992 population of at least 50,000, a population density of at least 1,000 persons per square mile, and an IRC territorial definition that approximates the city being compared. Territorial definitions do not always match official city limits. For example, figures for Birmingham, AL are actually for Jefferson County.

[28] In this analysis, tort states include both traditional tort states and "add-on" tort states. First-party health insurance coverage for auto injuries is available through medical payment (MP) policies in traditional tort states and through personal injury protection (PIP) policies in "add-on" tort states.

[29] Although Florida is listed here as having a strict verbal threshold, its descriptive criteria are considerably broader than those in Michigan and New York. Even in Michigan, which has the strictest verbal threshold in the country, increasing numbers of cases are being judged eligible for litigation.

primary coverage (BI in tort states and PIP in no-fault states) in each system are presented at the end of Table 2.

Table 2
Differences in Claiming Behavior between Cities and the Rest of the State

State	City	Bodily Injury (BI)				Personal Injury Protection (PIP)		
		Freq.	Sev.	Avg. Loss Cost	BI-to-PD Ratio	Freq.	Sev.	Avg. Loss Cost
AL	Birmingham	+10%	0%	+9%	-6%	*NA*	*NA*	*NA*
AZ	Phoenix	+34%	-8%	+24%	+15%	*NA*	*NA*	*NA*
AR	Little Rock	+55%	-7%	+44%	+16%	*NA*	*NA*	*NA*
CA	Los Angeles	+144%	-22%	+90%	+122%	*NA*	*NA*	*NA*
CO	Denver	+35%	-13%	+19%	+9%	+31%	+3%	+35%
CT	Hartford	+161%	-28%	+88%	+23%	+171%	-7%	+151%
DE	Wilmington	+59%	-11%	+41%	+12%	+74%	-10%	+56%
DC	DC Suburbs	+39%	+6%	+47%	+22%	*NA*	*NA*	*NA*
FL	Miami	+83%	-32%	+24%	+62%	+2%	+25%	+27%
GA	Atlanta	+52%	-14%	+31%	+21%	+47%	+10%	+61%
HI	Honolulu	+61%	-29%	+16%	+17%	+31%	-24%	-1%
ID	Boise	+21%	-11%	+8%	+4%	*NA*	*NA*	*NA*
IL	Chicago	+53%	-20%	+23%	+32%	*NA*	*NA*	*NA*
IN	Indianapolis	+32%	-3%	+27%	+13%	*NA*	*NA*	*NA*
IA	Des Moines	+51%	-2%	+49%	+9%	*NA*	*NA*	*NA*
KS	Wichita	+10%	-4%	+6%	-14%	+18%	-3%	+15%
KY	Louisville	+20%	-8%	+10%	-5%	+9%	-6%	+2%
LA	New Orleans	+49%	+4%	+55%	+34%	*NA*	*NA*	*NA*
ME	Portland	+29%	-8%	+18%	-2%	*NA*	*NA*	*NA*
MD	Baltimore	+121%	-6%	+106%	+69%	+140%	+14%	+173%
MA	Boston	+93%	+10%	+112%	+28%	+97%	+16%	+129%
MI	Detroit	+27%	-18%	+6%	*NA*	+23%	-45%	-33%
MN	Minneapolis	+63%	-3%	59%	+27%	+24%	+15%	+43%
MS	Jackson	-9%	-16%	-24%	-13%	*NA*	*NA*	*NA*
MO	Kansas City	+34%	-16%	+13%	+15%	*NA*	*NA*	*NA*
MT	Billings	+85%	-13%	+62%	+21%	*NA*	*NA*	*NA*
NE	Omaha	+100%	-21%	+58%	+36%	*NA*	*NA*	*NA*
NV	Las Vegas	+47%	+7%	+57%	+19%	*NA*	*NA*	*NA*
NH	Manchester	+50%	0%	+49%	+7%	*NA*	*NA*	*NA*
NJ	Newark	+244%	-18%	+182%	+142%	+119%	+13%	+148%

Table 2 (Continued)

State	City	Bodily Injury (BI)				Personal Injury Protection (PIP)		
		Freq.	Sev.	Avg. Loss Cost	BI-to-PD Ratio	Freq.	Sev.	Avg. Loss Cost
NM	**Albuquerque**	+43%	-3%	+39%	+14%	*NA*	*NA*	*NA*
NY	**New York City**	+234%	-29%	+140%	+167%	+37%	+36%	+86%
NC	**Charlotte**	+111%	-18%	+74%	+39%	*NA*	*NA*	*NA*
ND	**Fargo**	+51%	+15%	+72%	-1%	+52%	+3%	+56%
OH	**Cleveland**	+40%	+4%	+46%	+43%	*NA*	*NA*	*NA*
OK	**Tulsa**	+34%	+10%	+47%	+2%	*NA*	*NA*	*NA*
OR	**Portland**	+53%	-4%	+46%	+14%	+68%	-19%	+37%
PA	**Philadelphia**	+226%	-13%	+184%	+250%	*NA*	*NA*	*NA*
RI	**Providence**	+48%	-13%	+28%	+33%	*NA*	*NA*	*NA*
SC	**Charleston**	+50%	-7%	+40%	+1%	*NA*	*NA*	*NA*
SD	**Sioux Falls**	+73%	-25%	+30%	+19%	*NA*	*NA*	*NA*
TN	**Memphis**	+66%	-25%	+24%	+41%	*NA*	*NA*	*NA*
TX	**Houston**	+42%	+3%	+46%	+21%	+41%	+14%	+60%
UT	**Salt Lake City**	+40%	-2%	+36%	+11%	+30%	+2%	+33%
VA	**Norfolk & Area**	+47%	-17%	+23%	+23%	*NA*	*NA*	*NA*
WA	**Seattle**	+18%	+8%	+28%	-10%	-3%	+17%	+13%
WV	**Charleston**	+3%	-6%	-3%	-8%	*NA*	*NA*	*NA*
WI	**Milwaukee**	+95%	-16%	+64%	+49%	*NA*	*NA*	*NA*
Averages:								
All States		**+65%**	**-9%**	**+47%**	**+31%**	**+53%**	**+3%**	**+57%**
Tort States		**+57%**	**-8%**	**+43%**	**+28%**	*NA*	*NA*	*NA*
Strict Verbal N-F States		*NA*	*NA*	*NA*	*NA*	**+20%**	**+5%**	**+27%**
$/Weak Verbal N-F States		*NA*	*NA*	*NA*	*NA*	**+57%**	**+2%**	**+61%**

Source: Joint Economic Committee calculations and Insurance Research Council (1995).

For the 49 cities examined, the average BI claim frequency was 65 percent higher than the rest of the state. The pattern for PIP claims was similar, with cities averaging 53 percent more claims per 100 insured cars. Unadjusted BI claiming rates, however, are not perfect indicators of claiming behavior, since urban areas tend to have more accidents. As noted in Table 1 above, an alternative measure of claiming rates is the ratio of BI claims to property damage (PD) claims (called the BI-to-PD ratio), in which the number of PD claims serves as a proxy for the number of accidents. As might be expected, when the different accident rate is accounted for, the discrepancy in claiming frequency between cities and other areas is reduced. Nonetheless, the difference in BI claiming frequencies is startlingly higher—31 percent higher on average (see the bottom of column 4 in Table 2).

Although injury claims are more frequent in cities, the injuries caused by auto accidents tend to be less severe. The fatality rate for accidents on urban roads is less than half that for rural roads.[30] Even among crashes with at least one fatality, urban accidents are generally less severe, with 42 percent of survivors reporting no injury compared to 28 percent for rural accidents. Conversely, 25 percent of survivors of fatal accidents in urban areas suffer an incapacitating injury, versus 37 percent for rural accidents.[31] Reflecting these facts, the average BI claim in cities was 9 percent smaller than elsewhere in the same state, while PIP claims were just 3 percent larger.[32]

The final point of comparison, average loss cost, is perhaps the most important in determining the actual premium charged by insurance companies. Average loss cost is simply the total amount of injury payments made by insurers divided by the number of insured cars. It is, in other words, each policyholder's share of the direct cost of paying injury claims, not counting expenses such as administrative, personnel, or legal defense costs. The average loss cost, or pure premium, is the base from which total premiums are determined.[33] Any effort to reduce premiums must, ultimately, reduce average loss costs. As with claiming rates, the data in Table 2 indicate that loss costs in cities are substantially higher than elsewhere in the state. The average cost per insured driver to pay bodily injury claims is 47 percent higher in cities compared to other parts of the state. For PIP claims, the figure is 57 percent.

It is worth noting, however, that for the three states with strict verbal thresholds (Florida, Michigan, and New York), the city-suburb disparity in

---

[30] These data also indicate that there is only a negligible difference in the number of people injured or killed per accident. U.S. Department of Transportation, Federal Highway Administration, *Highway Statistics 1995* (Washington, DC: Government Printing Office, 1996), V-104.

[31] U.S. Department of Transportation, National Highway Traffic Safety Administration, *Rural and Urban Crashes: A Comparative Analysis*, DOT HS 808-450 (Washington, DC: NHTSA, 1996), 75.

[32] Injury severity is measured here as the size of the injury claim. Claim size, however, is an imperfect measure of the actual damage because the size of the claim is often a function of tort incentives presented to the claimant. See supra notes 11, 12, and 13, and accompanying text.

[33] See S.S. Huebner, Kenneth Black, Jr., and Bernard L. Webb, *Property and Liability Insurance*, 4th ed. (Upper Saddle River, NJ: Prentice Hall, 1996), 623-628.

average PIP loss costs is just 27 percent, less than one-half the 61 percent average for the other no-fault states.[34] Michigan, with the toughest verbal threshold in the country, is the only no-fault state where the average loss cost of PIP claims is significantly lower in the city than elsewhere. Since average loss cost represents the base used to determine overall premiums, these figures can be interpreted as a rough measure of the differences in BI and PIP premiums paid by residents of the different territories.[35]

One remarkable observation that comes from the data in Table 2 is that auto insurance problems are not just limited to major metropolises like Philadelphia and Los Angeles. Even cities such as Billings, Montana, and Charlotte, North Carolina, have average loss costs that exceed 60 percent of the average for the rest of the state. Bigger cities, in other words, are frequently the most expensive areas for insurance, even within otherwise "low cost" states. These figures underscore the importance of auto insurance reform for all urban centers.

2.2. Fraud and Claim Buildup

Another factor that increases the cost of auto insurance in cities is fraud and other abuse of the insurance system. The available data indicate that fraud and abuse are more common in large urban areas. The insurance system suffers from two types of abuse. The first type involves explicit fraud, including staged accidents, orchestrated visits to doctors' offices, and organized crime. The second type includes opportunistic claim buildup that results when individuals inflate their insurance claims for injuries that either are not real, are less severe than claimed, or are not even related to the auto accident in question.

The most comprehensive study of fraud by accident location is the 1996 report *Fraud and Buildup in Auto Injury Claims* by the IRC.[36] The report examined over 15,000 actual insurance claims from 1992, each of which had notes from claim adjusters identifying elements that suggested the presence of fraud and buildup. The IRC study included data for nine major

---

[34] For further discussion, see text accompanying infra note 133.

[35] This interpretation assumes that the markup from pure premium is uniform within a state. Although this generally appears to be the case (as indicated in Lamberty), the correlation between loss costs and premiums is weakened to the degree that state insurance regulations limit the use of location as a determinant of premiums. Steve Lamberty, "Urban and Non-Urban Auto Insurance Comparisons," *NAIC Research Quarterly*, 1, 4 (October 1995), 17.

[36] Insurance Research Council, *Fraud and Buildup in Auto Injury Claims* (Wheaton, IL: IRC, 1996).

cities (with populations of at least one million) and their surrounding suburbs, as well as other large central cities (with populations of 100,000 to one million) and their suburbs, medium cities, and small town/rural areas. Figure 4 presents the percentage of cases in each location for which there was a high degree of suspicion of fraud and buildup. A similar pattern is evident for both types of abuse: the greater the degree of urbanization, the more likely an injury claim will be fraudulent or include buildup. In major cities, for example, 14 percent of claims had a high degree of suspicion of fraud, and 26 percent had a high degree of suspicion of buildup. Rates for all other areas were progressively lower.

Figure 4
Claims with a High Degree of Suspicion of Fraud or Buildup

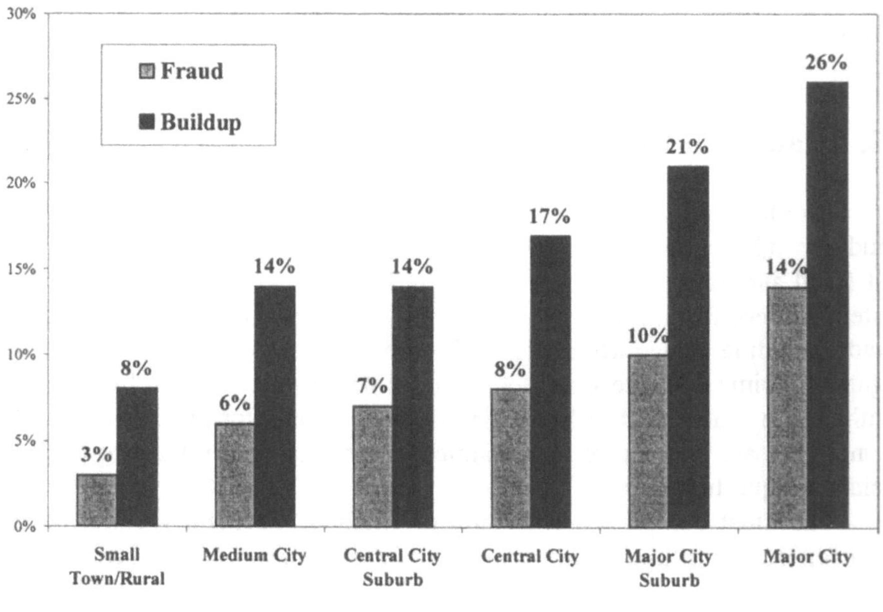

Source: Insurance Research Council (1996).

A more indirect indicator of fraud and buildup is the frequency of soft-tissue injuries. Soft-tissue injuries, such as sprains or strains, are real injuries, but because there is no way to verify their existence medically, they make ideal candidates for fraud and buildup. Figure 5 presents data on the distribution of injury types by accident location. In rural accidents, 40 percent of injury claims involve only sprains or strains. By comparison, nearly two-thirds (64 percent) of injury claims in central cities are non-verifiable.[37]

As noted above, the different forms of fraud and other abuse vary widely, ranging from opportunistic claim buildup committed by individuals to multi-million dollar fraud rings orchestrated by organized crime. Organized fraud and criminal rings are more common in inner cities. Dense urban centers generally have all the elements necessary for such crime rings to prosper: frequent accidents that can result in easily-faked injuries; an abundance of professionals capable of taking advantage of the system; and a supply of often needy, low-income individuals who may be enticed into breaking the law.

Figure 5
Types of Bodily Injury Claims by City Size

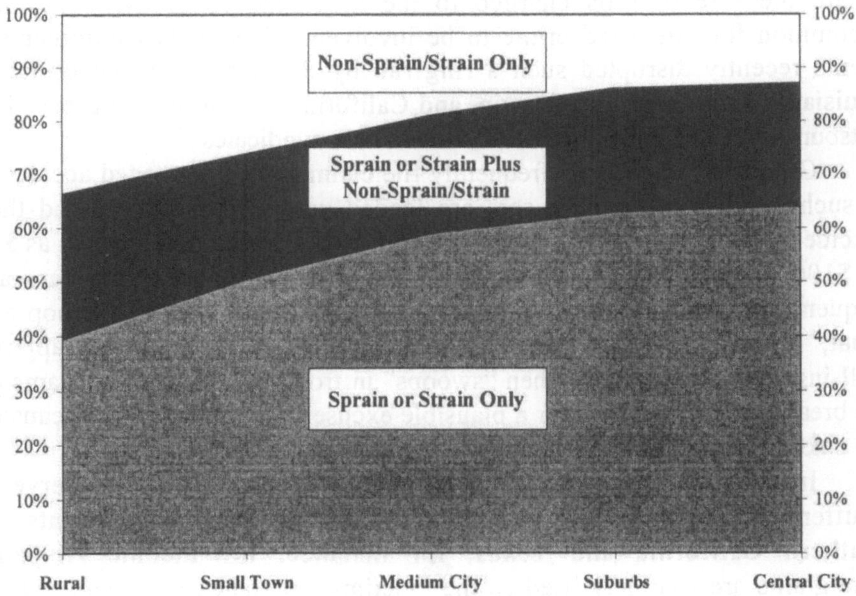

Source: Insurance Research Council (1994a).

One common type of fraud is "ghost riders," individuals who file insurance claims for accidents that either did not happen or did not involve them. In a 1993 New Jersey investigation of ghost riders, police staged a

[37] Insurance Research Council, *Auto Injuries: Claiming Behavior and Its Impact on Insurance Costs* (Oak Brook, IL: IRC, 1994), 20.

low-speed accident with a city bus, and 17 people climbed onto the bus *after* the accident and later filed insurance claims for their "injuries".[38] In a separate case, a bus driver witnessed an accident between two other vehicles and stopped to see if anyone needed help. Having heard the sound of a crash and seeing the bus driver get off the bus, 27 of the bus passengers assumed that their bus had crashed and filed insurance claims.[39]

Another type of abuse comes in the form of schemes that coordinate staged accidents, visits to doctors' offices, legal representation, and insurance claims. For example, a Boston chiropractor who was convicted of insurance fraud required that all patients to his clinics make at least 25 visits and receive at least $2,000 worth of medical treatments.[40] Another common technique is for fraud rings to utilize "runners" who use radio scanners to arrive at accident scenes ahead of police or emergency personnel, and then encourage individuals to file claims for non-existent injuries. Other schemes involve lawyers and doctors who work in conjunction with each other to inflate the size of bills charged to the insurance company. It is not uncommon for organized crime to be involved. Federal law enforcement agents recently disrupted such a ring run by Russian organized crime in Louisiana, Texas, Florida, Oregon, and California.[41] Another ring based in Pittsburgh has also been linked to Russian crime syndicates.[42]

Organized fraud rings frequently file claims based on staged accidents. In such cases, two or more cars are loaded up with passengers and then "accidentally" collide. Participants are then paid a fixed amount, such as $50 or $100 per accident, to file false injury claims. Innocent drivers are frequently unwitting participants. A common technique is the "swoop and squat," where one car pulls in front of a truck or other vehicle that appears well-insured. A second car then "swoops" in front the first car and slams on the breaks, giving the first car a plausible excuse to do likewise, thus causing the unknowing driver to collide into the schemer from behind.

Investigators often note that ethnic groups are targeted to serve as "stuffers", the individuals who ride in the cars that cause the accidents. In southern California and Texas, for instance, low-income Hispanic immigrants are routinely used as the "victims" in staged accidents. Other staged-accident rings have involved African-American, Filipino, Armenian, and Korean groups in Los Angeles; Vietnamese in Orange County,

---

[38] *The New York Times*, August 18, 1993.

[39] Ibid.

[40] *The Boston Globe*, April 19, 1995. Not coincidentally, Massachusetts law requires that injury claimants have at least $2,000 in medical bills before they can sue for pain and suffering.

[41] U.P.I., August 1, 1997.

[42] *The Pittsburgh Post-Gazette*, January 4, 1997.

California; Russian-Jews and Eastern Europeans in Pittsburgh and New York; and Haitians and Jamaicans in Florida.[43] Although the injuries that stuffers are instructed to claim are supposed to be fake, staged accidents have resulted in death or serious injury to stuffers and innocent drivers alike.[44] Ironically, these low-income stuffers are paid as little as $50 or $100 to risk their lives, even as the lawyers and doctors involved can bring in tens of thousands of dollars per accident.[45]

The problems of fraud and abuse of the insurance system are of real concern to low-income, inner-city residents. Indeed, such people suffer from both ends of the system. Not only do they have to pay high premiums because they live in high-cost territories, but they also are targets of organized crime rings that try to lure them into staged accident schemes. As Sean Mooney of the Insurance Information Institute put it:

> Residents of inner cities suffer from a number of social ills—low income, poor education, and reduced employment opportunities. In addition, inner-city residents are prey to drug dealers, thieves, and other criminals. It is now increasingly apparent that inner-city residents are also the prey of a newer parasite—the profiteers of hard-core insurance fraud. These profiteers recruit inner-city residents as their pawns in multi-million-dollar insurance fraud rings. To some extent insurance companies pay for these claims out of profits. But the real victims are the inner-city residents themselves who pay for the costs of insurance fraud and abuse through higher insurance premiums.[46]

Another detrimental consequence of greater fraud in inner cities is the potential for slower payment for real injuries. Fraud prevention efforts necessarily require that insurance companies investigate injury claims that appear to have elements of fraud or buildup before the claims are paid. Since inner-city injury claims are more likely to exhibit signs of fraud or buildup, payments to claimants for legitimate injuries can be delayed while insurance companies investigate suspicious cases.

---

[43] *The San Francisco Chronicle*, October 31, 1993; *The Los Angeles Times*, July 13, 1992; and *The Pittsburgh Post-Gazette*, March 12, 1997.

[44] *The Los Angeles Times*, July 13, 1992.

[45] For a comprehensive account of the long history of abuses by claimants and organized fraud rings, see Ken Dornstein, *Accidentally, on Purpose: The Making of a Personal Injury Underworld in America* (New York, NY: St. Martin's Press, 1996).

[46] Sean F. Mooney, "The Cost of Urban Auto Insurance" (New York, NY: Insurance Information Institute, 1992), 22.

The magnitude of the organized fraud schemes is often quite large. A fraud ring in south-central Los Angeles, for example, bilked insurers out of more than $20 million in medical and legal bills.[47] In Passaic County, New Jersey, hundreds of individuals have been charged with manufacturing over $75 million in bogus claims.[48] A chain of clinics run by two chiropractors in northern New Jersey has been charged with filing $52 million in bogus insurance claims.[49]

Consumers ultimately bear the cost of fraud and claim buildup through higher premiums. According to FBI Director Louis Freeh, "Every American household is burdened with over $200 annually in additional premiums to make up for this type of [insurance] fraud."[50] As previously noted, research by the RAND Institute for Civil Justice indicates that between 35 and 42 percent of injury claims occur as a result of the incentives of the tort system, totaling between $13 and $18 billion in higher premiums in 1993.[51]

2.3. Transaction Costs and Litigation

As in any industry, consumers suffer when transaction costs are too high. In the case of auto insurance, one of the biggest transaction costs is legal expenses. Clearly, lawyers play an important and necessary role in obtaining compensation for injured drivers in today's system. However, in many cases pain and suffering damages are awarded not to compensate the injured victims, but to pay for legal costs. According to Wolfram, "inflated elements of general damages, such as pain and suffering, are tolerated by courts as a rough measure of the plaintiff's attorney fees."[52]

Quite simply, attorney services are expensive, and consequently, high lawyer involvement can increase the cost of providing auto insurance. For personal injury lawsuits, the plaintiff's attorney generally takes 33 to 40 percent of the final award, regardless of how much time and effort are required to win the case. According to one study, attorney representation is associated with a 64 percent increase in the size of the insurance claim, even after controlling for environmental variables and injury type.[53] Defense

[47] California Department of Insurance, Fraud Division, *The Investigator* (Spring 1996).

[48] *Business Week*, June 30, 1997; and *The (Bergen, N.J.) Record*, June 11, 1997.

[49] *The New York Times*, April 22, 1997.

[50] U.S. Department of Justice, Federal Bureau of Investigation, Press release (Washington, DC: FBI, May 24, 1995).

[51] Carroll, Abrahamse, and Vaiana, 23.

[52] Wolfram, 528 at note 21.

[53] Mark J. Browne and Robert Puelz, "Statutory Rules, Attorney Involvement, and Automobile Liability Claims," *The Journal of Risk and Insurance*, 63, 1 (March 1996), 79.

attorneys are also highly paid (though on an hourly basis) and often seek to drag cases out as long as possible, hoping to force the plaintiff to accept a smaller award as well as to increase their own fees.

The available data indicate that attorney involvement is significantly higher in large cities relative to suburbs (Table 3). In both Baltimore and Los Angeles, approximately 9 out of every 10 bodily injury claimants hired an attorney in 1992.[54] While attorney representation in the suburbs of these cities was still high (78 percent), it was nonetheless significantly lower than the rate in the central city. The city-suburb differential was even greater in other cities. The attorney representation rate for PIP claimants in New York City, for example, was 60 percent higher than in the suburbs, and PIP claimants in Dallas/Ft. Worth were 74 percent more likely to hire an attorney than claimants in the suburbs. The average rate of attorney representation in these selected cities relative to their suburbs was 24 percent higher for BI claimants and 33 percent higher for PIP claimants.

Table 3
Attorney Representation for BI and PIP Claims in Selected Cities

	BI Claims			PIP Claims		
	City	Suburb	Ratio	City	Suburb	Ratio
Baltimore	89%	78%	1.14	80%	68%	1.18
Los Angeles	92%	78%	1.18	NA	NA	NA
Houston	72%	49%	1.47	52%	42%	1.24
Washington, DC	76%	63%	1.21	56%	50%	1.12
San Francisco	70%	55%	1.27	NA	NA	NA
Chicago	61%	47%	1.30	NA	NA	NA
Dallas/Fort Worth	53%	48%	1.10	47%	27%	1.74
Seattle	51%	39%	1.31	23%	29%	0.79
Phoenix	50%	38%	1.32	NA	NA	NA
Philadelphia	NA	NA	NA	77%	56%	1.38
New York	NA	NA	NA	64%	40%	1.60
Detroit	NA	NA	NA	36%	16%	2.25
Average	**68%**	**55%**	**1.24**	**54%**	**41%**	**1.33**

Source: Insurance Research Council (1994a).

[54] Insurance Research Council, *Claiming Behavior*, 48.

If the tort liability system were successful at compensating individuals, then the higher cost might be worth paying. The available data, however, suggest that having an attorney does not improve the speed of compensation for injured victims. For example, among small bodily injury claims ($500 or less), just 9 percent of claimants with an attorney received their final payment from the insurance company within 30 days, compared to 63 percent for non-represented claimants. For more serious injuries (over $2,500), three times as many attorney-represented claimants (45 percent) had to wait over a year for final payment compared to non-represented claimants (15 percent).[55]

Moreover, as previously indicated, the system performs badly with respect to the amount of compensation. A 1991 study by the RAND Institute for Civil Justice found that accident victims with less than $5,000 in economic losses receive compensation that is on average worth two to three times the amount of their losses.[56] The seriously injured, such as those with permanent or total disability, do not fare nearly as well. Such victims are often denied full recovery for their economic losses, and what they do receive can be delayed for years. According to RAND, individuals with economic losses of $25,000 to $100,000 are compensated for just over one-half (56 percent) of their losses on average. The very seriously injured (economic losses over $100,000) receive compensation worth just 9 percent of their damages.[57]

2.4. Uninsured Drivers

A major problem that contributes to higher premiums in urban areas is the number of uninsured motorists. All states require drivers to carry a minimum amount of liability insurance or to meet certain financial responsibility levels. Nonetheless, uninsured motorists are a widespread and costly problem in urban areas, where the concentration of low-income households places many families in the difficult position of choosing between purchasing basic necessities or complying with the law. As City Councilman Mark Ridley, who represents South Central Los Angeles, put it:

---

[55] Ibid., 72.

[56] Carroll, Kakalik, Pace, and Adams, 187.

[57] In many cases, the seriously injured are undercompensated even though they receive maximum compensation from the applicable insurance policy. That amount, however, is often capped at the limits chosen by those who injure them.

"It's a function of putting food on the table versus paying for car insurance. It's really obvious what one does."[58]

The problem of uninsured motorists is particularly severe in inner cities. According to one survey of 17 large cities, the average rate of uninsured motorist (UM) claims (per 100 property damage claims) is over three times higher in cities than in other areas of the same states.[59] Other insurance claim data also indicate that uninsured motorists are more frequent in central cities. As can be seen in Figure 6, 44 percent of all uninsured motorist claims resulted from accidents that took place in central cities, even though such accidents accounted for just 36 percent of all bodily injury (BI) claims.[60]

Figure 6
Accident Location of Injury Claims

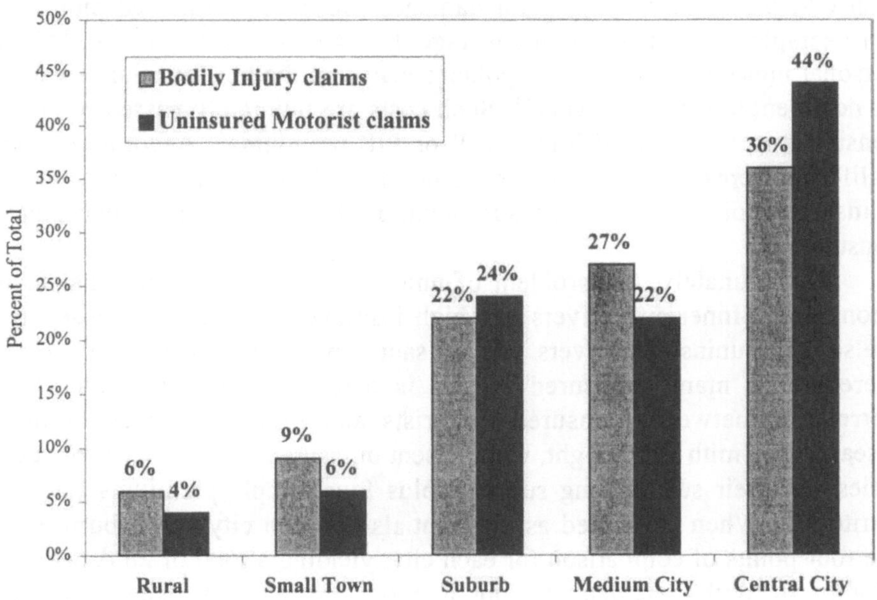

Source: Insurance Research Council (1994a).

The problem of uninsured motorists is well documented in California. A 1995 zip code level survey by the California Department of Insurance

[58] *The Los Angeles Times*, March 2, 1995.

[59] Insurance Services Office, Inc. and National Association of Independent Insurers, "Factors Affecting Urban Auto Insurance Costs" (New York, NY: ISO, Inc., 1988), 15.

[60] Insurance Research Council, *Claiming Behavior*, 14.

found that 28 percent of drivers in that state were uninsured, totaling roughly 5.8 million vehicles statewide.[61] In Los Angeles County, the figure was 37 percent, and in San Francisco it was nearly 33 percent. Certain zip codes had exceptionally high uninsured motorist rates. Some areas of Oakland and south central Los Angeles, for instance, had an uninsured motorist rate over 60 percent, while other zip codes in Los Angeles and San Diego had rates in excess of 90 percent.

The consequences of high rates of uninsured motorists are significant. The California study revealed that the state's insured drivers pay more than $1 billion a year in added premiums to protect themselves from uninsured motorists.[62] The overall premium effect of uninsured motorists, however, is significantly greater than just the cost of UM policies. As Eric Smith and Randall Wright explain in their 1992 *American Economic Review* article, "although the entire [insurance] package may be actuarially fair, the individual components are not."[63] In other words, insurance coverages other than UM may end up paying for damages caused by uninsured motorists. For example, first-party health coverage through medical payments (MP) or personal injury protection (PIP) policies may foot the bill for injuries caused by negligent uninsured drivers.[64] Such costs are ultimately passed on to the consumer in the form of higher MP or PIP premiums. According to the California Department of Insurance, other non-UM premium costs caused by uninsured motorists create an additional $1 billion burden to that state's consumers.[65]

Unfortunately, the problem of uninsured motorists is one that feeds upon itself. Inner-city drivers pay high insurance premiums because there are so many uninsured drivers. At the same time, however, the very reason there are so many uninsured drivers is that premiums are high. This correlation between uninsured motorists and premiums is apparent in research by Smith and Wright, who present uninsured motorist data for seven cities and their surrounding suburbs, plus four sample premiums for each territory.[66] When calculated as differentials between city and suburb, there are four points of comparison for each city, yielding a total of 28 data points (Figure 7). With these data, it is possible to compare the change in premiums with the change in uninsured motorists. As the trend line indicates, the

---

[61] *The Los Angeles Times*, March 2, 1995; *The San Francisco Chronicle*, March 2, 1995; and *The San Diego Union-Tribune*, March 3, 1995.

[62] *The San Francisco Chronicle*, March 2, 1995.

[63] Eric Smith and Randall Wright, "Why Is Automobile Insurance in Philadelphia So Damn Expensive?" *American Economic Review*, 82, 4 (September 1992), 759 at note 5.

[64] The same principle holds for property damage as well.

[65] *The Sacramento Bee*, March 19, 1995.

[66] Smith and Wright, 757.

greater the increase in uninsured motorists, the greater the increase in premiums. This pattern helps to confirm the contention that premium reductions would be somewhat effective in reducing the number of uninsured drivers.

Figure 7
Correlation between Uninsured Motorists and Premiums

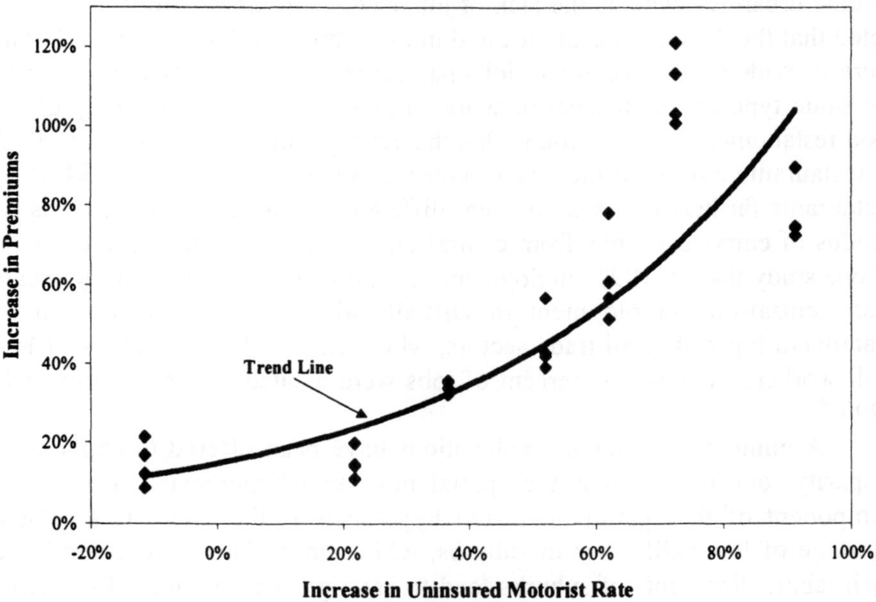

Source: Joint Economic Committee calculations and Smith and Wright data.

3. CONSEQUENCES OF HIGHER INSURANCE COSTS FOR URBAN AREAS

A number of adverse outcomes result from all of the problems that increase insurance costs in urban areas. First, by reducing the transportation options available to low-income workers, high urban premiums can reduce labor market efficiency and depress wages for low-skilled, inner-city residents. Second, there is the burden on taxpayers in the form of higher government expenses and lower tax receipts. Third, distrust towards the auto insurance system eventually can lead to a more generalized lack of respect for the law. Finally, large premium disparities arise between cities and suburbs. Such disparities underscore the higher cost of living in many cities and encourage middle-class families to move to the suburbs. Each of these outcomes is explored in greater detail below.

3.1. Inner-City Jobs

An important consequence of excessively high premiums for low-income urban residents is the lack of job access and job mobility. It is often noted that the "good" jobs are located in the suburbs of large cities.[67] In fact, there is evidence that suburban jobs pay more than inner-city jobs, even for the same type and skill level of work. For example, a 1989 survey of fast food restaurants in Atlanta found that the average entry-level wage was $3.79 in restaurants closest to the city's center, compared to an average $4.61 for restaurants farthest out, a 22 percent difference.[68] A related concern is the exodus of entry-level jobs from central cities, a trend evident in the finding of one study that by 1990 employment in suburban areas was actually greater than central-city employment in virtually all industrial sectors. In the manufacturing and retail trade sectors, which employ large numbers of low-skill workers, roughly 70 percent of jobs were located in suburban areas by 1990.[69]

A number of different explanations have been offered to explain this disparity, one of which is the spatial mismatch hypothesis. The central component of the spatial mismatch hypothesis is that there is a relative shortage of low-skill labor in suburbs, while inner cities have a surplus of such labor. Residents of suburbs tend to have greater amounts of education and training, and as a result there are fewer suburban residents to fill the demand for low-skill jobs. In order to attract workers to such positions, the market pushes up the average wage for such jobs. Inner cities, in contrast, face the opposite problem: there is a surplus of low-skill labor for local jobs, which exerts downward pressure on wages. Access to the better-paying suburban jobs is limited for inner-city residents because of their higher travel

---

67 For example, see Jane Gross, "Poor without Cars Find Trek to Work Is Now a Job," *New York Times*, November 18, 1997; Lorraine Woellert, "D.C. Students 'Go Where the Money Is'; Turn to Suburbs for Summer Jobs," *The Washington Times*, June 24, 1995; and William Julius Wilson, *When Work Disappears* (New York, NY: Vintage Books, 1996), 39-42.

68 Keith R. Ihlanfeldt and Madelyn V. Young, "The Spatial Distribution of Black Employment between the Central City and the Suburbs," *Economic Inquiry*, 34, 4 (October 1996), 693-707.

69 John D. Kasarda, "Industrial Restructuring and the Changing Location of Jobs," in *State of the Union: America in the 1990s, Volume I: Economic Trends*, ed. Reynolds Farley (New York, NY: Russell Sage Foundation, 1995), 235, 262.

costs, which either make finding a job more difficult or discourage inner-city residents from seeking suburban employment altogether.

This problem first became apparent in the aftermath of the 1965 Watts riots in Los Angeles. California Governor Edmund Brown appointed the McCone Commission to investigate the factors that led up to the outbreak of violence. The Commission identified inner-city employment as the "most serious immediate problem" and reported that transportation obstacles were an important element of the jobs problem:

> Our investigation has brought into clear focus the fact that the inadequate and costly public transportation currently existing throughout the Los Angeles area seriously restricts the residents of the disadvantaged areas such as south central Los Angeles. This lack of adequate transportation handicaps them in seeking and holding jobs, attending schools, shopping, and in fulfilling other needs. It has had a major influence in creating a sense of isolation, with its resultant frustrations, among the residents of south central Los Angeles, particularly the Watts area.[70]

The first formal research on the subject was published by John Kain of Harvard University. In his widely cited 1968 article, Kain identified the transportation problem faced by low-income and racial minorities who live in central cities.

> Frequently ghetto Negroes may be forced to choose between buying a private automobile and thus spending a disproportionate share of their low incomes on transportation, making a very long and circuitous trip by public transit (if any service is available at all), or forgoing the job altogether. Where the job in question is a marginal one, their choice may frequently be the latter. More often, they will not even seek out the job in the first instance because of the difficulties of reaching it from possible residence locations.[71]

In the three decades since the spatial mismatch hypothesis was first articulated, a large amount of research has been produced on the subject.[72]

---

[70] State of California, Governor's Commission on the Los Angeles Riots, *Violence in the City—An End or a Beginning?* (Los Angeles, CA: State of California, 1965), 65.

[71] John F. Kain, "Housing Segregation, Negro Employment, and Metropolitan Decentralization," *Quarterly Journal of Economics*, 82, 2 (May 1968), 181.

[72] For a review of evidence supporting the spatial mismatch hypothesis, see John F. Kain, "The Spatial Mismatch Hypothesis: Three Decades Later," *Housing Policy Debate*, 3, 2 (1992), 371-460. For an opposing view, see Brian D. Taylor and Paul M. Ong, "Spatial

Many of the issues related to the spatial mismatch hypothesis are still hotly debated, particularly the role played by residential segregation. Nonetheless, a significant amount of research has been produced which identifies the practical consequences associated with higher travel costs for inner-city residents. For instance, Keith Ihlanfeldt found that limits to job accessibility significantly increase minority unemployment, accounting for upwards of one-quarter of the difference between Hispanic and white employment levels.[73] Of particular relevance to this chapter, Holzer, Ihlanfeldt, and Sjoquist found that car ownership is associated with 12 percent higher wages for blacks, as well as shorter spells of unemployment.[74]

Research by John Kasarda and Kwok-fai Ting further suggests that public transportation remedies are not only inadequate, but that problems of job access have a disparate impact on inner-city women with little education:

> The deconcentration of metropolitan jobs, together with restricted transport choice, differentially impacts the least mobile—that is, less-educated inner-city women. These women are most likely to (1) depend entirely on public transportation, (2) travel close to home, (3) seek only jobs with short commute times, (4) avoid work that requires traveling through nearby dangerous areas (especially after dark), and (5) need to balance multiple domestic responsibilities with work schedules. As a result, job options for these women tend to be much more restricted spatially and temporally, often limiting them to low-paying and part-time work closer to home. These constraints no doubt pose strong work disincentives.[75]

Mismatch or Automobile Mismatch? An Examination of Race, Residence, and Commuting in U.S. Metropolitan Areas," *Urban Studies*, 32, 9 (1995), 1453-1473, who argue that employment obstacles faced by low-skilled, urban minorities are attributable not to a spatial mismatch, but to an "automobile mismatch," in which the lack of access to automobiles forces them to rely on inadequate public transit.

[73] Keith R. Ihlanfeldt, "Intra-Urban Job Accessibility and Hispanic Youth Employment Rates," *Journal of Urban Economics*, 33, 2 (March 1993), 254. Similar findings were reported by Katherine M. O'Regan and John M. Quigley, "Teenage Employment and the Spatial Isolation of Minority and Poverty Households—Comment," *Journal of Human Resources*, 31, 3 (Summer 1996), 692-702.

[74] Harry J. Holzer, Keith R. Ihlanfeldt, and David L. Sjoquist, "Work, Search, and Travel among White and Black Youth," *Journal of Urban Economics*, 35, 3 (May 1994), 340.

[75] John D. Kasarda and Kwok-fai Ting, "Joblessness and Poverty in America's Central Cities: Causes and Policy Prescriptions," *Housing Policy Debate*, 7, 2 (1996), 412.

The transportation obstacles associated with locating and holding down a job are a critical component of welfare reform.[76] The importance of owning a car for recipients of Aid to Families with Dependent Children (AFDC) was the subject of a 1996 article in *Social Work Research*.[77] Even after controlling for other factors like education and race, author Paul Ong found that automobile ownership granted significant benefits to welfare recipients in the form of higher rates of employment, more hours worked, and higher monthly earnings. On average, welfare recipients who owned an automobile were 12 percent more likely to work at all, worked an additional 23 hours per month, and brought home an additional $152 per month (Table 4).

Table 4
Effect of Automobile Ownership on Welfare Recipients

Work characteristic	Automobile Advantage
Worked at all	+12%
Average hours worked	+23
Average monthly earnings	+$152

Source: Ong.

These findings are consistent with a survey of local welfare administrators by the U.S. General Accounting Office that found that lack of transportation was a significant obstacle to moving individuals off welfare even when they were prepared to work.[78] Seventy-five percent of welfare administrators felt that lack of transportation was either a "major reason" (44 percent) or a "moderate reason" (31 percent) why welfare recipients failed to become employed. In fact, the survey results suggest that lack of transportation is a greater problem than lack of jobs, since just 26 percent cited "no jobs are available" as a "major reason" for failure to become employed. In addition, having access to a car can help welfare recipients to obtain better-paying, yet more distant jobs that will help keep them off public assistance. In Wisconsin, for instance, a preliminary analysis of that state's

[76] See Jane Gross, "Poor without Cars Find Trek to Work Is Now a Job," *New York Times*, November 18, 1997; and Carl F. Horowitz, "Off the Dole and Into Autos," *Investor's Business Daily*, January 13, 1998.

[77] Paul M. Ong, "Work and Automobile Ownership among Welfare Recipients," *Social Work Research*, 20, 4 (December 1996), 255-262.

[78] U.S. General Accounting Office, *Welfare to Work: Most AFDC Training Programs Not Emphasizing Job Placement*, HEHS-95-113 (Washington, DC: General Accounting Office, 1995), 84.

W-2 welfare reform plan found that there was a strong positive correlation between hourly wages and distance traveled to work.[79]

3.2. Fiscal Impact on State and Local Governments

The problems associated with the auto insurance system impose a significant burden on state and local governments, diverting scarce taxpayer dollars from other priorities. In 1995, state, county, and municipal governments owned and operated more than 3.3 million vehicles, most of which were trucks and buses.[80] The burden on taxpayers comes not only from the direct insurance and legal costs of maintaining such a large fleet, but also from such indirect costs as an eroding tax base and excess consumption of health care by public-aid recipients. Moreover, since local governments depend on state governments for roughly 30 percent of their revenue, the fiscal burden placed on states has important indirect consequences as well.[81]

3.2.1. Lawsuits against Cities

For some cities, the rising number of lawsuits brought against government agencies is a major problem. Automobile tort cases make up the single most common type of tort litigation brought against government, accounting for 44 percent of all tort cases where the government is the primary defendant.[82] One factor is the perception that the government has "deep pockets" and can afford a large settlement. This explanation is corroborated by the fact that a government agency is more likely to be hit with a large damage award than are other defendants. According to a survey of auto injury tort cases conducted by the U.S. Department of Justice, the government was the defendant in close to one-third (29 percent) of all jury

---

[79] John Pawasarat, "Initial Findings on Mobility and Employment of Public Assistance Recipients in Milwaukee County and Factors Relating to Changes in W-2 Regions Over Time," University of Wisconsin, Milwaukee, Employment and Training Institute (1997), on-line at <http://www.uwm.edu/dept/eti/afdcmobl.htm>.

[80] U.S. Department of Transportation, *Highway Statistics 1995*, II-4.

[81] U.S. Bureau of the Census, *Government Finances: 1991-92*, Series GF/92-5 (Washington, DC: Government Printing Office, 1996), 2.

[82] Analysis based on data from U.S. Department of Justice, Bureau of Justice Statistics, "Civil Justice Survey of State Courts, 1992," available on-line at the University of Michigan's Inter-University Consortium for Political and Social Research, on-line at <http://www.icpsr.umich.edu/index.html>.

verdicts in excess of $1 million, even though they represented less than 8 percent of all such jury verdicts.[83]

The strain on city governments from such lawsuits can be considerable. As former Corporation Counsel for the District of Columbia John Payton pointed out, litigated settlements must be paid no matter how excessive and may force spending reductions in other areas: "We're at the point where we can't afford to get hit. . . . Our options are limited. We [could] end up having to cut services, fire employees."[84]

Consider the problem of excess litigation for New York City alone. The cost of settling all personal injury lawsuits against the city increased from just $25 million in 1977 to $282 million in 1996, for a total increase of over 1,000 percent. With an average rate of growth of nearly 14 percent per year, liability payouts by New York City grew two and one-half times faster than the rate of inflation.[85] Cases related to auto accidents make up a major portion of those costs—more than $40 million, and between 60 and 75 percent of that amount ($24 to $30 million) went for "pain and suffering" claims.[86]

A broader measure of the overall liability costs faced by state and local governments comes from a survey of the membership of the National Institute of Municipal Law Officers, consisting mainly of legal counsels. The survey reveals that litigation costs for most cities grew at least 10 percent in 1991 and 1992.[87] For roughly one in five local governments, litigation costs in those two years grew by more than 30 percent. Even worse, the survey indicates that local governments in "poor or fair" fiscal condition have been hit the hardest. Nationwide, the study estimates that city governments spent roughly $6.45 billion on all forms of litigation costs in 1991. County governments were burdened with an additional $2.1 billion in

---

[83] The term "government" refers to any government agency. These figures refer only to jury verdict tort cases in state general jurisdiction courts. U.S. Department of Justice, Bureau of Justice Statistics, *Civil Jury Cases and Verdicts in Large Counties*, NCJ-154346 (Washington, DC: Bureau of Justice Statistics, 1995), 5.

[84] John Murawski, "District Slumps under Liability Strain," *Legal Times*, August 30, 1993.

[85] Paul A. Crotty, Corporation Counsel of the City of New York, "Shutting off the Money Faucet," *Citylaw* 2, 6 (December 1996), 125; and Council of Economic Advisers, *Economic Report of the President* (Washington, DC: Government Printing Office, 1998), 349.

[86] Rudolph Giuliani, Mayor of New York City, Statement submitted to the Senate Committee on Commerce, Science, and Transportation, U.S. Congress, September 24, 1996.

[87] The survey data did not indicate the portion of litigation and costs attributable to motor vehicle crashes. Susan A. MacManus and Patricia A. Turner, "Litigation as a Budgetary Constraint: Problem Areas and Costs," *Public Administration Review*, 53, 5 (September/October 1993), 462-472.

litigation costs, bringing the total cost to local government to approximately $8.5 billion in 1991.

Figure 8
Types of Tort Cases in 75 Most Populous Counties

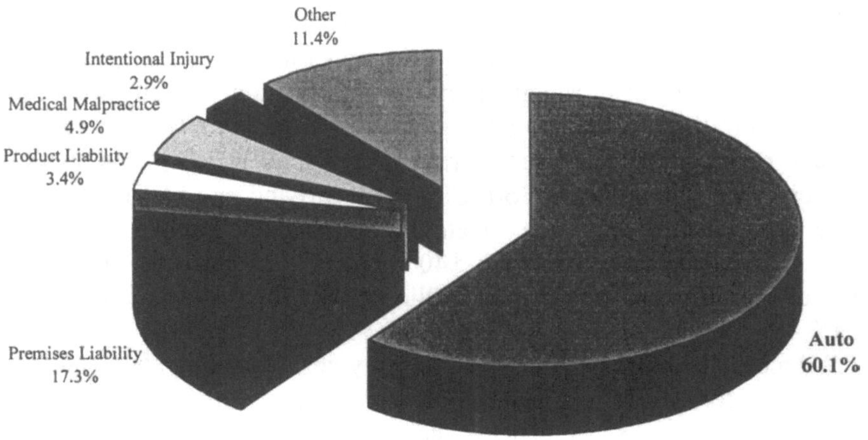

Source: U.S. Department of Justice, Bureau of Justice Statistics, Tort Cases in Large Counties.

3.2.2. Administration of Justice

A 1992 survey of the nation's 75 most populous counties by the U.S. Department of Justice found that auto accident-related lawsuits filed in state courts account for 60 percent of all tort cases—more than all other types of tort lawsuits combined (Figure 8).[88] The cost of providing the judicial infrastructure for these cases consumes resources that could be better used to aid cities. Just as importantly, the large number of auto-related lawsuits clogs the court system and causes delays in the administration of justice in other cases.

[88] Refers only to cases in state general jurisdiction courts. U.S. Department of Justice, Bureau of Justice Statistics, *Tort Cases in Large Counties*, NCJ-153177 (Washington, DC: Bureau of Justice Statistics, 1995), 2.

3.2.3. Health Care

An additional fiscal burden for state and local governments comes in the form of unnecessary consumption of medical services in order to increase a legal settlement for "pain and suffering" damages. According to the U.S. Department of Transportation, state Medicaid programs pay for close to 10 percent of all medical costs resulting from auto accidents, totaling $1.7 billion in 1994 alone.[89] If such costs continue to grow at the average rate for 1990 to 1994, state governments will spend approximately $9.8 billion over the next five years (1998 to 2002).[90] Unless the extent of fraud in government-paid services varies greatly from that in privately paid services, a significant portion of these expenses can be attributed to fraudulent and unnecessary services.[91]

3.2.4. Tax Base

Expensive auto insurance also affects local governments by contributing to the erosion of the tax base in two ways.

First, large premium disparities between central cities and suburbs create an additional incentive for middle-income households to leave the city. Although the stream of middle- and upper-income families out of central cities results from numerous problems—including crime, school quality, and

---

[89] State and federal government sources combined pay roughly one-quarter (24.2 percent) of all medical expenses from auto accidents. Other Department of Transportation studies have estimated the government's share to be even higher. A 1993 report estimated the government's share to be 26.4 percent, and a 1992 report put the figure at 29 percent. The 1992 report, however, cautioned that since payment information is usually only available for first-year costs, the long-term figure could be as high as 51 percent, since some victims are "rendered eligible for publicly assisted medical care as a consequence of the motor vehicle injury." The authoring agency for all three reports is the U.S. Department of Transportation, National Highway Traffic Safety Administration: *The Economic Cost of Motor Vehicle Crashes, 1994*, by Lawrence J. Blincoe, DOT HS 808-425 (Washington, DC: Government Printing Office, 1996), 46-47; *Saving Lives and Dollars—Highway Safety Contribution to Health Care Reform and Deficit Reduction* (Washington, DC: Government Printing Office, 1993), 3; and *Source of Payment for the Medical Cost of Motor Vehicle Injuries in the United States*, by Joan S. Harris, DOT HS 807-800 (Washington, DC: Government Printing Office, 1992), 7, 28.

[90] Growth rate of medical costs was calculated using methodology recommended by Blincoe. See supra note 89 and U.S. Department of Transportation, National Highway Traffic Safety Administration, *The Economic Cost of Motor Vehicle Crashes, 1990*, by Lawrence J. Blincoe and Barbara M. Faigin, DOT HS 807-876 (Washington, DC: Government Printing Office, 1992), I-3.

[91] See supra notes 11, 12, and 13, and accompanying text.

taxes—high auto insurance premiums exacerbate the already higher cost of living in cities.

Second, high insurance premiums reduce the number of registered automobiles, which in turn lowers registration receipts raised by state and local governments. In 1995, such fees at the state level accounted for $11.9 billion.[92] As with most goods, when the price increases, there is a reduction in the quantity purchased. In the case of cars, high insurance premiums significantly raise the long-term costs of owning a vehicle. According to a 1995 article in *Public Finance Quarterly*, authors Tim Pritchard and Larry DeBoer estimate that a 10 percent reduction in insurance costs would boost the number of registered automobiles by 4.6 to 5.6 percent.[93] This research suggests that if insurance premiums were reduced by close to one-quarter, state governments could raise an additional $1.2 billion in revenue.[94] Thus, spiraling insurance costs strain the fiscal resources of governments by reducing motor vehicle registration receipts from levels that would otherwise result.

3.3. Respect for the Law

Of all the consequences of an inefficient and costly auto insurance system, among the most troubling is how frustration eventually transforms into lack of respect for the law. Resentment towards the insurance system results from at least two sources. First, because premiums are so high (even for drivers with clean records), many individuals feel that they are not getting their money's worth out of auto insurance. Second, the perception that fraud and claim buildup is widespread helps to erode the social inhibition against insurance abuse. In other words, people begin to believe that claim buildup is acceptable behavior because "everybody does it." Together, high premiums and the perception of pervasive fraud combine to foster an attitude among some consumers that the insurance system is corrupt, unfair, or

[92] Amount does not include an additional $10.7 billion raised from other fees, such as driver's license fees, title taxes, fines and penalties, or other related charges. U.S. Department of Transportation, *Highway Statistics 1995*, IV-61.

[93] An increase in registrations does not necessarily mean more cars on the road. Some new cars may be purchased by individuals at the margin; other registrations may result from currently owned vehicles that are not now registered. Pritchard and DeBoer caution that the elasticity estimate is sensitive to the premium measure used and the instrumental variable technique. Tim Pritchard and Larry DeBoer, "The Effect of Taxes and Insurance Costs on Automobile Registrations in the United States," *Public Finance Quarterly*, 23, 3 (July 1995), 297.

[94] See infra Table 8 and accompanying text.

illegitimate. Because of such feelings, some individuals feel justified in abusing the insurance system. Common sense suggests that these attitudes get worse as premiums get higher and fraud appears more widespread, the very problems that are most evident in urban areas.

To a large degree, the perverse incentives of the tort system are responsible for these attitudes. Indirectly, the high cost of a litigious compensation system pushes premiums up. Directly, the way the system overcompensates minor injuries adds to the perception that fraud and claims abuse is pervasive. Injured drivers begin to feel that they too are entitled to "payback" for all the years they paid excessive premiums.

It should come as no surprise that drivers increasingly feel that they are participating in a giant lottery, where slight collisions causing minor property damage are treated by many as an opportunity to win the jackpot. Marjorie Berte, the director of the California Department of Consumer Affairs, articulated the problem in her 1991 book, *Hit Me—I Need the Money!*: "Because people have learned that they can get perhaps three times the amount of their actual economic losses, each claimant, regardless of how serious the injury, expects triple the value of his loss."[95]

Because the problems of high premiums and claims abuse are greater in inner cities, there is also more tolerance of claim buildup. According to a 1993 survey, 46 percent of large city residents felt that claim buildup was acceptable to make up for premiums paid in past years. Only 24 percent of suburban residents shared the same view.[96] Likewise, 25 percent of large city residents approved of receiving treatment after an injury has healed, compared to just 6 percent of suburban residents.[97]

The mandatory nature of auto insurance in many states also contributes to negative perceptions of the law, government, and other citizens. Approximately 44 percent of respondents in a survey of low-income families in Maricopa County, Arizona (which contains the city of Phoenix), felt that other drivers were not complying with the mandatory insurance law.[98] Perhaps of greater concern is the prevalence of this opinion among minorities in the survey, 53 percent of whom believed that the mandatory insurance law was not being followed by others. Attitudes towards law enforcement were similarly affected. When asked whether the police were a problem in enforcing the mandatory insurance law, only 22 percent of whites responded

---

[95] Marjorie M. Berte, *Hit Me—I Need the Money!* (San Francisco, CA: ICS Press, 1991), 38.

[96] Large cities are defined in the survey as having a population of one million or more. Insurance Research Council, *Public Attitude Monitor 1993* (Oak Brook, IL: IRC, 1993), 18, 20. See also supra note 36 and accompanying text.

[97] Ibid., 20.

[98] Maril, 17.

affirmatively, whereas 66 percent of minorities felt that they were. A common theme is reflected in the comments of one minority respondent who said ". . . I got stopped four times in one day by police, and they purposely wanted to know whether I had insurance."[99]

Resentment is further fueled by the often-stiff penalties imposed on drivers who lack auto insurance. For instance, a 1997 California law imposes fines ranging from a *minimum* of $1,375 to a maximum of $2,750 for first-time offenders of the state's mandated insurance law.[100] Ohio's effort to crack down on motorists violating the state's insurance requirements resulted in the suspension of more than 71,000 driver licenses in the first year of the new law.[101] Drivers in Louisiana and Oregon can now have their cars towed and impounded if they fail to carry proof of insurance.[102] Even without addressing the merits of mandatory insurance laws, it is clear why such penalties can undermine respect for the law: such laws punish low-income motorists who refuse to spend hundreds, if not thousands, of dollars annually to buy liability insurance. Despite the high price, however, liability insurance does not cover one dime of their own losses if they are injured, protects assets that they do not have, and contributes to a liability system that is perceived by many as corrupt and wasteful.[103]

3.4. City-Suburb Premium Disparities

One of the most vexing consequences of the problems described above is that an urban insurance policy can cost much more than a policy for the same coverage and same driver living in the suburbs. According to a 1991 survey of urban auto premiums by Robert Klein, then the Director of Research for the National Association of Insurance Commissioners (NAIC), the average liability premium is 32 percent higher in large cities than other parts of the same state (Figure 9).[104] A separate analysis by the NAIC similarly indicated that the average premium differential for cities ranged

---

[99] Ibid., 14.

[100] *The Los Angeles Times*, January 3, 1997.

[101] *The (Cincinnati) Call and Post*, November 7, 1996.

[102] *The (New Orleans) Times-Picayune*, December 31, 1997; and *The (Bend, OR) Bulletin*, August 1, 1996.

[103] For further discussion on these and related issues, see the section below on Poor and Low-Income Drivers, as well as the earlier section on Fraud and Claim Buildup.

[104] Robert Klein, "Reducing Urban Auto Insurance Costs," in *Affordable Auto Insurance for Urban Communities: The Universe of Possibilities*, 1995 Conference Proceedings, Milwaukee, Wisconsin, May 12-13 and Baltimore, Maryland, December 7-8, ed. Guila P. Parker and James L. Brown (Milwaukee, WI: Center for Consumer Affairs, 1995).

between 25 and 33 percent for different types of policies.[105] The absolute size of disparities can be quite large, easily exceeding $1,000 or $1,500 per year, per car.

Figure 9
Average Liability Premium for Cities and the Rest of the State

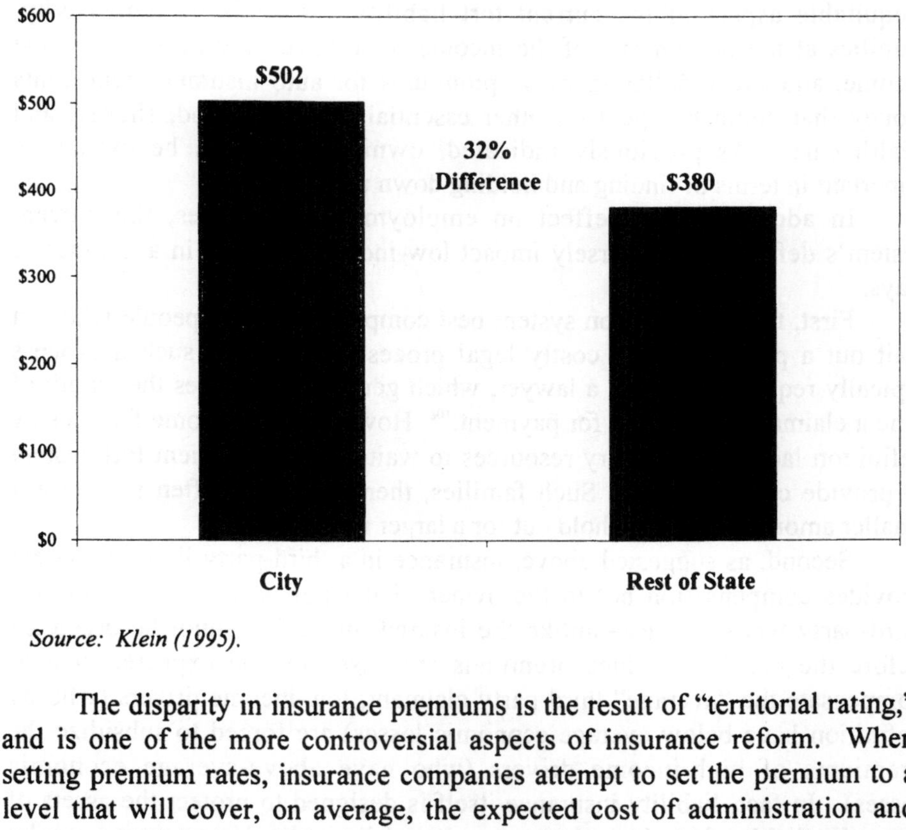

Source: Klein (1995).

The disparity in insurance premiums is the result of "territorial rating," and is one of the more controversial aspects of insurance reform. When setting premium rates, insurance companies attempt to set the premium to a level that will cover, on average, the expected cost of administration and payment for injuries. If insurance costs are higher in cities, then insurance companies must set higher urban premiums to cover the higher expected costs.

This chapter makes no attempt to resolve the many issues surrounding territorial rating, except to note that: (1) perhaps the most effective way to minimize its apparent disparate impact is to eliminate the perverse incentives which distort claiming behavior and push up costs; and (2) a system that pays

[105] Lamberty, 17.

policyholders for their own losses would more fairly reflect in the insurance premiums of the poor their lower wage losses suffered in accidents.[106]

4. POOR AND LOW-INCOME DRIVERS

The shortcomings of the auto insurance system are clearly evident in their deleterious impact on the poor. Indeed, perhaps the most manifestly inequitable aspect of the current tort liability system is its regressivity. Families at the bottom end of the income scale have very little disposable income, and every dollar spent on premiums for auto insurance represents money that could be spent on other essentials, such as food, shelter, and health care. As previously indicated, owning a car can be extremely important in terms of finding and holding down a job.[107]

In addition to the effect on employment and wages, the current system's deficiencies adversely impact low-income families in a number of ways.

First, the tort litigation system best compensates those people who can wait out a protracted and costly legal process. However, such a process typically requires retaining a lawyer, which generally increases the length of time a claimant has to wait for payment.[108] However, low-income families by definition lack the necessary resources to wait for an inefficient tort system to provide compensation. Such families, therefore, must often settle for a smaller amount rather than hold out for a larger award.

Second, as suggested above, insurance in a third-party liability system provides compensation not to the owner of the policy but to an unknown third-party whose losses—unlike the insured himself—cannot be predicted before the accident. Since premiums are based on the expected cost to compensate the "average" third-party claimant, low-income drivers (who by definition have below average economic losses) are forced to subsidize the premiums of high-income drivers (who have above-average economic losses). In fact, liability insurance itself is designed to protect the assets of the policyholder from lawsuits—a service of limited value to someone who has no assets. Since the poor generally have little in the way of assets, liability insurance affords them little protection. This type of system by its very nature provides no compensation to policyholders injured in single-car

[106] See text accompanying infra note 109.
[107] See text accompanying supra notes 67 through 79.
[108] See supra note 55 and accompanying text.

accidents, in an accident for which they are held responsible, or by uninsured drivers.[109]

Third, the regressivity of the current system is heightened by the fact that insurance represents a larger share of operating costs for older, less-valuable cars. According to a 1992 report from the Department of Transportation, the share of the ownership costs attributable to vehicle insurance steadily increases with the car's age.[110] For a brand new sub-compact car, auto insurance represents 13 percent of the total cost of owning and operating the car. For a six-year-old car of the same make and model, insurance doubles to 26 percent of total costs, even after dropping the optional property damage coverage, and after eight years, liability insurance is the single most expensive component of car ownership. By the 12th year, insurance premiums account for 33 percent of total ownership expenses and cost more than even vehicle repairs and maintenance. Since low-income households often purchase older, used vehicles, the deficiencies of the current system that drive up costs are magnified for families at the bottom of the income scale.[111]

Finally, because auto insurance is (to varying degrees) a legal requirement of owning a car, low-income families often must purchase an expensive liability policy that consumes a disproportionate share of their family budget. According to data from the Bureau of Labor Statistics, among households that have auto insurance, the wealthiest fifth spends 2.3 percent of their total household income on insurance premiums (Figure 10).[112] The poorest fifth of households, by comparison, spends 16.3 percent of their income on premiums when they purchase auto insurance, more than seven times the income share of the richest families.

---

[109] Additional insurance policies can be purchased at added cost to cover such contingencies (on a first-party basis). However, the point remains that the tort liability system itself has nothing to offer such accident victims.

[110] Costs are based on operation of typical 1991 vehicles in the suburbs of Baltimore, Maryland. The analysis assumes that insurance for the first five years meets Maryland's minimum liability requirements plus optional coverage for collision and comprehensive. The collision and comprehensive coverages are assumed to be dropped after the fifth year. U.S. Department of Transportation, Federal Highway Administration, *Cost of Owning & Operating Automobiles, Vans, & Light Trucks 1991*, FHWA-PL-92-019 (Washington, DC: FHA, 1992), 12-13.

[111] A survey by the U.S. Department of Energy found that the average age of vehicles in households eligible for food stamps was 11.8 years. U.S. Department of Energy, Energy Information Administration, *Household Vehicles Energy Consumption 1991*, DOE/EIA-0464 (Washington, DC: Government Printing Office, 1993), 42.

[112] These figures are only for those households reporting an expenditure on vehicle insurance. Joint Economic Committee calculations based on data from the U.S. Department of Labor, Bureau of Labor Statistics, "1995 Consumer Expenditure Survey."

Figure 10
Vehicle Insurance as a Share of Household Income

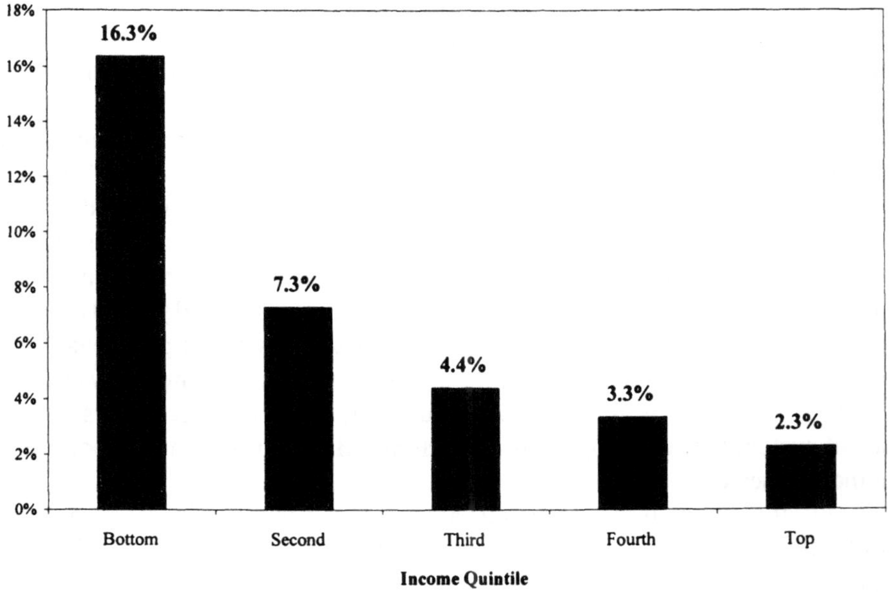

Source: Joint Economic Committee calculations and U.S. Department of Labor, "1995 Consumer Expenditure Survey."

The heavy financial burden imposed by auto insurance stands in stark contrast to the inexpensive cars that low-income families generally own. Given the high premiums charged in big cities like Los Angeles and New York, many low-income urban drivers end up spending more on auto insurance than the value of their car. Household surveys indicate that the average insurance expenditure by families in the bottom income quintile represents close to two-thirds (63 percent) the median value of their car (Figure 11).[113] In other words, the typical low-income household with auto insurance spends more on premiums in two years than the value of their automobile.

---

[113] These estimates were computed using insurance data from a survey of consumer expenditures and data on vehicle value from a survey of household assets. Although the data come from two different surveys, and therefore are not directly comparable, the household characteristics in each survey were similar enough to allow combination of the data. Data on average annual insurance expenditures (for households buying auto insurance) are from the U.S. Department of Labor, Bureau of Labor Statistics, "Consumer Expenditure Survey" (1991 and 1993). Data on median vehicle value (for households with a vehicle) are from U.S. Bureau of the Census, *Asset Ownership of Households: 1993* (Washington, DC: Government Printing Office, 1995), 6.

Figure 11
Vehicle Insurance as a Share of the Value of the Vehicles

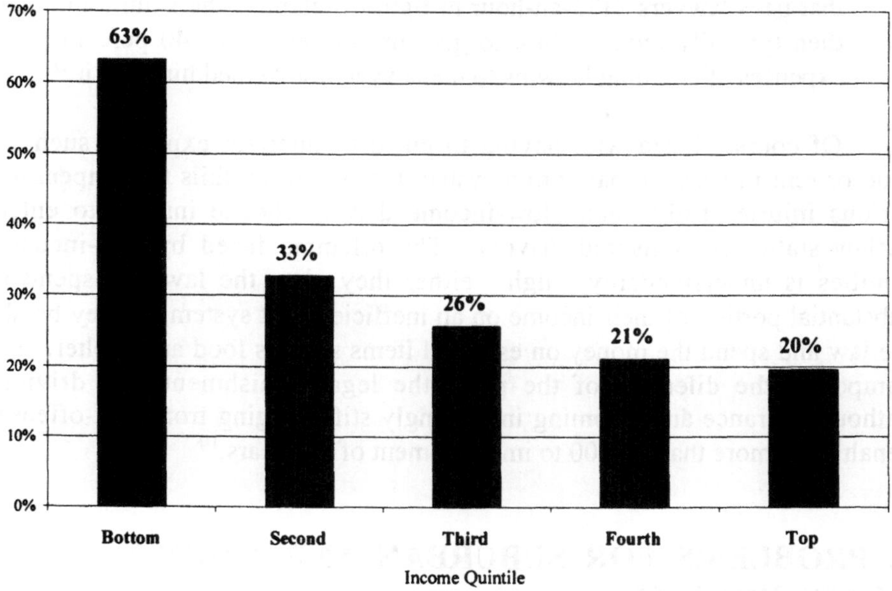

Source: Joint Economic Committee calculations and U.S. Bureau of the Census, Asset Ownership, *and U.S. Department of Labor, "1995 Consumer Expenditure Survey."*

Perhaps the best evidence of the burden of auto insurance on low-income families comes from the 1993 study of poor and near-poor families in Maricopa County, Arizona, cited earlier. According to this study, families with incomes below 50 percent of the poverty line (roughly $6,700) spend nearly one-third of their income (31.6 percent) on auto premiums when they purchase insurance.[114] Over half (50.9 percent) of all families living at or below 200 percent of the poverty line report having to put off other important expenses in order to pay their insurance premiums. The most common purchase that was put off was food, followed by rent or mortgage.

Although low-income families bear the brunt of the current system's inequities, the primary beneficiaries of the perverse incentives in the tort system are lawyers (who gain from excessive litigation) and medical professionals (who gain from buildup of unnecessary medical treatments). The irony of this situation was noted by consumer advocate Andrew Tobias in his testimony before the Senate Commerce Committee:

---

[114] Maril, 17. This figure differs from the Bureau of Labor Statistics figures cited earlier in two ways: (1) it is focused on a narrower and poorer segment of the population, and (2) it is based on a different household survey.

> As a practical matter, what this means is that today's $7-an-hour worker, if he obeys the law in most states, is forced to buy insurance that pays lawyers $125-an-hour to fight his claim, if he's hurt, and that then typically requires him to give up 33 percent or 40 percent plus expenses of anything he wins to the lawyer who helped him win it.[115]

Of course, faced with having to put off important expenses such as food or rent in order to pay into a system that too often fails to compensate serious injuries fully, many low-income drivers choose instead to enter outlaw status as uninsured drivers. The dilemma faced by low-income families is understandably tough: either they obey the law and spend a substantial portion of their income on an inefficient tort system, or they break the law and spend the money on essential items such as food and shelter. To compound the dilemma of the poor, the legal punishments for driving without insurance are becoming increasingly stiff, ranging from first-offense penalties of more than $1,300 to impoundment of their cars.[116]

5. PROBLEMS FOR SUBURBAN AND MIDDLE-CLASS DRIVERS

The fact that low-income and urban drivers are big losers under the present system does not mean that other drivers are winners—the auto insurance system is not a zero-sum game for consumers. Suburban and middle-class drivers face the same fundamental problem that urban and low-income drivers have: premiums are too high, yet policies fail to provide prompt and sensible payments for injuries.

Even in the suburbs of big cities, premiums can be painfully high. For example, in the suburbs of Camden, New Jersey, a married couple with one car and a 17-year-old daughter, all with clean driving records, would have to pay more than $2,000 a year for an insurance policy with relatively good coverage.[117] For a two-car family in Pasadena, California, where each parent has one speeding ticket and the 17-year-old son is an occasional driver, the average premium is over $4,700 per year.[118]

---

[115] Andrew Tobias, Testimony to the Senate Committee on Commerce, Science, and Transportation, U.S. Congress, July 17, 1997.

[116] See supra notes 100, 101, and 102, and accompanying text.

[117] New Jersey Department of Insurance, *1995 Automobile Insurance Premium Comparison Survey* (Trenton, NJ: Department of Insurance, 1995).

[118] California Department of Insurance, *1996 Automobile Premium Survey* (1997), online at <http://www.insurance.ca.gov/sab/autosurvey.html>.

While premiums for suburban residents may consume a smaller portion of the family budget compared to low-income drivers, they are nonetheless stunningly high, and in any event represent resources that could be spent on more productive uses. The financial consequences of the current system's shortcomings are magnified for such families because the average middle-income household owns two vehicles.[119] As with any family, excessively high premiums take money from the family budget that could be better spent on items such as education, health care, or a home mortgage. For example, data from the Bureau of Labor Statistics indicate that middle-income families on average spend two-and-one-half times more on vehicle insurance than on direct educational expenses.[120] However, as previously noted, despite such high premiums, the tort system does not offer quicker or more complete compensation.[121]

6. AUTO CHOICE SOLUTIONS

The proposed Auto Choice reform would help alleviate many of the problems associated with the current auto insurance system. Auto Choice represents real reform because it addresses the underlying cause of the problems, principally the incentives in the tort liability system to inflate medical claims and engage in litigation. By reducing these incentives, Auto Choice would lower premiums and at the same time increase the degree to which premium dollars are used for medical and wage losses for drivers who switch to a PPI policy.

Auto Choice promises to be effective in lowering premiums because it relies on market forces to reduce costs. Unlike health, life, or homeowners insurance policies, consumers in today's highly regulated auto insurance system are forced to purchase insurance coverage for pain and suffering losses. In economic terms, the present system "bundles" insurance for economic and non-economic losses, essentially giving consumers just one package of services. Auto Choice unbundles the two types of premiums and allows consumers to choose the amount of coverage they want for each type of loss. Auto Choice is therefore a market-based reform because it gives insurance providers greater leeway to meet the needs and preferences of their customers. In doing so, Auto Choice exposes the incentives of the current tort liability system to the pressures of market forces.

---

[119] U.S. Department of Labor, Bureau of Labor Statistics, "1995 Consumer Expenditure Survey."

[120] Ibid. Does not include educational expenses funded through tax payments.

[121] See text accompanying supra notes 55 and 56.

The premium savings from Auto Choice have been well documented in a series of studies by Stephen Carroll and Allan Abrahamse of the RAND Institute for Civil Justice.[122] Previous studies by the Joint Economic Committee used RAND's research findings to estimate potential premium savings from implementation of Auto Choice.[123] This section presents updated savings estimates of Auto Choice based on the 1998 RAND study, *The Effects of a Choice Automobile Insurance Plan on Insurance Costs and Compensation: An Updated Analysis.*

6.1. Premium Savings

According to RAND's 1998 study, Auto Choice would reduce the cost of compensating PPI drivers for personal injuries by about 45 percent.[124] Since personal injuries make up about one-half of the total premium (with property damage being the other half), these savings translate into roughly a one-quarter reduction in the overall premium. Based on RAND's findings and insurance industry data, Auto Choice would make available to consumers more than $35 billion in premium savings in 1998, and up to $193 billion over the next five years (1998 to 2002).[125]

---

[122] Stephen J. Carroll and Allan F. Abrahamse, *The Effects of a Choice Automobile Insurance Plan on Insurance Costs and Compensation: An Updated Analysis* (Santa Monica, CA: RAND, forthcoming 1998). See also Abrahamse and Carroll, *The Effects of a Choice Automobile Insurance Plan under Consideration by the Joint Economic Committee of the United States Congress* (Santa Monica, CA: RAND, 1997); and Abrahamse and Carroll, *The Effects of a Choice Auto Insurance Plan on Insurance Costs* (Santa Monica, CA: RAND, 1995).

[123] Joint Economic Committee, U.S. Congress, *The Benefits and Savings of Auto Choice* (1997) and *Improving the American Legal System: The Economic Benefits of Tort Reform* (1996).

[124] The savings estimates presented here are somewhat smaller than previous estimates, a change largely attributable to the fact that the present system has gotten worse at compensating accident victims. Between 1987 (the basis for previous estimates) and 1992 (the basis for the current estimates), the average economic loss in auto accidents grew faster than the average compensation. As a result, accident victims found it increasingly difficult to recover not only pain and suffering, but even their basic economic losses. This trend affects the savings estimates in two ways. First, because pain and suffering is harder to recover, there are less savings to be realized from eliminating such payments. Second, because the current system has gotten worse at paying economic losses, some of the savings are offset by increased compensation for serious injuries. For a fuller explanation, see Carroll and Abrahamse, Appendix B.

[125] Savings for a given year and state were obtained by following the methodology described in O'Connell, et al. (1996). Projections were made using historical data from A. M. Best Company, Inc., in Insurance Information Institute, *The Fact Book—Property/Casualty Insurance Facts* (New York, NY: Insurance Information Institute, annual); and Conning &

Table 5
Estimated 1998 Savings from Auto Choice

	Private	Commercial	Total
Average Premium Savings	22.8%	27.5%	23.7%
Average Savings per Car	$184	*NA*	*NA*
Savings for Low-Income Drivers	36.0%	*NA*	*NA*
Total Available Savings if 100% Switch (Billions)	$27.4	$8.1	$35.5

Source: Joint Economic Committee calculations using data from Carroll and Abrahamse.

The typical private passenger insurance policy would save approximately 23 percent, averaging $184 per car (Table 5).[126] Drivers who opted to remain with their state's current system would be largely unaffected. State-by-state savings are presented in Table 6.[127]

Co. (Hartford, CT: January 16, 1997). Because of data limitations, the RAND analysis did not examine the effect of Auto Choice on savings for commercial policies. This analysis assumes that commercial policies will experience the same personal injury savings as private passenger vehicles.

[126] The savings estimates presented here are based on the assumption that 100 percent of drivers switch to the new PPI policy. Percentage and average savings, however, are relatively insensitive to how many drivers elect PPI. See Carroll and Abrahamse, Section 3. Actual savings for a particular driver will depend on the specifics of his or her policy, as well as other individual risk factors. Differences between the average percentage savings presented here and the estimates in Carroll and Abrahamse are primarily attributable to the use in this analysis of more recent premium data to estimate savings for 1998; average savings in Carroll and Abrahamse are for 1992. Historical data are from the National Association of Insurance Commissioners.

[127] The RAND study uses 1992 data to estimate the effect of Auto Choice based on laws in effect as of 1988. Data problems or changes in state law since 1988 precluded RAND from estimating savings for four states. This analysis therefore assumes that savings for Hawaii (which modified its no-fault system in 1998) equals the average for all no-fault states. For the two states that repealed their no-fault systems (Georgia in 1991 and Connecticut in 1993), this analysis assumes that savings equal the average for all tort states. Two states (Pennsylvania and New Jersey) have limited choice systems already in place. In both cases, the savings estimate is a weighted average of savings from the full-tort and limited-tort

Table 6
State-by-State 1998 Savings from Auto Choice[a]

State	Personal Injury Savings	Overall Premium Savings		Total Potential Savings (Millions)	Average Savings
		Private Drivers	Low-Income		
Alabama	43%	16%	31%	$346	$113
Alaska	53%	23%	38%	$80	$216
Arizona	45%	25%	37%	$641	$229
Arkansas	60%	25%	42%	$354	$180
California	42%	21%	34%	$3,739	$193
Colorado	50%	26%	40%	$639	$230
Connecticut	44%	23%	33%	$596	$217
Delaware	44%	26%	36%	$141	$232
Florida	50%	29%	42%	$2,677	$249
Georgia	44%	16%	31%	$718	$129
Hawaii	47%	30%	39%	$248	$322
Idaho	18%	8%	13%	$46	$46
Illinois	38%	16%	28%	$1,002	$117
Indiana	51%	22%	36%	$691	$147
Iowa	67%	26%	47%	$370	$140
Kansas	27%	10%	18%	$137	$65
Kentucky	38%	18%	27%	$357	$134
Louisiana	60%	34%	49%	$962	$323
Maine	51%	24%	39%	$148	$124
Maryland	52%	26%	40%	$882	$221
Massachusetts	63%	35%	48%	$1,591	$285
Michigan	30%	14%	27%	$866	$124
Minnesota	39%	21%	31%	$568	$155
Mississippi	46%	19%	35%	$249	$142
Missouri	44%	18%	31%	$524	$134
Montana	57%	25%	44%	$119	$161
Nebraska	36%	14%	25%	$126	$87
Nevada	49%	27%	40%	$291	$259
New Hampshire	52%	24%	40%	$171	$159
New Jersey	47%	25%	38%	$1,800	$321
New Mexico	35%	17%	27%	$157	$146
New York	63%	32%	48%	$3,729	$385

policies. In the case of New Jersey, there were no reliable 1992 data, so this analysis assumes that savings for full-tort policies equal the national average for all tort states, and that savings for limited-tort policies equal the average for all no-fault states.

Table 6 (Continued)

State	Personal Injury Savings	Overall Premium Savings		Total Potential Savings (Millions)	Average Savings
		Private Drivers	Low-Income		
North Carolina	32%	16%	25%	$639	$102
North Dakota	75%	28%	54%	$93	$155
Ohio	44%	20%	33%	$1,092	$126
Oklahoma	52%	23%	38%	$399	$165
Oregon	48%	23%	36%	$426	$159
Pennsylvania	37%	19%	29%	$1,398	$149
Rhode Island	57%	31%	45%	$224	$313
South Carolina	38%	17%	28%	$337	$122
South Dakota	8%	4%	6%	$13	$22
Tennessee	45%	18%	31%	$484	$118
Texas	47%	25%	37%	$2,826	$202
Utah	61%	29%	45%	$271	$205
Vermont	26%	11%	20%	$36	$67
Virginia	37%	19%	28%	$652	$117
Washington	60%	33%	48%	$1,034	$242
West Virginia	55%	28%	44%	$298	$237
Wisconsin	23%	10%	17%	$261	$62
Wyoming	69%	26%	51%	$68	$165
U.S. Average	45%	23%	36%	$35,513	$184

[a] *Analysis assumes 100 percent of drivers switch. Based on state laws as of 1988 (see infra note 127). Percentage and average savings are relatively insensitive to how many drivers switch (see infra note 126).*
Source: Carroll and Abrahamse (1998) and Joint Economic Committee calculations.

Low-income drivers would enjoy significantly higher savings—36 percent on average. Since low-income families, by definition, have less disposable income, they often forgo the optional collision and comprehensive property damage coverages. As a result, the personal injury savings represent a larger share of their overall premium. The potential Auto Choice savings represent real purchasing power for low-income households. The average savings of $184 is the equivalent of five weeks of free groceries or nearly four months of free electricity.[128] In addition, to the degree that more affordable auto insurance enables low-income workers to own an

[128] U.S. Department of Labor, Bureau of Labor Statistics, "1995 Consumer Expenditure Survey."

automobile, Auto Choice will yield additional benefits in terms of better-paying jobs or reduced commute costs.[129]

Table 7 presents the illustrative effect of Auto Choice on premiums for hypothetical policyholders with clean driving records in five metropolitan areas.[130] These calculations take the average premium charged for hypothetical drivers (based on surveys of insurance companies by the relevant state regulatory agency) and estimate what the drivers would save if Auto Choice were enacted. The first row under each city lists the premium and savings for the urban driver, while the second row shows the estimates for the same driver in a nearby suburb. The third row under each city presents the city-suburb premium disparity. As the data indicate, Auto Choice offers substantial savings for urban drivers. In central Los Angeles, for example, a 38-year-old female could save nearly $1,200 per year on her insurance premium. Likewise, a young male living in Chicago could reduce his premium by over $600 per year. Clearly, drivers in urban areas stand to enjoy considerable premium savings if Auto Choice is enacted.

---

[129] For example, Ong's research found that welfare recipients who owned a car earned an additional $152 per month relative to welfare recipients without a car. See supra note 77 and accompanying text.

[130] These estimated savings are calculated using hypothetical driver profiles and average premiums charged for specific territories. Actual savings for a particular driver will depend on the specifics of their policy (especially the amount of personal injury coverage purchased), as well as other individual risk factors.

Table 7
Effect of Auto Choice on City and Suburb Premiums for Hypothetical Drivers[a]

	Average Premium under: Current Law	Average Premium under: Auto Choice	Savings[b]	
Los Angeles, CA: Female, age 38 (BI/PD 100/300/50; MP 5; UM 15/30)				
Los Angeles	$3,461	$2,281	34%	**$1,180**
Pomona	$1,827	$1,204	34%	**$623**
City-Suburb Difference	$1,634	$1,077	34%	**$557**
Chicago, IL: Male, age 20 (BI/PD 20/40/15; MP 1; UM 20/40)				
Chicago	$2,132	$1,540	28%	**$592**
Aurora	$1,064	$769	28%	**$295**
City-Suburb Difference	$1,068	$772	28%	**$296**
Baltimore, MD: Male, age 20 (BI/PD 20/40/10; PIP 2.5; UM 20/40/10)				
City of Baltimore	$3,214	$1,937	40%	**$1,277**
Baltimore County	$1,778	$1,072	40%	**$707**
City-Suburb Difference	$1,435	$865	40%	**$570**
New York, NY: Male, age 20 (BI 25/50/10; PIP 50; UM 25/50)				
Brooklyn	$2,270	$1,187	48%	**$1,083**
Mount Vernon/ Yonkers	$1,363	$712	48%	**$650**
City-Suburb Difference	$907	$474	48%	**$433**
Dallas, TX: Female, under age 21 (BI/PD 20/40/15)				
Harris County	$1,297	$812	37%	**$485**
Ellis County	$870	$545	37%	**$325**
City-Suburb Difference	$427	$267	37%	**$160**

[a] *All drivers in these examples have clean driving records. Policy limits for bodily injury and property damage policies are listed as "BI/PD 15/30/5," where the numbers*

refer to the liability coverage (in $1,000s) on BI per person, BI per accident, and PD per accident, respectively. Uninsured motorist (UM) policies take the same form as BI policies. Other policies are medical payments (MP) and personal injury protection (PIP).

[b] *Percentage savings equals the low-income savings estimate, or savings for policies with liability coverage only.*

Source: Joint Economic Committee calculations using data from the relevant state regulatory agency and Insurance News Network, "States," on-line at <http://www.insure.com/states/>.

6.2. City-Suburb Premium Disparities and Savings

Table 7 also illustrates the effect of Auto Choice on city-suburb premium disparities. In Baltimore, the city-suburb premium difference for a 20-year-old male would fall from more than $1,400 under current law to $865, a drop of 40 percent. In New York City, the city-suburb disparity for a single 20-year-old male would be cut by over $430 per year, or 48 percent. Nationwide, premiums for liability-only policies would be reduced by 36 percent on average.[131] Although city premiums would still be higher than suburban premiums, the dollar difference between the two would be reduced significantly.

The evidence presented in this chapter suggests that inner cities may enjoy significantly larger savings than those estimated by RAND. The RAND analysis estimates what it would cost to provide auto insurance without coverage for pain-and-suffering damages, assuming that there is *no* change in claiming behavior. In this sense, the RAND estimates are quite conservative, since there is compelling evidence that the potential to recover pain and suffering is a major contributing factor to insurance costs.[132] As the data in Section 2 so clearly indicate, excess claiming behavior is a principal reason why premiums are so high in central cities. Because Auto Choice eliminates the incentive for such excess claiming behavior for those who choose it, the premium savings for many urban drivers are likely to be significantly greater than the RAND estimates, thus further reducing both the dollar and percentage difference between city and suburb premiums.

Empirical confirmation of the potential rate-flattening effect of Auto Choice is found by examining the city-suburb disparities in insurance costs

---

[131] The RAND analysis of Auto Choice estimates personal injury savings by state, but not by city. Mathematically, since premiums in both the city and suburb examples are being reduced by the same percentage, the ratio of city to suburb premiums would not change. However, the disparity in absolute terms would be reduced by the same percentage that overall premiums are reduced.

[132] See supra notes 11, 12, and 13, and accompanying text.

for the three no-fault states that currently have a strict verbal threshold. Of the 14 states that had a no-fault system during the 1989 to 1991 period, only Florida, Michigan, and New York have what is called a "strict verbal threshold," where victims must suffer a specific type of injury (such as permanent disability) before they can sue for pain-and-suffering damages. Relative to no-fault states with monetary thresholds, there is far less incentive to inflate medical claims artificially in order to surpass the threshold.[133] Based on the data listed in Table 2, the city-suburb difference in average loss cost (ALC) for PIP claimants in Florida, Michigan, and New York is 27 percent, whereas the average for the other 11 no-fault states is 61 percent. In other words, the city-suburb premium disparity for states with a strict verbal threshold is less than one-half the disparity in other no-fault states. Moreover, average loss costs in the state with the toughest verbal threshold in the country, Michigan, are actually lower in the city than elsewhere in the state.[134] This relationship confirms the conclusion that implementation of the Auto Choice reform will significantly reduce the premium disparity between cities and suburbs.

Previous attempts to address premium disparities between cities and suburbs have typically focused on requiring suburban and rural drivers to pay higher insurance rates in order to lower premiums in heavily urbanized areas. Although such subsidies may in fact flatten rates, they do nothing to remedy the problems that drive up urban premiums in the first place. A further drawback of this approach is the attendant resentment felt by the drivers who are expected to finance the subsidy through higher rates. One of the appealing aspects of the Auto Choice reform is that it reduces city-suburb premium disparities by addressing the underlying cost factors.

6.3. Savings to State and Local Governments

Auto Choice would provide government at all levels some degree of fiscal relief. State Medicaid programs pay for roughly 10 percent of all medical expenses from auto accidents.[135] As discussed above, a substantial portion of these costs are for unnecessary medical treatments incurred in response to the perverse incentives of the tort liability system. Depending on how many consumers choose a PPI policy, Auto Choice could significantly

---

[133] Even in strict verbal threshold states, however, once the threshold has been crossed there is still a powerful incentive to inflate damages in order to maximize the pain-and-suffering award.

[134] See supra note 27.

[135] U.S. Department of Transportation, *Motor Vehicle Crashes*, 46.

reduce the taxpayer's share of this excess consumption of health care. Moreover, the significant rate reductions will make auto insurance affordable for many motorists who are currently uninsured. Because many of these drivers are poor, their purchase of first-party health coverage would reduce their dependence on government-provided health benefits.

A more quantifiable source of savings comes in the form of vehicle registration fees. In 1995, state governments raised $11.9 billion from fees for personal and commercial motor vehicle registrations. Using the lower bound estimate of insurance price elasticity from Pritchard and DeBoer,[136] the premium reductions produced by Auto Choice would increase the number of registered vehicles by roughly 11 percent. Based on this assumption and 1995 data, increased motor vehicle registrations from Auto Choice would have increased state government receipts by around $1.2 billion.[137] The estimates in Table 8 suggest the rough order of magnitude of the potential revenue gains, although these estimates are sensitive to the assumption that the elasticity effect of insurance price reductions is the same for all states.

6.4. Jobs and Urban Renewal

Despite billions of dollars in aid from the federal government, many of the nation's large cities continue to suffer from a range of problems, including economic stagnation or decline, high rates of crime, racial tension, high cost of living, and a declining tax base. Obviously, no single piece of legislation could hope to satisfactorily address all of these problems. The proposed Auto Choice reform, however, would help alleviate many of the pressures that have contributed to the long-standing problems of cities.

Although the automobile may seem to be a surprising choice to aid in urban renewal, history suggests that geographic mobility is a potent social tool. Historically, access to transportation has been of greatest value to ordinary people. Affordable travel grants individuals the ability to change their location, and with it the opportunity to change their social and economic well being. As the economist Robert L. Heilbroner noted:

---

[136] See supra note 93 and accompanying text.

[137] Estimated premium savings are listed in Table 6. See also supra notes 92 and 93.

Table 8
Potential Effect of Auto Choice on
Motor Vehicle Registration Receipts in 1995 (in Millions)

State	Revenue	State	Revenue
Alabama	$4.4	Montana	$1.4
Alaska	$2.5	Nebraska	$3.0
Arizona	$8.6	Nevada	$7.2
Arkansas	$6.5	New Hampshire	$4.6
California	$339.9	New Jersey	$27.6
Colorado	$11.4	New Mexico	$4.1
Connecticut	$14.2	New York	$50.6
Delaware	$1.8	North Carolina	$13.1
Florida	$45.5	North Dakota	$4.9
Georgia	$13.1	Ohio	$36.5
Hawaii	$9.2	Oklahoma	$28.9
Idaho	$1.1	Oregon	$5.9
Illinois	$42.3	Pennsylvania	$35.7
Indiana	$16.8	Rhode Island	$4.1
Iowa	$30.6	South Carolina	$4.5
Kansas	$5.0	South Dakota	$0.6
Kentucky	$3.2	Tennessee	$9.4
Louisiana	$9.9	Texas	$79.7
Maine	$3.8	Utah	$3.3
Maryland	$16.1	Vermont	$1.3
Massachusetts	$24.7	Virginia	$4.4
Michigan	$31.9	Washington	$129.1
Minnesota	$40.1	West Virginia	$7.3
Mississippi	$5.3	Wisconsin	$10.7
Missouri	$15.4	Wyoming	$4.0
		All U.S.	**$1,217.7**

Source: Joint Economic Committee calculations using data from U.S. Department of Transportation, Highway Statistics 1995 *(1996) and Pritchard and DeBoer (1995).*

Yet these reflections on the impact of the automobile still fail to do justice to its quintessential contribution to our lives. This is its gift of mobility itself—not mobility as a dollar-spreading device or a mechanical substitute for personal movement, but as a direct enhancement of life, as an enlargement of life's boundaries and opportunities. This is so enormous, so radical a transformation that its effect can no longer be measured or appreciated by mere figures. It is nothing less than the unshackling of the age-old bonds of locality; it is the grant of geographic choice and economic freedom on a hitherto unimagined scale.[138]

The economic importance of mobility is highlighted by the discussion of job accessibility above. The federal government has recognized and tried to address these issues with additional spending programs. The Department of Transportation has proposed spending $600 million over the next six years on the Access to Jobs program.[139] Transportation assistance is one of the components of the Department of Labor's $3 billion Welfare-to-Work grant program.[140] In addition, some state and local governments have sought to address the problem by expanding public transportation programs.[141] Although these programs may have merit, they nonetheless represent increases in the size of government and a burden to the taxpayer. Auto Choice is an attractive alternative because it would directly address the transportation barriers faced by low-income and inner-city workers by making car ownership more affordable, without creating a new government program or engendering dependence on public assistance.

6.5. Improved Compensation for Injuries

In addition to reducing premiums, Auto Choice virtually guarantees that everyone injured in an auto accident will have access to greater amounts of compensation than is available today—even for those buying minimum policy limits. This result is true for drivers regardless of whether they choose to remain in their state's current system or switch to the new PPI policy. This conclusion follows from the fact that in today's system, accident victims are compensated from two sources, their own first-party auto health coverage

---

[138] Robert L. Heilbroner, "Halfway to the Moon on Wheels," *Petroleum Today* (Spring 1960), 1-3, quoted in John B. Rae, *The Road and the Car in American Life* (Cambridge, MA: MIT Press, 1971), 370.

[139] Office of Management and Budget, *Budget of the United States Government, Fiscal Year 1998* (Washington, DC: Government Printing Office, 1998), 87-88.

[140] U.S. Department of Labor, Employment and Training Administration, ETA Press release, "Labor Secretary Herman Kicks-Off Nationwide Welfare-to-Work Tour," (Washington, DC: Employment and Training Administration, 11/17/97).

[141] Most of the research surveyed here has found that traditional public transportation systems suffer from a number of inherent limitations. For example, Kain and Meyer found that efforts to expand public transportation failed to compensate for low automobile ownership rates among blacks. John F. Kain and John R. Meyer, "Transportation and Poverty," *The Public Interest*, 18 (Winter 1970), 75-87. Wilson and Kasarda and Ting also document the inadequacies of public transportation (supra notes 67 and 75).

(if any) and the negligent driver's liability policy (if any). Auto Choice would increase the amount of compensation available from both sources.

In terms of collection from first-party health coverages (such as MP policies), drivers residing in a tort state who switch to Auto Choice would generally increase their available compensation by a factor of at least three or four. For example, most medical payment coverages purchased today have limits of $5,000 or less.[142] In contrast, minimum PPI limits in 33 of the existing 37 (roughly three out of four) tort states would be at least $15,000.[143] These figures significantly understate the magnitude of increased compensation, since most states make the purchase of first-party health coverage optional. Thus, many drivers would switch from having zero first-party health coverage under the current system, to $15,000 or more under Auto Choice, a vast improvement for all drivers. It would be of particular benefit to the approximately 30 percent of injured drivers who have no recovery under the tort system—for injuries sustained in single-car accidents, by at-fault drivers, or caused by uninsured motorists.[144]

On top of expanded first-party health coverage, Auto Choice preserves the right of injured PPI drivers to sue the negligent party for any economic losses above their PPI policy limits. Regardless of whether the negligent driver chose TMC or PPI, they would still be required to carry liability insurance at least to their state's financial responsibility level.[145] PPI drivers would therefore be able to recover greater amounts of their economic losses on a first-party basis, plus recover at least everything they could have under the old tort system on a third-party basis.

Even drivers who opted to remain in their state's existing system would be better off, since they would have access to compensation not only from their own TMC policy but also from the negligent PPI driver's supplemental liability insurance. Both TMC and PPI drivers would further benefit from any reduction in the number of uninsured motorists that results from the premium reductions.

Thus, even if PPI drivers choose to purchase policies with the *minimum* limits, they would still on average recover more of their economic loss than in today's system. However, if drivers choose instead to spend part or all of their premium savings on additional coverage (for example, by raising their limits to $250,000), they stand to be dramatically better off

---

[142] Insurance Research Council, *Claiming Behavior*, 76.

[143] Insurance Information Institute, *The Fact Book*, 112-113.

[144] Carroll and Abrahamse, 12 at note 24.

[145] The RAND analysis assumes that since drivers who switch to PPI would have the same amount of assets to protect, they would purchase supplemental liability coverage at the same levels that they now buy.

under Auto Choice. Traditionally, drivers who suffer catastrophic losses have fared the worst under the current tort system. Whereas the current tort system compensates such victims for just 9 percent of their losses,[146] under Auto Choice, drivers would at least have the opportunity to buy affordable coverage for such incidents. Consumers would finally be empowered to purchase an insurance policy that covers all economic losses up to limits that they choose. This sort of consumer choice stands in stark contrast to the present fault-based system. Since accident victims in the tort system are compensated by the insurance company of the negligent driver, compensation limits are often set by the very wrongdoer who caused the accident. With first-party PPI coverage, Auto Choice puts consumers in control of the limits of their compensation.

In addition to increasing the amount of compensation, Auto Choice would provide it more quickly to accident victims because of the reduced need for time-consuming litigation as a means of determining compensation. The fact that the tort system relies on litigation in the clogged court system to resolve negligence means that compensation for injuries can be delayed for months and even years. In contrast, the Auto Choice reform described here would require PPI claims to be paid within 30 days.

Finally, it is important to note that the first-party health coverage provided by Auto Choice is of greatest value to lower-income households. Such households may have limited employer-provided health benefits or lack private health insurance altogether. When the tort system malfunctions and fails to compensate injuries, the people who suffer the most are those who have no alternative source of health coverage. Auto Choice offers these families the opportunity to purchase more affordable health insurance to cover their injuries from auto accidents.

7. CONCLUSION

Auto insurance is first and foremost about compensating people for injuries they suffer in car accidents. Today's system of compensating people through a third-party liability system, however, has failed in this goal: the system malfunctions on many levels, even as premiums are growing one-and-one-half times faster than inflation. In other words, the system costs too much and does not give consumers their money's worth.

The shortcomings of the present tort liability system make all consumers losers. Low-income families are burdened with high and often

[146] Carroll, et al., 187.

mandatory insurance premiums that can consume up to one-third of household income. Urban residents suffer from high costs, large city-suburb premium disparities, organized fraud rings, and obstacles to job opportunities. Finally, suburban and rural drivers must not only pay excessively high premiums, but also run the risk of being injured by an uninsured motorist or becoming the target of a frivolous lawsuit.

While no single reform could hope to remedy all the problems identified in this chapter, Auto Choice represents real reform because it addresses the underlying causes. For those who choose it, Auto Choice would eliminate the powerful incentives to inflate medical and wage losses and to engage in unnecessary litigation. Consumers would benefit from substantial premium reductions, with average savings of $184 per car. Accident victims would also benefit from a system that compensates medical and wage losses more surely and more quickly than today's system.

Auto Choice would particularly benefit low-income and inner-city drivers. Low-income motorists could see their premiums cut by 36 percent and would benefit from a first-party system that more fairly reflects their lower expected economic losses. Residents of inner cities would enjoy significant premium savings as well as see the disparity between city and suburban premiums greatly diminish. Urban areas would further benefit from a reduction in the high cost of living and reduced fiscal strain on government. In addition, by making legal car ownership more affordable, Auto Choice would enhance the ability of poor, inner-city workers to find and maintain better-paying jobs.

Finally, Auto Choice has the added appeal of achieving these benefits without an expensive government program or burdensome regulations. Indeed, it seems that as the auto insurance system worsens with respect to cost and injury compensation, increased government intervention is frequently offered as a solution, including mandated rate-rollbacks, harsher penalties for uninsured drivers, and subsidization of urban premiums by suburban drivers. Rather than expanding the role of government, Auto Choice relies on market forces to offer all consumers a more effective and less costly way to compensate auto injuries. Moreover, by addressing the problems that afflict all motorists, Auto Choice generates numerous benefits that specifically accrue to low-income and inner-city families.

References

Abrahamse, Allan F., and Stephen J. Carroll, 1995, *The Effects of a Choice Auto Insurance Plan on Insurance Costs*, Santa Monica, CA: RAND Corporation, Institute for Civil Justice.

Abrahamse, Allan F., and Stephen J. Carroll, 1997, *The Effects of a Choice Automobile Insurance Plan under Consideration by the Joint Economic Committee of the United States Congress*, Santa Monica, CA: RAND Corporation, Institute for Civil Justice.

Berte, Marjorie M., 1991, *Hit Me—I Need the Money!*, San Francisco, CA: ICS Press, 1991.

Browne, Mark J., and Robert Puelz, 1996, Statutory Rules, Attorney Involvement, and Automobile Liability Claims, *The Journal of Risk and Insurance*, 63, 1, 77-94.

California Department of Insurance, 1997, *1996 Automobile Premium Survey*, on-line at <http://www.insurance.ca.gov/sab/autosurvey.html>.

Carroll, Stephen J, and Allan Abrahamse, 1998, *The Effects of a Choice Automobile Insurance Plan on Insurance Costs and Compensation: An Updated Analysis*, Santa Monica, CA: RAND Corporation, Institute for Civil Justice.

Carroll, Stephen J., Allan Abrahamse, and Mary Vaiana, 1995, *The Costs of Excess Medical Claims for Automobile Personal Injuries*, Santa Monica, CA: RAND Corporation, Institute for Civil Justice.

Carroll, Stephen J., James S. Kakalik, Nicholas M. Pace, and John L. Adams, 1991, No-Fault Approaches to Compensating People Injured in Automobile Accidents, Santa Monica, CA: RAND Corporation, Institute for Civil Justice.

Conning and Co., 1997, Data provided to the Joint Economic Committee of the U.S. Congress, January 16, Hartford, CT: Conning and Co.

Council of Economic Advisers, 1998, *Economic Report of the President*, Washington, DC: Government Printing Office.

Crotty, Paul A., 1996, Shutting off the Money Faucet, *Citylaw*, 2, 6, 125-129.

Dornstein, Ken, 1996, *Accidentally, on Purpose: The Making of a Personal Injury Underworld in America*, New York, NY: St. Martin's Press.

Fleming, John G., 1966, The Collateral Source Rule and Loss Allocation in Tort Law, *California Law Review*, 54, 4, 1478-1549.

Giuliani, Rudolph, 1996, Statement submitted to the Senate Committee on Commerce, Science, and Transportation, U.S. Congress, September 24.

Heilbroner, Robert L., 1960, Halfway to the Moon on Wheels, *Petroleum Today*, Spring, 1-3. (Cited in *The Road and the Car in American Life*, 1971, by John B. Rae, Cambridge, MA: MIT Press, 370.)

Highway Loss Data Institute, 1995, Atlas of Automobile Injury and Collision Losses in Large Metropolitan Areas, Arlington, VA: HLDI.

Holzer, Harry J., Keith R. Ihlanfeldt, and David L. Sjoquist, 1994, Work, Search, and Travel among White and Black Youth, *Journal of Urban Economics*, 35, 3, 320-345.

Huebner, S. S., Kenneth Black, Jr., and Bernard L. Webb, 1996, *Property and Liability Insurance*, 4th Edition, Upper Saddle River, NJ: Prentice Hall.

Ihlanfeldt, Keith R., 1993, Intra-Urban Job Accessibility and Hispanic Youth Employment Rates, *Journal of Urban Economics*, 33, 2, 254-271.

Ihlanfeldt, Keith R., and Madelyn V. Young, 1996, The Spatial Distribution of Black Employment between the Central City and the Suburbs, *Economic Inquiry*, 34, 4, 693-707.

Insurance Information Institute, 1997, Data provided to the Joint Economic Committee of the U.S. Congress, April 30, New York, NY: III.

Insurance Information Institute, annual, *The Fact Book—Property/Casualty Insurance Facts*, New York, NY: III.

Insurance News Network, *States*, on-line at <http://www.insure.com/states/>.

Insurance Research Council, 1991, *Automobile Injury Claims in Hawaii*, Oak Brook, IL: IRC.

Insurance Research Council, 1993, *Public Attitude Monitor 1993*, Oak Brook, IL: IRC.

Insurance Research Council, 1994a, *Auto Injuries: Claiming Behavior and Its Impact on Insurance Costs*, Oak Brook, IL: IRC.

Insurance Research Council, 1994b, *Paying for Auto Injuries: A Consumer Panel Survey of Auto Accident Victims*, Oak Brook, IL: IRC.

Insurance Research Council, 1995, *Trends in Auto Injury Claims*, 2nd Edition, Wheaton, IL: IRC.

Insurance Research Council, 1996, *Fraud and Buildup in Auto Injury Claims*, Wheaton, IL: IRC.

Insurance Services Office, Inc. and National Association of Independent Insurers, 1988, *Factors Affecting Urban Auto Insurance Costs*, New York: ISO and NAII.

Joint Economic Committee, U.S. Congress, 1996, *Improving the American Legal System: The Economic Benefits of Tort Reform*, Washington, DC: JEC of the U.S. Congress.

Joint Economic Committee, U.S. Congress, 1997, *The Benefits and Savings of Auto Choice*, Washington, DC: JEC of the U.S. Congress.

Kain, John F., 1968, Housing Segregation, Negro Employment, and Metropolitan Decentralization, *Quarterly Journal of Economics*, 82, 2, 175-197.

Kain, John F., 1992, The Spatial Mismatch Hypothesis: Three Decades Later, *Housing Policy Debate*, 3, 2, 371-460.

Kain, John F., and John R. Meyer, 1970, Transportation and Poverty, *The Public Interest*, 18, 75-87.

Kasarda, John D., 1995, Industrial Restructuring and the Changing Location of Jobs, in *State of the Union: America in the 1990s, Volume I: Economic Trends* (Reynolds Farley, ed.), New York, NY: Russell Sage Foundation.

Kasarda, John D., and Kwok-fai Ting, 1996, Joblessness and Poverty in America's Central Cities: Causes and Policy Prescriptions, *Housing Policy Debate*, 7, 2, 387-419.

Klein, Robert, 1995, Reducing Urban Auto Insurance Costs, in *Affordable Auto Insurance for Urban Communities: The Universe of Possibilities* (Guila P. Parker and James L. Brown, eds.), Milwaukee, WI: Center for Consumer Affairs.

Lamberty, Steve, 1995, Urban and Non-Urban Auto Insurance Comparisons, *NAIC Research Quarterly*, 1, 4, 14-19.

MacManus, Susan A., and Patricia A. Turner, 1993, Litigation as a Budgetary Constraint: Problem Areas and Costs, *Public Administration Review*, 53, 5, 462-472.

Maril, Robert Lee, 1993, The Impact of Mandatory Auto Insurance upon Low Income Residents of Maricopa County, Arizona, unpublished manuscript.

Marter, Sarah S., and Herbert I. Weisberg, 1992, Medical Expenses and the Massachusetts Automobile Tort Reform Law: A First Review of 1989 Bodily Injury Liability Claims, *Journal of Insurance Regulation*, 10, 4, 462-514.

Mooney, Sean F., 1992, *The Cost of Urban Auto Insurance*, New York, NY: Insurance Information Institute.

National Association of Independent Insurers, 1997, Data provided to the Joint Economic Committee from the NAII Auto Compilation, January 17, Des Plaines, IL: NAII.

National Association of Insurance Commissioners, annual, *State Average Expenditures and Premiums for Personal Automobile Insurance*, Kansas City, MO: NAIC.

New Jersey Department of Insurance, 1995, *1995 Automobile Insurance Premium Comparison Survey*, Trenton, NJ: NJDOI.

O'Connell, Jeffrey, Stephen Carroll, Michael Horowitz, and Allan Abrahamse, 1993, Consumer Choice in the Auto Insurance Market, *Maryland Law Review*, 52, 4, 1016-1062.

O'Connell, Jeffrey, Stephen Carroll, Michael Horowitz, Allan Abrahamse, and Paul Jamieson, 1996, The Comparative Costs of Allowing Consumer Choice for Auto Insurance in All Fifty States, *Maryland Law Review*, 55, 1, 160-222.

O'Connell, Jeffrey, Stephen Carroll, Michael Horowitz, Allan Abrahamse, and Daniel Kaiser, 1995, The Costs of Consumer Choice for Auto Insurance in States without No-Fault Insurance, *Maryland Law Review*, 54, 2, 281-351.

Office of Management and Budget, 1998, *Budget of the United States Government, Fiscal Year 1998*, Washington, DC: Government Printing Office.

Ong, Paul M., 1996, Work and Automobile Ownership among Welfare Recipients, *Social Work Research*, 20, 4, 255-262.

O'Regan, Katherine M., and John M. Quigley, 1996, Teenage Employment and the Spatial Isolation of Minority and Poverty Households—Comment, *Journal of Human Resources*, 31, 3, 692-702.

Pawasarat, John, 1997, *Initial Findings on Mobility and Employment of Public Assistance Recipients in Milwaukee County and Factors Relating to Changes in W-2 Regions over Time*, University of Wisconsin—Milwaukee, Employment and Training Institute, on-line at <http://www.uwm.edu/dept/eti/afdcmobl.htm>.

Pennsylvania Department of Insurance, 1995, cited in *Pennsylvania Auto Insurance Premiums* (1997, Insurance News Network), on-line at <http://www.insure.com/states/pa/>.

Pritchard, Tim, and Larry DeBoer, 1995, The Effect of Taxes and Insurance Costs on Automobile Registrations in the United States, *Public Finance Quarterly*, 23, 3, 283-304.

Smith, Eric, and Randall Wright, 1992, Why Is Automobile Insurance in Philadelphia So Damn Expensive?, *American Economic Review*, 82, 4, 756-772.

State of California, Governor's Commission on the Los Angeles Riots, 1965, Violence in the City—An End or a Beginning?, Los Angeles, CA: State of California.

Taylor, Brian D., and Paul M. Ong, 1995, Spatial Mismatch or Automobile Mismatch? An Examination of Race, Residence, and Commuting in U.S. Metropolitan Areas, *Urban Studies*, 32, 9, 1453-1473.

Tobias, Andrew, 1997, Testimony to the Senate Committee on Commerce, Science, and Transportation, U.S. Congress, July 17.

U.S. Bureau of the Census, 1995, *Asset Ownership of Households: 1993*, Washington, DC: Government Printing Office.

U.S. Bureau of the Census, 1996, *Government Finances: 1991-92*, Series GF/92-5, Washington, DC: Government Printing Office.

U.S. Department of Energy, Energy Information Administration, 1993, Household Vehicles Energy Consumption 1991, DOE/EIA-0464, Washington, DC: Government Printing Office.

U.S. Department of Justice, Bureau of Justice Statistics, 1995, *Civil Jury Cases and Verdicts in Large Counties*, NCJ-154346, Washington, DC: BJS.

U.S. Department of Justice, Bureau of Justice Statistics, 1995, *Tort Cases in Large Counties*, NCJ-153177, Washington, DC: BJS.

U.S. Department of Justice, Bureau of Justice Statistics, *Civil Justice Survey of State Courts, 1992*, cited in the University of Michigan's Inter-university Consortium for Political and Social Research, on-line at <http://www.icpsr.umich.edu/index.html>.

U.S. Department of Justice, Federal Bureau of Investigation, 1995, Press release, May 24, Washington, DC: FBI.

U.S. Department of Labor, Bureau of Labor Statistics, 1997, *1995 Consumer Expenditure Survey*, on-line at <http://stats.bls.gov/blshome.html>.

U.S. Department of Labor, Bureau of Labor Statistics, 1997, unpublished data from the *1995 Consumer Expenditure Survey*, Washington, DC: BLS.

U.S. Department of Labor, Bureau of Labor Statistics, 1998, *Consumer Prices Indexes*, on-line at <http://stats.bls.gov/cpihome.htm>.

U.S. Department of Labor, Employment and Training Administration, 1997, Press release, November 17, "Labor Secretary Herman Kicks-off Nationwide Welfare-to-Work Tour," Washington, DC: ETA.

U.S. Department of Transportation, Federal Highway Administration, 1992, *Cost of Owning and Operating Automobiles, Vans, and Light Trucks 1991*, FHWA-PL-92-019, Washington, DC: FHA.

U.S. Department of Transportation, Federal Highway Administration, 1996, *Highway Statistics 1995*, Washington, DC: Government Printing Office.

U.S. Department of Transportation, National Highway Traffic Safety Administration, 1992, *Source of Payment for the Medical Cost of Motor Vehicle Injuries in the United States* (by Joan S. Harris), DOT HS 807-800, Washington, DC: Government Printing Office.

U.S. Department of Transportation, National Highway Traffic Safety Administration, 1992, *The Economic Cost of Motor Vehicle Crashes, 1990* (by Lawrence J. Blincoe and Barbara M. Faigin), DOT HS 807-876, Washington, DC: Government Printing Office.

U.S. Department of Transportation, National Highway Traffic Safety Administration, 1993, *Saving Lives and Dollars—Highway Safety Contribution to Health Care Reform and Deficit Reduction*, Washington, DC: Government Printing Office.

U.S. Department of Transportation, National Highway Traffic Safety Administration, 1996, *The Economic Cost of Motor Vehicle Crashes, 1994* (by Lawrence J. Blincoe), DOT HS 808-425, Washington, DC: Government Printing Office.

U.S. Department of Transportation, National Highway Traffic Safety Administration, 1996, *Rural and Urban Crashes: A Comparative Analysis*, DOT HS 808-450, Washington, DC: NHTSA.

U.S. General Accounting Office, 1995, *Welfare to Work: Most AFDC Training Programs not Emphasizing Job Placement*, HEHS-95-113, Washington, DC: GAO.

Whitman, Christine Todd, 1997, Testimony to the Joint Economic Committee, U.S. Congress, March 19.

Wilson, William Julius, 1996, *When Work Disappears*, New York, NY: Vintage Books.

Wolfram, Charles W., 1986, *Modern Legal Ethics*, St. Paul, MN: West Publishing Co.

11
MORE FOR LESS UNDER AUTO CHOICE
Fewer Dollars for Lawyers, Fraud, Pain and Suffering, and Insurance Companies Mean Lower Premiums and *Better Compensation for Motorists*

Peter Kinzler
Coalition for Auto-Insurance Reform

Jeffrey O'Connell
University of Virginia

1. INTRODUCTION

Opponents of the federal Auto Choice Reform Act[1] contend that any premium savings the legislation would produce would come at too great a price—the loss of benefits for injured people. If that were truly the case, then the opponents would have a legitimate argument. In fact, there is so much waste in the present system that the personal injury protection (PIP) reform option of Auto Choice, by eliminating the waste, can provide both dramatically lower premiums *and* better compensation of economic loss, primarily medical bills and lost wages.

Much work has already been done to document the potential cost savings under Auto Choice. The federal Joint Economic Committee has estimated that, if all motorists selected the PIP option, the savings from lower premiums would aggregate to $35 billion a year.[2] The most recent RAND Institute for Civil Justice study estimates that the savings for the average PIP

---

[1] S. 837 and H.R. 1475, 106th Cong., 1st Sess. (1999). (The sponsors of the bills in the 106th Congress intended to introduce nearly identical bills in the 107th Congress.)

[2] Joint Economic Committee (JEC), Auto Choice: Impact on Cities and the Poor, 34-36 (March 1998). Preliminary work by the author of the study indicates that the use of the new, higher RAND estimates cited in note 3 infra would increase aggregate savings to approximately $41 billion in 2001 and $493 billion for the period from 2001 to 2110.

driver would be approximately 57 percent.[3] By contrast, little work has been done on the compensation effects of Auto Choice. This chapter explores the compensation issues through both aggregate data and the use of concrete examples of how injured people fare under the tort system and how they would fare under different Auto Choice accident scenarios.

Compensation under the tort system: "It's like homeowner's insurance that pays triple if your stereo's stolen (or you say it was) but only 9 percent if the house burns down."[4] The starting point for discussion of any legislative reform is always the present system. In this instance, the predominant system in the U.S. is the tort and liability insurance system, which is the sole "option" in 35 states.[5] The failure of this system to provide prompt and adequate compensation of the economic loss of injured persons, particularly for those with very serious injuries, has been documented in many comprehensive and widely accepted studies.[6]

For people injured by the negligence of others, the tort system holds out the promise of a full recovery of losses, both economic and non-economic. However, this theoretical possibility is tempered by two harsh realities that undermine the promise. The first is the practical world of the tort system itself. Inasmuch as recovery is contingent upon establishing the legal fault of another person and one's freedom from fault,[7] one's own negligent contributions to an accident—as perceived by a claims adjuster or a

---

[3] Stephen J. Carroll, Allan F. Abrahamse, The Effects of a Choice Automobile Insurance Plan on Insurance Costs and Compensation: An Analysis Based on 1997 Data, 19 (RAND Institute for Civil Justice, 1999) [hereafter cited as Carroll and Abrahamse].

[4] Testimony of Andrew Tobias, Hearing on S. 1860, Auto Choice Reform Act, before the Committee on Commerce, Science, and Transportation, U.S. Senate, S. Hrg. 104-613, 116 (September 24, 1996).

[5] Ten other states mandate some form of no-fault insurance that requires the payment of medical and wage losses and limits the right to sue for pain and suffering, and two states require drivers to purchase no-fault benefits but do not restrict the right to sue. Only three states—New Jersey, Pennsylvania, and Kentucky—permit motorists some form of limited choice between two different insurance systems, a no-fault system and a tort system.

[6] See, e.g., Columbia University Council for Research in the Social Sciences, Report by the Committee to study Compensation for Automobile Accidents (1932); U.S. Department of Transportation, Motor Vehicle Crash Losses and Their Compensation in the U.S., A Report to the Congress and the President (March 1971); and Stephen Carroll, James Kakalik, Nicholas Pace, John Adams, No-Fault Approaches to Compensating People Injured in Automobile Accidents (RAND Institute for Civil Justice, 1991) [Hereafter cited as Carroll, et al.].

[7] These fault requirements of the tort system preclude recovery in about 30 percent of all cases, with the largest single category of people without any recovery being those involved in single-car accidents. Many of these people had no complicity in their injuries, as is the case when a person who is driving carefully is injured when his or her car skids on the ice and hits a tree. U.S. Department of Transportation, National Highway Traffic Safety Administration, Traffic Safety Facts 1997, 90 (1998).

jury—may reduce or even eliminate a recovery. If an injured person has to litigate a claim, then the competency of one's own attorney and that of the defendant, as well as rulings by the judge and the sympathies of the jury, create even greater uncertainty as to the outcome. These variables also mean that people who are injured in a similar fashion often recover vastly different sums. Worst of all, seriously injured people, faced with the prospect of a long wait for a trial whose outcome is uncertain, have strong incentives to settle for less than the full value of their losses in order to get money they may need badly to pay for medical and rehabilitation bills and to provide some funds to tide them over while they are out of work—especially if they are less well-off to start with.

Even if an injured person can withstand the theoretical and practical problems of the tort system to win a large judgment, there is still no guarantee of a large recovery. The second harsh reality an injured person must face is that, at the end of this ordeal, the size of one's recovery from a defendant is contingent almost exclusively on the insurance coverage of the defendant.[8] Unfortunately, most defendants either are uninsured or lack the amount of insurance coverage needed to pay for the medical bills and lost wages of a seriously injured person.[9] Unless one is fortunate enough to be injured by the negligence of someone such as Bill Gates or the federal

---

[8] Only 5 percent of all payments to a claimant come from an at-fault driver personally. Insurance Research Council, Paying for Auto Injuries: A Consumer Panel Survey of Auto Accident Victims, Edition 37 (September 1999). In reality, people settle within the defendant's "policy limits," the amount of bodily injury liability insurance carried by the at-fault driver. Any difference between the claimant's loss and the defendant's policy limits is left unpaid unless the claimant can make up the difference from his or her own insurance sources (if any)—e.g., health insurance, underinsured motorist coverage, and Medical Payments (MedPay) coverage (all of which one pays for oneself), federal and state government programs (if one qualifies), and one's own savings.

[9] The RAND Institute for Civil Justice estimates that 15 percent of all drivers are uninsured (Carroll and Abrahamse, supra note 3 at 25), while the Insurance Research Council (IRC) estimates that 14 percent of drivers are uninsured (Insurance Research Council, August 12, 1999 Press Release, Uninsured Motorists). The IRC data show that 52 percent of all policyholders carry $50,000 or less of liability insurance (with most of such policyholders carrying $25,000 or less) to cover the losses of one other person in the event that the insured should be found liable in an accident. Most of the rest of the drivers carry $100,000 of coverage. Insurance Research Council, Injuries in Auto Accidents: An Analysis of Auto Insurance Claims, note 7 at 104 (June 1999). When one factors in the uninsured population, nearly 60 percent of all drivers carry $50,000 or less of insurance coverage, not nearly enough to begin to pay the economic loss of a seriously injured person. As to what limits apply when the at fault insured hurts more than one person (so-called "per accident" limits), see Jeffrey O'Connell, et al., The Comparative Costs of Allowing Consumer Choice for Auto Insurance in All Fifty States, 55 Maryland Law Review, 160, Appendix C, col. 4, at 214-22 and note 4 at 222 (1996).

government, a seriously injured person can expect to receive far less than is needed to cover his or her economic loss, not to mention non-economic loss.

The realities of the tort and liability insurance system produce a compensation system that is the exact opposite of what injured people need: one in which people with relatively minor injuries recover, on average, far more than their economic loss, while those with the most demonstrably serious injuries, with a few lucky exceptions, recover only a tiny fraction of their economic loss. These results have been documented most recently by the RAND Institute for Civil Justice. RAND has found that while people with economic loss between $500 and $1,000 recover, on average, 250 percent of those losses, people with economic loss between $25,000 and $100,000 recover on average only 56 percent of their economic loss, while those with economic loss over $100,000 recover only 9 percent.[10] These figures are gross recovery numbers, before plaintiff attorneys take their fees. Although plaintiff attorneys are free to reduce their fees in order to provide more for their clients, the literature is devoid of any such instances, even where the victim's loss is great and the attorney's time is insubstantial. It is these figures that led consumer author and activist Andrew Tobias to liken automobile bodily injury liability insurance coverage to "homeowner's insurance that pays triple if your stereo's stolen (or you say it was) but only 9 percent if the house burns down."[11]

1.1. The Tort and Liability Insurance System: *Not so good for injured people, but great for attorneys, con artists, and insurers*

If the premiums collected from motorists are not going to compensate the economic loss of seriously injured persons, then where are they going? The answer is simple—and very disturbing. While motorists pay excessive premiums for too little compensation for injuries, attorneys and quick-buck artists are getting rich and insurers are benefiting by simply taking a percentage of a pie that is unnecessarily large.

The Joint Economic Committee has found that, from each dollar of premium for bodily injury liability coverage, the following amounts are paid out:

- 28.4 cents go to plaintiff and defense attorneys to handle claims, including litigation;

---

[10] Carroll et al., supra note 6 at 21-22.

[11] See supra note 4.

- 12.6 cents go for fraudulent and excessive claims, everything from staged accidents to the more common padding of claims in response to the pain-and-suffering incentives of the tort system (the more medical bills one can accumulate—paid by one's own health insurance—the more payment for "pain and suffering"); and
- 16.9 cents go for non-economic loss.[12]

How much is paid for legitimate medical bills, lost wages, and other economic loss? Only 14.5 cents.[13] Can anyone possibly give a passing grade to a system that pays twice as much for attorneys as it does for the economic loss of victims, and more than three times as much for attorneys and pain and suffering combined as for economic loss?

And these figures do not include insurer costs. What do insurers receive from a dollar of premium? The primary insurer costs are 15.2 cents for commissions and selling expenses and another 10.1 cents for other overhead expenses. Insurers' rate of return on net worth, which in recent years has come primarily from their investments rather than from underwriting, has averaged about 10 percent over the past decade, somewhat less than other major industries. However, this is a situation where insurers benefit from benign neglect. The higher the premium, the more absolute

[12] While such loss is a legitimate form of loss, as the RAND data cited in the text above indicate, almost all of this money is being paid to people with minor injuries rather than to people with serious injuries (i.e., those with the most demonstrable pain and suffering).

[13] Joint Economic Committee (JEC), Auto Choice: Impact on Cities and the Poor, 5 (March 1998). The JEC numbers are based on bodily injury liability insurance figures only. They show what dollars one gets under the tort system, i.e., what dollars are paid for damages caused by a driver's negligence. They do not include payments made under the Medical Payments (MedPay) portion of an insured's auto insurance policy. MedPay is a discretionary coverage and it is not negligence-based. Instead, MedPay benefits are paid by one's own insurer, without regard to fault. The failure to include MedPay payments does not have much impact on the total amount of dollars paid for bodily injuries in tort states because MedPay payments are relatively small, with an average payment in 1997 of $1,949. Insurance Research Council, Injuries in Auto Accidents: An Analysis of Auto Insurance Claims, 46 (June 1999). Under the Auto Choice legislation, people who elect the new PIP system would receive most of their compensation on the same basis one receives MedPay benefits today. However, the payments would be much larger, particularly in serious injury cases, because the minimum required PIP benefits are much higher than the average amount of MedPay benefits people carry. On the other hand, RAND, in its chart that describes compensation under the tort system by categories of economic loss, includes payments from MedPay. Thus, the RAND approach, while showing the reality of how one fares in a tort and liability insurance state today, somewhat overstates the benefits of the tort system itself, under which one is legally entitled to a recovery only if the other driver is at fault. Even so, RAND's data show gross undercompensation of economic loss in serious injury cases.

dollars a 10 percent rate of return will produce. So insurers also benefit from the existence of the bloated tort and liability insurance system.[14]

1.2. The Auto Choice Reform:
Transferring dollars from quick-buck artists to lower premiums and *better compensation of economic loss*

The seeming paradox of Auto Choice—that it can provide both dramatically lower premiums and better compensation—disappears with the description of the extraordinary amount of resources that are wasted in the tort system on things other than the compensation of economic loss. Auto Choice would accomplish its twin goals by offering motorists the opportunity to opt out of the costly, inefficient, and inequitable tort and liability insurance system and elect, instead, a primarily first-party (i.e., payable by one's own insurer), non-fault-based insurance option that focuses on the efficient delivery of compensation for economic loss.

Under the new PIP system of Auto Choice, far more of the bodily insurance premium would wind up in the pockets of injured persons for their economic loss. Where would the money come from?

First, the 12.6 cents that now go for fraudulent and excessive claims under the tort system, as a result of the pain and suffering incentives of that tort system,[15] would be available for other uses because the PIP system covers only economic loss.

---

[14] Of course, insurers only benefit from higher costs if they can get an adequate rate of return. Recent overcapacity among auto insurers, coupled with rises in medical cost inflation, a flat stock market that has reduced insurers' investment income and regulators who have sometimes not been quick to permit premium increases to address higher costs, led to significant underwriting losses in the first half of 2000. Auto insurers' combined ratio on private passenger vehicles (a measure of underwriting profitability for which a lower value indicates higher profits) was 109.9 during the first six months of 2000, up from 103.9 for the first six months of 1999. That means that insurers lost $9.90 on each $100 of insurance they sold. While auto insurance was still profitable because of the money insurers earned on their investments, a flat stock market reduced investment income significantly. A. M. Best, P/C Results Weaken amid Market Firming, Viewpoint (September 25, 2000). If these trends continue, then auto insurers may also find themselves the victims of the costly tort system if they cannot earn enough to cover their costs or, for stock companies, if the lower rate of return encourages investors to seek more profitable companies.

[15] In the tort system, liability insurers will end up paying a not-at-fault injured party two to three times the amount of his or her economic loss as compensation for non-economic loss. Otherwise, such loss cannot be readily quantified. This payment provides strong incentives for injured parties to make extra visits to medical practitioners in order to get a higher award. This system works in favor of injured persons only when the insurance

Second, for the same reason, the 16.9 cents that is paid for non-economic loss also would be available.

Third, the PIP reform also would lower insurers' claim costs.

Fourth, because most payments would be made on a first-party basis without the need for litigation or lawyers to dispute claims, a significant portion of the 28 cents that presently are used to pay attorneys would be available for other purposes.

The first three changes would free up over 30 cents—or more than twice the amount presently paid to injured people for legitimate economic loss—out of the existing bodily injury liability insurance premium dollar to use for both lower premiums and more compensation of economic loss.[16] The fourth change, moving primarily to a first-party, non-fault-based system, would also free up more of the premium dollar. Some of the dollars—approximately 57 percent under the RAND estimate—would be used to cut premiums. The rest would be used to pay more of the economic loss of injured people. Instead of receiving only 14.5 cents out of every premium dollar for their economic loss, injured people would likely receive more than three times that amount from these sources. That would represent in excess of a 200 percent increase in the percentage of the premium dollar that would go for legitimate economic loss.[17]

---

coverage of the other driver is sufficient to cover such losses. As the discussion in the text and the RAND data indicate, such overpayment is typically available only when the injuries are relatively minor.

[16] Savings from the reduction in excessive medical claims would increase somewhat RAND's projected cost savings of 57 percent. RAND does not include these savings in its estimate but acknowledges "[t]hat to the extent that the distributions of claimed economic losses reflect excess claiming in response to the current system, . . . [t]he choice plan might thus result in greater savings than those reported here." Carroll and Abrahamse, supra note 3 at 6. It is also important to note that both RAND and the JEC (supra note 2) estimate only savings for auto insurance policyholders. The $35 to $41 billion annual estimated savings (if all drivers elected to purchase the required amount of new PIP coverage) does not include the savings that would inure to health insurance policyholders to the extent that auto insurance under the PIP system would pick up costs presently borne by health insurers under the tort system. Examples of such costs would be payments for the 30 percent of people who are ineligible for payment under the tort system (to the extent that their losses exceed the level of their MedPay coverage) and payments for medical care that are not recovered from health insurers' policyholders years later when the policyholders recover from the other drivers' liability insurance through a tort claim.

[17] We calculate the increase in the percentage of the premium dollar that goes to pay for legitimate economic loss by holding constant the portion of the premium that goes for insurer expenses and moving all or substantial portions of three categories of costs in the tort system—fraudulent and excessive claims, pain and suffering, and attorneys' fees—into payments for economic loss. We start with a tort system baseline of 14.5 cents for legitimate economic loss, as determined by the JEC, supra note 2. For the PIP system, we add the following amounts to the 14.5 cent figure: (1) 12.6 cents that will no longer be paid for the

fraudulent and excessive claims that are a response to the incentives of the tort system, (2) 16.9 cents that will no longer be paid for pain and suffering in a PIP system that does not permit such suits, and (3) 8 cents (a conservative estimate) that will no longer be paid to attorneys because far more claims will be resolved strictly through the payment of first-party PIP claims with no attorney involvement. Adding these four figures together produces a total net payout to injured people for economic loss of approximately 52 cents on the PIP premium dollar. That represents more than a 200 percent increase in the percentage of the premium dollar that will pay for net economic loss under the PIP system as compared to the tort system.

How does one reconcile this huge increase in the percentage of the premium dollar paid as compensation for economic loss with RAND's estimate of an increase of about 15 percent in total payments for compensation for economic loss if all motorists select the PIP system? Carroll and Abrahamse, supra note 3 at 24 (with a minor adjustment for purposes of this discussion from an assumption that one-half of all motorists would elect PIP to one that all motorists would elect PIP). The answer lies in the fact that the allocation of the premium dollar and the total amount of economic compensation paid to victims are two different matters—"apples and oranges." While far more of the premium dollar is paid to injured people to cover their economic loss under the PIP system as opposed to the tort system, the PIP premium dollar would be less than one-half the size of the tort premium dollar (because of the 57 percent reduction in costs). Thus, the more efficient use of the PIP dollar to compensate economic loss does not translate into a similar percentage increase in absolute dollars paid for economic compensation.

In addition, as discussed in note 16 supra, unlike the JEC (supra note 2), RAND does not separate fraudulent and excessive claims for medical losses from legitimate economic loss claims in its estimate of dollars paid for economic loss under the tort system. Elsewhere, RAND has estimated such claims at 35 percent to 42 percent of all medical claims. Stephen Carroll, Allan Abrahamse, and Mary Vaiana, The Costs of Excess Medical Claims for Automobile Passenger Injuries, 23 (RAND Institute for Civil Justice, 1995). Removing such payments from RAND's "before" or existing tort system numbers would result in a significant reduction in RAND's tort system baseline. Because such claims are in response to the pain and suffering incentives of the tort system, they do not appear in the PIP compensation numbers. Thus, reducing the economic compensation numbers for the tort system to eliminate excess claims would result in a significantly higher increase in the absolute numbers of dollars that would be paid for economic compensation under the PIP alternative of the Auto Choice plan.

When RAND's numbers are revised to (1) account for excess medical claims, and (2) reflect the reduction by more than one-half in the size of the PIP premium dollar, they would show a very substantial increase in the absolute amount of money that would be paid to injured people to cover their economic loss, one that is consistent with the more than 200 percent increase reflected in the percentage of the PIP premium dollar that would go for the payment of such loss.

There is one other important factor to consider here. To the extent that motorists elect the PIP system but choose to purchase higher PIP benefits instead of reducing their insurance premiums, they would receive an even higher percentage of their premium dollar back in payments for economic loss (because there would be fewer lawsuits and thus lower payments to both plaintiff and defense attorneys) and also a much higher absolute dollar increase in the amount of auto insurance paid for economic loss. See the discussion of compensation for PIP insureds who choose higher benefits instead of reduced premiums in the text, infra. According to a highly respected insurance actuary, they could purchase about $300,000 of PIP benefits if they chose to keep their premiums level.

1.3. Injured People Would Fare Better under Auto Choice

The extra compensation for economic loss benefits two categories of injured people: (1) those with no recovery under the tort system,[18] such as people involved in single-car accidents, and (2) those with serious injuries who have a tort claim but cannot recover full compensation from the other driver for even their economic loss. Under the PIP system, all motorists insured for PIP—except for those who engage in egregious conduct such as drunk driving—would be entitled to PIP benefits for any economic loss, up to their PIP policy limits. The most common minimum limits under State law would be $25,000. In addition, section 4(31) of S. 837 and H.R. 1475 provides for the payment of uncompensated economic loss from a third party at fault in causing this loss, with no offset for plaintiff attorneys' fees. Attorneys are thus paid a reasonable fee in addition to the payment to the injured person. The additional first-party non-fault-based benefits, coupled with the additional third-party at-fault benefits, would mean that PIP drivers who are seriously injured would receive better compensation, on average, than they would have under the tort system alone. Because uncompensated economic loss is treated the same way for people who elect to stay in the modified version of their state system, called tort maintenance coverage (TMC) under the legislation, a seriously injured TMC insured would also, on average, receive better compensation under Auto Choice than under the present system. That the average person would receive better compensation is not a guarantee that everyone would fare better in every case. There would be a small percentage of people who would have fared better under the tort system. However, a valid test of legislation is not that it would necessarily make everyone better off, but that it would improve the lot of the vast majority of people. As the compensation comparisons below indicate, Auto Choice passes that test with flying colors.

1.4. Compensation under Auto Choice

Motorists choose between two insurance options under Auto Choice. As indicated above, the personal injury protection (PIP) coverage protects insured motorists and their family members against economic loss from personal injury, *without regard to fault.* In the event of an accident, one files

---

[18] People who are not entitled to recovery because of the rules of the tort system can recover something if they have purchased MedPay coverage, the first-party no-fault coverage that approximately 86 percent of motorists carry in tort states. However, the typical policy covers only $5,000 or less for medical losses and nothing for lost wages.

a claim with one's own (first-party) insurer for medical bills and lost wages. A person who elects PIP coverage would relinquish the right to sue other drivers except for uncompensated economic loss. In turn, the PIP driver would be insulated from any lawsuits except for uncompensated economic loss. "Uncompensated economic loss" is defined in section 4(31) of the legislation as any economic loss beyond the limits of the insured's own coverage for such loss from all sources, such as PIP benefits and health insurance benefits. It does not include non-economic loss, such as pain and suffering. As also indicated earlier, it does include a reasonable attorney's fee.

Alternatively, a motorist may elect to stay with a modified version of the law that already exists in one's own state. For 35 states, that is the tort system. A person who elects the tort system must purchase "tort maintenance coverage" (TMC) in case one is involved in an accident with a PIP driver. This coverage is similar to uninsured motorist (UM) coverage in that the TMC insured's own (first-party) insurer pays him or her for both economic and non-economic damages if it can be established that another person was at fault.

Here is how injured people would be compensated under the four basic accident scenarios:

(1) *TMC insured v. TMC insured*. If two individuals who have elected the tort maintenance system are involved in an accident in a tort state, they may sue each other on an at-fault basis.[19]

(2) *PIP insured v. PIP insured*. If two individuals who have chosen the PIP system are involved in an accident, each person recovers economic damages to the limits of his or her own PIP policy. If the loss exceeds the policy's coverage plus any other coverage (i.e., collateral source) available to pay for the injury, the injured person may sue the other PIP insured for uncompensated economic loss on an at-fault basis.

(3) *PIP insured v. TMC insured, where the TMC insured is at fault*. The PIP insured recovers first from his or her own insurer, up to the limits of the policy. The PIP insured may also recover any uncompensated economic loss from the TMC driver on an at-fault basis.

(4) *TMC insured v. PIP insured, where the PIP insured is at fault*. The TMC insured recovers from his or her own TMC coverage first, just as if the

[19] Under section 8(a)(1) of S. 837 and H.R. 1475, supra note 1, in a no-fault state, two TMC drivers who are involved in an accident would recover according to the rules of that state. They would recover no-fault benefits and could sue for any excess economic loss or pain and suffering pursuant to the rules governing such lawsuits in the state. The text discussion focuses on TMC drivers in tort states because there are 35 tort jurisdictions and only 13 which either offer or mandate no-fault insurance.

PIP insured were an uninsured motorist. The TMC insured may recover for both economic and non-economic damages, to the extent of the TMC coverage. The TMC insured may also recover any uncompensated economic loss from the PIP driver on an at-fault basis. In addition, the TMC insured may recover non-economic damages from uninsured or underinsured motorist coverage on an at-fault basis (as well as any uncompensated economic loss above the PIP driver's tort liability limits).

The following chart demonstrates these four scenarios:

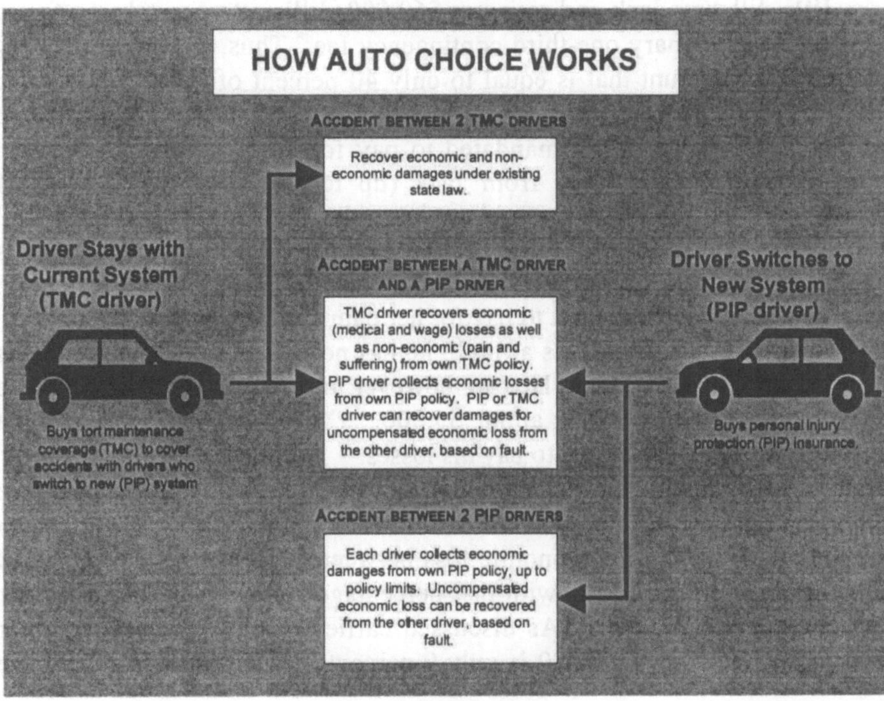

1.5. Comparisons of Likely Compensation under Tort and Auto Choice

What would these changes mean in practice for injured people? A few comparisons of how people would fare under the tort system and the PIP system should demonstrate how much better off seriously injured people would be under Auto Choice. For purposes of illustration, let us use the following example of two people who are seriously injured in an accident, assuming that each motorist carries the average bodily injury liability coverage of $60,000:[20]

Example. Assume Jack and Jill each incur $100,000 of medical expenses and lost wages in an accident in which Jack is completely at fault.

1.5.1. Jack and Jill under Today's Tort System

Jill. Jill sues Jack and recovers $60,000. Jill's attorney takes a fee of $20,000, the customary one-third contingency fee. Thus, Jill's net recovery is $40,000, an amount that is equal to only 40 percent of her full economic loss.[21] Even if Jill is insured in a tort state where her own underinsured motorist (UIM) coverage is mandated to pay for any amount in excess of what Jill is able to recover from Jack (up to the limits of Jill's UIM coverage), her UIM coverage would net her only another $27,000, for a total of $67,000.[22] By definition, in this best-case scenario for Jill, in which she is completely free from fault, she recovers only two-thirds of her full economic loss, and there is no money left to pay for her pain and suffering.

Jack. Because Jack was at fault, he has no one to sue and so recovers nothing from the tort system. He can, however, utilize any MedPay coverage he has purchased to recover about $5,000. Otherwise, he is left almost completely to his own devices to pay his losses.

These results are consistent with the RAND data that show an average gross recovery today (before the reduction for the plaintiff attorney's fee), in a serious injury case with economic loss between $25,000 and $100,000, of only 56 percent of such loss, with that percentage far lower as the economic loss approaches $100,000. (As discussed earlier, the average recovery for economic losses over $100,000 is only 9 percent.) Inasmuch as the average

---

[20] See discussion, supra note 9.

[21] This amount is close to RAND's average gross recovery of 56 percent for losses between $25,000 and $100,000 (supra note 6, and accompanying text). In fact, RAND's 56 percent is an average for this category, one that starts at close to 100 percent at $25,000 and declines rapidly as it approaches $100,000. Id. Jill may also recover $5,000 from her MedPay coverage, but typically her insurer has a subrogation claim against the other driver for that amount, so it does not affect her net recovery of $40,000.

[22] According to State Farm Mutual Insurance Companies, as of October 16, 1996, 15 of the 35 tort states required drivers to purchase UIM coverage that is "excess" of the other driver's coverage, i.e., that pays an injured insured for any loss that is not compensated by the resources of the at-fault driver (up to the limits of one's own UIM coverage). In the example cited in the text, Jill files a suit against Jack for $100,000. Because Jack has only $60,000 of bodily injury liability coverage, Jill's own UIM coverage provides the other $40,000 of benefits. If Jill's attorney takes the customary one-third contingency fee (which is based on the full $100,000 recovery), then Jill's net recovery will be only $67,000.

recovery in serious injury cases is only a small fraction of one's economic loss, one's "right to sue" for non-economic loss is most often largely illusory.

1.5.2. Jack and Jill as PIP Motorists

Section 3(1)(B) of S. 837 and H.R. 1475 describes the PIP system. Recall that: (1) under the PIP system, accident victims are compensated by their own insurers for their medical bills and lost wages up to the limits of their policies, regardless of fault (the collection of benefits from one's own first-party insurer is after all the way most insurance works, such as health insurance and homeowners insurance); (2) once PIP insureds have exhausted their first-party benefits, they can sue other drivers (whether PIP or TMC insureds) on an at-fault basis for any economic loss not covered by their policies and they, too, may be sued by other drivers on an at-fault basis for uncompensated economic loss; and (3) uncompensated economic loss includes the payment of a reasonable attorney's fee. The PIP system does not pay benefits for non-economic loss,[23] nor can one sue or be sued for non-economic loss.

Let us examine two PIP scenarios: (1) where Jack and Jill each select the minimum amount of required PIP benefits (about $25,000[24]), and (2) where Jack and Jill each select a much higher amount of coverage that they can purchase for what their tort liability insurance would have cost (normally about $300,000, according to a highly respected insurance industry actuary).

(1) Where Jack and Jill each select $25,000 of PIP benefits.

Jill (with the minimum required PIP coverage). Jill, who was not negligent, first collects $25,000 in PIP benefits from her own insurer. Then she sues Jack based on fault for the remaining $75,000 of economic loss. Jack's insurance pays his full policy limits of $60,000. Thus, Jill nets $85,000—in the majority of states, more than twice the $40,000 she would

---

[23] While the basic system does not provide for first-party benefits for non-economic loss, an insured could choose to purchase such coverage for an additional premium. Under one view, first-party coverage for non-economic loss would be more valuable because it would cover all such injuries, not just those caused by another's negligence. And, according to an estimate by an actuary of a large insurer, PIP plus a schedule of benefits for non-economic loss in serious injury cases would still be less expensive than traditional tort liability insurance, in part because there would be much lower legal costs associated with the payment of non-economic loss.

[24] As of 1996, 24 states had long-standing $25,000 financial responsibility limits. The next largest number—10—require $20,000. See Jeffrey O'Connell, et al., supra note 9.

have received under the tort system.[25] And her insurance costs about half the amount her tort liability insurance used to cost.[26]

Jack (with the minimum required PIP coverage). Jack has no third-party claim because he was at fault. However, he is entitled to $25,000 of first-party PIP benefits, or about 5 times what he would have received under the tort system (assuming he has $5,000 of MedPay coverage). Once again, as with Jill, his PIP coverage costs about one-half of what his tort liability insurance policy cost him.

Jack and Jill, as PIP insureds, would recover the same amounts even if the other driver were a TMC insured because, under the legislation, PIP insureds recover their first-party PIP benefits regardless of the insurance carried by the other driver and can sue either an at-fault PIP or TMC motorist for uncompensated economic loss.

(2) Where Jack and Jill each purchase $300,000 of PIP benefits.

Now, let's examine what would happen if the average driver chose to purchase PIP but to forgo the cost savings and, instead, spent the same amount of money on PIP benefits that he or she is spending on bodily injury premiums under the tort system today. That would amount to approximately $300,000 of PIP benefits per insured, according to one estimate by the chief actuary of a large auto insurer.

Jill (with $300,000 of PIP coverage). Jill would recover $100,000 from her PIP coverage, her full economic loss. She would have no need to sue Jack (nor, in this case, any right to sue Jack because she has no uncompensated economic loss)—nor to worry about whether Jack had third-party liability coverage and, if so, how much. By comparison with the tort system recovery, Jill would recover between 50 percent[27] and 150 percent[28]

---

[25] Jill receives her full $25,000 of PIP benefits with no offset from her $60,000 recovery from Jack. Supra note 21 cites the fact that Jill's MedPay benefits under the tort system would be subject to a subrogation claim by her own insurer from her tort recovery from Jack. By contrast, the PIP system does not permit Jill's insurer any subrogation rights against her recovery from Jack for the $25,000 in PIP benefits it has paid her (or for any level of PIP benefits she may choose). Jill's net recovery for economic loss under the PIP system would be 21 percent higher than her recovery in a tort state where her UIM coverage was in excess of Jack's bodily injury liability coverage (i.e., $85,000 is 21 percent greater than $67,000, the amount she would have recovered in an excess UIM state in the example cited in the text).

[26] Carroll and Abrahamse, supra note 3 at 23.

[27] If Jill lived in a tort state where her own UIM coverage was "excess" of any recovery from Jack's third-party bodily injury liability coverage, then, as noted in the text accompanying supra note 22 discussing her tort system recovery, she would recover approximately $67,000. Under the PIP system described here, she would recover $100,000, which is 50 percent more.

[28] If Jill lived in a tort state where her UIM coverage would not pay for any loss beyond that covered by Jack's third-party coverage, then her net recovery would be $40,000

more (using figures from Jill in the tort system above), for the same price as tort liability insurance. Of course, Jill's percentage recovery would be far greater if her losses exceeded $100,000, because her losses would be covered up to $300,000 under PIP while they would be capped between $40,000 and $67,000 under tort.[29] If her economic loss were $300,000, then her guaranteed PIP recovery would be between 3.5 and 6.5 times the amount of protection. And for the same price. Moreover, each member of Jill's family would be covered up to $300,000. Under the tort system, the family's total recovery would be capped by the average multi-person policy limit of $120,000[30] (minus plaintiff attorneys' fees).

Jack (with $300,000 of PIP coverage). Jack, who was at fault and would have been entitled to only $5,000 under any MedPay coverage under his tort liability policy, would be entitled to the full $100,000 of his economic loss under PIP—20 times his likely recovery from his MedPay coverage in the tort system. His own insurer would pay him for the loss.

Injured PIP insureds, regardless of the level of PIP benefits they chose, would also be better off because (1) they would be entitled to their benefits in all of the 30 percent of accidents in which there is no tort recovery (and only a very limited MedPay recovery) because there was no tortfeasor or because the injured person was the one at fault, and (2) PIP benefits must be paid within 30 days of submission of a bill, far faster than the lump-sum payments at the end of the claims process under the tort system. While MedPay coverage pays promptly, because it also is a first-party, non-fault based coverage, once it is exhausted there would be no further interim payments until the claim or lawsuit were resolved. The availability of PIP's prompt payment of losses as they accrue will mean faster and more complete rehabilitation.

(see text accompanying supra note 21). Her $100,000 recovery under the PIP system would be 2.5 times, or 150 percent, greater.

[29] See the discussion in the text of Jill's recovery under the tort system, depending upon whether or not she resided in a state where her own UIM coverage was excess of any recovery from Jack's third-party bodily injury liability coverage.

[30] Bodily injury liability coverage is typically sold with a per-person and a per-accident limit. The per-accident limit establishes the maximum coverage for all individuals injured by an at-fault driver in any one accident. It is normally twice the per-person limit. Thus, we use a $120,000 per-accident figure because the average per-person amount is approximately $60,000, as discussed in the text supra with respect to compensation under the tort system.

1.5.3. Jack and Jill as TMC Motorists

Section 3(1)(A) of S. 837 and H.R. 1475 describes the TMC system. According to RAND analyses, the TMC system will provide for average premiums and injury compensation levels comparable to those in existence in a state on the date of enactment of this bill.[31] As indicated above, the TMC system builds on the existing liability system in a tort state.[32] A TMC insured would continue to purchase third-party bodily injury liability coverage, the same as today's coverage in that it protects the assets of the insured against at-fault claims by others against the insured. In addition, as also indicated above, the TMC insured would purchase a new supplemental coverage called tort maintenance coverage or TMC, that works like UM coverage today. When a TMC insured is involved in an accident with a PIP driver, the TMC insured can recover both economic and non-economic loss from his or her own insurer if the requisite at-fault liability of the other driver can be established. The TMC insured can sue the PIP driver on the same at-fault basis for any uncompensated economic loss.

While there is an added charge for TMC, the TMC insured's premiums stay the same because of an offset: This offset is the byproduct of the fact that a TMC driver has to pay less to a PIP driver in an accident when the TMC driver is at fault. The TMC driver does not have to pay any economic loss covered by the PIP insured's policy and only has to pay for the PIP insured's uncompensated economic loss, not for non-economic loss. In short, although TMC insureds insure for their own economic and non-economic loss payable when a PIP insured is at fault, their insurance costs will remain the same because they will no longer have to cover most of the PIP insured's losses when the TMC driver is at fault.[33]

There would be three accident scenario possibilities involving Jack and Jill as TMC motorists. In the first, Jack and Jill both select the TMC system. In this scenario, Auto Choice provides that there would be no change from the tort system—if Jack were at fault and Jill not, Jill would recover just as she did in the original tort example; Jack would not.

Recoveries would change only if either Jack or Jill were a TMC driver and the other were a PIP driver. We discuss Jack and Jill only as the TMC insured because we have already described how they would fare if they were the PIP insured.

---

[31] Carroll and Abrahamse, supra note 3 at 7, 23.

[32] The TMC system would also apply in a no-fault state, with TMC coverage paying for any economic loss not covered by one's no-fault benefits and for pain and suffering in cases that cross the tort threshold.

[33] Carroll and Abrahamse, supra note 3 at 26-27.

Jill (as a TMC insured not at fault). First, Jill collects $60,000 from her own insurer under TMC.[34] If Jill uses an attorney to collect her TMC benefits, she will pay the attorney approximately $20,000. Thus, Jill nets $40,000 from her TMC. Now, however, she can sue Jack for her remaining $40,000 of uncompensated economic loss.[35] Jack's $60,000 bodily injury liability policy pays Jill's remaining $40,000 of uncompensated economic loss with no offset for her attorney's fee. Under the Auto Choice Reform Act definition of uncompensated economic loss,[36] Jill's attorney is paid a reasonable fee, separate from the amount that Jack's policy pays Jill for her uncompensated economic loss. So Jill nets $80,000 from these two sources—$40,000 from her TMC coverage and $40,000 from Jack's bodily injury liability coverage for uncompensated economic loss. Her recovery is twice as large as the $40,000 she would have netted from Jack's bodily injury liability insurance coverage under the tort system.[37] In addition, under section 7(b) of S. 837 and H.R. 1475, Jill can utilize her UM coverage or her UIM coverage to pay for the shortfall in both economic and non-economic loss. As a result, her total recovery in many states will exceed her economic loss of $100,000. And her premium will not change.

Jack (as a TMC insured at fault). Because Jack is completely at fault, his selection of the fault-based TMC system means that he would have no recovery from a free-from-fault Jill as a PIP insured. His only recovery would be from his MedPay coverage, if he had purchased it.

Compared to today's insurance system, the injured not-at-fault TMC insured would actually be *better off* in the average serious injury case where

---

[34] RAND assumes in its costing of tort maintenance insurance that the TMC driver will buy the same amount of coverage for TMC as for bodily injury liability. Carroll and Abrahamse, supra note 3, at 17.

[35] In this case, Jill's uncompensated economic loss is only $40,000, because she has already received $60,000 for economic loss from her TMC coverage. The fact that Jill chooses to retain an attorney and pay the attorney a fee in her TMC claim against her own insurer does not alter the fact that she has received compensation for $60,000 of economic loss.

[36] See definition (31), uncompensated economic loss, in S. 837 and H.R. 1475, supra note 1.

[37] As discussed earlier in the text accompanying supra note 21, Jill's sole source of recovery in the majority of tort states would be Jack's bodily injury liability insurance, or a net of $40,000. The TMC system would provide better compensation even in the 15 states where UM and UIM coverage pay for any loss that is in excess of the injured person's recovery from the at-fault driver. As discussed in the text describing recovery under the tort system in a tort state where UIM is "excess" of the at-fault driver's bodily injury liability coverage (supra note 22), Jill would net $40,000 from Jack's $60,000 of coverage (with the rest going to her attorney) and another $27,000 from her UIM coverage (with the other $13,000 going to her attorney). That is less than the $80,000 she would receive from the combination of her TMC coverage and Jack's bodily injury liability coverage.

a PIP driver is at fault because he or she now has three pots of money to recover from: (1) his or her own TMC coverage, (2) the at-fault PIP driver's coverage for uncompensated economic loss, and (3) the TMC insured's UM coverage or UIM coverage, if his or her economic or non-economic loss exceeds the amount of the first three coverages.[38] By contrast, today one would have at most two coverages (the other driver's bodily injury liability coverage and, if applicable, one's own UM coverage or UIM coverage).

In almost all cases, then, the accident victim would be better off with the new TMC coverage because the three pots of money would provide more compensation than is available from the one or two sources of recovery under the tort system. One would be worse off only in the rare instance where the other driver is completely at fault and happens to be Bill Gates, a U.S. government vehicle or some such other "deep pocket" defendant.

1.5.4. The PIP System in Real-World Situations

Let us close with two actual cases that illustrate how Auto Choice could make a difference in the lives of people.

Robert Demichelis II. Robert Demichelis II sustained a traumatic brain injury in a single car crash in the tort state of Illinois in 1980. As his father, Robert Demichelis, testified at a Senate hearing:

> Robert, at age 23, 18 years ago, was in the prime of his life, had just graduated from college, had accepted a job with a Big 8 accounting firm in Chicago. The car that he was driving careened off a metal guard railing and veered into a concrete abutment dividing the east-west lanes of a four-lane major highway. Robert had a serious head injury. It was diagnosed subsequently as a closed-head injury, with frontal and parietal lobe damage.
>
> He was in the hospital for 5 weeks. The first 2 weeks he was in a coma. Doctors were able to stem the brain swelling without surgery. From that point, we transferred him to the George Washington University Hospital here in Washington, and he underwent 3 more weeks of rehabilitation. He spent a month at the Psychiatric Institute, exhausting all of his psychiatric benefits under his health insurance policy. He ended up exhausting all of his other benefits under his health insurance policy, and still has not achieved 100 percent recovery.

---

[38] The third coverage would apply under section 7(b) of S. 837 and H.R. 1475, supra note 1.

> And yet, while his employer's health insurance paid for the majority of his health insurance expenses until the policy capped, he had no benefit from his automobile insurance policy. *If he had a first-party protection insurance policy, such as that offered to consumers in this bill, it would have been a much different story and a much more rapid recovery* [emphasis added].[39]

Under the PIP option of Auto Choice, Robert Demichelis II, who received nothing under his tort liability insurance, would have been entitled to at least $25,000 of PIP benefits. Had he spent as much on his PIP coverage as he did on the tort liability coverage that paid him nothing, he would have been guaranteed $300,000 in PIP benefits that would have been paid in addition to his health insurance benefits. Robert and his whole family would have been much better off, both financially and, as his father testified, in terms of rehabilitation and a return to a productive life.

Rosemary Pryor. Rosemary Pryor suffered a spinal cord injury in a crash in the State of Michigan in 1974 when the driver of the truck she was riding in lost control of the truck and hit a tree. The accident occurred one year after Michigan had adopted a no-fault automobile insurance law which, as with the PIP option of Auto Choice, provides for the payment of economic loss benefits without regard to fault. Had Ms. Pryor suffered the injury one year earlier under the pre-existing tort system, the host-guest statute of the tort system would have precluded any tort recovery whatsoever. Under Michigan's no-fault law, as of 1977, she had received $52,000 of benefits for lost wages and medical and rehabilitation services, including the remodeling of her house to meet her needs and a car with hand controls so that she could get around and attend college.[40] These first-party benefits—which would also be available under the PIP system of Auto Choice[41]—helped her remake

[39] Testimony of Robert J. Demichelis, Hearing on S. 625, The Auto Choice Reform Act, before the Committee on Commerce, Science, and Transportation, U.S. Senate, S. Hrg. 105-1021 57-58 (September 9, 1998).

[40] Testimony of Rosemary Prior, State No-Fault Automobile Insurance Experiences, Hearings before the Subcommittee on Consumer Protection and Finance, Committee on Interstate and Foreign Commerce, U.S. House of Representatives, Serial No. 95-41, 683, 697-98 (June 13, 1977).

[41] Section 6(a)(1)(B) of S. 837 and H.R. 1475, supra note 1, provides that, in a state already having a no-fault law (such as Michigan), the minimum required PIP benefits shall be equal to the required level of no-fault benefits in that state. The Michigan law entitled Rosemary Pryor and all other drivers to unlimited benefits for medical and rehabilitation loss. People in Michigan who elected the PIP option of Auto Choice would continue to have the unlimited medical and rehabilitation benefits required by Michigan law today. For a list of no-fault states and their required coverages, see O'Connell, et al., supra note 9.

her life. She was able to return to and complete college and enter the workforce.

1.5.5. The Aggregation of Examples:
The quantification of greater benefits for economic loss under Auto Choice

In sum, under PIP, there would be three main sources of economic benefits that would increase recoveries over what they would have been in the tort system. First, the 30 percent of injured people with no tort system recovery would, in the average state, recover $25,000 in PIP benefits. That is approximately five times more than the $5,000 they would be entitled to if they carried the average amount of MedPay coverage under their tort system coverage.[42] Second, for seriously injured people who recover far less than their economic loss under the tort system, the $25,000 in PIP benefits will be a second source of payment for economic loss, in addition to their tort recovery.[43] Third, under both the PIP and TMC systems, people with a tort claim for uncompensated economic loss would not see their gross recovery reduced by about one-third to pay their attorney because, under Auto Choice, plaintiff attorneys receive a reasonable fee in addition to their clients' tort recovery. Inasmuch as the average bodily injury liability insurance coverage is about $60,000, that would mean an additional $20,000 in net recovery for uncompensated economic loss in most serious injury cases.

The effect of these three additional sources of economic loss recovery on RAND's profile of recovery in serious injury cases is substantial. For example, recall that RAND found that the gross recovery for people with economic loss between $25,000 and $100,000 was 56 percent of such loss under the tort system. If one adjusts RAND's numbers to a net figure by eliminating the payment of plaintiff attorneys' fees in successful tort claims, then the net figure dips to approximately 42 percent.[44] Adding another

---

[42] Their PIP benefits would also be more valuable because 100 percent of PIP motorists would be required to have them. By contrast, MedPay coverage is optional and only about 86 percent of drivers in tort states carry it (National Association of Independent Insurers, Automobile Experience, 1992). Moreover, PIP covers both medical and work loss, while MedPay covers only medical loss.

[43] See supra note 25.

[44] In order to convert RAND's gross economic compensation figure of 56 percent for economic loss between $25,000 and $100,000 to a net figure, one must eliminate the amount that plaintiffs pay their attorneys. Inasmuch as RAND found that 30 percent of plaintiffs recovered nothing from the tort system (see supra note 7), most of the 56 percent recovery figure went to the 70 percent of plaintiffs who had a tort recovery. A small amount also was paid to claimants with MedPay claims. Putting that amount to the side for the moment, RAND data show that successful tort claimants pay their attorneys an average fee of 31

$20,000 for those with no tort recovery and up to $40,000 for those with a tort recovery and losses of at least $85,000 would represent a substantial increase in recovery for serious injury. And these figures are based on the assumption that all motorists would choose only the minimum required coverage. To the extent that many motorists elect to use their savings to purchase higher levels of PIP benefits instead, the profile of recovery for economic loss would be even better. As stated above, a PIP motorist who chose to forgo the cost savings entirely could afford to purchase approximately $300,000 of PIP benefits for each member of his or her family. Motorists who elect this level of PIP benefits would, of course, be assured 100 percent of their economic loss up to at least $300,000 (and there would also be the possibility of some tort recovery for any uncompensated economic loss). That would be a far cry from RAND's findings of a 9 percent gross recovery of economic loss in the worst injury cases, those that average over $100,000.

2. CONCLUSION

The RAND Institute for Civil Justice and the Joint Economic Committee studies of the 1990s have demonstrated clearly that the federal Auto Choice Reform Act would produce substantial savings in bodily injury premiums. The combination of examples and quantification of aggregate benefits discussed in this chapter demonstrate that Auto Choice would also significantly increase economic loss benefits for the average seriously injured person and for the vast majority of injured individuals. It would not do this by magic. Instead, Auto Choice would achieve both substantial increases in economic loss benefits and lower premiums the hard way (at least politically)—by transferring dollars from people who make a living off the tort system to injured people. The money saved by eliminating most lawsuits, along with the attendant attorneys' fees on both sides, pain and suffering damages, and the fraud generated by the pain-and-suffering

---

percent. Thirty-one percent of 56 percent is 17 percent. Reducing 56 percent by 17 percent produces a net recovery figure of 39 percent. The actual net economic compensation figure would be slightly higher because of MedPay claims, but certainly not above about 42 percent.[1]

The author wishes to thank Peter Kinzler for background information and helpful comments on an earlier draft of this chapter.

incentives of the tort system, would indeed enable motorists to enjoy both lower premiums and better coverage of economic loss.

12
THE POLITICAL FEASIBILITY OF CHOICE NO-FAULT INSURANCE

Edward L. Lascher, Jr.[1]
California State University, Sacramento

1. INTRODUCTION

Much of this book addresses the following two questions: (1) How does choice no-fault insurance work? and (2) What are the effects of choice no-fault under different design arrangements? These are crucial issues. Yet given how frequently even well supported automobile insurance reform efforts have collapsed in the political realm, those concerned about real-world public policy may find the following question equally important: (3) What is the political feasibility of moving to a choice no-fault system?

It is significant that, at least in the U.S., public discussion of choice options has overtaken debate over mandatory no-fault schemes in large part because no-fault advocates believe the former are more politically feasible. Some prominent long-time no-fault advocates, such as University of Virginia Law Professor Jeffrey O'Connell, have focused mainly on the choice approach in recent years, and have been explicit about its potential political advantages. Thus, O'Connell, et al. (1993) wrote in a law review article:

> [T]he issue of high—and rising—auto insurance costs assures that interest in "choice" auto insurance can be expected, at least at the state level. That is so, argue proponents of change, because such proposals could radically drive down the high cost of insurance while also having the political virtue of arguably freeing the debate from the claims that reform involves involuntary surrender of rights by consumers.

I concur with the argument that, on balance and for the foreseeable future, it is easier to establish a choice system in the U.S. than a mandatory no-fault system (this is decidedly *not* true in Canada, however, for reasons I will discuss later). Yet choice no-fault is itself a difficult sell, and choice proposals pose some unique political dangers. For this reason it is important to be more precise about the political advantages and disadvantages of the choice route.

My discussion is organized as follows. Initially I indicate why it is plausible to think that choice no-fault has political feasibility advantages. Next I draw specific lessons relevant to the implementation of no-fault at the state/provincial level, based on case studies and other information. This section is largely based on my own previously published work (Lascher, 1999), although I also draw from other sources. I then turn more briefly to implementation of choice no-fault at the level of the U.S. national government, giving consideration to the "The Auto Choice Reform Act" discussed at length in other chapters. Finally, I summarize where this analysis leaves us with respect to likely future public policy actions.

Before proceeding further, a word of caution is in order. Because there have been so few successful efforts to implement no-fault of any kind in recent years, it is impossible to draw political lessons with anything approaching statistical rigor. I have attempted to draw lessons based on the preponderance of the evidence; I do not claim any sort of conclusive empirical demonstration for them.

2. WHY CHOICE NO-FAULT MAY BE MORE POLITICALLY FEASIBLE

In both the U.S. and Canada, (a) automobile insurance regulation is handled at the subnational (i.e., state/provincial) level, and (b) tort is the default system for loss recovery following automobile accidents. Furthermore, adoption of no-fault requires statutory change. Consequently, the political feasibility of any sort of no-fault turns on what is necessary to convince subnational legislatures to adopt an enabling law.

Before examining the empirical evidence from actual recent battles over insurance reform, one can posit four reasons why legislatures might more readily back choice no-fault than mandatory no-fault proposals.

2.1. Less Uniform Opposition from Attorney-Legislators

It has long been noted that attorney-legislators commonly form a base of opposition to no-fault; systematic empirical work comparing lawmakers who are and are not attorneys tends to support this claim (Dyer, 1976; Lascher, 1999, pp. 82-85). Such opposition presumably is based upon self-interest (at least for some lawmakers who expect to do further personal injury work), ideological opposition to any measures limiting the "right to sue" (see especially Miller, 1995, pp. 17-28), and professional solidarity. Choice plans may partially alleviate attorney-legislators' concerns, since some of these plans allow people to retain full tort rights if they choose, and those who so choose might still need legal counsel. But the word "partially" is key; attorney-legislators might still have concern about loss of tort remedies through misunderstanding or coercion, for example.

2.2. Reducing Other Lawmakers' Concerns about Loss of Tort Rights

While many lawmakers are attorneys, this group tends to remain a minority within legislative bodies, especially at the subnational level. Furthermore, a National Council of State Legislatures (1996) study showed that the proportion of attorneys in American state legislatures had declined since the 1970s; in 1976 over 22 percent of state lawmakers were attorneys, while by 1995 that proportion had dropped to under 16 percent. Hence, attorney-legislators opposed to no-fault must build coalitions with other lawmakers to defeat no-fault plans. Yet non-lawyers themselves often feel a strong personal commitment to preserving citizens' "rights", and lawyers are often adept at raising such issues in legislative bodies and framing issues in terms of rights (Miller, 1995). Choice may alleviate these concerns.

2.3 Alleviating Lawmakers' Worries about Imposing Losses on Constituents

Aside from their own concerns about tort rights, legislators can generally be expected to show reluctance in imposing losses on constituents. A large political science literature demonstrates that politicians are loath to reduce or eliminate benefits currently available to voters (see especially Weaver and Rockman, 1993; Pal and Weaver, forthcoming), even if doing so leads to other desirable consequences, and even if these other benefits are greater in the aggregate. A notable feature of mandatory no-fault plans is that they require that the average citizen gives up something. Typically what's lost is the ability to obtain compensation for non-economic losses under at least some circumstances. True, citizens may obtain rate reduction or stabilization as a result, outcomes that can have great salience for constituents (Lascher, 1999, pp. 28-34). But this fact has to be demonstrated to constituents (who are likely to believe that "promises are cheap"), and does not change the fact that some citizens may *worry* about what will happen to them in an accident, while others will *in fact* find themselves unable to sue for damages in circumstances where people previously could do so. In short, from a legislator's viewpoint, adopting mandatory no-fault may be seen as the equivalent of giving constituents unpleasant medicine. This is not something lawmakers like to do. From that vantage, the potential advantage of the choice plan is that it removes direct responsibility for policy costs from lawmakers themselves. Under choice, legislators do not make constituents give up the tort remedy; citizens do this themselves. One can easily see why this might be much more comfortable for lawmakers. Furthermore, a credible argument can be made that the notion of "giving citizens a choice" has a positive valence in itself, as evidenced by its common use in other policy debates (e.g., the debate over school vouchers and the debate over abortion).

2.4. Reducing Interest Group Opposition to No-Fault

No-fault plans in North America have prompted strong interest group opposition, notably from trial lawyer organizations, but sometimes from others as well, including some consumer groups (especially those associated with consumer advocate Ralph Nader). Because they may be seen as more favorable to consumers, choice plans might cause such groups to move toward positions of neutrality and support. This might have implications for campaign contributions and other types of support. Potentially even more important is that elimination of group opposition might reduce concerns about imposing losses, since groups often play a key role in reminding constituents about the losses they experience (in effect, this can be seen as the traditional function of campaign "hit pieces").

Balanced against these advantages are some potential disadvantages. Notably, the greater uncertainty about the rate effects of choice no-fault may dampen support among lawmakers. As stressed elsewhere in this volume, for example, potential savings from choice are sometimes dependent on the number of people who choose to give up full tort remedies. Such uncertainty can also reduce group support for no-fault, especially from insurance companies that may not want to be responsible for rate reductions if cost savings are slow to appear. Additionally, the very complexity of the choice model may be a strike against it.

3. CASE STUDIES AND OTHER EMPIRICAL EVIDENCE

I turn now to the recent experience of American states and Canadian provinces with respect to no-fault proposals. The key lessons I draw from these experiences are summarized in the paragraphs that follow. Some of these lessons relate directly to the possible political advantages of choice no-fault mentioned earlier, while others are broader in nature.

3.1. Continued Trial Lawyer Opposition

While in theory one might envision a softening of trial attorney opposition to no-fault if offered in the choice form, in practice this has not happened. Trial attorneys have been vociferous opponents to both mandatory and choice no-fault proposals, and have not softened their stance when the former were converted to the latter (as occurred in Rhode Island in the mid-1990s). Indeed, one is tempted to claim that trial lawyers are opposed to no-fault in all its permutations, and will remain opposed through eternity or the end of lawsuits, whichever comes first. The sharp stance of trial lawyers is underscored by the testimony of Association of Trial Lawyers of America (ATLA) President Mark Mandell before the U.S. Senate Committee on Commerce, Science, and Transportation (1998). Testifying against S. 625, "The Auto Choice Reform Act," Mandell (p. 42) began his remarks with the following argument:

> Some of the people who have already spoken in opposition to S. 625 have said they wanted to make it clear that they are not opposed to the concept of no-fault. They oppose the bill on State rights grounds. I would like to make it clear that I am personally opposed to the concept of no-fault. It leads to less personal responsibility, less personal responsibility in driving. It provides very minimal benefits to people who are injured [. . . .] It leads to the loss of very significant rights American citizens have, including the right to sue for pain and suffering, or quality of life damage.

In a prepared statement submitted with his testimony, Mandell made clear (p. 45) that the trial lawyers organization believed choice plans should be lumped with mandatory no-fault.

ATLA fundamentally objects to any automobile insurance system in which negligent or reckless motorists bear virtually no civil liability to those they injure. A fundamental feature of no-fault insurance plans, including the so-called "auto choice" plan in S. 625, is that negligent and reckless drivers are virtually immune from civil liability, and that motorists must instead file damage claims with their own insurers regardless of fault. ATLA opposes any legislation that so erodes personal responsibility.

It should be noted that while Mandell's statement illustrates the strong trial lawyer opposition to choice systems, his actual characterization of choice plans is questionable, since at least some versions of choice (e.g., those operating in New Jersey and Pennsylvania) do not provide the immunity to negligent drivers he claims.

3.2. Endangering Insurance Company Support

In both the U.S. and Canada, insurance companies traditionally have been supportive of strong no-fault plans.[2] This support has come in various forms, including funding of public relations campaigns on behalf of no-fault proposals. But insurance company support for no-fault has not been unanimous, and the extent of support has been highly contingent on the specifics of the proposal, in contrast to the uniform opposition from trial lawyers.[3] For example, when Hawaii flirted with adoption of pure no-fault in 1995 (the state legislature actually passing a bill to implement a system that was later vetoed by the governor), much of the industry withheld support. As suggested in the previous section of this chapter, insurance companies indeed seem to worry about the uncertainty of cost savings under choice plans, especially when combined with legislative requirements that rates be lowered to reflect such savings. Exactly such worries caused insurance companies in Rhode Island to withdraw their support for a 1993 no-fault plan that was converted to a choice proposal (Lascher, 1999, p. 81). Similarly, the Insurance Federation of Pennsylvania opposed legislation introduced in 1989 that combined choice no-fault with medical cost controls and mandatory rate cuts (Lascher, 1999, p. 57). Additionally, the Hawaii experience suggests that companies may worry when projected consumer savings are very great, since this may threaten the companies' revenue base.

---

[2] For a discussion of the role of the insurance industry in adoption of a strong no-fault system in Ontario, see O'Donnell (1991).

[3] Regarding the extensive divisions within the insurance industry with respect to political support for no-fault, see especially Davies (1998).

3.3. Opposition from Trial Attorneys and Insurance Companies Not Entirely Bad

During the last wave of sharply increasing automobile insurance rates in the late 1980s and early 1990s, many American states considered no-fault proposals. A striking fact is that the greatest success occurred in Pennsylvania, where a choice plan was enacted. Yet that plan was opposed by both trial attorney and insurance company organizations as well as the Pennsylvania Medical Society.[4] This may be counter-intuitive, but the connection to the success of the Pennsylvania legislation is clear. The stances taken by the major groups offered then Pennsylvania Governor Robert Casey and his allies an opportunity to "run against the special interests." Many state lawmakers appeared to take group opposition to the plan as a signal that it really must be pro-consumer. And in this regard it is important to note that polls have shown that both attorneys and insurance companies are relatively unpopular among the public at large.

Interestingly, a study of California voters' attitudes toward an array of insurance initiatives on the 1998 general election ballot also indicates that ordinary citizens use industry support as a negative cue (Lupia, 1994). That study demonstrated that when California voters determined the industry was behind a particular initiative (i.e., a no-fault plan) they moved against it, while moving to support a plan that the industry strongly opposed (i.e., the controversial *Proposition 103* that was narrowly passed, thereby establishing a tight regulatory system in the state).

3.4. *Prima Facie* Evidence of Political Feasibility

If we take leading politicians as generally good judges of political feasibility, then the actions taken in the Pennsylvania and Rhode Island cases I studied provide *prima facie* evidence for the greater feasibility of choice no-fault. In both cases political leaders who had advocated mandatory schemes dropped them in favor of choice proposals. (Pennsylvania's governor dropped his plan after it failed in 1988, while Rhode Island's state senate leader converted his 1993 plan after the original proposal encountered stiff opposition.) Also, in both cases political insiders indicated explicitly during interviews that the changes were based on judgments about what was necessary to obtain adequate legislative support. And in Rhode Island, the state senate bill sponsor who doubled as majority floor leader underscored

---

[4] For a more in-depth discussion of the Pennsylvania case, see Lascher (1999), ch. 4.

the very positive value placed on "giving consumers a choice," returning to that theme time and again during floor debate (Kelly, 1993). For example, in his opening statement he indicated as follows:

> Basically all I'm asking you to do tonight is for this chamber to say to the people in the state of Rhode Island: "We are going to offer you a choice as a consumer [sic]. We're going to give you a choice the same way you have in health care [to choose a health-care plan] . . . ." And the purpose of my legislation tonight is to offer consumers that choice in insurance.

It is less clear exactly from which legislators no-fault supporters hoped to win support, and why. However, at least in Rhode Island, the target seemed to be non-attorney legislators; attorney-lawmakers were generally considered a "lost cause." It is not apparent whether the expected greater support from non-lawyer legislators was based on their own perceived concerns about limiting tort rights or the general reluctance to impose direct losses on constituents.

3.5. Not Much Progress at the Subnational Level Absent Sharp Rate Increases

One of the things that emerges with a relatively high degree of certainty from previous research is the strong connection between large rate increases and serious consideration of no-fault of any form (see also Harrington, 1994). My surveys of people knowledgeable about insurance issues indicated that major insurance reform was simply off the active political agenda in jurisdictions with stable and average to low insurance rates. Even in jurisdictions with relatively high rates, insurance tends to be a major issue only when rates are also climbing quickly, as was the case in several jurisdictions in the late 1980s and early 1990s, including California, Hawaii, New Jersey, Pennsylvania, Rhode Island, and Ontario. Not coincidentally, no-fault was on the decision agenda in all such places. And with rates growing more slowly in recent years, no-fault has fallen off the radar screen even in several of these jurisdictions.

3.6. Political Feasibility Advantages Unique to U.S., Not Salient in Canada

As I have argued at greater length elsewhere, strong no-fault proposals traveled a much easier political path in Canada during the last era of sharply escalating rates (Lascher, 1998; Lascher, 1999, ch. 7). Not only were a relatively larger number of proposals enacted, but the no-fault laws themselves were much stronger. During one five-year period, Manitoba and Saskatchewan adopted pure no-fault schemes, eliminating lawsuits altogether, while Ontario adopted no-fault with a verbal threshold "much stronger and tighter than any existing verbal threshold in the United States" (O'Donnell, 1991, p. 202). Put simply, moving to the choice option does not appear politically necessary in Canada.

While there are other possible explanations for the variance between the two countries (notably, what may be a greater degree of litigiousness in the U.S.), the institutional differences between the American and Canadian subnational governments are most plausibly the cause of the different outcomes. In the American states, no-fault proposals are considered by governments following the separation-of-powers model, while Canadian provincial governments all use the Westminster parliamentary system. Power is more concentrated and veto points are fewer in the provinces. Cross-national case studies indicate that the separation-of-powers system makes it especially difficult for the U.S. national government to impose losses on interest groups (Weaver and Rockman, 1993). My research found the same pattern at the subnational level with respect to automobile insurance reform. And more recent studies comparing the American and Canadian national governments on a range of policy issues (e.g., smoking, gun control, abortion) tend to confirm that loss imposition is easier in Canada (Pal and Weaver, forthcoming).

4. THE FEDERAL CHOICE BILL

Mandatory no-fault proposals were considered in the U.S. Congress in the 1970s, even coming to a favorable floor vote in the Senate in 1974 (the House failed to act because of the Nixon impeachment proceedings, and subsequent bills did not get that far). Interestingly, much of the support for a national no-fault bill came from the left end of the spectrum, including liberal icon Senator Phil Hart, most consumer groups, and labor unions.

Since the 1970s, the vast majority of American legislative activity has been at the state level. However, bills to establish a federal choice system were introduced in the Senate in the 104th Congress (1996), reintroduced in the Senate and introduced in the House in the 105th Congress (1997-98), reintroduced again in the next Congress, and are now pending as well. The principal author in the Senate has been Mitch McConnell (R-Kentucky), while the principal author in the House has been Majority Leader Richard Armey (R-Texas); the backing of both legislators signals support from the Republican leadership. While most of the remaining sponsors have been Republicans, the legislation has garnered support from a few Democrats, notably those with "New Democrat" links, including Representative James Moran (D-Virginia) and Senator Joseph Lieberman (D-Connecticut). Respected veteran Daniel Moynihan (D-New York), who retired after the 2000 term, also supported the legislation. Support also has come from prominent Democrats outside the Congress, including former Massachusetts Governor Michael Dukakis (see his preface to this book), Democratic National Committee Treasurer Andrew Tobias, and Denver Mayor Wellington Webb.

The federal choice bill was based on the plan developed by Jeffrey O'Connell and Robert Joost, and there is reason to think that its legislative sponsors accepted the originators' argument that this was a more politically feasible approach than mandatory no-fault. Additionally, bill provisions allowing states to "opt out" of the choice system were consistent with generally expressed Republican support for deference to state decision making (states' rights concerns also had been stressed by Republican opponents of mandatory no-fault in the 1970s). Armey emphasized this point in his testimony before the Senate Committee on Commerce, Science, and Transportation on behalf of the original 1997 bill (see <http://armey.house.gov/ac-sentest.htm>):

> [T]he concept of freedom upon which Auto Choice is built does not apply exclusively to individuals; it applies to the states as well. Unlike other proposals that emanate from Washington, the Auto Choice Reform Act is not a mandate on states, nor does it usurp their authority to regulate automobile insurance. Nor does it employ a "carrot and stick" approach to coerce states to participate. The cherished principle of federalism is preserved. The fact of the matter is, states are free to opt out of Auto Choice at any time—and without fear of federal reprisal.

The above passage certainly reinforces the notion that choice legislation at the national level faces a major additional burden: potentially being seen as an intrusion into a policy area traditionally left to the states. Armey's effort to counter this argument underscores its importance.[5]

The choice bill carries other political burdens as well. Not surprisingly, trial lawyer opposition remains firm, and trial lawyers have strong links (and are major campaign contributors) to many Democratic legislators. Furthermore, with rates relatively stable in most places, automobile insurance has not been a prominent public concern in recent years. Explaining how the complex choice proposal would work remains a challenge. Representative Armey is also a polarizing figure, considered anathema by many liberal groups.

Nevertheless, there are reasons to think that the advent of the Bush Administration creates a brief window of opportunity for choice no-fault proponents. President George W. Bush has long supported tort reform and voiced opposition to the trial lawyers' agenda, as did his father during his own presidency. While he was not an active supporter of no-fault as governor of Texas, President Bush is likely to be sympathetic to the idea. It is also well known that the close and controversial 2000 presidential election, as well as the very narrow partisan division in Congress, has encouraged action on items that can draw bipartisan support. The history of no-fault suggests that, properly framed, it can fit this bill. Third, one of the main Democratic supporters, Senator Joseph Lieberman, appears to have emerged with enhanced prestige from his narrow loss as the Democratic vice-presidential candidate. If Lieberman were to assume some leadership on the issue, the chances for passage likely would be enhanced.

5. CONCLUSION

What does this analysis lead us to expect in the foreseeable future? First, choice no-fault proposals are likely to surface again in a number of American states. No-fault itself has shown a remarkable ability to appear and reappear on the political agenda over the last 30 years, contrary to premature reports of its political demise. Furthermore, there is good reason to think both that the choice proposal has political advantages relative to mandatory alternatives and that political supporters recognize these benefits. Second, the real action at the state level will occur if and when there is another round of significantly escalating rates. Third, the prospects for enactment of a *federal* law appear to have brightened for the near future with

---

[5] On the significance of concerns about consistency with federalist principles, see also Taylor (1998).

the results of the 2000 elections. Of course, the usual caveat applies to all of these points: it is difficult to make predictions, especially about the future.

References

Armey, Richard., 1997, Testimony before Senate Commerce Committee on Auto Choice, July 17, 1997, on-line at <http://armey.house.gov/ac-sentest.htm>.

Davies, Jack, 1998, A No-Fault History, *William Mitchell Law Review*, 24, 839-847.

Dyer, James A., 1976, Do Lawyers Vote Differently? A Study of Voting on No-Fault Insurance, *Journal of Politics*, 38, 452-456.

Harrington, Scott E., 1994, State Decisions to Limit Tort Liability: An Empirical Analysis of No-Fault Automobile Insurance Laws, *The Journal of Risk and Insurance*, 61, 276-294.

Kelly, Paul., 1993, Comments during floor debate on 93S-529, Rhode Island State Senate, May 11.

Lascher, Edward L., Jr., 1998, Loss Imposition and Institutional Characteristics: Learning from Automobile Insurance Reform in North America, *Canadian Journal of Political Science*, 31, 143-164.

Lascher, Edward L., Jr., 1999, *The Politics of Automobile Insurance Reform: Ideas, Institutions, and Public Policy in North America*, Washington, DC: Georgetown University Press.

Lupia, Arthur, 1994, Shortcuts versus Encyclopedias: Information and Voting Behavior in California Insurance Reform Elections, *American Political Science Review*, 88, 63-76.

Miller, Mark C., 1995, *The High Priests of American Politics: The Role of Lawyers in American Political Institutions*, Knoxville, TN: The University of Tennessee Press.

National Council of State Legislatures, 1996, *State Legislators' Occupations: 1993 and 1995*, Denver, CO: NCSL.

O'Connell, Jeffrey, Stephen Carroll, Michael Horowitz, and Allan Abrahamse, 1993, Consumer Choice in the Auto Insurance Market, *Maryland Law Review*, 52, 1016-1062.

O'Donnell, Allan, 1991, *Automobile Insurance in Ontario*, Toronto, Ontario: Butterworths.

Pal, Leslie, and R. Kent Weaver, forthcoming, *The Politics of Pain: Political Institutions and Loss Imposition in the United States and Canada*, Washington, DC: The Brookings Institution.

Taylor, Stuart, Jr., 1998, How to Save $30 Billion a Year in Car Insurance, *The National Journal*, June 6, 1283-1284.

U.S. Senate Committee on Commerce, Science, and Transportation, 1998, *S. 625, The Auto Choice Reform Act*, S. Hrg., 105-1021.

Weaver, R. Kent, and Bert A. Rockman, eds., 1993, *Do Institutions Matter? Government Capabilities in the United States and Abroad*, Washington, DC: The Brookings Institution.

Index

MIX
Papier aus verantwortungsvollen Quellen
Paper from responsible sources
FSC® C105338

If you have any concerns about our products,
you can contact us on
ProductSafety@springernature.com

In case Publisher is established outside the EU,
the EU authorized representative is:
Springer Nature Customer Service Center GmbH
Europaplatz 3, 69115 Heidelberg, Germany

Printed by Libri Plureos GmbH
in Hamburg, Germany